ADOLF GALLAND

The Authorised Biography

Dedication

This book is dedicated to fighter pilots
throughout the world, who give of their best
without pause to count the cost

ADOLF GALLAND

The Authorised Biography

DAVID BAKER

Windrow & Greene

© David Baker 1996

This edition published in Great Britain 1996 by
Windrow & Greene Ltd
5 Gerrard Street
London W1V 7LJ

Printed and bound in
the United States of America

Typesetting by BookEns Ltd
Royston, Herts, England

A CIP catalogue entry for this book is
available from the British Library

ISBN 1 85915 017 9

Contents

Foreword

I first came to know of Adolf Galland as a famous German pilot during the 1950s when, as a young boy, my admiration for fighter pilots everywhere was absolute. They were both role models and heroes. In the 1960s I had reason to read his doctrine of air combat presented as a lecture to NATO pilots; and in the 1970s I heard him speak at a US fighter base in North America. In the 1980s I used the life and career of this extraordinary man in my own lectures on air power to young pilots taking academic degrees; and finally, in the 1990s, I decided to write my own story of his life. In one way or another he has been a part of my life for more than 40 years.

In 1990 I met 'Dolfo' for the first time in private at his home above the beautiful town of Oberwinter not far from the Rhine bridge at Remagen – which has its own memorial to recent history. We spoke at length about a new book on his life, and discussed many aspects of his career. It was only then that I began to realise that all I had known up to that point was only a fraction of his story; and the events which we discussed over several days eclipsed in drama any fictional adventure I could have imagined. As a starting point, his autobiography published in 1953 was a very modest account of his career. I found others who could tell me much more about this man; and from declassified intelligence reports I began to get the full measure of the highs and lows of an astonishingly full life.

I wrote this book not in unblemished adoration of a proud and honourable officer, but as a true story of human endurance against odds, of principled strength in the face of unscrupulous deceit, and of service beyond the call of duty. This is what I found at the end of my quest for the real story behind the legend. I believe that much which has been said about Adolf Galland in the past starts and finishes with the public record of the valiant soldier; I was as intrigued to discover the loyal friend, dedicated in wartime to the men both above and below his rank, and committed to a personal set of moral principles. 'Dolfo' suffered both physical injury and crushing personal defeat several times in his life; but with iron determination and stoic endurance he simply refused to give in – to the very end. The events described in this book – violent, heroic, and tragic – must be judged in the light of the times in which they happened. The Germany of the 1930s and 1940s was a world distant from our modern Europe. Adolf Galland, like all men, was a product of his time and place; the story of his life is woven into a panorama of total war, of intrigue, of terrible loss and of human bravery under a totalitarian regime which changed the face of the 20th century, and transformed the world from the Atlantic to the Caspian.

Adolf Galland's story is more than the tale of a talented fighter pilot with great physical courage. It follows the fortunes of a man who showed determination in the face of adversity; who could not suffer fools or knaves; who sometimes showed the intolerance of a resolute spirit, but who strove to reconcile the demands of honour and duty with a decent human consideration of others. It is also a story about the group of men of whom Galland was an exemplar, formed and framed by the turbulence of their times. Among that remarkable peer group of young men – by at least one measure, the greatest fighting airmen in history – Adolf Galland sought to be the first and the best; and in several senses he achieved it.

Glossary

Use of German words

This book contains a large number of German words, particularly referring to Luftwaffe organisation. In all cases the nouns are capitalised (as they are in written German) and adjectives are in lower case. The German umlaut is conventionally represented here as a letter 'e' following the vowel, e.g. Fuehrer, Goering. German words have different forms in the plural, often but not always adding 'en' or 'n' to the singular form; where the plural form is unchanged from the singular we show here (pl.-). Rather than attempt formal capitalised translations – which can only be approximate – of the more complex German appointment titles, we have chosen to use general translations in lower case, e.g. Fuehrungsstab der Oberkommando der Luftwaffe is here simply 'Luftwaffe operations staff'.

Luftwaffe units

The basic combat unit was the Staffel (pl.Staffeln) of between 9 and 16 aircraft, led by a Staffelkapitaen (pl.-kapitaene), usually an Oberleutnant. Three (or rarely, late in the war, four) Staffeln and a command staff element (Stab) usually of two aircraft formed a Gruppe (pl.Gruppen) of between 30 and 60 aircraft, led by a Gruppenkommandeur (pl.-kommandeure), usually a Hauptmann or Major. Three (later in the war, often four) Gruppen and a Stab element normally of four aircraft formed the Geschwader (pl.-), which thus had a serviceable strength of anything between about 90 and 150 aircraft, led by the Geschwaderkommodore (pl.-), usually an Oberstleutnant.

Although these units do not correspond directly in terms of strength or organisation with RAF and USAAF units, where they are translated in this book we use 'wing', 'group' and 'squadron' for Geschwader, Gruppe and Staffel respectively.

Staffeln were numbered in a single sequence throughout the Geschwader, e.g. 1./JG26 to 9./JG26 in a Geschwader of three Gruppen each of three Staffeln. Gruppen bore Roman numerals, e.g. III./JG26 was the 3rd Gruppe of Geschwader JG26, and comprised Staffeln 7., 8. and 9./JG26.

.

Unit category prefixes

The Geschwader – and occasionally, when formed as a single group for independent operations, the Gruppe – was identified by a number (the various coding conventions used at different periods are mentioned in the relevant chapter notes); and by a prefix indicating the category of aircraft – e.g., Jagdgeschwader (JG), Kampfgeschwader (KG), etc. There were many of these, but the examples found in this book, with their standard abbreviations, are as follows:

Ergaenzungs- (ErgGr)	Operational training group
Erprobungs- (EGr, Ekdo)	Experimental group, command
Jagd- (JG)	Single-engined fighter wing
Kampf- (KG)	Bomber wing
Lehr- (LG)	Tactical development wing
Nachtjagd- (NJG)	Night fighter wing
Schlacht- (SGr, SG)	Ground-attack group, wing
Stuka- (StG)	Dive-bomber wing
Zerstoerer- (ZG)	Twin-engined fighter wing

Ranks

In several cases there is no exact equivalence between Luftwaffe, Royal Air Force and United States Army Air Force ranks, e.g. the non-commissioned grades. A rough comparative table would be:

Luftwaffe	*RAF*	*USAAF*
Generalfeldmarschall	Marshal of the RAF	5-star General
Generaloberst (Genobst)	Air Chief Marshal (ACM)	General
General der Flieger (Gen)	Air Marshal (AM)	Lieutenant General
Generalleutnant (Genlt)	Air Vice Marshal (AVM)	Major General
Generalmajor (Genmaj)	Air Commodore (Air Cdre)	Brigadier General
Oberst (Obst)	Group Captain (Gp Capt)	Colonel
Oberstleutnant (Obstlt)	Wing Commander (Wg Cdr)	Lieutenant Colonel
Major (Maj)	Squadron Leader (Sqn Ldr)	Major
Hauptmann (Hptmn)	Flight Lieutenant (Flt Lt)	Captain
Oberleutnant (Oblt)	Flying Officer (Flg Off)	1st Lieutenant
Leutnant (Lt)	Pilot Officer (Plt Off)	2nd Lieutenant
Oberfeldwebel (Ofw)	Flight Sergeant (Flt Sgt)	Master Sergeant
Feldwebel (Fw)	Sergeant (Sgt)	1st Sergeant?
Unterfeldwebel (Ufw)	–	Tech./Staff Sgt.?
Unteroffizier (Uffz)	Corporal (Cpl)	Sergeant
Obergefreiter (Ogefr)	Lance Corporal (L/Cpl)	Corporal
Gefreiter (Gefr)	Leading Aircraftman (AC1)	PFC

CHAPTER 1

March 1912 – February 1932

Germany was a fragmented nation united only by a common tongue when, some time in 1742, a French Huguenot refugee named Galland was given employment as a bailiff on the estate of Count Graf von Westerholt near Essen in Westphalia. He would be the first in a long line of Gallands who would tend the sprawling Westerholt estate; but while his German descendants would sustain this commitment to the family which gave their ancestor a new home and a respectable place in society, the Gallands would give up the Protestant faith which had made them exiles, and became loyal Roman Catholics. Catholicism was both a faith and a code through which life's rules could be expressed. Everything about the Galland family bespoke a sense of tradition and formality. Loyalty and obedience were unquestionable; no transgressions could be excused, and rules were enforced with patriarchal harshness.

Germany's new-found unity in the second half of the 19th century provided a platform of national pride upon which respect for tradition, stern self-discipline, and dedication to the service of nation and Kaiser were the foundations for an honourable life.

Into this world, on 19 March 1912, was born the second son of Adolf and Anna Galland – Adolf the younger, who would eventually become the youngest general in the German armed forces.

Situated just outside the landowner's walled house, the solid home where the young Adolf grew up was typical for a middle-class country family of the period. From the attic window a view resplendent in greens and browns stretched away across avenues of conifers and hardwoods to fields and woodlands clothing a gently rolling landscape, tended carefully over the centuries. Adolf Galland senior took his responsibilities to his employer seriously; and he extended to his growing family the same discipline which he demanded of his workers. Retribution for minor indiscretions could be severe and painful. Anna Galland was a haven of peace and understanding, occasionally intervening to temper the punishments meted out by their father to Adolf and his elder brother Fritz, to their eternal gratitude. Almost two years his senior, Fritz was a constant source of irritation and antagonism, and there was little love lost between the boys. When Adolf was barely two and a half years old he was presented with a second brother; born in October 1914, Wilhelm-Ferdinand was very different from Fritz, and Adolf became his affectionate protector and staunch friend from the outset.

Although the young Adolf saw his father as the personification of all he was taught to believe in, his unyielding domestic rule was not greatly missed after he went off to fight in the Great War as an officer in the Kaiser's army – although Anna Galland was not about to condone wanton abandonment of her husband's code while he was away fighting for his country. The war that began on 14 August 1914 did not touch the young Galland in any material way; he was too young to understand, and too busy learning his way around the Westerholt estate to care much for what lay beyond its boundaries.

It is not fanciful to trace the first seeds of Galland's success as a fighting pilot to his life around the Westerholt estate when he was barely of school age. Although his father was only at home for brief periods during the war, the boy had a solid early grounding in the safe handling and use of guns, in marksmanship and, very soon afterwards, in the skills of stalking and hunting living prey. When only five years old Adolf had his first shooting lessons, and within a year he had shot his first hare.

Although still only six when the Great War ended in November 1918, Adolf was peripherally aware of the deep anguish caused to his, and almost every other family in Germany. Most of the 1,700,000 German citizens lost in 1914-18 were non-professional soldiers claimed for service from ordinary civilian homes. His father alone lost seven brothers, and the sadness was impossible to veil. The next of kin to every German lost received a small black book bearing inscriptions and illuminated drawings of Christ receiving the worthy souls in Heaven. It had been an unforgettable moment when the first little black book arrived from the German War Ministry to mark the death of one of Adolf's uncles; and he kept that book until the end of his life.

Quite soon after hostilities ended Galland's father returned to take up again the management of the Westerholt estate. For most Germans all the comforting certainties of prewar life had been swept away; it was a time of want, of political turmoil, and of humiliation. Yet Adolf senior and Anna Galland wanted nothing more than a return to things as they had been in 1914; and for this middle-class family leading a secure rural life, there was a reasonable chance of escaping the harsher realities endured by the urban poor. They chose to have a fourth child, and in November 1919 Adolf's youngest brother Paul was born.

In some ways life for the children was even easier after the war. Adolf senior was less ready to use the stick, and the two younger boys escaped the sterner regime suffered by Fritz and Adolf when they were the only children. Now that there were four, rigid discipline was tempered with a degree of informality which even 'Papa' Galland found relaxing. He gave the family members nicknames, and young Adolf was known as 'Keffer'.

As a growing child and adolescent young Adolf had many interests, and found reward in practical things. He was no academic, preferring sports and handicrafts to art and philosophy. Despite his strict religious upbringing the Catholic church held no particular appeal for him, although he would always adhere to Christian codes of conduct for family and daily life. He felt some attraction to music, however; at 14 years of age he began violin lessons, and worked hard at them for two years, before giving the instrument up because he felt himself to be a mediocre player. He later explained that this was not a fit of pique at not being the best, but simply a recognition that to continue would be a waste of time and resources which could be more effectively applied elsewhere.

What did matter to him were technical things, ingenious little devices that puzzled and challenged him. He spent hours putting Meccano sets together; and he was not content merely to indulge his delight in such things, but soon turned his talents into money. Having taught himself the basic principles of radio, he made little crystal sets which he sold to the local farmers who rented land from the Westerholt estate. His practical bent led him to build wooden model aeroplanes, sometimes fitting them with miniature motors and flying them on short hops. Something about the thought of flying seemed to touch an instinctive chord, and he eagerly sought out books recounting the exploits of the airmen of the Great War, who in the Germany of the early postwar years were immortalised in print as gallant heroes of the Fatherland. The young Adolf learned about Max Immelmann, one of the earliest air aces, who gave his name to a daring manoeuvre; Oswald Boelcke, the first great leader of a squadron of fighting airmen; and Manfred von Richthofen, the legendary 'Red Baron', with 80 victories the highest scoring fighter pilot of the war. He also learned of Hermann Goering, a successor to von Richthofen as leader of Jagdgeschwader Nr.1 – the first 'Flying Circus', so called from its colourfully painted aircraft and tent hangars. In time he would come to know him better.

Although Adolf felt drawn to the stories of these men and their adventurous war, free to fight across the skies man against man, man against machine, they seemed to inhabit a world utterly distant from his own. At school he had to struggle to keep up; he saw no link between the mundane tedium of the classroom and the real world outside. The classics positively bored him, while science, wildlife and sport – all subjects he loved – seemed to get so little priority. He didn't really care about his grades, and despite pressure from his father to study harder it all seemed to no avail. It was as though he was waiting for something to spring into his life and add the spark of commitment.

In these formative years his character and personality took shape. The young Adolf was highly opinionated and specific in his views. His religious upbringing played some part in developing his inclinations. Early on he showed a deep hatred of communism, and in later life this was to influence him in several key political and military judgements. Linked to this, and due in no small part to his father's influence, he would come to share with many conservative Germans – men and women who would have no sympathy for Nazi ideology – a distrust for the Slav peoples who had historically been seen as a threat to Europe from the east.

As every second child in a large family has found, Adolf was in a difficult position. As the eldest, Fritz was marked as his father's successor in the long line of Westerholt bailiffs. Young Wilhelm-Ferdinand and Paul were largely free from expectations and could follow their own paths. Only Adolf felt challenged by his older brother and excluded from the privileges kept for Fritz. It was this sense of coming second that spurred Adolf to succeed, even to eclipse his brother. Matters came to a head when Fritz wooed away from Adolf, albeit temporarily, a local girl of stunning attractions. Stung into action, Adolf got his girl back more as a warning to Fritz than out of any real devotion. Adolf was forming an implacable will to be a high achiever – not just to participate creditably in life's game, but to be the first and the best. His upbringing shaped his stubborn refusal to fit into a preconceived role. It was both his strength and his weakness. In later years Adolf would steadfastly refuse to play the game according to rules dictated by a discredited authority; this would be his undoing as a soldier, but the making of him as a man.

* * *

The much-needed spark to release and focus Adolf's energy appeared in his life when, in early 1927, a group of sailplane enthusiasts brought the first gliders to the Borkenberge, a stretch of rolling heathland on a corner of the Westerholt estate. It was to these cropped hillocks that the members of the Gelsenkirchen Luftsportverein – air sports club – came to hone their skills; and Adolf made the 30km (20-mile) trek on foot or horse-drawn wagon to watch the enthusiastic helpers prepare the slender-winged gliders. It was a revelation. For the first time he knew exactly what he wanted from life: he wanted to fly – and the immediate goal was to experience this silent, soaring freedom which looked so effortless. But that was easier said than done, especially as he was barely 15 years old; and the young Adolf came alive to the possibilities that study and instruction might afford.

For Germans, gliding was to become a national sport. The Treaty of Versailles of June 1919 had forbidden Germany to build, own or operate military aircraft. Now, just eight years later, the next generation of Germans were taking to the skies without engines, as the simplest way to build expertise in the control of aircraft. Adolf Galland would later testify, time and again, that you could tell a pilot who had first learned to fly a glider: he simply 'felt' the air, and exploited it to the full.

Sports flying of all kinds became popular when the Reichswehr (German armed forces) organised Sportflug GmbH; ten flying schools were set up across Germany, with at least one in each of the seven military districts. Army flying officers were reassigned to these, keeping their hand in and attracting the interest of air-minded German youth. Of all flying sports gliding was the most attractive. *Flugsport* magazine launched a series of gliding competitions in the Rhoen region, mountainous country between the rivers Fulda, Werra, and the Franconian Saale; first held in 1920, these contests quickly became the national arena for gliding prowess. Two influential army officers did much to advance this interest. On 31 October 1920 Hptmn Helmut Wilberg[1] of the Truppenamt (the army's secret General Staff, technically forbidden by the Versailles Treaty) recommended encouragement of gliding to his chief, Gen Hans von Seeckt[2]; and one of von Seeckt's staff, Maj Kurt Student[3], was an active participant in the Rhoen meetings.

A major expansion of civilian aviation was taking hold as protocols to the Treaty of Versailles relaxed some constraints on the development of passenger and transport aircraft. During 1927 and 1928 German aircraft would carry more passengers and fly a greater cumulative distance than the combined passenger aircraft of France, Britain and Italy. Adolf Galland was one of the boys who determined to find a place for himself at the heart of this revolution.

In 1927 Adolf set himself to acquire the essential working knowledge of aerodynamics and the structural theory of gliders. Before long the local schools were drawn into these daring activities on the Borkenberge, and the vocational high school at Gelsenkirchen began to make simple gliders. Soon they were turning out modifications to existing designs, one of which was the Zogling, a lightweight trainer which Adolf helped to build. His first abortive attempt at becoming airborne, during Easter 1927, was an event he would never forget. As he would recall later: 'My heart was beating fast as I sat with the joystick between my knees on the little board above the skid-beam. My friends strapped me to the centre strut. Theoretically I knew every move, every reaction; but how would it go in practice?' Predictably, without practical experience all the theory in the world comes down to earth – which is what the little glider did as the inexperienced Adolf pulled back too sharply on the stick. Instead of rising it stalled, and he returned to the ground with a sickening crunch in the first of several crashes which he would experience over the next 18 years. Apart from a few broken wires there was little damage, and on his next attempt Adolf was more successful; but it was all too obvious that there was more to flying than pointing in the right direction and pulling the joystick.

Over the months which followed he thoughtfully applied the lessons which he had studied hard to master, and came to understand the vagaries of the weather. This inherent 'feel' for the atmosphere was the one aspect of flying that could only be learned through gliding; meteorology is as important to the glider pilot as the theory of aerodynamics, and Adolf applied himself to both. The challenge to be the first and the best had taken root; now was the time to grasp it.

The opportunity came through the graduated system of examinations for sailplane pilots. A licence to fly gliders whenever and wherever the law permitted could only be obtained after successfully passing three tests – A, B and C certificates – which in turn would lead to a final test giving professional status as a glider pilot. Each test was more demanding than the last; success would only come by degrees, although there were experienced glider pilots around to help. One in particular, Georg Ismer, did much to help Adolf understand the aerodynamics of gliders and their control techniques. Galland was a committed student tutored by demanding instructors; and by now he had the support of his father, but only in so far as this enthusiasm acted as stimulus, and not a replacement, for his schoolwork. 'Papa' Galland even came up with a motorcycle, which greatly eased the journeys between home and the Borkenberge.

The effort paid off in 1929, when a 34-second flight above the Borkenberge brought Adolf the handsome blue and white gull badge marking success in the A test. After a total of five flights in the same season he qualified for his B badge. For his C certificate he had to remain aloft for five minutes, a feat demanding the controlled use of thermals which, at the age of 17, Adolf had yet to master. There would be more flights to build greater experience, and yet more study of weather systems and the delicate balance between lift and drag.

All this inevitably distracted the boy from his academic studies, which by this time required him to attend the Hindenburg Gymnasium school at Buer. On hearing from the school that Adolf was seriously behind in his results and in danger of losing his place, 'Papa' was not amused, and threatened him with a flying ban unless his marks improved. Adolf had to tread a delicate line between the lure of the Borkenberge slopes and the tedium of school, and the next year was frustration personified. Compelled to devote more time to his school work, Adolf was unable to pick and choose when he travelled to the Borkenberge in pursuit of his longed-for C badge. The low, rolling heathland offered few opportunities for thermal soaring, and when they did he was never able to take advantage of them. The magic five minutes aloft were elusive for all the Borkenberge enthusiasts; so far the record stood at 4min 45sec, frustratingly short of the required time, although the young Galland had managed to stay aloft for 3min 15sec already.

Persistence, and the threat of being grounded, paid off in better school results, a place in the Upper First – and a chance to participate in the 1931 gliding championships in the Rhoen. The Mecca for soaring enthusiasts across Germany, the Rhoen mountains lay approximately 40km (25 miles) north-east of Frankfurt; they had drawn glider pilots since before World War I. Their tops frequently shrouded in mist, these majestic slopes were awe-inspiring to the 18-year-old Galland when he finally arrived at Easter 1931. One slope stood out as a spectacular place to find thermals – the Wasserkuppe, 950m (3,100ft) high. Now Galland was able to rub shoulders with the great names in gliding and soaring from all over Germany and abroad; it was the best possible opportunity for him to pick brains and compare techniques. Within a few days he had managed to get airborne in a Falke, and remained aloft for a full ten minutes before he was urgently signalled to land. At last he had his C class certificate; but a full professional licence still required a flight of at least one hour.

That autumn Galland was back on the Wasserkuppe to attend an international competition. With fellow members of the Gelsenkirchen club he helped ready their pride and joy, a glider called Meyer II with an 18m (60ft) wingspan, in which Adolf soared above the mountain slopes for the required hour. On his return home he was presented with his certificate of qualification as a glider pilot by the President of Westphalia; he was only the third pilot from the region to attain this standard. Now he could fly outside practice areas, make cross-country flights, exhibit at air shows, even train other pilots if he so desired. The benevolent Count von Westerholt, much impressed by his bailiff's second son, decided that the achievement merited some reward.

'Papa' Galland had mused with the count over his son's fortunes in the air and his struggles in the classroom. The count resolved to motivate the young man, offering to buy him his own glider if he successfully passed his matriculation from the Hindenburg Gymnasium. This he did, in February 1932; the incentive had worked, compounded by the knowledge that the hated schoolroom was now behind him and he could turn his full attention to flying. As part of his matriculation every pupil had to prepare a thesis of his own choosing. For his final essay Galland prepared detailed plans and description of a trailer designed to haul a sailplane; but this was no ordinary trailer. As well as containing the dismantled components it provided shelter, eating facilities and sleeping accommodation for the launch crew and its pilot! On his final report from the school, where the pupil's preferred profession was noted, his tutor simply wrote, 'Galland wants to be a pilot.'

Adolf got his glider, a much-coveted Grunau Baby tailored to his own specification, three days after the final examination. It arrived from Silesia, having been hauled across Germany by rail while its proud owner was busy recruiting helpers to build the trailer. Galland was growing up, acquiring the attributes that would single him out for leadership a decade hence; it was to him that the glider club now looked for leadership and direction, and he had little difficulty in getting the members to pitch in. When materials ran out, they scrounged; when funds ran low, they begged and borrowed until the job was done.

Suspicious of what he believed to be a diversion from the serious matter of choosing a suitable profession, even 'Papa' Galland had to admire the young man for his ingenuity and single-minded refusal to give in. Young Adolf had gained a lot since the day when the Gelsenkirchen Club came to rent land on the Westerholt estate; now he wanted to give something back, while making a name for himself. He wanted nothing less than to put the Westerholt flying club firmly on the gliding map. The endurance record for soaring above the Borkenberge was 47 minutes. With the excellent design and superb handling qualities of the Grunau Baby, that record could surely be improved upon.

At first conditions were marginal; but by 27 February, just 12 days after the glider arrived, Adolf was determined to make an attempt. It was still dark, and driving sleet numbed the hands of volunteers straining to pull the tiny glider up the Rauher Hang hill. Skating across the frozen ground it plunged into the air, only to smack hard down again on the solid turf. It was barely 09.25 when the second attempt was made, under a brooding sky and in biting wind.

Slowly, in ever-widening circles, Galland caught the wind and gained height. After about 30 minutes he had climbed 90m (300ft), and now began the delicate task of sweeping ever closer to the hillside to catch the rising currents, such as they were. Caught in a particularly violent updraught, his Baby was almost thrown to the ground, but he recovered to gain more height still. As the minutes ticked away Galland could see the coveted record edging into his grasp. At last he made it – 47 minutes aloft above the Borkenberge – and celebrated by eating half a bar of chocolate, throwing the other half down to his cheering, capering supporters on the frozen hill below. On and on he flew: one hour went by, then two, and still he kept the Baby perched at that elusive point between soaring flight and a stall. Already the hard-pressed little glider was creaking at the seams; it had been put through more than 320 turns, and aileron control wires were slackening to the point where it became increasingly difficult to maintain lateral control. It was prudent to land, and gradually the Baby returned to earth. Galland had been aloft for 2hr 6min 5sec; Borkenberge could now lay claim to being an official gliding site, and the Gelsenkirchen Club was formally accepted as a branch of the Luftsport Verband.

Adolf Galland approached his 20th birthday in the knowledge that he had found his own challenge, charted his own course, and set his sights firmly on a future in flying. He had already excelled far beyond his own expectations of a few years earlier. Against the objectives he had set for himself, he had become the first and the best. There would be several times throughout his life when he would match that achievement again.

Notes to Chapter 1

1 Helmut Wilberg, as a captain, set up and headed in 1923-27 the Air Defence Referat (nearest equivalent term would be 'desk') within the Truppenamt to form an air force department within the army.
2 Hans von Seeckt, head of the Reichswehr 1920-26, remodelled the army under the Weimar Republic and the strict terms of the Treaty of Versailles. His aim was to ensure a cadre of excellence whose every member was a potential leader and instructor when restrictions were lifted and a larger army became practical.
3 Kurt Student fought in the German air force in World War I, and became Inspector of Airborne Forces in 1938. He was responsible for many of the classic German paratroop operations of the war, and rose to the rank of Generaloberst commanding Army Group H.

CHAPTER 2

March 1932 – April 1933

Adolf Galland had already confronted his father with his ambition to become a professional pilot. It happened just before matriculation when 'Papa' took his son on a walk through the Westerholt estate, recalling how he had taught Adolf to shoot and to hunt, how he had given him that elusive instinct for stalking prey, and how – to the lad's distress – he had given him his first taste of pipe tobacco. But conversation quickly turned to the realities of life in a wider world where Adolf would have to make his way in dangerous and unpredictable times. Beneficiaries of a somewhat detached rural existence, the Gallands were nevertheless perfectly aware of how hard life was for many people in Germany. More than six million Germans were out of work with little or no prospect of employment.

In 1922 escalating inflation followed a flight of capital abroad, stagnant trade and a deepening balance of payments crisis; the heavy reparations claimed by the victorious powers made these conditions impossible to correct. In 1923 French troops occupied the Ruhr, provoking passive resistance and a temporary halt to reparations payments; in retaliation the French blockaded the Rhineland and virtually cut it off from the rest of Germany, worsening the financial crisis. In little more than 18 months the value of the mark against the dollar went from RM162 to RM4.2 billion. Food riots broke out as barter replaced currency. Across Germany a storm of despairing anger fanned support for a range of extremist factions which threatened to plunge the country into civil war. Communists in Saxony and Thuringia joined left-wing socialists in an attempt to seize control of the Reich; in Bavaria officials refused to obey calls from Berlin for the suppression of extremist parties such as Adolf Hitler's National Socialists. In attempting a putsch in Munich early in November 1923 Hitler overreached himself; his party was dissolved, and he himself was sent to Landsberg prison following trial in April 1924. Later in the decade the reconstituted party would rise again to challenge the precarious order presided over by Field Marshal von Hindenburg. Successive, ineffective governments and continual readjustment of the reparations payment schedule stifled growth and rekindled the flames of dissent.

In September 1930 the communists and the Nazis both recorded major gains in elections. The government led by Heinrich Bruening struggled to maintain stability amid a chaos orchestrated by both left and right. On 13 March 1932 a mandatory election for president saw Hindenburg challenged by four candidates, one of whom was Hitler; a re-run one month later left Hitler in second place. This particular event was only weeks away as the Gallands, father and son, walked and talked in the Westerholt woods.

The dilemma that faced the 19-year-old Adolf was very real. Jobs were desperately scarce; but he had very specific ideas about what he wanted. Reluctant at first, 'Papa' Galland warmed to the idea when he saw the sheer determination and enthusiasm with which his son was fixed upon a career in flying. The odds were heavily against success: there were far too many hopeful young would-be pilots chasing far too few openings. Nevertheless, 'Papa' Galland put his heart and soul behind his son, and when the walk in the woods was over Adolf had a staunch supporter. It was a turning point in his relationship with his father. From that day forward he had nothing but respect for him, and would always remember how his father had allowed himself to be persuaded that what his son wanted, his son was going to get.

Shortly afterwards Galland applied for one of just 20 positions that year in the Deutsche Verkehrsfliegerschule or DVS (commercial flying school) – as did about 4,000 others in 1932. The odds were daunting, although his glider flying gave him some advantages. From these thousands of applicants about 100 were picked to attend a ten-day selection course at Braunschweig, about 55km (35 miles) south-east of Hannover; and Galland's name was among the chosen few.

The DVS had four flying schools including Braunschweig; the others were at Warnemuende near Rostock, at Schleissheim outside Munich, and at List on the North Sea island of Sylt. All were heavily subsidised by Deutsche Luft Hansa (DLH), created on 6 January 1926 from the two major German airlines of the day – Deutsche Aero Lloyd and Junkers Luftverkehr – with 36 per cent government capitalisation. There had followed an unprecedented expansion in routes and destinations. Only the DVS could carry a pupil progressively through the five licence grades certifying a pilot for all types of aircraft. These were graded according to the number of engines, the number of people carried and the flight weight, from the basic A1 grade licensing a pilot to fly a single-engined, single-seat aircraft with a flight weight of up to 500kg (1,100lb), to the B2, for twin-engined aircraft of 5,000kg (11,025lb) with up to seven passengers. The C licence was for any aircraft type.

By 1930 DLH was Europe's leading airline, and would become the *de facto* training school for Germany's military pilots and the cradle of her military aircraft development, neither of which were permitted under the terms of Versailles. With heavy government funding DLH was able to stay one step ahead of the international competition in new airliners, feeding the nascent German aircraft industry with specifications to keep DLH equipped with German aircraft and engines – with predictable support from the military, against the expectation of less restricted days. Those days were coming a lot quicker than Adolf Galland or his fellows realised as they arrived at Braunschweig. But flying for Europe's premier airline was an appealing enough prospect; only the previous year the company had introduced into service the giant Junkers G38, a massive 24,385kg (24 ton) four-engined airliner capable of carrying 34 passengers at 200kph (127mph) for 3,500km (2,150 miles).

There is no doubt that German transport aircraft were ahead of the competition throughout the 1930s, though lacking the markets available to the American, British and French industries. Over the next six years DLH were to specify and introduce into service three aircraft that would play central military roles in World War II: the ubiquitous Junkers Ju52 transport entered service in 1932, and the Heinkel He111 by 1936; and the Focke-Wulf Fw200 – the first four-engined landplane to have a trans-Atlantic capability – carried DLH passengers from 1938.

Life at Braunschweig proved tough and uncompromising. Dressed in blue civilian clothes, applicants were subjected to a disciplinary regimen that was military in its rigour. Scurrying from the modern barrack blocks to their various classrooms, examination rooms, instruction halls and interview boards, they endured psychological as well as technical tests. Evaluation was thorough and highly selective; DLH wanted highly trained and disciplined pilots, and the army wanted a pool of airmen from which the core of a modern air arm could emerge when the time was ripe. No one knew then that, when it did emerge, the air force would become a military service in its own right rather than an element of the army.

* * *

At the end of ten days 18 applicants were selected to go forward for DLH flight training, and Adolf Galland was among them. He was jubilant at this confirmation that he was among the best, but the going got tougher as the real instruction began. Constantly under threat of expulsion if they failed to perform as expected, the trainees got used to working and studying under pressure. Anyone who faltered could look forward to 50 Reichsmarks in his pocket and a train ride home. It was a fitting preparation for military life.

Most instructors were veterans of the 1914-18 war, who brought to their task a military style which did not endear them to their students. Proudly aware that they had been selected from among several thousand applicants, the trainees were unwilling to be brow-beaten like raw recruits. Yet there were some instructors who retained their military bearing while offering much that the trainees could identify with. One such was the principal of the flying school, Oberst Alfred Keller. A former bomber pilot who had conducted raids on London during the war, and who had been awarded Germany's highest award for bravery – the Ordre pour le Merite – Keller achieved the right balance between maintaining discipline and allowing the freedom to explore individual talent and aptitude. A daunting figure at first sight, he understand how to lead young men, and more than once gave Adolf Galland the confidence to carry on.

An Albatros L101 provided Galland's first experience at the controls of a powered aeroplane when he was taken into the air by an instructor named Stutz. Powered by a 110hp Argus inverted inline engine, the L101 was a high-wing monoplane with tandem seats; it had a cruising speed of just under 160kph (100mph), a ceiling of just over 4,900m (16,000ft) and a range of 740km (460 miles) in ideal conditions. Last in a long line of Albatros types, the L101 was a pleasant aeroplane to fly.

On a subsequent flight Galland made a heavy landing and broke the undercarriage, denting his confidence and raising the spectre of that rail ticket home. He was further shaken by an incident in which two Klemm trainers collided in midair while he was leading a three-plane formation; fortunately, no one was killed. As flight leader it was Galland's role to make distinct signals when changing direction; by inference, the conclusion that poor formation tactics had led to the accident implicated Galland, and he took the judgement badly.

Aware that incidents like these boded ill for his prospects, Galland decided to apply for service with the 18th Infantry Regiment at Paderborn. He soon passed the entrance examination, unbeknown to his instructors at Braunschweig, and carried on with his training while awaiting the call to report, fully convinced that his two accidents would sooner or later result in his dismissal from flying school. Several weeks went by without further word; imagining that the backlog of applicants for regimental service had placed him far down the list – if not off it altogether – Galland settled back into the rhythm of the flying school.

He was soon gaining greater confidence in his flying abilities, and enjoying the freedom that came from cross-country flights. The Albatros L75 was a stout two-seat biplane specifically designed for flying schools; powered by a 350hp BMW engine, with a cruising speed of around 180kph (110mph) and a range of about 1,600km (990 miles), it made an admirable cross-country aeroplane, its design sympathetic to pupil error. By the summer of 1932 Galland had obtained his B1 certificate (for single-engined aircraft of 2,500kg/5,512lb with three passengers), and things began to look up. Just when he began to feel that he might, after all, have a future in aviation, the army summoned him to Paderborn.

There was nothing he could do but request permission from Keller to leave the school and join his regiment. But the colonel was not inclined to be co-operative; he assured Galland that he had every prospect of graduating from flying school if he kept to the task, and refused to release him. This was just what the young man needed; encouraged by this endorsement, he wrote to decline the offer of a career in the infantry with some considerable relief. Galland took a pragmatic view of military service; he believed that it was a German's destiny to serve his country in an appropriate capacity, and recognised that stern discipline was a necessary part of service. But he saw the army as intractable and unyielding; he preferred the freedom to express himself and apply his skills in a self-selective way. This view of the army was shaped in no small part by the arrogant and dismissive attitude of several Reichswehr officers who attended the flying school along with the civilian students.

Now it was time to focus seriously on getting his B2 certificate, which required 150 hours' flying time. In one sense he was encouraged by the steady attrition rate among the 18 pupils who had made it to Braunschweig; by Christmas 1932 only half would remain, yet he was one of them, and it became clear that if he worked hard enough he would pass. In the coming months Galland would indeed work hard; but he did manage to get some time in on the only sailplane at Braunschweig, where little attention was paid to anything other than powered flight.

There was also time to renew his links with the soaring club on the

Borkenberge. During late summer Galland heard about a new sailplane built by the club to the specification of Georg Ismer, and that autumn he went along to see for himself. The club members had dubbed this glider 'Keffer' after Adolf's nickname, and there was nothing for it but to try it out for himself. Hauled into the air by rubber catapult ropes, the glider proved unstable; the tail immediately dropped, causing the aircraft to stall and nose into the ground. Striking his head on the cockpit rim, Adolf suffered mild concussion and a few bleeding cuts in the first of several crashes which would remodel his dark and handsome features.

No sooner had Galland returned from the Gelsenkirchen flying club than he was sent to the aerobatic school at Schleissheim, where he learned skills that would stand him in good stead during the years to come. He acquired the techniques of inverted flight, rolls, loops, steep dives and complex integrated manoeuvres. With his background in sailplanes Galland found these lessons much to his liking, and became confident where others felt uncertainty. By Christmas he had recorded the necessary 150 hours, passed his B2 test, and was well on the way to becoming a fully qualified pilot.

Early in 1933 Galland was sent to the seaplane training base at Warnemuende on the Baltic coast. Here he was instructed in the basic handling of flying boats and seaplanes, logging 25 hours' instruction in aircraft of this type. A lot of what the trainees learned was related to maritime navigation and seemed to have little to do with flying; uninterested in seamanship, Galland failed to see the point of this exercise. Soon it was back to Schleissheim, and more familiar territory – until he was summoned for an intriguing interview.

It was from Schleissheim that Galland and four other trainees were directed by the school authorities to go to the Zentrale der Verkehrsflieger Schule (ZVS – Central Airline Pilot School) in Berlin. They were not told why. When they arrived they were taken into a private room, and introduced to matters with which they had not previously concerned themselves. They were told, by officials dressed in civilian clothes, that in contravention of the Versailles terms Germany had a secret training programme for military pilots; and they were asked whether they were interested in volunteering for it. They were told that they would fly high-performance aircraft, and that they would get the chance to learn high-speed manoeuvres. All five accepted, and returned to Schleissheim to participate in this clandestine course. Thus for the first time the politics of the period played a direct part in the life of the young Adolf Galland. Unknown to the excited young pilots, Germany was set on a course that was lead inexorably to dictatorship and war.

* * *

The Nazi party had made impressive gains in the elections of 24 April 1932, becoming the majority party in the Prussian state. The fate of Germany's democracy was sealed on 30 May when President Hindenburg replaced Breuning with Franz von Papen as head of government. He promptly lifted a ban on the Nazi SA (Sturmabteilung) storm troopers, and put Kurt von Schleicher in as minister of defence. Elections to the Reichstag held on 31 July saw further Nazi gains; but in a subsequent election on 6 November they lost nearly two million votes to the communists. Horrified, Schleicher forced von Papen to resign and took office himself. Unable to get the various parties to agree to power-sharing, Schleicher inveigled Hindenburg into approving a deal with the Nazis; and from 30 January 1933 the National Socialist German Workers' Party received three out of 11 seats in the coalition cabinet.

Hitler became Reichskanzler (chancellor); Wilhelm Frick became the Reich interior minister, and Hermann Goering the Prussian interior minister and Reich minister without portfolio. Four days later Hitler appointed Goering Reichskommissar fuer die Luftfahrt (Reich Commissioner for Aviation). Fearing a political take-over of military aviation the new defence minister, Gen Werner von Blomberg, merged the army and navy aviation offices on 1 April and effectively blocked any interference from Goering. But this measure lasted barely a month, and sweeping changes by the Nazi leadership denied the army and navy the control over air power which they sought to retain.

Back at Schleissheim there was a sense of expectancy in the air; but Galland had never been much concerned about politics, and failed to grasp the significance of what was happening. He did know, however, that his flying career might suddenly take a very different tack and carry him into a more exciting future. Hermann Goering, the charismatic Nazi with a strong military aviation pedigree, was now in government. Of Hitler, Galland had little knowledge or interest; anything not involved with aviation was unlikely to hold his attention for long.

Training was under the control of Maj Beyer, who had been one of the first batch of officers slipped into Russia for clandestine military flying training at a base set up for that purpose at Lipetsk in 1923 – a much deeper and darker secret than the use of DLH training centres to recruit military pilots. Adolf Galland's dawning career, had he but known it, was the end product of a long conspiracy to build not only the manpower but also the technology for a modern air force. By the time Lipetsk closed at the end of September 1933 – when the more open expansion of military aviation in Germany ended its usefulness – about 450 flying personnel had been trained there over eight seasons (including some 120 pilots and 100 navigators), with a further 450 trained in ground duties. These formed the core of instructors who would train Germany's resurgent air arm[1].

When Adolf Galland returned to Schleissheim in early 1933 to participate in the military training course he had the chance to fly Albatros and Heinkel biplanes. The course as a whole proved to be poorly conceived, however, including a range of only vaguely relevant topics such as 1914-18 air tactics, aviation history and the principles of aerial combat, all of which would soon be revealed as out of date for an emerging generation of aircraft. The poor quality of the tutorials generally reflected the calibre of the teachers. Despite its disappointments the course did give Galland 25 hours in the air, sometimes with the heady experience of firing live ammunition at simulated – if unconvincing – ground targets. These mock attacks did instil an enthusiasm for combat, and tempered with realism the swashbuckling notions of air fighting which many of the pupils had brought to Schleissheim.

In the outside world events were moving fast. Toward the end of Galland's course at Schleissheim Germany's democratic government ran its course to extinction, proving impotent against the manipulations of Adolf Hitler. With no one party in control of the coalition, Hitler persuaded the cabinet to hold another election on 5 March 1933. In the meantime, as head of the Prussian police, Goering purged its leadership of non-Nazis, drafted in 50,000 SA and SS members as police auxiliaries, and forbade interference with political demonstrations. One week before the elections, on 27 February 1933, the Reichstag building was burned down by an SS Sondergruppe under orders from Reinhard Heydrich[2]; the outrage was blamed on a retarded Dutchman, the Nazis publicly held the communists responsible, and unleashed the SA and the SS. By the evening of the 28th, 4,000 communist officials and party members had been arrested. Despite this manipulation of public fear of foreigners and communists Hitler only barely managed to get a majority in the elections by doing a deal with the Nationalist party.

By deft manoeuvring Hitler pushed through on 23 March the so-called 'Enabling Law' – an act which set aside the constitution and enabled Hitler to act independently of the Reichstag or the president. Thus was formed the legal framework for the dictatorship which would be unveiled as the Third Reich. On 14 July 1933 Germany became a one-party state when the opposition groups voluntarily disbanded.

Notes to Chapter 2

1 The story of the secret interwar plan to preserve and build upon the nucleus of a German military air arm is long and involved, but it may be traced to the memorandum of 18 May 1919 from Hptmn Wilberg to Gen von Seekt, then military advisor to the Armistice Commission, on the Reichswehr's future needs in aircraft and personnel. Although the signatory of the order disbanding the German air service, von Seeckt saw to it that 120 army and 20 navy pilots were retained. From that group came the instructors who would soon be sent to the secret training ground in Russia.

Following a German-Soviet trade agreement in May 1921, Gen von Seeckt persuaded the Russians that Soviet defences could benefit from German industrial expertise, including that of aircraft manufacturers. Taken in, and never averse to secrecy, the Russians agreed at Rapallo in April 1922 a treaty covering trade and the exchange of technical information. The secret German training base was in due course established at Lipetsk on the Voronezh, about 500km (310 miles) south-east of Moscow. Orders for Dutch Fokker aircraft were originally born of the 1923 Ruhr crisis and German fear that the occupation of the Rhineland might lead to war with the Allies. The crisis abated, but an order for 50 type DXIII sesquiplane fighters – then, at 270kph (170mph), the fastest fighter in the world – was retained; and by highly devious means the aircraft, and British surplus machine guns to arm them, were secretly delivered to Lipetsk.

The field, set up to resemble a Russian base, housed an average of 200 personnel of which 50, interspersed with Russian personnel, were responsible for training. The first courses began during summer 1926; and in time even joint field exercises would be held in conjunction with Russian forces. During this period the German aircraft industry had been evolving on the back of other plots to evade the Versailles restrictions, and several key World War II aircraft types were flown at Lipetsk. The whole conspiracy came to an end with the accession to power of the virulently anti-communist Nazis.

2 Head of the Sicherheitsdienst (SD – SS Security Service), Reinhard Heydrich was Deputy Protector of Bohemia and Moravia with headquarters in occupied Prague from 1941. While serving as such he was ambushed and killed by Czech partisans.

CHAPTER 3

May 1933 – March 1935

One man above all others who would influence Galland's life for the next 12 years was now assuming powers that would put him at the head of Europe's most powerful air force. Dissatisfied with his position as head of the essentially civilian Reich Commission for Aviation, Goering enlisted Hitler's support in engineering a change in the law. On 27 April 1933 Hindenburg succumbed to their pressure to upgrade the commission to the status of a ministry – the Reichsluftfahrtminister-ium (RLM, German Aviation Ministry) – thus automatically elevating Goering to equal rank with defence minister von Blomberg. On 15 May all the many and varied German military aviation projects were brought under the authority of the RLM. Within days of his appointment as Reich commissioner for aviation Goering had named Erhard Milch as his deputy, and on 22 February Milch was made state secretary of aviation[1].

At the end of the course at Schleissheim in May 1933 Galland was ordered to attend a special meeting at the Behrenstrasse in Berlin. He was one of 12 'civilian' pilots in the group of about 70 airmen who converged from various similar clandestine programmes; the others were military officers and NCOs. The meeting was addressed by Goering; and it was at this first encounter that Galland fell under the spell of this articulate, magnetic, larger-than-life personality.

Goering addressed his assembled recruits – the nucleus of what would become the new Luftwaffe – with enthusiasm and a sense of purpose. Galland was impressed; Goering seemed to make sense, appeared to have thought through a logical plan for the development and expansion of the Third Reich's air power, and gave an impression of culture and education. Indeed Goering impressed most of those at the meeting, with a sense that Germany's leaders offered a spirit of restored pride and a real chance to take part in a new adventure. In such company Goering could trade on the aura of having led Jagdgeschwader Nr.1 some months after the death of its founding commander Manfred von Richthofen; to these young fliers he seemed a natural leader for Germany's new aviation programme. In reality, Goering surrounded himself with ingratiating cronies and had none of the essential attributes of a true leader, as Galland would discover to his cost[2].

Goering told the group at the Behrenstrasse of plans to have done with the restrictions of Versailles, and to build all the elements of a strong air force; for the time being, however, these activities would remain secret. The 70 young airmen were told that what they were doing was part of a well-planned programme. The young would be enlisted for air competitions using the widely established Ring der Flieger. These were to be organised into the Deutscher Luftsportverband (DLV – German Air Sport Association) with Bruno Loerzer, another World War I ace, as president. Only the preceding month Goering had put the active members of the DLV into grey-blue uniforms; the organisation would help spread an air of militarism among the country's air-minded youth. Finally, Goering told his audience that they were to attend a special air combat training course in Italy.

* * *

The German pilots would travel in civilian clothes, in two separate parties: one to Udine in northern Italy, the other to the old World War I airship base at Grotaglie in the south. In July 1933 the two groups gathered at Frankfurt-am-Main for three days of lectures and security briefings before being despatched by train to their respective destinations, Galland's group crossing the Brenner under the guise of Tyrolean recruits. The train took them to Bari on the Adriatic coast, headquarters for one of Italy's four Air Zones.

The deception did not end when they crossed into Italy: they were greeted at Bari by a group of Italians in civilian clothes who ushered them into military vehicles disguised as civilian transport. That their hosts were officers from the Grotaglie flying school became evident when the transport came to a halt several miles outside Bari. To the puzzlement of their visitors the Italians disappeared into an olive grove, only to reappear in resplendent white Regia Aeronautica summer uniforms complete with 'plumes like banana-skin peelings'. They seemed to Galland more like musicians in a marching band, and he could not help wondering what sort of toy soldiers these men were. Rejoining the German airmen in their new splendour, the Italians seemed to assume an air of superiority which grated on their travel-worn guests as they rattled off down the dusty road to the flying school.

No sooner had they arrived at Grotaglie than the Germans were shepherded into barracks and issued old, faded air force recruits' uniforms. The prospect of a two-month stay became distinctly tedious when the Germans found themselves kept under almost constant watch, drilled, and treated generally like ignorant and undisciplined conscripts. They were not allowed to leave the airfield, and lacked any opportunity for diversion or company – particularly female company. Clearly, someone had failed to brief the Italians on the newcomers' level of military and flying experience. Galland, as frustrated by this treatment as his companions, was a frequent instigator of humourous banter hurled at the Italians; but in the absence of a fluent common language the message did not seem to penetrate. When the Germans were given worn-out Breda biplane trainers for initial orientation it was the last straw.

Galland's opportunity to demonstrate the misunderstanding came when the Italians boasted of the latest record by one of their pilots, an inverted flight of 90 minutes' duration. Taking off in a Breda, Galland promptly flipped the little biplane and proceeded to fly up and down the airfield inverted. The Italians' initial annoyance changed to respect as time passed; Galland did not feel confident that he had got his message across until he had been droning back and forth upside down for a full 45 minutes.

Having shown what they were capable of, there was some opportunity for Galland and his colleagues to practice air-to-ground strafing, much to their enjoyment – though to the consternation of Italian soldiers in trenches holding balloons as targets, who were accustomed to the Regia Aeronautica's more sedate training regime. At Grotaglie Galland and his group managed to get in about 60 hours' flying time, but in reality they learned very little of practical value. It was a strange experience for Galland: to all intents and purposes he was receiving fighter combat training, but he did not belong to any formal military unit – not even to an air force.

None too soon the two-month course was over; and at least their time was to be handsomely rewarded. Still burdened by their bogus Tyrolean identity, Galland and his friends were given a two-week holiday, and more than enough spending money to enjoy themselves. Galland visited Rome, Naples, Capri and Milan; the concentrated impact of Italy's spectacular artistic and architectural heritage made a real and lasting impression on him – as also did the diversions of good food, fine wine and beautiful women. (This last interest was often reciprocated; and so began a full-hearted, if sometimes hazardous involvement with the opposite sex that would far outlast his youth. Even in his later years, despite the scars of time and several crashes, women would melt before his charisma, his dark good looks, and a certain tantalising aura of hidden danger.)

* * *

In September 1933 Galland returned to Germany. He found time for some glider flying, and won another prize in a local contest, before reporting to the Zentrale der Verkehrsflieger Schule at Braunschweig/Broitzem. At the ZVS he completed a course on instrument flying and received tuition in the techniques of piloting heavy transport aircraft, logging another 50 hours' flying time.

The following month Galland began life as a Lufthansa pilot and, for a brief period, had time to explore and enjoy the relaxing ambience of southern Spain. Flying either a Rohrbach-Roland or a Junkers G24 airliner, Galland would take passengers twice a week from Stuttgart to Barcelona via Geneva and Marseilles. The G24 trimotor was a relatively old design (it first flew in 1925), but it was a comfortable aircraft for its three crew and up to nine passengers. Galland found Spain much to his liking, relaxing whenever he could at shady pavement bars, or walking under the palms of the Catalonian coast. He liked the Mediterranean climate, the affable people, the warm hospitality, the free and friendly manners – it was all so different from the culture of the cold north, and Galland took it to his heart. He was 21 years old, healthy, good-looking, a pilot with the best airline in Europe, and often far from home in exotic surroundings. He was flying for a living, and his secure and ordered working life had some appeal. But the excitement of military aviation, which he had been allowed to taste, was lacking.

In December 1933 he was called to the ZVS in Berlin, where officials gave him an invitation which confronted him with these hard choices. Did he wish to volunteer for military service with a view to joining the now not-so-secret air force as a commissioned officer? Galland was one of 70 in the group assembled in Berlin, and most found the choice a difficult one. Although young, the aviators had their feet on the first rungs of a ladder that could lead to steady work far into the future. They had achieved this by unremitting work and against great odds, in a country traumatised by relatively recent hyperinflation and mass unemployment. Yet, while civilian flying offered stability it had little of the excitement they associated with military aviation. Again, if it should ever come to war, it was better to be on the inside having risen through the ranks than to be drafted in at the convenience of the government. So it was that, largely because of the promise of adventure rather than through any serious ambition to help develop the emerging air force, most of the young men in the group opted for military service.

* * *

Unavoidably, this would mean a period with the army, pounding the parade ground and polishing boots. It was with a certain wistfulness for the pleasures of Spain that Galland reported to his barrack room sergeant of the 10th Infantry Regiment at the Grenadier Barracks, Dresden, on 15 February 1934. His professional career as a military aviator was starting at the bottom, in the rank of rifleman. For three months his group – a motley collection of airline and meteorological pilots and flying instructors – endured infantry basic training. Sometimes they drilled and double-marched all day; other days were spent polishing and cleaning parade clothing and equipment. It had nothing to do with flying, and everything to do with instilling the military discipline to carry out orders without question or sentiment. It was all very soul-destroying, but – according to the sergeant-major – character-building …

In May, presuming their characters built, the army moved them on to Infantry School, also in Dresden, and Galland received the rank of officer cadet. Here the group underwent further infantry training and officer schooling, before proceeding to air combat theory at the War Academy. The syllabus was solidly based on the experience of World War I, and had little relevance to modern conflict; the army saw the use of aircraft in terms of support for ground operations, and had little concept of an independent air force for strategic use. The young aviators, on the other hand, knew full well the dangers of such limited thinking.

While Galland was garrisoned at Dresden Germany stumbled further toward the abyss. The SA had grown vastly in size, and its leader Ernst Roehm had an ambitious agenda of his own. Formed by Hitler in 1920 to provide the Nazi party with physical muscle in the days of mass street politics, the movement had outgrown its usefulness: it was an embarrassment to a government in power; it worried influential elements who were otherwise prepared to see Hitler as a way forward for Germany; and it was becoming a focus for political causes left behind by Hitler's rise to power. The army's Gen von Blomberg had reason to seek assurances from Hitler that he would not allow the SA to infiltrate the army. The generals, politically conservative and loyal to the 87-year-old President von Hindenburg, were potentially a source of serious opposition to Hitler.

In return for his promises of a dramatic cut in the SA, military expansion, and a commitment that the armed forces would be the sole 'bearers of arms', the army staff agreed to support Hitler for president on Hindenburg's death. Events conspired to bring matters to a head; Himmler's SS had been growing increasingly restless about the Roehm faction; so, at his and Goering's urging, Hitler struck. On 30 June 1934, in a purge known as the 'Night of the Long Knives', SS troops snatched Roehm and other SA leaders for summary execution; at the same time a wide range of Hitler's other political adversaries throughout Germany were eliminated, under the pretence of forestalling a putsch. The SA was emasculated forever; Hitler had kept his pact with the military, and would receive his reward little more than a month afterwards.

On 2 August 1934 the old president died. True to their word, the army and navy approved Hitler's decision to merge the posts of Reichskanzler and president. On that day Adolf Galland, along with every other person under military authority, bound themselves by a new declaration:

'I swear by God this sacred oath, that I will yield unconditional obedience to the Fuehrer of the German Reich and Volk, Adolf Hitler, the Supreme Commander of the Wehrmacht, and, as a brave soldier, will be ready at any time to lay down my life for this oath.'

Within three weeks a national plebiscite returned the National Socialist Party to power with 88 per cent of the 43.5 million votes cast. Already, since achieving power in July 1933, the Nazis had poured massive funds into public works, road building and improvements to the national infrastructure. By the end of 1934 unemployment stood at 2.6 million, a fall of more than 3.4 million in two years. In the coming year rearmament on a massive scale would turn unemployment into a dramatic labour shortage. A year later the arms budget would stand at RM10 billion – five times what it was when Hitler came to power.

* * *

For Galland, to whom the carefully slanted official version of the Roehm incident had seemed like the timely crushing of a dangerous political conspiracy, the nation suddenly seemed to be coming alive. His own prospects seemed bright, if confused. In October 1934 he was discharged from the army with the rank of Kettenfuehrer, equivalent to lieutenant in the forthcoming Luftwaffe; and he received his Flugzeugfuehrerabzeichen (aircraft commander's badge – in practice, his pilot's qualification brevet.) It was ironic that there was as yet no German air force for him to join; but everything was to change in 1935, and the new year would bring a posting that just five years earlier would have been beyond his wildest dream.

When Galland left Dresden he wore on his grey-blue DLV uniform the breast wings and bird collar emblems signifying the rank of pilot officer. His first posting was back to Schleissheim. Technically Galland was back in the civilian flying organisation, but this was a brief interlude. He was now one of approximately 900 flying officers, 200 flak officers and 17,000 men in the 'air force in waiting'. Schleissheim was in the throes of being transformed from a pseudo-civilian flying school into the primary military training ground for a new air force. Here Galland began a ten-week course to put the edge back on his flying skills and aeronautical theory, blunted by his ten months as a soldier. He hoped to be posted before long to a flying unit as an open and unashamed member of a national air force; but there was a catch.

Briefings about the impending announcement of Germany's nascent air force were frequent. There were classroom sessions on how the new air force would be organised and administered, and what sort of equipment it was going to receive. Only a small cadre of founding members – the group to which Galland belonged – would be seasoned aviators, the rest being trainees recruited from the ranks of inexperienced enthusiasts. There would be a pressing need for instructors.

Galland knew that his performance at Schleissheim could either propel him to an active service unit – a prospect with immense attractions; or condemn him to the boredom of a training school. The last thing in the world he wanted was to be an instructor. The best pilots were urgently needed to inspire and train the recruits, while the rest would be sent to operational squadrons. Treading a delicate line between mediocrity and excellence, Galland determined to place his flight rating at about the average, in the hope of avoiding dangerous prominence. Each week brought further news of Staffeln (squadrons) being formed across Germany as the pace of expansion picked up. The first flying unit to be set up after Hitler assumed power in 1933 had been the Reklamefliegerabteilung (Propaganda Detachment) comprising three squadrons, one each at Berlin-Staaken, Neuhausen near Koenigsberg in East Prussia, and Furth near Nuremberg. Under the command of Maj Robert Ritter von Greim[3], the first operational unit had been established on 1 April 1934 and given the grand title of Jagdgeschwader 132[4], set up at Doeberitz-Damm close to Berlin with the task of training fighter and dive-bomber crews. Throughout that year the units built up toward a strength of five reconnaissance squadrons, three fighter squadrons, five bomber squadrons and a stand-by unit at the disposal of the Ministry of Defence. These squadrons were to be equipped with Arado Ar65 and Heinkel He51 fighters and He50 dive-bombers.

In February 1935 Goering came to visit , sweeping through the buildings and hangars and across the concrete aprons on a specially conducted tour. Galland would remember that the new Reich Minister for Aviation seemed to light the place up with his sheer charisma. He gave the impression of gathering into himself all the dreams and aspirations of the men around him, harnessing them into a focused hope for the future. There was more to come. At Schloss Mittenheim, Goering gave the young aviators a glimpse into the future of the new air force. He described how for two years the Nazi party, and now the government of Germany, had worked to build up manpower and inject new resources into the aviation industry so that, when called upon, it could supply large numbers of combat aircraft. Galland listened intently; he knew that dreams had their place in setting goals, but the realities depended on an expanded industrial base, stronger research and development, and a well run training programme for air and ground crew. Goering spoke confidently of the increased output already achieved in the two years since Hitler came to power – manpower levels in the airframe industry had risen from 4,000 workers in 1933 to 16,900 just a year later, and by the end of the decade would exceed 210,000. By this date the production plan set up on 1 January 1934 had achieved an output of 2,105 aircraft in 13 months[5].

On 26 February 1935 Hitler signed the decree establishing what he referred to as the Reichsluftwaffe, publicly unveiling an independent air force distinct from the army – Reichsheer – and navy – Reichsmarine. (He had personally selected the title of the new service, but it quickly became formalised as the Luftwaffe.) The decree took effect from 1 March, on which date the Luftwaffe had 20 squadrons of land and sea-based aircraft, 20 flying stations, and the special reserve unit with the RLM. The airline DLH also represented an auxiliary bombing force – the airliners they used to fly passengers around Europe could be converted into bombers within a few hours.

The timing of the announcement, with regard to the probable reactions of the Allied powers, had always been considered critical, given Germany's unreadiness for any armed confrontation. In the event the official unveiling of the Luftwaffe made little difference; the intelligence services of the other European governments had already revealed – at least in secret, to their accountable bodies – the existence for some years past of a German air force. Yet the threat of military action by Germany's neighbours had shaped the very structure of the Luftwaffe; and the question of just what kind of air force to build had exercised the generals for a decade or more.

In simplistic terms, the argument was between those who saw the aircraft's role as fulfilling the tactical needs of the army for ground support, reconnaissance and liaison; and those convinced by the theory of strategic air power advanced by such writers as the Italian Giulio Douhet, author of the internationally influential *Command of the Air*. Until the late 1920s the army was more or less united behind the first view; but the claims of a strategic air force would be voiced by such far-sighted staff officers as Obst Hans Jeschonnek[6], Obstlt Helmuth Felmy, Obst Walther Wever, and Genlt Wilhelm Adam. Most tellingly, they were advanced in a secret memorandum of May 1933 from Dr Robert Knauss to Erhard Milch.

Broadly, Knauss defined Germany's dilemma as buying time to build up her strength without pre-emptive interference from her potential enemies to east and west. He proposed a deterrent strategy reminiscent of von Tirpitz's naval plan of pre-1914, with a strong strategic bomber force taking the place of the 'risk-fleet' of heavy battleships. Knauss argued that for the price of two divisions, or two battleships, Germany could produce 400 strategic bombers. Given the fear of unacceptable damage from air assault which was general throughout Europe in the 1930s, this fleet would be a sufficient deterrent to preventitive war while Germany rearmed.

This analysis appealed to Milch, to Deputy Fuehrer Rudolf Hess, and ultimately to Hitler (Goering seems to have been strangely ambivalent). Accordingly, in January 1934 Milch put together a production plan calling for 4,021 aircraft including 822 heavy bombers, 590 reconnaissance or ground-attack aircraft, 51 dive-bombers and 251 fighters, plus 1,760 trainers, and miscellaneous naval and communication types.

In the event, however, a combination of army influence and the limitations of skilled labour shortages and a basic research and development programme would shape the compromise air force which Germany actually got. Inevitably, the many army officers transferred into the command and staff levels of the new Luftwaffe brought with them a core belief in victory through rapid mechanised warfare, which tilted the culture in favour of tactical support. Nevertheless, it should be remembered that Knauss's stated objective was indeed achieved: Europe was intimidated, and Germany did rearm.

* * *

The first day of March, when the new Luftwaffe officially came into being, was declared Air Force Day, and celebrated by special flying displays and parades[7]. Public awareness was important to the recruiting campaign; and on 14 March the links with the air service of 1914-18 were ostentatiously underlined when Jagdgeschwader 132 was redesignated Jagdgeschwader 'Richthofen' Nr.2 (in deference to the first Jagdgeschwader, JG1, formed by Manfred von Richthofen in 1917, the reconstituted group took the next number in sequence).

Although hardly a surprise to their political leadership, the formal announcement of the Luftwaffe sent echoes of public concern reverberating around the countries of Europe. In 1933, when Germany had no armed forces to speak of, Hitler's assumption of total power had caused concern: now doubts about Nazi intentions grew apace with the Wehrmacht. There was in fact no immediate, formal declaration to Germany's neighbours, and the first discussion about the Luftwaffe came on 15 March in an interview given by Goering to Ward Price, correspondent of the London *Daily Mail*. Until 1935 Nazi politics had been internal German affairs; from this year on Hitler would walk a fine, internationally-exposed line between acceptable politics and the provocation of precipitate reaction. Later in March Germany proclaimed the doctrine of Wehrbefreiung (lit: 'liberation of arms'), thus declaring German sovereignty over issues relating to national defence, and implicitly burying the Versailles restrictions. On 25 March Hitler boasted to the British foreign secretary, Sir John Simon, that the Luftwaffe was already bigger than the Royal Air Force[8].

Notes on Chapter 3

1 A captain in the World War I air service, Milch joined Deutsche Luft Hansa in 1926, becoming its chief executive three years later. DLH financed Goering in his lean years before political power brought its rewards, and Milch organised clandestine activities for the 'black' air force prior to 1933, seeing to it that the airline sponsored many projects helpful to the future Luftwaffe.

2 In conversation with the author, Galland said that in his view Goering would have made a much better Reichskanzler than Hitler, because he had little interest in party politics and would have left the government to run the country. Through private

conversations Galland also came to form the view that Goering abhorred the thought of war, and much preferred to enjoy at his leisure the fruits of power, such as his already not inconsiderable gallery of art treasures. Galland believed that a Germany led by Goering would not have taken the risk of attacking Poland.

3 Gen Ritter von Greim would be flown by Hanna Reitsch into Berlin to report to the Fuehrer's bunker on 26 April 1945 – the last outside visitors – leaving on the 30th just after the news of Himmler's negotiations reached Hitler, and the Russian forces got to within a block of the bunker.

4 The designation '132' represented coded information defining the unit. The first digit (1) stood for the unit's number within the Luftkreis or Air District; the second identified the type of unit, in this case (3) for fighter; and the third, (2), the number of the Luftkreis.

5 As part of their long-term planning the army had kept a research and development base alive long before DLH's commercial orders became available. Evading detection by the Allied Control Commission, Ernst Heinkel built during the 1920s various prototypes to army specifications, which were tested at Lipetsk, as were Arado and Dornier designs. The latter company had designs built in Japan and Switzerland and set up facilities in Italy. The armed forces also maintained secret aviation research stations at Rechlin in Mecklenburg, and Travemunde.

6 Jeschonnek was commissioned as a lieutenant at the age of 16, and flew with Jagdstaffel 40 in the Great War. He served in the Army Ordnance Corps between 1923 and 1928, completed General Staff training, and served in the Reichswehr Inspectorate before joining Kampfgeschwader 152 in 1934. As a general he was Chief of the Luftwaffe General Staff from 1939 until he commited suicide in 1943.

7 As so often, great affairs had more basic human consequences. For the graduates of Schleissheim being in the vanguard of change meant that for the first time in the history of the Germany military, and to the outrage of traditionalists, officers were to wear collars and ties under an open-collar tunic – the new Luftwaffe uniform was largely based on that of the Deutscher Luftsportverband.

8 In fact, of 2,500 aircraft theoretically available, fewer than 800 were serviceable; and Hitler was including aircraft that were militarily irrelevant, such as trainers.

CHAPTER 4

April 1935 – April 1937

During March 1935 Galland got his longed-for orders to report to JG2, the Luftwaffe's first fighter unit, then under the command of Maj Wieck and based at Doeberitz. Everything had worked perfectly: his performance at Schleissheim had been good enough to get him a top posting, but not so impressive as to single him out as an instructor. Now at last he was free of schools and training – free to join not only a fighter unit, but the one chosen to carry the legacy of Germany's greatest fighter pilot.

Soon after arriving at I./JG2[1] on 1 April, Galland was assigned to help set up and staff II Gruppe which was to be located at Jueterbog-Damm. (During this early phase of the Luftwaffe's build-up units were hard put to reach establishment. When Galland reported to Doeberitz only I Gruppe had yet formed.) Expansion was being attempted so quickly that it swept the graduate officers into a frenzy of activity which left little time for leisure. Every day brought a succession of rosters, logistical problems, manpower assignments – a blizzard of paperwork, when all the brand new lieutenant wanted was to get back into the air. The weeks raced by, and aircraft for II Gruppe began to arrive during the summer. Everything had had to be built from scratch: barracks, hangars, administration offices – even the roads to the still unfinished airfield, where Galland would soon be flying the new Heinkel He51 single-seat fighter biplane.

The first production aircraft, the He51A-1, came off the production line during April, and was delivered to II./JG2 first. The new fighter had vicissitudes that caught the pilots by surprise. With heavier loadings than the comparatively docile Arado Ar65 flown by I Gruppe, the He51 had about the same all-up weight but a BMW engine which was 50 per cent more powerful – and it showed in performance. Galland was impressed with the new fighter, and explored every aspect of its potential for high-speed manoeuvres. He soon found he had an aptitude for this type of flying and, encouraged by II Gruppe commanding officer Maj Rheitel, set about practising for air displays and competitions. Galland specialised in low altitude aerobatics – the most dangerous, albeit spectacular, type of flying; but Rheitel had no intention of letting one of his young turks write off one of the gleaming new Heinkels, and Galland had to perform his aerial antics in the standard training biplane of the day, the two-seat Focke-Wulf Fw44 Stieglitz.

It was in this aircraft that Galland the amateur engineer met Galland the pilot. He devised a method, implemented by the unit mechanics, of fitting a special carburettor which allowed him to fly the Stieglitz inverted. Seeking better negative response from the elevators he also had them modified, which improved performance in a spin and helped maintain an inverted nose-up attitude. Spinning was part of Galland's low-altitude display – not a trick for those of a nervous disposition.

One day in October 1935 he took the Stieglitz up for a practice session to try out the modifications in a series of well-rehearsed manoeuvres. He decided to give himself a cautious extra 760m (2,500ft), just in case. The modified Stieglitz took off and Galland put in a few basic flick turns and slow rolls to get the feel of the modified elevators. All seemed well – a few unfamiliar responses, but nothing to cause a problem. Now it was time to throw the biplane into the classic aerobatic manoeuvres. It was when Galland tried to perform his spectacular spin recovery that things went badly wrong.

He went into the spin as he always had, and counted through the three turns, at completion of which he had the aircraft under control – but something felt wrong. The turns had taken a few seconds longer than they ever had before, but the Stieglitz was falling to earth at the usual rate. The result was inevitable: there was not enough altitude to recover fully. Galland could see it happening several seconds before it did. With both hands tugging the stick fully back into his stomach, there was nothing else he could do.

As the biplane sliced into the ground it broke up in a cloud of flying turf and dirt, with tangled pieces of wing and fuselage hurtling from the impact. Wrenched from its mountings, the seat slammed forward, burying Galland's face in the instrument panel. Blood and tissue mixed with twisted metal and splintered glass, reshaping Galland's features forever. Mercifully he lost consciousness immediately, and would never remember the impact that nearly took his life.

From all over the airfield fellow pilots and ground crew sprinted to the scene, as smoke and dust drifted lazily across the appalling mass of torn fabric and crushed metal. It took some time and effort to extricate him from the smashed cockpit, carefully freeing his bloodied head from the instrument panel. (One of the pilots who eased him from the crushed cockpit that day was Douglas Pitcairn, who would be his commanding officer at 3./J88 in the Spanish Civil War.) Hardly recognisable and only barely alive, Galland was rushed to Jueterbog army hospital, and into the immediate and expert care of Prof Dr Sauerbruch and an experienced surgeon from Berlin. Under the new regime they were at the hospital on national service, and as luck would have it they were uniquely placed to give Galland the best possible care.

* * *

The surgeons worked on Galland's multiple skull fractures while he lay in a coma, oblivious to his condition. If he lived it would take months for his injuries to heal. Over the next three days Galland's condition hung in the balance; summoned from Westerholt, his parents stayed by the bedside of their 23-year-old son night and day. He found them there when he came round, and needed them most. They explained that he was very lucky to be alive, and gently urged him to abandon all hope of ever flying an aeroplane again.

It was time to count the cost. Apart from a very serious set of cranial fractures, the front of his face had been flattened, his nose had been badly broken and broadened, and there was serious damage to the cornea of his left eye from glass splinters. On discharge from the hospital he was declared medically unfit for flying and sent back to II./JG2, where his commanding officer took a sympathetic view of Galland's dilemma. He had joined the Luftwaffe to fly; even the post of instructor had horrified him – nothing short of active service in a fighter unit was tolerable.

Maj Rheitel had more reason to be understanding than most. He too had fought hard for the opportunity to fly and fight during World War I, when aviation was considered in many circles a very primitive occupation for a military man. He believed in instinctive ability over bureaucratic restrictions; and he knew what an asset his Gruppe had in Galland. After an informal chat with his young officer, Rheitel decided to give him a chance to prove himself. Conveniently pretending to have mislaid the damning medical report, Rheitel let Galland get back in the air to see for himself how his pilot fared. It was all the convalescence Galland needed; he luxuriated in being back where he felt he belonged. He would need to be at his best: new aircraft were on the horizon to test the mettle of the very best pilots.

Throughout 1935 major decisions were being taken about a revolutionary new concept: the all-metal monoplane fighter with enclosed cockpit and retractable undercarriage. On 28 May 1935, less than two months after Galland had joined JG2, Messerschmitt's test pilot Hans Knotsch put the Bf109[2] prototype into the air for the first time. Four other contenders for a Luftwaffe production order put to the air that year, and a competitive evaluation was held at Travemunde. Three of the four, including the Bf109, had Rolls-Royce Kestrel engines. At the end of the competition only two types stood any chance of selection: the Bf109, and Heinkel's He112 gull-wing design. Many favoured the Heinkel, but the Bf109 was eventually selected as the Luftwaffe's primary monoplane fighter.

Galland's ability to keep flying for his Gruppe hinged on Maj Rheitel keeping secret the medical report that declared him unfit. His eye was healed, although sight was a problem, and the other physical injuries disappeared with time. The sheer volume of documentation pouring into the unit literally papered over the report as the expansion of the Geschwader continued. During early 1936 Galland kept up his flying and showed no lasting effects from his crash; a successful return to the air was capped by a magnificent holiday on the Baltic during the summer.

That year brought Galland a new prize, and further reassurance of his recovered eyesight. Obst Ernst Udet – a World War I ace whose 62 victories put him second only to von Richthofen, and a passionate hunter – organised a clay pigeon shooting competition to encourage the general standard of marksmanship. Ten Luftwaffe officers would be selected, to compete against the best shots in the country. Galland saw this opportunity as a personal challenge; he entered, and made the team. In the subsequent shooting championship in Berlin they beat the civilian team with ease. To Galland's astonishment and lifelong delight, each team member was given a matched pair of fine Merkel over-and-under shotguns to keep.

Early that year III Gruppe had been formed, and by summer had its new equipment, the Arado Ar68; by this time I Gruppe had replaced most of its Ar65s with He51s. The Ar68 – in the event, the Luftwaffe's last biplane fighter – was a decided improvement over the He51; but, with even higher wing loading and sharper performance, it was sometimes a handful to fly. Nevertheless, if manoeuvrability was the criterion for measuring fighter performance then it was a major step forward, and Galland was keen to try it out.

He got his chance in October 1936, almost a year after his near-fatal crash. Taking off in an Ar68 from Bernburg airfield, he soon noticed a problem with the engine; it was misfiring badly, and Galland decided at once to swing round and put down. Coming back toward the grass landing strip he failed to notice a row of tall lights extending above a long row of fruit trees lying across his approach path. Intent upon nursing his engine, and partly dazzled by the sun, he swept majestically over the fruit trees and straight into one of the light poles. The Ar68 lost its wings on one side, slewed round and crashed into the ground. Once again Galland's face was cut, his shin was splintered, and he suffered widespread abrasions and bruising. Suffering from concussion, he was quickly taken to hospital; and that was when the secret of his medical status came out.

Galland was hospitalised for several weeks; the hospital administration naturally needed his records, and this time they had to be retrieved and dusted off. The situation was clear: Galland had been flying for almost a year after being declared unfit. Quite how Maj Rheitel explained himself, Galland never knew. Rumours of courts martial came to nothing; but an investigation was held, and an order issued grounding Galland without further notice.

Adolf Galland had other ideas. He worked on the medical staff to convince them that he had been wrongly diagnosed, claiming that although there were still tiny shards of glass in his left eye he had perfect vision. In the absence of any other physical defect they had no right to ground him, particularly when the Luftwaffe needed all the experienced men it could lay hands on. The doctors agreed to send him to a special diagnostic hospital at Magdeburg. During his stay there Galland appealed for help to visiting brother officers; and one of them managed to get hold of the eye test charts. Time and again he studied the charts, using his good eye at close range to memorise the sequence of letters, first forwards, then in reverse. When the test came he simply recited the letters from memory – with just the right degree of natural hesitation. Not one doctor thought to call his bluff by putting together his own sequence of letters. At the end of the visit to Magdeburg no one could find any medical reason to ground him, and he returned in triumph to his astonished squadron.

For the time being that meant continuing to fly Heinkel and Arado biplanes. Many Luftwaffe officers – both the old guard, and young pilots too – regarded the prospect of closed-cockpit monoplanes and retractable landing gear with some unease. Willi Messerschmitt's new Bf109 would give them an edge over the competition, but at a price which concerned some pilots. The heavy wing loading of the monoplane design made the aircraft less manoeuvrable than the biplanes it replaced, although it did have a top speed of almost 465kph (290mph) – some 160kph (100mph) faster than the Ar68. Manoeuvrability, it was argued by Galland and others, is more important that outright speed. There was also concern about the closed cockpit, which it was feared would seriously reduce visibility: never was the maxim 'he who sees first, kills first' truer than in a fighter cockpit.

Another worry was the automatic leading edge slats, designed to pop out and improve aileron control near the stall. This aspect of the design was probably the most controversial, and it was feared that the slats would open automatically during aerobatics. It was also argued that the retractable landing gear would cause problems for pilots used to a fixed undercarriage; and that battle damage which rendered the gear inoperable could write off an aeroplane that might otherwise live to fight another day. (Learning to cope with retractable undercarriages was indeed a problem for many air forces, but they became familiar soon enough.)

Ironically, it was the Spitfire which clinched the argument in favour of the Bf109. The Messerschmitt represented, to some extent, the same design and aero-engineering philosophy as the Spitfire. Powered by a 1,172hp Rolls-Royce Merlin, the Spitfire first flew in March 1936, and soon displayed a top speed of 500kph (316mph). By early July the RAF had ordered some 310 Spitfires; the watchful RLM interpreted this as a vote for speed, and chose the Bf109[3], markedly faster than the He112. (In years to come many pilots would muse over whether the He112 would not, in fact, have been a better fighter.)

Christmas 1936 passed, and 1937 promised to bring the Jagdgeschwader 'Richthofen' this new challenge. It was decided that II./JG2 at Jueterbog-Damm should be the first unit to receive the Bf109B when it rolled off the production line, followed by I./JG2 at Doeberitz. Events on a more distant stage would intervene, however. Spain was now to play a part in Adolf Galland's career for a second time.

* * *

Spain's political, social, and regional differences had become polarised over several years; and it was against a background of anarchy, bloodshed and savage factional hatreds that the Civil War proper broke out in July 1936. The defining act was the Nationalist rising, spearheaded by elements of the army, against the Popular Front government of the Second Republic. Both Republican and Nationalist camps were coalitions of diverse interests; the explicitly Marxist Republic drew its internal support from many elements of the left, the Nationalists from the conservative right. Internationally, the Republic would be supported and supplied largely by the USSR and France, the Nationalists by Fascist Italy and Germany. The Nationalist leader Gen Francisco Franco appealed for German support on 23 July, within days of the rising, and received a swift response. A confidential call for volunteers to fight in Spain reached Luftwaffe units by 27 July; and the first 86 men set sail from Hamburg with six He51 fighters on 31 July.

By autumn 1936 some 4,500 German servicemen – mostly aviation, artillery and armoured specialists – had been shipped to Spain; and November saw the creation of a formal military organisation, the Condor Legion, commanded by Generalmajor Hugo Sperrle. The decision to escalate Luftwaffe involvement stemmed in part from the poor showing made by the aircraft initially sent. The He51 fell prey to faster Russian fighters like the stubby Polikarpov I-16 monoplane; and most German aircraft seemed to be on the ragged edge when it came to holding their own against designs from America, Russia and France. It was apparent that the modern aeronautical technology which Germany was only now putting on the production line already existed elsewhere. In 1937 the Luftwaffe would send to Spain several examples of its 'next-generation' combat aircraft – the Messerschmitt Bf109, Heinkel He111, Junkers Ju87, Dornier Do17 and Henschel Hs126 – to test their effectiveness.

All Galland and his comrades knew about these volunteers initially was that faces would disappear from the mess. When they reappeared months later, with suntans and more money than they knew how to spend, their thrilling stories of a mobile war between aircraft and pilots from several countries made them the centre of attention. Unsurprisingly, Galland found the prospect of returning to Spain – with the chance of flexing his wings in combat, and the certainty of high pay – irresistible. In April 1937 he responded to one of the now frequent invitations by confidential notice; granted leave of absence by his CO, he made his own way to the government building in Berlin which housed the secretive hive of activity known as 'Sonderstab W'. On presentation of his documents from JG2 the formalities were swift and minimal.

He was ordered not to reveal his destination to anyone, in or out of uniform, before arriving in Spain. Once there, all mail home was to be addressed to 'Max Winkler, Berlin SW68' for opening and forwarding. From Berlin he was sent to Doeberitz, where various small parties soon assembled into a group of 370 airmen. In a large gymnasium they were ordered to strip off their uniforms – which caused Galland an uneasy pang – and were issued civilian clothes, papers and travelling money. A rail journey, ostensibly as tourists from the 'Strength through Joy' movement bound for Genoa, took them to Hamburg, and a rusty old liner flying the Panamanian flag.

The voyage which followed was one of the worst experiences of Galland's life. Their quarters, deep in the bowels of the ship, were appallingly crude and filthy; the crew appeared to be professional gun-runners; and once beyond territorial waters Captain van Ehren insisted that the passengers stay below decks, in conditions of unrelieved squalor. With some difficulty, given their disguises, it was eventually established that Galland was the senior German officer. He tried to maintain some sort of order, but discipline became such a serious problem that he was obliged to have some troublemakers lashed to the mast. The supposedly seven-day voyage was delayed by engine trouble and by bad weather in the Bay of Biscay, adding to the misery and bad temper below decks; the food rations were cut, and then the water. Galland was seriously worried about mutiny when, after 12 days at sea, they finally sighted El Ferrol on 8 May 1937.

From El Ferrol a tedious, 500km (310 mile) rail journey took the volunteers across northern Spain to the town of Vitoria in the province of Castilla y Leùn. Here a major concentration of Franco's forces in the north was anchored on the Navarra Brigades, highly motivated troops familiar with the region. Because of the accepted superiority of the Luftwaffe planning staffs the Condor Legion was in overall control of Spanish, German and Italian air units throughout the region.

Galland and his men would wear olive-brown uniforms, assuming false Condor Legion ranks as, ostensibly, individual mercenaries fighting for pay. Galland was instantly 'promoted' to the rank of captain, and given three stars to wear on the shabby uniform (which reminded him depressingly of that of the National Socialist Labour Service, the RAD). All in all, it was not quite what he had imagined; and his spirits were not improved when he discovered what his initial duties were to be.

Notes to Chapter 4

1 I./JG2 – the first Gruppe of Jagdgeschwader 2. The Jagdgeschwader of the new Luftwaffe were divided into three Gruppen, each of which had three Staffeln of nine aircraft. At full strength JG2 should have had about 94 aircraft, counting Geschwader and Gruppen staff machines. For a fuller explanation of Luftwaffe unit designations see Glossary.

2 The confusion over the type prefix arises from the original registration of the company as Bayerische Flugzeugwerke AG on 30 July 1926, the model 109 therefore bearing the prefix Bf. On 11 July 1938 the management changed the name to Messerschmitt AG, with Willi Messerschmitt as chairman and managing director; henceforward all new designs carried the prefix Me, e.g. Me163, Me262, etc.

3 The Bf109B was powered by a 720hp Junkers Jumo 210 engine, giving a maximum 400kph (255mph) at sea level but 465kph (290mph) at 4,000m (13,120ft). By comparison, the Spitfire Mk I with its 1,030hp Merlin engine had a top speed of 465kph (290mph) at sea level and 580kph (362mph) at 5,640m (18,500ft). However, the Spitfire would not enter squadron service for another 18 months, by which time the 1,175hp Daimler-Benz DB601 engine would give the Bf109E a comparable performance.

CHAPTER 5

May 1937 – July 1938

At Vitoria Galland joined Jagdgruppe 88, the Condor Legion's fighter unit, which consisted in May 1937 of three Staffeln equipped with the He51. To his frustration, the new arrival found himself assigned to 3./J88 on administrative duties, overseeing maintenance and repair. For several weeks he supervised the arrival of aircraft, set up repair shops and organised motor transport; he even acquired a new nickname – 'Capitano'.

Jagdgruppe 88 had formed on 3 November 1936 under the command of Hubertus von Merhart. Eighteen He51s had arrived at Sevilla by freighter, ostensibly to serve as fighters – the role for which they had been designed, but in which this war would find them outclassed. By early December 1936 J88 had three Staffeln ready for action: 1./J88 under Hptmn Werner Palm, 2./J88 under Hptmn Otto Lehmann and 3./J88 under Hptmn Juergen Roth. The first credited enemy kill was a Soviet Polikarpov I-16 shot down by Hptmn Palm on 16 December. For much of the time the Jagdgruppe was kept busy escorting Ju52 bombers. There was excitement on 14 March when the first Bf109B-1s arrived with 2./J88, now commanded by Oblt Guenther Luetzow.

By the end of March 1937 Franco had concentrated his forces – and, with the agreement of the Condor Legion staff, the air elements – against the northern front from Bilbao to Gijùn. The main offensive in the northern sector began on 31 March, just over a month before Galland arrived in Spain. The pilots faced little opposition from Republican aircraft in this sector, but enemy ground fire was effective. The difficulty of distinguishing civilian from military targets in the conditions of civil war led to a cavalier attitude in attacks on roads and bridges. In the most notorious miscalculation the market town of Guernica was attacked indiscriminately by Condor Legion He111B-1 and Do17 bombers for three hours on the evening of 26 April. Some 300 people were killed and 900 injured, many of them by a second wave of Ju52s which caught civilians who had thought it safe to leave shelter. The military objectives, a bridge and road junction east of the town, were completely undamaged.

When Condor Legion pilots flew across the area to report damage next day they were appalled. A pilot from 1./J88, Oblt Harro Harder, noted in his diary that '[Guernica] has been totally destroyed, and not by the Reds as all the local newspapers report, but by German and Italian bombers. It is the opinion of all of us that it was a rotten trick to destroy such a militarily unimportant city as Guernica ...' When Galland arrived at Vitoria he found those who had witnessed the episode shocked and depressed. The Luftwaffe in general, and the Condor Legion in particular, would never be allowed to forget Guernica, where the difficulty of hitting a specific target without precision bombing equipment became all too apparent.

During the first month of Galland's stay at Vitoria the Bf109 proved itself against the opposition. Guenther Luetzow had been the first Bf109 pilot to claim a kill when he shot down a Polikarpov I-15 on 14 April. Now the He51 was to be relegated to the ground-attack role, leaving the much faster monoplane to contend for air superiority. While Galland endured his frustration at organising repair work and logistics – only occasionally arranging his duties well enough to allow him to keep his hand in with flights in the He51 – the 'Iron Ring' around Bilbao was broken by the Navarra Brigades, and the town fell to the Nationalists on 12 June. Galland's long-awaited baptism of fire was one consequence.

In an attempt to free the Nationalist hold on Madrid, Gen Miaja's Republican forces mounted an advance from the west southward past Brunete, breaching Franco's lines and weakening his attack on Santander. To help stem the tide the Nationalists switched attention to the south; 1. and 2./J88 moved down to Escalona and Avila, 3./J88 to Villa del Prado with a forward base about 64km (40 miles) from Avila. Headquartered at Avila by 8 July, Stab/J88 was put in charge of all Nationalist air units – some 200 aircraft. The Republicans had assembled about twice that number.

On 24 July 1937 Galland saw action for the first time, near Brunete – flat terrain, with no features to mask an aircraft's approach, and heavily defended by AA guns (which had claimed an He51 only five days earlier). Gotthardt Handrick, the Olympic athlete who had recently taken command of J88, was one of eight pilots who took off to suppress the flak and support the infantry that day. Whenever he could get airborne in his He51 Galland flew with Oblt Harder's 1 Staffel; others flying that day included Harder, Lt Reutter, Ofw Wilfert, Uffzs Beurer and Kolbow and Gefr Terry. Of that flight, Harder was to write later:

'I divided the Staffel into four pairs. We flew as far as Brunete at low level, then climbed. We observed the bombing by the Spanish squadrons... then we made our attack on the anti-aircraft positions. We were greeted by a real display of fireworks. Shells burst above, beside and below us ... We went over to low-level attack and were met by intense 20mm fire from every direction. I was able to make out one of the AA positions clearly. I dived, pinning them down with machine gun fire, and dropped my whole load (six 10kg/22lb bombs). Everywhere we looked there were He51s dancing and attacking through the anti-aircraft fire. The battle lasted about eight minutes, until we had dropped all our bombs. Then we assembled and headed off in the direction of Brunete to support the infantry. As soon as they saw us they launched their assault. Although we had almost no ammunition or bombs, we so shook the Red infantry by several dangerous attacks that they left their positions and ran away in headlong flight.'

The He51s flew twice more that day; during the evening sortie Lt Reutter was shot down and killed. Harder's diary again: 'Our nerves are shot. This latest loss just about finished me off. The staff medical officer urgently requested three weeks leave for the five senior pilots of my Staffel. Beurer, whose aircraft had taken numerous hits that morning, had already broken down. The rest of us were not far away from it.'

The Republican heavy AA guns particularly threatened the slow Junkers Ju52s – converted airliners which still doubled as bombers, even though the He111 and Do17 were now being introduced in larger numbers. J88 were required to neutralise the AA guns in the bombers' path, running the gauntlet of hostile fire. Galland, coming fresh to the work, found that he revelled in these ground-strafing missions. With engines straining at full throttle the stubby biplanes would plummet out of the sky and hurtle towards the AA positions. Every so often flying wires or metal skin would give out the ringing whine of a ricochet, or the fuselage would shudder as bullets plucked through the canvas. The heat, the vortices of dust and smoke whipped into patterns by the propeller at low altitude, the sheer thrill of being shot at as he charged through the dense and acrid air in an open cockpit – all of it sent the adrenaline coursing, just as he had imagined it a thousand times before. But the hunter within – the instinct to stalk and kill, shaped by generations of ancestors and awakened by his father in the Westerholt woods – still sought release; and he yearned for the challenge of a one-on-one duel.

* * *

In this war there were no rule books: the Staffel pilots devised their own ways of achieving results, and it was in Spain that the tactics for the new age of air warfare began to evolve. There was some official expectation that the Legion pilots would report back their evaluations of aircraft and their employment, but few found the time or the inclination to do so. Galland was different; even without the pressure from Berlin he would have been eager to compile his own records – analysing his observations, evaluating techniques, devising new methods, and trying to make tactical and strategic sense of this overwhelming new experience, for the benefit of other pilots.

During his first month in action Galland demonstrated the three separate facets of his character that would fashion him for leadership in the next few years. He was a very capable pilot, and a very brave fighting man; and he could analyse the battle, thinking several steps ahead.

In this same period the brotherhood-in-arms of a fighting unit made a deep and lasting impression on him. The loyalty and respect that he quickly came to feel for his fellow pilots, and for the unsung ground crews who kept them in the air, were never to leave him. In his first two months in Spain Galland saw the effect of war on ordinary men. He experienced daily the intensity with which they went into battle, and the withering effect of a few hours in combat upon even the strongest. Spain instilled in him a deep respect for fighting men everywhere, linked by a common bond transcending nationality or politics; and throughout his career this would govern his treatment of friend and foe alike.

At the end of July elements of J88 moved to Alar del Rey, north of Burgos, and Calahorra, north-west of Tudela. By this date the Gruppe had 18 He51s and nine Bf109s, the latter deployed with 1. and 2.Staffeln. Galland had done well in his initial period with 3./J88, setting it up for the operations which he was now heavily involved in planning and implementing on a daily basis. On 27 July he received due recompense when he was given command of the Staffel, succeeding Hptmn Douglas Pitcairn, and from 1 August he was promoted to Oberleutnant; now he could begin to apply his own tactics and views on leadership.

It was at this period that Galland introduced a new weapon. Most He51s carried a single 170-litre long range belly tank, but their short range missions made this unnecessary. Galland had his mechanics fill the tanks with 87 octane fuel and attach two 10kg (22lb) bombs. Jettisoning the tank produced an impact-detonated fire bomb, highly effective over about 100sq/m (1,000sq/ft). The other Staffeln copied the idea – to the consternation of the supply depot over the sudden run on 87 octane fuel and metal tanks. An improved version featured a mixture of used fuel oil and four bombs instead of two.

The new Staffelkapitaen forged a close relationship with the mechanics, getting to understand their work and their needs – a policy he would pursue throughout his flying career, and which would stand him in good stead. (Even today, pilots marvel at the range of field modifications he was able to carry out – all with the help of men he trusted, who knew what he wanted and could count on his respect.) As a boy Galland had read how in 1918 von Richthofen had encouraged the culture of field servicing and attention to detail; his pilots were made to take responsibility for the condition of their aircraft and its armament – 'No gun jams itself!' It was an ethic he was naturally inclined to pursue now he had a Staffel of his own, demanding meticulous preparation for flight to minimise mechanical or armament failure during combat. In World War II Galland worked tirelessly to weld together his pilots, the aircraft they flew, and the skills of the ground crews to a single, focused objective: effective combat operations. He could be quite fanatical about this, extending it even to the private lives of his men; Galland wanted no pilot on his squadron whose personal entanglements diluted his energy and commitment to battle.

A more relaxed tradition echoing the days of the Great War aces was the Staffel insignia, an unofficial but cherished good luck symbol. When Galland took over command of 3./J88 the Staffel carried the emblem of a certain famous cartoon mouse. Originally introduced by his predecessor Douglas Pitcairn, the mouse – distinguished from its less bellicose Hollywood original by an axe, a pistol and a parachute harness – would follow Galland as his personal insignia throughout World War II. His He51 also carried the type number 2 and the individual aircraft number 78 each side of the Nationalist insignia on the fuselage.

* * *

In the heat of the Spanish summer the He51 pilots of J88 were flying a very different war from the one they wanted. Ostensibly fighters, the stubby little biplanes were no match for the Republicans' Russian I-15, or the even more formidable I-16 monoplane. (Aircraft identification was sketchy in Spain; the I-15 was often misleadingly called a 'Curtiss', and was nicknamed 'Chato' by the Nationalists; the I-16 was called a 'Boeing', 'Rata' or 'Mosca'[2].) The I-16 gradually became the primary Republican fighter, relegating the I-15 to a ground-attack role. Now it was the turn of the monoplanes to 'ride shotgun' while the once-proud biplane fighters trucked bombs around the lower sky.

In the month when Galland took over 3./J88 the Republicans captured Reinosa, an important arms centre. Staffeln 1. and 3./J88 moved east to Orzales, while pilots of 2./J88 increased their scores against Chato biplanes; in fierce fighting on 21 and 22 August, Luetzow, Pingel and Flegel got one apiece. Now the battle was joined for Asturias, and on 2 September J88 moved to the Santander region. A week later Galland's He51s ran into stiff opposition:

'We were attacked by enemy fighters, six Ratas and four Curtisses. It immediately developed into a wild dogfight. A broken layer of cloud at 1,500m (5,000ft) had allowed the enemy to take us by surprise. With unexpected speed we formed a defensive circle, all the while harassed by the superior enemy. One of our machines had been hit, was losing oil and had to head back across the front. Our defensive circle was broken. A wild chase began. Each of us had one of these fellows on his tail, and we tried to shake them off by flying low over the ground between the steep walls of the mountain valleys. The Rata behind me fired like mad . . .

'During the dogfight I had seen a parachute going down. I didn't know who it was and had no time for such thoughts. Back at our aerodrome at Santander we first looked at each other in wide-eyed astonishment, and then determined that another of our number was missing. We had just finished counting the hits (37 round, 4 horizontal), when the last one appeared in the sky. Teniente Eduard Neumann had taken the liberty of shooting down a Curtiss. It crashed on the airfield at Llanes.'

In recalling this action at leisure Galland was sympathetic to his men; on the day he took a very different view, claiming that they had broken the circle and panicked, each charging about the valley trying to save his own life. After landing he gave them a severe dressing down, which only ceased when Neumann appeared to report his victory. Incidents like this taught Galland valuable lessons in leadership.

On 21 September 3./J88 moved again, to an airstrip near Llanes. They haunted the roads behind the Republican lines, watching for the tell-tale glint of sun on metal or a plume of dust; but very little activity was spotted. In due course they realised that the enemy moved their supplies during twilight or at night. Galland described a take-off just as the sun was going down:

'We flew along in the last red glimmer of the sun a few metres above the calm water of the Bay of Biscay, 65-90km (40-55 miles) deep in enemy territory. Then we turned back toward land, climbed to more than 900m (3,000ft), and soon the first salvo from 18 machine guns and numerous bomb racks was striking communications traffic and troops, munitions and supply transport. Then we turned back in the direction of the front, attacking anything that showed itself on the roads and railway lines. We dubbed this new tactic "the evening blessing", and were extremely pleased with our success . . .'

Although the pace of operations was demanding, there was occasionally time to relax and soak in Spanish pleasures. For Galland one of the most alluring was the hunting. Parties of pilots would drive from Avila some 65km (40 miles) into the mountains of the Parador de Gredos, returning with trophies for their hastily decked-out mess rooms. (To the end of his life one of Galland's proudest trophies was the head of a rare ibex bagged during summer 1937.) It was in Spain that Galland acquired his weakness for thick Brazilian cigars, a habit that would become his unmistakable trademark. There were also the pleasures of the cellar, and the table; and many a dashing legionary hurled himself into pursuit of a pair of dark eyes ... During that long, hot summer at the front life took on a strange flavour all its own. The pilots would go to war in their open cockpits wearing nothing more than underpants and fur boots. Formalities were kept to a minimum, but in the air – where it mattered – discipline was tight.

That autumn a drive against Republican forces around Gijùn and Aviles led to the first major encounter between I-16s and the Bf109s of 1./J88. Six I-16s (three flown by Russians) and three I-15s took off from Carreno to attack He111 bombers escorted by six Bf109Bs; the biplanes hit the bombers while the I-16s went for the escorts, shooting down two.

In six weeks of fighting for Gijùn and Aviles, 3./J88 had expended an average 25,000 rounds of ammunition a day; for much of this period they had flown several sorties daily – sometimes six or seven – driving home attacks on roads, railways and communication centres. It was time for a rest; the Gruppe personnel flew south to Leùn, leaving the Asturian hills to the rain and murk of late autumn, and the aircraft to a thorough overhaul. 1./J88 'Marabou' under Harder had recently completed conversion to Bf109s, giving its remaining He51s to a new 4.Staffel which formed on 2 November under Eberhardt. Schlichting's 2./J88 'Zylinder' also had Bf109s; but still 3./J88 'Mickymaus' under Galland soldiered on with the He51. (Galland's squadron was to relinquish biplanes for Bf109Cs only in mid-1938, after he had completed his tour of duty; he would not get to fly the Messerschmitt in combat for another two years[3].)

The effectiveness of 3./J88, though limited by the He51's small warload, was significant. As leader of the only Condor Legion Staffel wholly committed to the ground-attack role, Galland's reports played a part in a policy debate then raging over the development of a purpose-designed dive-bomber, as opposed to the use of fighters – suitably modified and armed – for ground-strafing. Ernst Udet[4], promoted Inspector of Fighter and Dive-bomber Forces in February 1936, and to head of the Technical Office that June, was a keen advocate of the Sturzkampffleugzeug (Stuka) concept: an aircraft designed to deliver bombs on pinpoint targets in a high speed, high angle dive. A leading opponent was Obstlt Wolfram von Richthofen (a cousin of the 'Red Baron'); as Condor Legion chief of staff, he used Galland's reports to support the opposing case for the 'Schlachtflieger'. In January 1937 a trials unit, VK/88, was set up to test the Henschel Hs123 biplane, the Bf109, the He112, and the new gull-winged Ju87 dive-bomber for suitability as a close-support assault aircraft. In January 1938 I./ StG 162 'Immelmann' sent three of its new Ju87A-1 pre-production aircraft to Spain for operational evaluation.

A surprise Republican offensive at Teruel in December 1937 sent J88 to a forward base at Calamocha. Disgusted by the inefficiency and disruption inseparable from these frequent moves, Galland had his men turn to and convert a 12-coach train into a permanent mobile squadron headquarters, with offices, accomodation, mess, and other facilities. Using a locomotive on temporary loan from the national railways, the whole squadron could move together to new bases, the aircraft flying in as normal. The idea was later copied by several other units.

At Calamocha the strain of low-level combat missions was not eased by temperatures which plunged to -17C; pilots and ground crews suffered greatly in these freezing conditions. Christmas came as a mixed blessing for the legionaries. The pilot Hajo Herrmann remembered: 'Christmas in a foreign country. Christmas at war ... On the afternoon of Christmas Eve we drove to Salamanca to see a German film. It was evocative of house and home, country and loved ones, so much so that when it was over and we were on our way back, most of us sat in the bus subdued and silent. Later we sang "Silent Night".' On New Year's Day 1938 Galland led a particularly intensive assault on a Republican armoured column, and his He51s were peppered with shrapnel from their own bombs. On another occasion – the closest he came to serious injury – ground fire put one bullet through the wing, another cleanly through a cockpit handle and into the instrument panel, and a third through his boot, grazing his foot. Keeping the aircraft operational in the freezing cold and snow was a constant challenge; when a pre-heater arrived at Calamocha it was put into almost constant use warming up the engines before flight.

On 8 January Teruel fell to the Republicans. The fighting went on without respite for the rest of January and most of February, with Condor Legion bombers raiding Teruel from Zaragoza, El Burgo de Osma, Alfaro and Bunuel. In mid-February Lt Haas's Kette of three Ju87 Stukas arrived at Calamocha; their first mission on 17 February failed due to navigation problems. (Later operations, out of Sevilla, would prove more successful, especially after examples of the new Ju87B arrived later in 1938[5].)

The devastated ruins of Teruel were retaken by the Nationalists on 21 February; and shortly thereafter J88 moved to Gallur on the Ebro river north-west of Zaragoza. A Nationalist offensive along the Ebro towards the Mediterranean began on 9 March, and in support the Condor Legion made constant attacks on enemy troops and armour in the northern sector of the advance. Again, 1. and 2./J88 escorted the bombers while 3.Staffel kept in close contact with the advancing ground units. On 15 April the Nationalists reached the Mediterranean at Vinaroz. Testimony to Galland's expertise is found in an account by Oblt Wilhelm Balthasar, who had recently joined J88 (and who would go on to become the leading ace of the 1940 French campaign, receiving the Oak Leaves to the Knight's Cross.) Of one attack led by Galland he would recall:

'The Reds have established themselves at the edge of a high plateau in very well fortified positions. We have already made two attacks on this trench system. Those people up there are heroic defenders and good shots. Galland had the cards shot right out of his hands on the last sortie. We almost always had reason to regret coming up against those fellows. We have thought out a completely new approach; we'll smoke out the nest. Galland hasn't loaded any bombs this time, instead a drop tank full of petrol fitted with a detonator ...

'Flying in a line, we wind through the terrain like a snake, exploiting the cover offered by every small valley, every tree, every hedge. Up front Galland flies so skilfully that I frequently lose sight of him. Now he pulls up, wings over to the left, and goes down in a steep dive. Is he going to pull out? My God – he's going to ram the target! Then the tank separates and falls right in the centre of the position. There is a dull thump and a bright flash reaches the sky. A glowing firestorm pours into the trenches. They're already running, forced to flee back across the broad flat plateau.'

During this period of intense activity air-to-air victories among the Bf109 pilots became more frequent. Harder had already recorded ten kills, while Fw Boddem and Lt Seiler had nine each. As in World War I, individual combat kills were becoming a measure of personal prowess. Galland ached to get command of a Bf109 Staffel; but he had already outstayed his tenure in Spain.

Volunteer pilots usually saw four to six months' action before returning to Germany, and Galland had already been in Spain for almost a year. Requests that he appoint a replacement had been deflected largely because he was now a Staffelkapitaen, and could convincingly claim that experienced leadership was vital given the regular rotation of other pilots. He played the system for as long as he could, hoping to keep command long enough for the coveted Messerschmitts to arrive; but such appointments were felt too valuable for future Luftwaffe Staffel and Gruppe commanders for Berlin to be put off indefinitely. Galland rejected as totally unsuitable for command the first replacement they sent out – which was his prerogative. The second candidate, Hptmn Hubert Hering, arrived on 22 March; there was no obvious reason to reject him, and Berlin would never tolerate it anyway. Just eight days later Hptmn Hering collided with another He51 piloted by Lt Manfred Michaelis while returning to Lanaja from a sortie into the Alcaraz sector; both pilots were killed.

Galland had begun to believe that he really might get just a brief period flying fighter patrols in the Bf109 when, one evening in the bar of the Hotel Christina in Sevilla, a young German came up and introduced himself as Galland's successor, Lt Werner Moelders[6.] He came with a message from Berlin to the effect that this was the best man they could send and he would have to do. At first inclined to look for some flaw that Berlin could not ignore, Galland came to admire and respect him, recognizing another serious student of tactics and air combat. They flew together for a month, and Galland thought him a natural leader. Although this quiet, unassuming young Roman Catholic officer would bring a more studious style to the job, Galland had no qualms about entrusting 3.Staffel to his mature hands; and on 24 May 1938 command was formally transferred. In less than seven months Moelders would be back in Berlin having achieved recognition out of all proportion to his rank; and within little more than two years he and Galland would be vying with one another for the highest laurels their country could bestow.

* * *

Before Galland returned to Germany he took leave to visit Tetuane in Spanish

Morocco, accompanied by J88 commander Gotthardt Handrick and Oblt Schellmann from 1.Staffel. There was time, too, for a final taste of the relaxing pleasures of Andalusia; but at last, in August, the day came for the inevitable return to a more formal routine. As Galland flew home in a lumbering Ju52 with a contingent of other time-expired volunteers, he could reflect on the experiences of an extraordinary year.

Before leaving Spain Galland had finally got the chance to make ten flights in the Bf109; and he was mightily impressed. Here at last was the mount he had been waiting for; in the narrow cockpit of that sleek fuselage, feeling the exhilaration of its sheer speed, he knew instinctively that this was where his passions for flying and for the hunt would come lethally together. It was a tantalising glimpse of a world he knew would be his, one day.

His faithful, much-patched He51 had carried him safely through 280 sorties over enemy territory, in the thick of the fight, in baking heat and numbing cold. The Heinkel had given Galland his first taste of combat and, through the skill with which he handled his position in the Staffel, his first command. For a while he had been king in his own kingdom, with responsibility to carry out the Gruppe orders but with flexibility to run his own show.

He had done much work beside flying and fighting, and he hoped that the flow of reports back to Berlin had at least begun to inform that giant administrative machine which often seemed unaware of the lessons being learned down south in this grubby war. His experience here had laid the foundations for a reflective analysis of the way operational units were organised, how they flew and how they fought.

Galland thought too about the concerns voiced by many of his comrades over the kind of war that they were fighting in. In J88 there had been plenty of opportunity to see how Franco's Nationalists treated civilians, and to recognize their indifference to the real issues around which this war had supposedly ignited. The medieval gulf between the richest and poorest in Spain was openly discussed in the mess. The volunteers had also formed a poor opinion of the military discipline and efficiency of their allies, and a respect for their enemies. It was not an uncommon joke in the mess for pilots to wonder if they could change sides, so that they could take advantage of Nationalist negligence to pick off easy targets instead of facing the well-concealed Republican guns.

What Galland was totally unprepared for, as the Ju52 droned north, was his return to a Byzantine world of power politics, to which almost every official in Berlin subscribed.

Notes to Chapter 5

1 These were not the first Bf109s in Spain; three pre-production aircraft (V-4, V-5 and V-6) were delivered in January for operational evaluation.

2 The Polikarpov I-15 biplane, powered by a licence-built 480hp Bristol Jupiter radial engine and carrying four 7.62mm machine guns, was relatively slow but very manoeuvrable, easily out-turning the early Bf109s. The altogether more dangerous Polikarpov I-16 was a next-generation monoplane fighter with two 20mm ShVAK and

two 7.62mm ShKAS guns and a top speed of 521kph (326mph) at sea level.

3 The Bf109C had a 730hp Junkers Jumo 210 engine with fuel injection, two 7.92mm MG17 machine guns in the wings and two above the engine; the Bf109B had the standard armament for which the series had been designed, two MG17s above the engine and a third firing through the propeller boss. In August 1938 3./J88 would begin to re-equip with the Bf109D-1, which had two cowling machine guns and two wing MG17s, and the 680hp Jumo 210 of the B. In Germany a few Bf109Ds received the more powerful Daimler-Benz DB600 delivering 986hp, and a three-bladed propeller; but concentration on the deterrent bomber fleet gave the similarly powered He111 priority. The DB600 Bf109D had a top speed of 570kph (355mph), about 130kph (80mph) faster than the 109C; but even this was only an interim version before the 109E with its 1,100hp DB601A. Designed for the DB601, the Bf109 had been rushed into operational use with a less powerful engine; it was seriously under-powered in its early versions, and the definitive engine was available in quantity only in late 1938. The airframe was capable of carrying the much more powerful DB601 series; there was a great relative increase in performance between the Bf109B and the Bf109F, which first flew in 1940. By that time the Bf109 was markedly superior to the early Spitfire; but the series would peak at this point, gradually falling behind other designs like the Fw190, and the later marks of Spitfire and P-51 Mustang.

4 After his heroic World War I service Udet led a colourful and adventurous life as a barnstorming pilot, amateur explorer and international playboy. An attractive, impressionable personality, it was with difficulty that he was wooed into the new Luftwaffe by Goering in June 1935 with the rank of Oberst. He would commit suicide in 1941 as a Generalleutnant.

5 With a bomb load of up to 450kg (1,000lb), routinely deliverable to within 7m (21ft) of a pinpoint target, the Ju87 was much more effective than the biplane Hs123 with its four 50kg (110lb) bombs. With effective air brakes, it could be controlled in a true 90-degree dive at a constant 600kph (370mph) – a unique capability.

6 A graduate of Dresden military academy, Moelders had applied for the clandestine Luftwaffe in 1934, but chronic motion sickness almost led to his rejection. Plagued by nausea throughout training at Braunschweig and Schleissheim and after posting to Stukageschwader 'Immelmann', he gradually mastered this reaction. In 1936 he was posted as an instructor to Jagdfliegerschule 1 under Theo Osterkamp, where he trained several future aces including Helmut Wick, Walter Oesau and Hans Hahn before the Oberkommando der Luftwaffe sent him to Spain.

CHAPTER 6

August 1938 – August 1939

Although it had been only 15 months since he sailed for Spain, when Galland returned to Germany in August 1938 it seemed to him that he found the country transformed. In the five years since Hitler came to power the nation had been mobilised and regimented almost beyond recognition. The contrasts between ramshackle, war-torn Spain and the new Germany made the impact all the greater. People were better off; almost everyone was in work; the country was running like a Swiss watch, and everything was organised by the state. Fed the Party line by Propaganda Minister Joseph Goebbels, the majority of ordinary Germans believed that fundamentally Hitler was doing a good job: the years of want and uncertainty seemed to be over, and Germany could stand tall again on the international stage

.But there was very little sense of freedom. Galland missed the expressions of individual wit and cynicism which had been commonplace in Spain. In every facet of life the Party increasingly controlled the choices of ordinary people, who were denied a place in the decision-making structure. The new Germany was like an automated machine – a machine waiting for some undefined but inescapable purpose to become clear. Galland felt confused, and surprisingly out of place; it was as if he was caught in a time machine, unprepared as the future rushed to meet him. To many thoughtful observers outside Germany, where there was no state control of information, it appeared all too clear that what the country was rushing towards was war.

There was nowhere in Berlin that Galland felt more uncomfortable than in the massive six-storey barrack blocks of the new RLM building on the Wilhelm-strasse, to which he was ordered to report on arrival. It seemed to be populated by military prima donnas and bureaucratic stuffed shirts, all of them stalking the endless corridors and courtyards stiffly – not so much from any natural military bearing, as to avoid creasing their colourful new uniforms. For all its modernity, Galland saw the RLM as a museum of patronising mannequins quite aloof from the realities of modern combat.

For a while he was able to escape to Westerholt for leave with family and friends, catching up on domestic news. The older Gallands had mixed feelings about the state of their nation. The renewed sense of unity and purpose was, for Germans of their generation, a very positive aspect to set against their unease over the strident authoritarianism of the state; it gave them a feeling of directed action, of damage being repaired and old wrongs righted. On the other hand, the economic situation was not an unmixed blessing for the middle classes. Germany's apparently booming wealth was achieved partly by reckless currency and credit manipulations; savings and dividends were low, and although prices had risen 25 per cent in a few years, wages had actually fallen.

The great mass of the German people felt a deep revulsion for war. They believed that Hitler was leading them, by properly robust but essentially peaceful means, to total liberation from the hated legacy of Versailles, and unequivocal restoration of national prosperity and pride. Their tragedy, and the world's, was that he was knowingly mobilising them to march down a path of aggressive expansion – the only path by which his vision was in fact attainable. During these years Hitler gambled recklessly, but successfully, that the traumatic memories of 1914-18 would sufficiently deter the other European powers from military confrontation before Germany was strong enough to face them. Even while the German forces remained dwarfed by those of France – Hitler's main concern – he pushed through the first steps of his planned expansion by a combination of diplomatic brinkmanship, undercover thuggery, and stage management of public opinion.

That war was in fact inevitable was perhaps most nakedly revealed at Hitler's meeting on 5 November 1937 with war minister Werner von Blomberg, foreign minister Constantin von Neurath, and the three service chiefs – Genobst Werner von Fritsch, Adm Erich Raeder and Genobst Goering. On that occasion the prospect of war with one or more neighbouring countries was openly accepted, as the price of the policy aim: to 'secure and preserve the racial community and to enlarge it' by acquiring 'living space' in the east. Various anticipated scenarios – specifically, possible international reactions to an annexation of Austria and the elimination of Czechoslovakia – would affect the exact course of events; but it was accepted that competitive rearmament would in any case make war inescapable by 1943.

Within three months of that meeting Hitler had freed himself of the hampering presence of those he contemptuously called 'the old moralists'. War minister von Blomberg and Gen Fritsch were forced from their posts by sexual scandals, at least partly engineered by the SS. The German cabinet met for the last time on 4 February 1938. From that date the War Ministry was abolished, replaced by the High Command of the Armed Forces (OKW), headed by the compliant Genlt Wilhelm Keitel; and Hitler himself became commander in chief of the armed forces. Wholesale dismissals and transfers of general officers followed.

It is known that this reshuffle did not in fact emasculate the potential resistance to Hitler among the traditional military leadership. Men like Genlt Ludwig Beck, the army chief of staff until August 1938, and his successor Gen Franz Halder, were all too aware of Germany's unreadiness for war in 1938, and feared that Hitler's recklessness would lead them to military disaster. Halder's determination to prevent this, if necessary by a military coup against Hitler, was only disarmed by the Fuehrer's astonishing success in securing the Allied powers' agreement, at Munich in September 1938, to German dismemberment of Czechoslovakia (ostensibly justified by the supposed plight of the 3 million Sudeten German minority within that state, which dated only from 1918). At that time war genuinely seemed imminent; and during this crisis Adolf Galland was one of thousands of staff officers spurred into frenzied activity behind the scenes.

* * *

Recalled early from a peaceful leave in Westphalia in summer 1938, Galland reported to the RLM to work on the staff of a certain Obstlt Dr Gnamm. Against the background of a worsening political crisis over German demands on Czechoslovakia, and contingency planning for war with that country (under the code name 'Case Green'), his initial task was to prepare reports and recommendations on the subject of close air support of ground troops, based on his experience in Spain. He found Gnamm a pleasant and understanding boss, sympathetic to the frustrations of his battle-proven young colleague. Although his own work was limited to tactical considerations, Galland inevitably gained some insight into the level and pace of preparations for the war with France and Britain which the Czechoslovakian crisis was thought likely to ignite.

Galland's reports and briefings on the potential for battlefield close-support by the new 'Schlachtgruppen' which were then being planned were not accepted uncritically. There was at that time a general belief that 'the bomber will always get through', and that the Luftwaffe's fast, well-armed Heinkels and Dorniers would provide a more effective means of hitting the enemy even in a battlefield environment. Galland argued that the relative success of the Condor Legion bombers, upon which this argument was partly based, was due to their freedom from high calibre fighter opposition in Spain – circumstances which could not be assumed to apply in a war against first class powers.

His arguments for the importance of the closest co-ordination between support aircraft and ground forces were accepted. He was able to quote specific instances of the vital importance of air attacks being delivered immediately before ground advances, so as to leave the enemy no respite to recover. This was the simplest extension of the effective artillery/infantry tactics of 1916-18; but there was still a frustrating pessimism, among officers lacking modern combat experience, about the practical feasibility of such tight air/ground liaison.

Even while pressing his arguments, Galland regarded the whole issue as a distraction from his ambition to beccome an operational fighter pilot, and in later years claimed to have forgotten what he had written. His reports do survive, however, and show a wide-ranging and incisive mind at work, able to synthesise clearly from a mass of data. Subjects include the Italians' preference for heavy calibre aircraft machine guns; Galland criticised the light machine guns employed on early German aircraft, and pointed to the advantages of multi-gun configurations. The balance between rate of fire and amount of metal on the target each second was clearly a key to kill probabilities. Early Bf109s had 7.92mm MG17 machine guns firing at a rate of 1,180 rounds per minute, but the 20mm MG FF licence-built Oerlikon cannon experimentally fitted in the wing positions of some C-models had the equivalent weight of fire per second of one and a half machine guns. The MG FF had shown good results when tested in Spain with the Heinkel He112V-4, which carried two cannon in the wings and two MG17s in the upper cowling. Galland considered the ability of ground-attack aircraft to operate safely without fighter escorts as vital. He also argued the dramatic improvement in operational effectiveness afforded by drop tanks.

In the midst of all this report writing Gnamm and Galland were thrust into a very different activity. On 21 April Hitler had asked the OKW to prepare final war plans for an invasion of Czechoslovakia on 1 October. Wolfram von Richthofen had convinced the now-Marshal Goering, Oberbefehlshaber der Luftwaffe (commander-in-chief of the Luftwaffe), that ground-attack units were preferable in some operations to Stuka dive-bombers. The 'Schlachtflieger' concept was defined as a more or less direct and continuous participation in the land battle, while dive-bombing implied a sudden pin-point attack on targets behind the front line. Obstlt Gnamm was given orders to form, by 1 September, two Schlachtgeschwader with a combined total of 10 Gruppen for deployment if 'Case Green' was activated.

As Gnamm's adjutant, Galland was thrown into a non-stop race to meet the deadline. His experience in setting up 3./J88 in Spain in the previous year stood him in good stead. He knew what a close-support unit would need – but a Staffel was hardly preparation for two full wings with all their aircraft, equipment and essential resources. They could scrape together the aircraft, but they represented a sorry mixture of the old and the incapable. There was the ubiquitous He51, and its forebear, the 1920s-vintage He46; the Arado Ar66 was a trainer capable of carrying only a handful of 2kg (4lb) anti-personnel bomblets. The Henschel Hs123, a response to the first specified requirement for a dive-bomber, had a superior performance and carried up to four 50kg (110lb) bombs or clusters of anti-personnel bombs in underwing canisters as well as two MG17 machine guns. Galland's allocation of aircraft types to particular units recognized the Henschel's relative superiority; he recommended that two of the 10 Schlachtfliegergruppen – SGr10 commanded by Hptmn Graf von Pfeil, and SGr50 commanded by Hptmn von Koratzki – should receive the Hs123 exclusively.

Pilots were as worrying a problem. Galland felt that the training schools were pushing out pilots quite unready for operational duty in order to 'make up the numbers', and he established rosters for them to continue their training at their respective airfields. Moreover, the NCOs were inexperienced and many were inadequate for their duties. It was a sad picture of a hastily prepared force with obsolescent equipment; but against all odds the Schlachtfliegergruppen were ready. Obstlt Gnamm took command of one of them, and retained Galland as his adjutant.

Now they could only wait for the word that would launch them against a well trained army of 800,000 men behind strong fortifications, covered by Avia B-534 fighters armed with a 20mm cannon and up to four machine guns, and backed by a modern, technically-sophisticated state. As adjutant Galland had frustratingly little opportunity to fly. On the apparent threshold of war young pilots naturally sought out Galland and other Spanish veterans, eager for their advice on real combat. Galland tried to be helpful; but he knew this war would not be much like Spain.

Under a barrage of propaganda intense international negotiations were taking place. Germany was not ready for war, and the general staff were all too aware of the fact. At the time Galland had no idea how close to mutiny the generals came that September; he would only become aware of such issues years later, as a general himself, when the Luftwaffe fell from favour and serious questions were raised about Hitler's place as head of state[1].

As the crucial date of 1 October approached international attention focused on Czechoslovakia and German demands that its people and the lands they occupied be 'returned' to the Reich (the Sudeten Germans were in fact former Austrian citizens.) As history would record, there was never any real threat of war with Britain or France, neither of which was willing to face hostilities for the sake of a small eastern European republic, however tragically unjust its fate. Britain was pledged to fight only in the event of a direct attack on France, and was concerned above all to try to avoid a general outbreak of war. The danger seemed very real at the time, however. While Prime Minister Neville Chamberlain was attempting to negotiate with an apparently incensed and ever more demanding Hitler at Godesberg on 22 September, Keitel was passing orders that preparations for Case Green should actually be advanced.

On his airfield in eastern Germany that evening, Adolf Galland took the phone call: Case Green had gone to a second level alert – it was on for 1 October, but might be brought forward. War was a week away, at most. His commanding officer was away at a meeting; Galland decided to stay up for him, so that Gnamm was sure to get the message as early as possible. In the event Galland stayed up until morning, pacing the line of biplanes under the night sky as he smoked, and wondered. The next few days passed in a frenzy of final preparations.

Chamberlain returned to London on the 24th; and on Monday 26 September Hitler ordered the assault divisions forward to their jumping-off positions. Galland's Schlachtflieger received preparatory orders for their move to forward airfields in Upper Silesia. According to plan, the road transport rolled south and east towards the pre-assigned locations. Constant telephone communication was maintained between Obstlt Gnamm and the commanders of the field units he was to support.

In London and Paris civilians began evacuating and mobilisation orders were issued. In a final exchange of telephone calls between Berlin, London, Paris and Rome on 27 and 28 September the four-power conference at Munich on the 29th and 30th was agreed. The outcome was preordained; Hitler, the most ruthless of the gamblers in the game, had won; a great area of Czechoslovakia, with all its resources, would be handed over to him, leaving the rump of the country notionally still protected by international guarantees but actually indefensible.

On their darkened airfield, Obstlt Gnamm and his adjutant received the call on the evening of the 28th: stand down, but be ready to execute Case Green a day later than scheduled. Galland recalled that he was sitting in the corner of Gnamm's office, chewing on a Spanish cigar; and that when the message arrived, he shifted it from one corner of his mouth to the other, as he and his commanding officer gazed silently at one another. Each knew exactly what the other was thinking.

Meeting with Chamberlain earlier that day, Czech Prime Minister Jan Masaryk had said: 'If you have sacrificed my nation to preserve the peace of the world, I will be the first to applaud you. But if not, gentlemen, God help your souls.'

* * *

Instead of fighting their way into the Sudetenland, the Luftwaffe made a ceremonial crossing of the frontier; within two days Galland flew to the airfield assigned to the Schlachtflieger units, and watched an impressive airborne assault exercise. The peaceful implementation of the invasion plan between 1 and 8 September was a colossal exercise to test the planning by the OKW and Luftwaffefuehrungsstab (Air Force Operations Staff). In total the Luftwaffe had managed to put up 1,230 operational aircraft out of a strength of 2,900. Galland, like most Germans, was immensely impressed with what had been achieved without a shot being fired; but he had no illusions about how far the Luftwafffe still fell short of a world-class air force.

Galland feared that he was in danger of getting 'type-cast' as solely a close-support expert, and he now renewed his lobbying of RLM contacts for a posting to a fighter unit. He was encouraged by the massive expansion of the Luftwaffe ordered by Hitler and Goering within two weeks of Munich; the leadership was fully conscious of the threat posed by the British and French forces, which was starkly confirmed by Luftwaffe intelligence[2].

The OKL began to work out an expansion programme covering the next four years. This envisaged 13 Seekampfgeschwader – bomber wings exclusively for operations against naval targets – in addition to 30 Kampfgeschwader as a strategic bomber force. On 14 October 1938 Goering announced an ambitious plan to enlarge the Luftwaffe five-fold by April 1942. In fact much of 1938 was spent re-tooling for the variety of new types, and industry was unable to greatly increase the monthly production rate of 450-500 aircraft before 1939, or to exceed 700 per month by autumn that year. The Technisches Amt planned to have 45,700 aircraft available by spring of 1942, by building an average of 13,000 annually. The aim was a force of more than 10,000 operational combat aircraft with 8,000 in reserve: 4,300 fighters (Bf109s), 3,300 heavy fighters and ground-attack aircraft (Bf110s and Me210s), 2,000 dive-bombers (Ju87s) and almost 11,000 medium and heavy bombers (He111s, He177s, Do17s)[3]. The emphasis on bombers, leaving single-seat fighters with only some 25 per cent of the total, was significant.

At last Galland's pleading paid off; and late in 1938 he was transferred to Boeblingen near Stuttgart, to set up an as yet undesignated Jagdgruppe and to command a Staffel. Jagdgruppe Boeblingen was soon receiving sleek new Messerschmitt Bf109Ds; and Galland – this time applying himself to the inevitable administrative work with a new spring in his step and a gleam in his eye – lost no time in assigning them to his best pilots and getting them into the air.

In November 1938 chief of operations staff Obst Jeschonnek set out the force strengths for the expanded Luftwaffe; Staffeln operating all other types were to have 12 aircraft each, but fighter squadrons were to have 18 with no increase in personnel. This provided a reserve for accidents and, more importantly, spare aircraft to get the pilots of damaged fighters straight back into the air in wartime conditions. However, of the total less than one in ten Geschwader would operate fighters, emphasising the Blitzkrieg concept of pre-emptive attack rather than providing a rounded force for defensive as well as offensive operations.

For several months Galland had the time of his life, working up the Gruppe into an efficient fighting unit. During that winter and spring 1939 there were numerous exercises, some of which were instigated by the newly forming Kampfgeschwader, and some of which he himself set up to test new tactical concepts. Tactics were officially based on the use of fighters to clear a path for the bombers through opposing fighters, rather than on staying with the bombers to defend them. During these exercises Galland continued to feel concern over his superiors' confidence that 'the bombers will always get through'. The Luftwaffe kept a close eye on developments in Britain, and Galland knew that modern monoplane fighters were also joining the RAF. No.19 Squadron at Duxord, Cambridgshire had received its first Spitfires in August 1938, and by that Christmas the RAF had 50. By Munich the RAF also had 12 fully operational squadrons of the sturdy eight-gun Hurricane, which would bear the brunt of Fighter Command operations until well after the Battle of Britain. These would be the aircraft which, in little more than a year, would confirm Galland's belief in the folly of making bombers rely on their own defences.

Galland got more time to develop new tactics and explore the potential of the Bf109D than he envisaged. His Gruppenkommandeur, Hptmn Graf von Pfeil, fell ill early in Galland's assignment, and shortly after returning he disappeared once more to get married. Galland took over the Gruppe with delight; he revelled in the responsibility, honing his Staffel and the work schedules of the entire Jagdgruppe to a high state of effectiveness. There was much work to be done.

One major change followed the recommendations of Galland's successor at 3./ J88, Werner Moelders. The quiet young officer had excelled in aerial combat; in little more than six months he had shot down 14 aircraft – the Condor Legion's highest score. When Moelders returned he wrote up the tactics he and 3. Staffel had practised; and it was these that Galland incorporated into his exercises. (Another Spanish ace, Johannes Trautloft, became an instructor, and wrote Moelders' tactics into the flight manual later used by all fighter pilots.)

The Bf109 was so much faster than the aircraft it replaced that it demanded a completely new approach. Interwar biplane fighters still used World War I tactics – flying in close formation for mutual defence and ease of hand signalling. In the new era of radio communications, greatly superior machine guns, and closing speeds between combatants of up to 965kph (600mph), close formations became obsolete – indeed downright dangerous. Another drawback was visibility; tightly packed formations simply did not have enough all-round vision, and were themselves too visible.

What Moelders devised was a Rotte (plural Rotten) of two aircraft flying about 180m (600ft) apart, with the Rottenfuehrer or leader slightly ahead of his 'Katchmarek' or wingman. Each would look inward, thus covering the other's blind zones. Two such Rotten flying side by side would make a Schwarme (plural Schwaerme) of four aircraft laid out in the configuration of the fingertips of the human hand. The elements of this 'finger four' formation would be equidistant from each other, spanning 550m (1,800ft) of sky, one Rotte advanced slightly ahead of the other. A Staffel would consist of three fighter Schwaerme stepped back up behind each other in altitude. Moelders also solved the potential problem of holding formation when making a turn. For a 90 degree right turn, the aircraft on the extreme left would turn first, bringing him over and behind his wingman, who would then turn himself, followed by the third and the fourth pilots with a couple of seconds between each. In this way the aircraft would reverse formation, those formerly on the left becoming the pair on the right.

The pairs and the stepped-up 'finger four' formations solved all the problems associated with operating high-speed combat aircraft; in time they would be copied, albeit with modifications, by the fliers of all the major combatant powers. Some airmen found it hard to abandon the doctrines laid down by the first great fighter leaders; Galland was receptive, and his respect for Moelders grew – alongside his envy of his successor's opportunity to fly the Bf109 in combat. When Galland finally got the chance himself, envy would turn into comradely but outright competition to be the first and the best.

Galland's happy labours with his unit did not preclude an active social life, however. Flying in Spain had been a profitable business; he bought himself a handsome BMW cabriolet and gave his Opel saloon to young Wilhelm, then 24 years old and keen to follow in big brother's footsteps. The new car did nothing to tone down his exuberant image; the sight of him roaring through the streets, top down and cigar gripped between teeth, brought envious stares from men and thoughtful glances from women – off duty, the demanding perfectionist was the image of the carefree fighter pilot.

* * *

During those carefree days Galland's future – among tens of millions of others – was being mapped out by powers far beyond his knowledge.

Even as his troops completed the peaceful occupation of the Sudetenland Hitler asked Keitel for his assessment of forces necessary to take over the remainder of Czechoslovakia. On 21 October 1938 Hitler ordered the OKW to prepare for the 'liquidation' of the rump of Czechoslovakia and the occupation of Memel (the Baltic region of East Prussia lost at Versailles). Just three days later foreign minister von Ribbentrop met the Polish ambassador to demand German access to the city of Danzig, isolated beyond a Polish corridor by the redrawing of maps at Versailles. Hitler was already looking beyond the final destruction of Czechoslovakia – which he achieved in March 1939, dividing any possible resistance by playing on Slovakian fears of Hungary. German troops occupied Bohemia and Moravia on the 14th, and Slovakia on the 16th, tossing some territory to Hungary as payment for her connivance. By 23 March Hitler was delivering a speech to 'liberated' Germans in the Stadttheatre in Memel: Lithuania had ceded the territory without a shot.

However, the contemptuous occupation of the remnant of Czechoslovakia brought about a complete change in British foreign policy. There was unanimous agreement that Hitler had to be made to understand that Britain would no longer tolerate territorial banditry. On 31 March Chamberlain publicly stated that in the event of any military threat to Poland's independence Britain would 'lend the Polish government all support in their power', adding that France too had given Warsaw such an assurance. Three days later Hitler issued a top secret directive to the armed forces bearing the codename 'Case White' – the plan for the invasion of Poland.

Hitler was, nevertheless, shaken by the British initiative and bemused by Britain's attitude. He was to remain obsessively anxious to avoid war with Britain until the very eve of his invasion of Poland (indeed, there is evidence that until at least May 1941 he still believed in the possibility of a separate negotiated peace[4].)

Now both Germany and the Western Allies secretly explored the possibility of pacts with Stalin's Russia – a power almost equally distasteful to all of them, and as it proved, at this date simply an unacceptable ally for the British.

On 23 May, after concluding the 'Pact of Steel' with Italy, Hitler informed his senior military chiefs that war with Poland was inevitable; that a simultaneous campaign against France and Britain must be avoided; that if it came to war, Germany should thrust not for Paris but through the Low Countries to the Channel coast, to secure air and naval bases from which Britain could be strangled by the destruction of her fleet and the cutting off of her vital imports – the only way to defeat her. It is too often forgotten that Hitler had a clear prior vision of the sequential steps towards his aim of eliminating Western interference with his destiny to expand the German Reich into the east[5].

During the politically explosive summer of 1939 the Luftwaffe began to feel the results of Goering's expansion programme. New equipment began to arrive with the field units; many more trainees were emerging from the flying schools; and by mid-1939, less than a year after the sobering experience of the Munich mobilisation, there was a general optimism that the Luftwaffe was the match of any air force in Europe.

* * *

On 28 March 1939 Republican Madrid surrendered, and the Spanish Civil War was over. After a huge victory parade through the streets of the capital on 22 May the Condor Legion returned home. The men who had fought in Spain would bring to their own forces recent combat experience which very few other nations could boast. Unfortunately for the Luftwaffe, that experience would only emphasise a doctrine that would ultimately leave Germany defenceless: the decisive nature of offensive tactical operations in Spain would obscure the fighter's role as a defensive interceptor.

When the ships carrying the legionaries home docked at the St Pauli pier in Hamburg their welcome was rapturous. From there they were transported to the outskirts of Berlin and a specially prepared tented camp at 'Sonderstab Doeberitz', where a great reunion began; Galland took the train up from Stuttgart – he had been seconded to a decorations vetting committee. On 6 June, after a few days' sunny rest, convoys of buses carried the 14,000 former legionaries into

Berlin to parade before their Fuehrer. New brown Reich Labour Service uniforms had been provided, as an approximation of what the veterans had worn in Spain; the combination of itchy uniforms, hot sun, and an interminable wait while ranks of men were presented with Spanish medals was excruciating. In addition to these campaign medals were just 27 awards of Germany's Spanish Cross in Gold with Diamonds; of these, 14 recipients were from J88 – Galland, Moelders, Balthasar and Harder among them.

At last, they formed up in ranks of nine to march behind the three commanding officers of the Condor Legion through the Brandenburg Gate, up the 'Lustgarten', and past Hitler on a specially decked podium in front of the Technical School. After the march past Galland was one of a group of legionaries taken to the new Reichskanzlei to be presented to Hitler. Galland marvelled at the sheer magnificence of the huge building, set with marble, decorated with fine drapes and relief sculptures, lit through tall windows, entered through tall doors – it was like a Wagnerian opera set in permanent testimony to the grand ambitions of a single man. Only in the presentation rooms were there carpets, the long broad corridors ringing to the steel-tipped boots of guards and officials; everyone seemed to be in uniform, and it crossed Galland's mind that civilian clothes would simply look out of place in such an edifice.

He recalled later that this building, for him, was the embodiment of what had been accomplished in Germany since Hitler came to power six years earlier. His first encounter with the man responsible for it all was an anti-climax. Galland was irritated at the order not to smoke in the presence of the Fuehrer, which he thought unmilitary; under the Prussian code a gentleman simply did not interfere with another's freedom of personal choice. Sweating in his prickly olive-green uniform, the young pilot ached for the relaxation of a cigar. At last, after a brief few words from Hitler and a quick handshake, the airmen had tea and left – which, while grateful for the honour, they were glad enough to do.

* * *

So far, 1939 had been an eventful year for the Luftwaffe. Changes at the top of the command structure gave Erhard Milch added responsibilities. In a move during February that combined the offices of secretary of state for air and the inspector-general of the Luftwaffe, he was placed in charge of the Central Department at the Air Ministry, superior to Udet, to the air defence chief, and the chiefs of training services and the signals command. Obst Jeschonnek replaced Gen Stumpff as chief of the general staff.

A new organisational structure divided the greater part of the flying formations into seven Fliegerdivision allocated between three Luftflotten. Covering northern and eastern Germany, Luftflotte 1 had headquarters in Berlin and was commanded by Genlt Albert Kesselring, a veteran of the army general staff during World War I and a founding member of the new Luftwaffe. Luftflotte 2 covered north-west Germany with headquarters at Braunschweig, and was commanded by Helmuth Felmy. Luftflotte 3, responsible for south-west Germany and led by Hugo Sperrle, was headquartered at Munich. In March the Austrian air force units were merged with air elements from Silesia, Bohemia and Moravia and absorbed into the Luftwaffe as Luftflotte 4; commanded by Gen Alexander Loehr, an Austrian who had joined the Luftwaffe after the Anschluss, it had headquarters in Vienna and covered Austria, south-east Germany and Czechoslovakia[6].

Before and after the Condor Legion parade Galland was involved with 'Map Study 1939', which was a veiled exercise for the planned assault on Poland. This provided a much better mechanism for identifying problems than had been the case during the Czechoslovakian crisis. Galland had a better opportunity to plan and rehearse procedures and to co-ordinate Staffel operations within the Geschwader; he took a leading role in setting up the administrative infrastructure governing communications and the movement of information – something Galland was good at, although he hated such work.

The type of pilot coming through the training system had not changed much, but the way they had been taught to fly was a great improvement[7]. Galland found less time had to be spent compensating for inadequate training, and throughout the first seven months of 1939 he relished the chance to flex the Staffel in combat exercises. The placing of all flying training on a military basis from 1936 now ensured that new pilots arriving with the Staffeln had a greater sense of discipline and control. Galland was still very much aware, however, that the Luftwaffe, now in the process of equipping with modern combat aircraft and integrating thousands of new aircrew, was still only five years old. There had been no time to build a generation of experienced aviators able to assume the responsibilities of middle rank and leadership. The Luftwaffe was a force top-heavy with senior commanders trained in another age of warfare, manned largely by very young pilots with little or no combat experience.

Great effort had gone into showing off Germany's new aviation industry, and specially equipped and prepared examples of service aircraft or military prototypes won a number of international speed records in 1937-38. Visits to facilities by foreign dignitaries were also stage managed to impress the international community with an air of invincibility. Yet perhaps Goering and his staff were also deceived into false expectations by their own propaganda machine. The RLM Technisches Amt showered the leadership with ambitious projects; 1939 was indeed a heady time for aviation research and development. Most exciting of all were developments in aircraft propulsion for airframes yet to be designed, and here Germany was genuinely well in the lead[8]. These seductive possibilities did nothing to eliminate the more immediate problems of the Luftwaffe on the brink of world war.

It was in August 1939 that Goering made his famous boast that 'the Ruhr will not be subjected to a single bomb. If an enemy bomber reaches the Ruhr... you can call me Meier.' Galland would later assert that Goering's vainglorious poses stemmed from an uneasy awareness, even then, of being swept along by a tide of events over which his imagined influence was diminishing. His overconfident claims for his Luftwaffe were his attempt to persuade Hitler of his continued importance to the Reich.

There was much reason for Galland to feel enthusiastic about his life that summer, however; and it was without the slightest warning that, early in August, a bitter blow fell. He stared in total disbelief at a teletype ordering him to report at once to II.(Sch)/LG2 at Tutow. Lehrgeschwader 2 was the last place on earth he wanted to go. It was bad enough to lose his Bf109 Staffel, just when he had honed his flying skills to a razor edge; but a training and operational conversion unit was the bottom of the barrel – let alone a ground-attack unit!

In a way he had only himself to blame – and men like Werner Moelders. It was as a result of the recommendations sent back from Spain to the OKL by Galland, Moelders and others that a Lehrdivision had been set up at Greifswald in 1937. Its purpose was to apply the Spanish lessons to tactics evolved for each separate aircraft coming out of prototype stage into development for the operational units. Lehr units performed remarkable service converting basic aircraft types into effective fighting machines, and developing the operational manuals to guide the crews in their use. With the proliferation of new types coming from the manufacturers, these instructional units were the only buffer between untried machines and safe operational deployments. The Lehrgeschwader comprised separate Staffeln each assigned a particular type of aircraft. A Staffelkapitaen with II.Gruppe of LG2 had dropped out, and Galland was to replace him. When he arrived by train from Stuttgart he learned that he was to work up on the Henschel Hs123 biplane dive-bomber – hardly a novelty in need of operational evaluation. But by this date the Lehrgeschwader had become quasi-combat units; with fewer new aircraft to test, it had lost its special status. II.(Sch)/LG2 was in fact the old SGr10, which Galland had helped to set up at Tutow the previous year; after that crisis the biplane Schlachtgruppen had been dispersed.

No sooner had Galland arrived at Tutow than he received orders to leave for a week or so at the research facility at Rechlin, there to fill the role of an operations development test pilot, charged with evaluating the Fw189 and Hs129 for their potential under service conditions. The Fw189, a tactical reconnaissance and army co-operation monoplane with an unusual twin-boom configuration, had surprisingly poor all-round vision given the extensive glazing. Still mourning his Bf109, Galland was unimpressed. The Henschel Hs129 was altogether different. This was a truly modern aircraft for the Schlachtflieger, a tough gun-platform complete with bulletproof windscreen, enclosed cockpit, two 465hp Argus in-line engines and a good view forward where a close-support pilot wanted it.

Back at Tutow he at once found himself in the throes of working up to a massive air exercise as a prelude to 'Case White'. In the skies east of Cottbus, over terrain resembling Poland, very large formations of aircraft carried out exercises integrated with ground units. In mid-August the weather took a turn for the worse with rain, fog and low cloud; this caused problems in integrating ground and air operations, which was a new challenge for most. The difficulties were soon overcome, and what many had predicted would be a disaster was generally successful – apart from an isolated but spectacular episode in which 13 Ju87 Stukas dived straight into the ground in low fog, killing all 26 aircrew members.

Only the armed services were aware of how far Hitler's plans extended for an attack on Poland. To Germany at large, Hitler was again standing firm in the face of resistance from intransigent neighbours unwilling to give back to Germany territory and suffering German populations unjustly seized at Versailles. Meanwhile, Hitler and Stalin were conducting in secret the grisly dance of mutual cynicism which would culminate, on 23 August, in the unholy embrace of the German-Soviet non-aggression pact. Germany was to have a free hand in Poland, which would be partitioned between them; Russia was to take most of the Baltic coast states and Finland. Despite warnings from a number of sources that Britain and France would this time stand firm, and depite a continuing insistence on the need to isolate Poland and to avoid simultaneous war in both west and east, the Fuehrer informed his generals on the 22nd that he would give the order to invade Poland on 26 August. The optimistic view that Britain would not, in the end, fight for Poland was held not only by sycophants like von Ribbentrop. Even Halder had noted in his unpublished diary, after a meeting on 14 August: 'Not even England has the money nowadays to fight a world war. What would England fight for? You don't get yourself killed for an ally.'

By mid-August instructions had already gone out for the faked Polish incursion into German territory which would give Hitler his pretext. Now, in the last week of the month, all across Germany the Wehrmacht made ready. X-Hour was to be 04.30 on Saturday 26 August. On the 22nd the Luftwaffe operations staff set up its battle headquarters at Wildpark Werder near Potsdam. Late on the afternoon of the 24th Goering sent the warning order to all units: 'Unterstellungsverhaltnis Weiss'. From that hour and on into the following morning Luftwaffe units left for their forward positions. With the rest of Maj Werner Spielvogel's II.(Sch) Gruppe LG2, Galland found himself at Alten-Rosenberg. The excitement crackled throughout the unit; but Galland would recall that for him – perhaps because he was denied the elation of leading a Bf109 Staffel in these momentous days; perhaps because he was one of the relatively few who had actually seen war close up – this excitement was mixed with uncertainty.

A sense of foreboding at the highest level was even now to cause a last minute delay. Prime Minister Chamberlain wrote to Hitler affirming that 'the announce-ment of a German-Soviet agreement is taken in some quarters in Berlin to indicate that intervention by Great Britain on behalf of Poland is no longer a contingency that can be reckoned with. No greater mistake could be made.' On the afternoon of Friday 25 August Hitler received absolute assurances that Britain and France would fight if need be. Halder's diary reveals that just nine hours before the invasion was due to be unleashed Hitler ordered all preparations for 'Case White' to be suspended. Much later, as they walked and talked at one of his hunting lodges, Goering would tell Galland that this moment was the turning point for Hitler. The Fuehrer had telephoned Goering, deeply concerned that he was about to plunge Germany into a two-front battle for survival. Goering asked him if the halt in movements was permanent; Hitler replied that he did not really know: 'We will have to see whether we can eliminate British intervention.' Even Halder wrote in his secret diary that night, 'Fuehrer considerably shaken.' In certain quarters in the army and the Abwehr there was a flash of joyous relief. It was to be short-lived.

The postponement order reached Galland's unit at 08.10 on the Friday evening; it was still light enough for the airmen to wander around the field, gathering in knots to exchange what information or rumours they could glean. By early on the Saturday afternoon Obstlt von Richthofen, commanding the ground-attack units of Fliegerfuehrer zbV ('Special Purposes Flying Command'), had passed new orders to II.(Sch)/LG2. The attack was rescheduled for 04.45 on Friday 1 September. They had a few more days on their sealed and guarded airfield to make final checks and preparations. Galland would be kept occupied; Maj Spielvogel drew heavily on his Staffel commander's combat experience.

Overnight Hitler had recovered his nerve; he would have his war against Poland come what may. In the meantime he would try to confuse and divert the British and French by creating uncertainty as to his intentions; and he would issue strict orders against any military provocation against them, forcing them to take responsibility for any declaration of war. His later pronouncements show that he believed that a quick victory over Poland could be followed by a redeployment to face the Western Allies. He requested Mussolini, who had declared himself unwilling to get dragged into war with the democracies, to make at least some demonstration to tie down British and French forces; and stated that 'this winter, at latest in the spring, I shall attack the West with forces at least equal to those of France and Britain.' Halder's diary reported him 'very calm and clear' that Saturday afternoon.

Notes to Chapter 6

1   In the closing years of his life Galland would comment upon these matters to the author. A product of his time, he was brought up to the Prussian virtues of duty, service and loyalty. He said that he had always believed that the use of force by a military junta to overthrow a political system was fundamentally wrong, an unsoldierly act which would plunge the nation into anarchy as factions struggled for power. He was never able to address the distinction between the passive acceptance of an unjust ruler, and the moral right to prevent unjustified violence in the service of political ambition. Galland admitted that the assassination of Hitler and other senior Nazis had been discussed in some circles in the Luftwaffe when the war was going badly for Germany, and that he had opposed such discussion. To the end of his days Galland believed that Germany need not have gone to war at all to achieve her legitimate aims in Europe.

2   The 5th Branch of the OKL Desk VI was responsible for intelligence on foreign air forces. Desk VI was headed by Hans Jeschonnek before he became Luftwaffe Chief of Staff in February 1939, to be replaced by the much less effective Obst Joseph 'Beppo' Schmidt for the first half of the war. During the Blitz German bomber crews profited from prewar work, receiving impressive target atlases with overprinted aerial photographs. Wartime intelligence on e.g. RAF loss rates was much less accurate.

3   The cost of this programme was RM60 billion, equal to total German expenditure on arms between 1933 and 1939. Moreover, such a fleet would have required 85 per cent of world aviation fuel production.

4   Galland discussed this subject at length with the author, citing several private wartime meetings with Hitler during which the latter freely voiced his puzzled respect for the British people, and his desire for some accomodation with the British Empire which would leave each power freedom of action in what he considered their natural spheres. Hitler seemed to think that as a fighting man Galland might have insights to offer, and quizzed him relentlessly about his combat experiences and his opinion of the British.

The reader should note that descriptions in this book of events from April 1939 take account of information volunteered by Galland based on his conversations with Hitler.

5   Condensed from verbatim minutes taken by Hitler's adjutant, Obstlt Rudolf Schmundt. Present at this meeting were Hermann Goering, Grossadmiral Raeder, Generals von Brauchitsch, Halder and Keitel of the army, General Erhard Milch of the Luftwaffe and Konteradmiral Otto Schniewind, naval chief of staff.

6   In March 1939 the Luftwaffe could boast 83 Gruppen with 254 Staffeln; by 1 July, 276 Staffeln; by 1 September, 302 Staffeln. On 1 May a new system of numerical unit designation was introduced which would last throughout the war. Geschwader numbers would now indicate the parent Luftflotte. Geschwader numbered 1-25 would be under Luftflotte 1, 26-50 under Luftflotte 2, 51-75 under Luftflotte 3 and 76-100 under Luftflotte 4.

7   All recruits went first to a Fliegerausbildungsregiment (pilot training regiment) for at least six months, acquiring military discipline, physical fitness, and rudimentary radio and map reading. Flying crew candidates spent two months at a Fluganwaerterkompanie to learn the rudiments of flying before posting to an elementary flying school (A/B Grade school); elementary training involved 100-150 hours' flying time. During the B classes trainees were screened for suitability for fighter, bomber or reconnaissance aircraft, after which they were sent forward to the relevant schools. On graduating from the A/B Grade pilots were given their 'wings'. Prospective fighter pilots went from the B Grade school to fighter school for a three-month course on elementary types before maturing to the Bf109 and Bf110; here the pilot flew for about 50 hours, so that he reached his operational squadron with about 200 hours in all. By the end of summer 1939 between 75 and 100 training schools – about half of them A/B Grade – were turning out some 12,000 pilots a year.

Even with a good flow of trained aircrew the Luftwaffe was only just able to meet the needs of a complex operation such as Poland. It was possible to shape force structures around the capabilities and assets of a particular enemy; but the OKL knew very well that the Luftwaffe would not be ready before 1942 to conduct total war on any front. Hitler dismissed such warnings as conservative, persuaded by Goering's overconfident predictions.

8   A world first on 20 June 1939 saw the diminutive Heinkel He176, powered by a liquid propellant rocket motor, take to the skies. On 27 August the Heinkel He178 became the first aircraft to fly powered by a turbojet engine. Messerschmitt had been working on what would become the rocket-powered Me163 since that January; and was completing the basic design of the P1065 turbojet fighter, later to become the Me262, in August. Contrary to myth, Britain was not the first country to fly a jet-propelled aircraft. Although much conceptual and design work had been done by Frank Whittle, in Germany his contemporary Dr Hans Joachim Pabst von Ohain produced the first engine to power an aircraft in flight. Second was the Italian Caproni-Campini CC2 in August 1940, followed by the British Gloster E.28/39 in May 1941.

CHAPTER 7

September 1939 – January 1940

The first shots of 'Case White' are usually said to have been fired at the Polish garrison of Westerplatte in Danzig at 04.45 on 1 September 1939 by the German battleship *Schleswig-Holstein*. In fact, it was exactly 11 minutes earlier when Oblt Bruno Dilley and two fellow Stuka pilots of 3./StG 1 from Elbing dropped their bombs on the detonation points to prevent the Poles from blowing Dirschau bridge over the Vistula.

On that day total Luftwaffe strength (within the margins of slightly conflicting sources) stood at 4,093 aircraft, of which 3,646 were serviceable – an impressively high rate of 89 per cent.

Of these, 1,179 (29 per cent) were fighters, 1,176 bombers, and 366 Stukas. However, 408 of the fighters were not Bf109s, but Zerstoerer[1] or 'destroyers' – heavy escort fighters doubling in the ground-attack role. So dominant was the Blitzkrieg concept that 313 Bf109s were assigned to the Zerstoerer role alongside the 95 available Bf110s. Of the 1,056 Bf109s on strength at the end of August almost two-thirds (631) were of the much improved Bf109E variant, fully equal to the British Hurricane and marginally better under some conditions even than the Spitfire. Of the rest, the more heavily armed C and D models were, reluctantly, allocated to escort duty.

For the attack on Poland the Luftwaffe had at its disposal a total of about 1,600 front-line aircraft with 288 reconnaissance and transport aircraft under the direct control of the army. Of the Luftwaffe's front-line total approximately 650 were bombers, 220 dive-bombers, 40 ground-attack, 210 fighters and 475 transport and reconnaissance types. In addition approximately 216 fighters were reserved for the defence of eastern Germany. Command of air forces was under Goering at his headquarters in Potsdam; operations were divided between Luftflotte 1 (east) under Genlt Albert Kesselring, with HQ at Henningsholm, Stettin, and Luftflotte 4 (south-east) under Gen Alexander Loehr with HQ at Reichenbach, Silesia. Luftflotte 1 operated with Army Group North under Gen von Bock, supporting the 3rd and 4th Armies in Prussia, while Luftflotte 4 was assigned to Army Group South under Gen von Rundstedt, supporting the 8th, 10th and 14th Armies. Galland's 4.Staffel,II.(Sch)/LG2 came under von Richthofen's Fliegerfuehrer zbV, headquartered at Oppeln under Luftflotte 4. The Gruppe's Hs123 close-support aircraft were to be among the first aircraft to attack, working closely with Gen von Reichenau's 10th Army on the Silesian front. (Elements of Luftflotten 2 and 3 would also be deployed from the fifth day of the campaign.)

The Polskie Powiertrzne Sily Zbrojne (Polish air force) could deploy 437 front-line aircraft including 156 bombers and 161 fighters as well as 120 general purpose aircraft. Their equipment was outclassed by the Luftwaffe, and they had fewer reserve aircrew. The best Polish fighter squadrons had a total of 128 examples of the PZL P-11c, a high-wing monoplane with a fixed undercarriage and two 7.7mm machine guns; it was highly manoeuvrable, but its top speed of only 390kph (242mph) allowed most German types to avoid combat at will[2]. Since June a reorganisation of the air force had separated total assets between a tactical air force and an army support air force, the latter being tied to the movements and demands of ground forces. During August the Poles had moved their best aircraft back from the border to concealed bases in the eastern areas. At their former airfields redundant and unserviceable machines were left exposed (thus giving rise later to the surprisingly long-lived myth that the Polish Air Force was destroyed on the ground).

The French had asked the Poles to prepare landing grounds for five bomber squadrons which would bomb Germany en route, take up position in Poland and support the Polish air force in raids on Germany from the east. When Poland came under attack France would engage the Luftwaffe immediately from the west and attack Germany as far as the Oder river. In the event none of this took place; but the Polish air force drew up its strategy based on help pledged by France and Britain. The British did send 100 Fairey Battle light bombers, 14 Hurricanes and one Spitfire; these were on their way when war broke out, but were diverted.

* * *

In the early morning hours of Friday 1 September, II.(Sch)/LG2 prepared for their first mission in support of troops of von Reichenau's 10th Army. The squadrons had been assigned specific times and targets, and the crews were told to expect updates based on reconnaissance flights as the day progressed. Led by Oblt Otto Weiss, 1.Staffel would take off first, followed by Galland's 4.Staffel; the whole Gruppe, with 36 serviceable Henschel Hs123A-1s, would be airborne shortly after dawn. That morning the rising heat would turn early mist into dense fog over large areas of western Poland; but conditions were better to the south, and Maj Spielvogel was optimistic. The fog that hampered the medium bombers and Stukas would work to the benefit of the close-support groups; the Henschels could hedge-hop to their targets and come upon the enemy without warning.

The Gruppe had been assigned as target a concentration of troops and light armour at the Polish village of Pryzstain. The Polish army had deployed along the border, its fortified defensive positions linked by batteries and heavily defended outposts. The German armour would punch through, rolling over the outposts and leaving flanking squadrons to circle back and attack the fortifications from the rear while the main forces moved on. It was the first job of the close-support aircraft to hammer the defended outposts linking the fortifications, and to support the Panzers on the flanks mopping up defended pockets. Sorties carried out later this first day would turn their attentions to the fortified areas, where heavy anti-aircraft fire could be expected.

In the damp pre-dawn darkness the Henschels' nine-cylinder BMW radials barked into life, blue tongues of flame spitting from the exhaust rings. As he strapped himself into the high-perched cockpit of the metal biplane, its growling engine sending a shiver through the fuselage, Galland thought how different this was from Spain. He was no longer the hired man of a foreign army, able to walk away from a war which was not his. He was about to play a part in the greatest collision of arms since World War I; nearly two million men would clash in a struggle whose consequences could reverberate across Europe. There could be no going back, short of final victory.

At his forward command post nearby at Grunsruh another Spanish veteran was thinking the same thoughts. Gen Wolfram von Richthofen would confide to his diary: 'Now the war was surely in earnest. Thought until now it would only be political or confined to a show of force. Am thinking about France and England, and believe no longer in the possibility of a political settlement after what is being done now .. .Very worried about the future.'

Shuddering under the power of their 880hp engines, the Henschels rumbled across the grass and into the air, circling in a wide arc as the first dawn light illuminated their ungainly shapes. For all its ugliness, grotesque after his sharklike Bf109, Galland liked the Hs123. Bulkier than his old He51, it had a slightly lower wing loading, was more manoeuvrable and, although just a shade smaller all round than the Heinkel, had more power; at 305kph (190mph) it was about as fast as the He51 at sea level but had an extra 32kph (20mph) at altitude.

With the sun still not fully up the aircraft circled over the gathering troops, buzzing like angry hornets, bobbing and bouncing. They carried clusters of 2kg (4.4lb) anti-personnel bombs in racks under the lower wing; some carried four 50kg (110lb) SC bombs each, and others were on the flank of the formation, ready to strafe the fleeing troops. Working to a specific timetable, the first formation of Henschels moved out across the frontier. Otto Weiss led 1.Staffel in, nosing over his stubby biplane, pointing now with his arm extended for others to follow him down. With engines howling the Henschels drove towards the ground, hurled their bombs at the village, then pulled up to left or right before climbing more slowly to reform away from the answering fire and the rising smoke.

Now it was Galland's turn to nose over and lead the charge, shouting an inaudible 'Horrido!' as he had so many times in Spanish skies. He was at war again – and today his Staffel were armed with 'flambos', light petroleum bombs, like the weapons he had devised for 3./J88. Bursting and flaming among the tightly packed targets, they caused chaos and confusion. In moments it was over, and time to turn for base to rearm. Von Reichenau's troops were pouring over the frontier below, and high above the Henschels streams of other aircraft were heading east for their assigned targets.

Again and again they returned that day, to bomb troop concentrations and supply dumps and strafe the moving traffic. After the first attack the Poles put up intensive AA fire and a constant barrage from small arms and machine guns; each time they dived the marauding Henschels ran a gauntlet of fire and metal. At the end of the first day the Army High Command summary report praised the sustained air support delivered by Maj Spielvogel's II.(Sch)/LG2. The tactics and the battle plans to which Galland had contributed no small part were a complete success.

In the northern sector Luftflotte 1, hampered all day by bad weather, was grounded long before dusk; but further south Luftflotte 4 kept up the attacks. Sortie after sortie pounded the Polish army and tactical targets were reached on time or ahead of schedule. Von Richthofen was confused, nevertheless, that little communication was coming up from 10th Army; and he decided to fly out across the front line in a Fieseler Fi156 Storch, equipped only with a lap map and a field radio, to see for himself how the ground war was going. Circling close to Pryzstain, he had first hand evidence of its stubborn defence when a hail of rifle and machine gun fire riddled the tail of his Storch and severed a fuel line; he only just made it back to his potato-field airstrip.

The emptiness of the known Polish airfields, and the low level of fighter interference, had been puzzling the commanders. As the bomber raids continued the next day, 2 September, more and more Luftwaffe units began to report Polish fighter reaction; in one ominous episode that afternoon two P-11s were shot down – for the loss of three Bf110s. The outnumbered, outgunned Poles were fighting back with determination and tenacity.

Otto Weiss and Adolf Galland led their Staffeln on several sorties that day, taking some losses from ground fire. At first they spent some time waiting for targets to be called in from forward army units, but gradually the local commanders got used to calling upon Spielvogel's Henschels. The 10th and 14th Armies were making headway deep into Polish territory.

By 3 September opposition was beginning to stiffen, and Galland's 4.Staffel was being committed increasingly to the 1st Panzer Division. Charging far ahead of XVIth Army Corps, 1st Panzer was rounding the heavily defended Tschenstochau region and moving toward the Warte river. Galland flew Staffel strikes along this corridor of Panzers, clearing out stubborn resistance and scattering troops falling back to rear defensive positions. Sortie after sortie returned without ever having seen Polish air activity; but the AA fire was intense and accurate. Complementing the Stuka attacks called up by 1st Panzer, Galland was able to deploy his aircraft in co-ordination with activity on the ground; what he had learned in Spain about the importance of synchronised air strikes and ground movement was applied with success.

On the morning of 3 September 1st and 4th Panzer Divisions crossed the Warte, and pushed on towards Kamiensk under increasingly heavy air attack; fighters were called in to clean up. There was a call from XIth Army Corps for dive-bomber attacks on Dzialoszyn to soften up the city; after the Ju87s went in with 225kg (500lb) bombs the Hs123s hurled anti-personnel bombs and strafed with cannon fire from underwing pods. With 10th Army's left wing secured and the armour pouring forwards, von Richthofen's Stukas and Henschels were moved south to work on the right flank. Galland was surprised by the ferocity of the Polish resistance, and that of the massively outnumbered air force in particular; wherever their dwindling resources could be brought to bear, they tore into the German ranks. It would not be the last battlefield where he had reason to wonder at Polish tenacity.

On 4 September units of the 7th Polish Division came under incessant strafing and bombing runs from Galland's Staffel. With strategic targets now the priority of the Heinkels and Dorniers, tactical air support became even more important. Over the next three days the strafing Henschels pressed home their attacks in the vanguard of 10th Army as it pushed toward the Vistula. Yet in this first week of war the ambivalence of army attitudes towards air support became clear. To a surprising extent ground commanders seemed oblivious to the help they could get from II.(Sch)/LG2, and often Weiss and Galland had to search out worthwhile targets for themselves. There seemed to be a reluctance in some quarters to call in air strikes for fear of mistaken targeting. There were a few accidents; but a major step towards compensating for the difficulty in communicating the exact location of the front line – frequently moving at the pace of a rolling tank – was made when von Richthofen put liaison officers in the air above the ground forces. In this way accidents were minimised; but Galland was particularly critical of the lack of care shown by German soldiers in the clear marking of their positions.

In the first four days of the war in Poland the Luftwaffe had flown a total 8,552 sorties, of which more than 4,800 were against railways, highways and military facilities and more than 3,700 were against enemy batteries and strongpoints. Air strikes against transport facilities had prevented the Poles from marshalling eight of their 45 infantry divisions and five of their 16 cavalry divisions.

On 7 September XVIth Corps' two Panzer divisions broke through the Piotrkow defences; on the 8th, 1st Panzer Division reached the Vistula less than 20 miles from Warsaw. By now all enemy movement on the routes Poznan-Kutno-Warsaw, Krakow-Radom-Deblin and Krakow-Tarnow-Lvov had been halted. Throughout that afternoon II.(Sch)/LG2 flew intensive sorties, smashing communication lines, upsetting Polish troop movements, clearing out minor pockets of resistance identified by ground commanders, and cutting roads into Warsaw.

At 17.00 on the 8th Gen von Reichenau ordered Warsaw to be taken by force. This was more than a propaganda objective: Warsaw commands a stretch of the Vistula, and Polish forces escaping into the vast hinterland beyond might regroup. By this date the Gruppe had relocated to a stud farm at Wolborz near Tomaszow, in the latest of a series of 'strip-hopping' moves across Poland which impressed even the former commander of the 3./J88 railway headquarters. The priority was to get forward to support the advancing Panzers with minimum delay for the flight from the airstrip to the front. As an airfield Wolborz was marginal, but it satisfied the criterion applied: if you could drive a car at 30mph in a straight line without excessive bumps, it would do. The stubby little Henschels were adept at getting into the air from an 180m (600ft) take-off, and down again in less.

On 9 September Major Spielvogel set out in his Fieseler Storch to reconnoitre the battlefront for the Warsaw operation. Piloted by Uffz Szigorra, the Storch flew over the devastated Okecie airfield and on toward the Mokotow and Okhata districts, where Major Spielvogel saw advancing German armour. Braving enemy fire, he ordered Szigorra to fly on so that he could fix targets for Weiss and Galland to attack. Crossing an embankment along the Warsaw-Radom railway line the Storch was hit by gunfire, and the pilot wounded in the stomach. Spielvogel snatched the control stick; all he could do was set down in the street ahead, in a hail of gunfire. He managed to pull Szigorra from the aircraft before, hit in the head, he fell dead. There was great sadness in his Gruppe; Werner Spielvogel had been a much liked and respected commander. Hptmn Otto Weiss took over command, and the pace of operations continued unrelentingly.

The 4th Panzer Division had broken into the built-up area of Warsaw and was coming under increasingly intense fire from the eastern bank of the Vistula. Gun batteries situated in the Praga district to the east were pounding Wehrmacht tanks and infantry. Von Richthofen ordered an all-out attack by Ju87s and Hs123s, the former hitting the big guns at Praga, the latter hitting defenders in the western suburbs. From airfields at Tschenstochau and Kruszyna, 140 Ju87Bs from the five Gruppen of StG77 took off for the first major raid on Warsaw. On the other side of the city Weiss and Galland harried ground defenders, shooting up everything in sight. At full throttle they led sortie after sortie up and down the open streets on the edge of Warsaw; but the narrower streets closer in toward the city centre made close-support flying impossible.

By this time the 35th Panzer Regiment and 12th Rifle Regiment were at the railway station, but their flanks were wide open to an encirclement attack. It was the old story of street fighting: there were simply too many streets to cover, too many alleyways and courtyards and cellars in which to hide an army – or swallow one up. Galland was ordered to pull back his Staffel rather than risk hitting Wehrmacht infantry or waste his efforts by exposing the Henschels to point-blank ground fire.

As Gen Reinhardt was ordering his forward regiments to pull back, a fresh threat altered the picture. The rapid advance on Warsaw and the middle Vistula by 10th Army had caused problems for the all-infantry 8th Army on its left flank, which was moving north-east via Lodz. Now 8th Army came under attack from Gen Kutrzeba's Poznan Army, a fresh force of four divisions and two cavalry brigades which, moving by night and lying up by day, had reached Kutno on the night of 9 September. It had remained hidden for several days and its precise location was only revealed when it began a major offensive across the Bzura river against 8th Army. The Wehrmacht consequently swung 10th Army around from the outskirts of Warsaw, to trap the Poznan Army and demolish it. A maximum air effort was ordered to support 8th and 10th Armies. On 11 September the situation reached a pivotal point. Galland and his fellow Staffel leaders were briefed by Weiss to carry out low level attacks on Polish columns moving near Piatek and Bielawy south of the Bzura.

No exact locations were known; the Henschels would be searching for an enemy army moving south across unfamiliar territory and at an ill-defined pace. This was the kind of running battle they did best. For two days the combined efforts of medium bombers, dive-bombers and close-support aircraft pounded away at the Poznan Army, wearing down its mobility, slowing its advance and blunting its cutting edge. By the night of 12 September Galland had flown his highest number of operations in a single day, achieving ten sorties during the daylight hours. Engines ran almost non-stop as aircraft came and went: rearming, refuelling, bouncing off again down the rough airstrips – keeping a conveyor belt of bombs and gunfire pouring into the battle of the Bzura. That night Gen Kutrzeba pulled his divisions back and regrouped for a run to Warsaw and Modlin. It was the turning point; as his forces opened out in their movement back and east they became vulnerable, and over the next several days continuous attacks wore down their resistance. On 16-17 September a series of non-stop low level attacks shattered everything that moved. On 18 September a relieved II.(Sch) Gruppe could at last afford to reduce the hectic frequency of its sorties.

Hitler had arrived to visit the front on 11 September, and during his tour Galland had his second encounter with the Fuehrer and his entourage. Just as at the Reichskanzlei in June, Hitler had an air of detachment and seemed not to mix well with those around him. He stopped for a while and had a meal with the personnel of Galland's Staffel, eating a bowl of soup innocent of the pieces of meat which were served to everyone else: not only a non-smoker, but a vegetarian too. … Galland was surprised at the triviality of the awkward smalltalk his Fuehrer exchanged with the airmen. For Galland, success should crown achievement merited by talent and skill; he failed to detect any such spark in this withdrawn, out-of-touch, seemingly ordinary man. He was puzzled that Germany should put so much trust in this figure; and noted with unease the ingratiating manner of those around him. Germany needed great strength from its leadership, but it also needed acceptance from the world beyond its borders. What it did not need was puppets who passively let their strings be pulled by this isolated-seeming figure. It was a worry that would return.

The intense period of fighting was beginning to wane as the centre of the struggle shifted toward Warsaw. For another week or more there would be a furious bombing campaign to break the city's stubborn resistance. For Galland the modest respite was welcome and timely; more than two weeks of non-stop flying and fighting was beginning to take its toll. Losses had been tolerable, but the level of attrition could not have been sustained over a long period. By 19 September resistance had diminished to the point that Luftwaffe units could start withdrawing from Poland; and the Schlachtflieger could count the cost.

Of the 36 aircraft with which II.(Sch)/LG2 had taken part in those first attacks, 26 remained – many of them damaged, though flyable. An attrition rate of 28 per cent in little more than two weeks was high, but unsurprising for ground-attack operations. By the time Galland's Polish campaign finished on 21 September he had flown 87 missions, but had personally seen Polish fighters in the air only three times; so far as Galland had seen, not one Henschel had been attacked in the air.

The ferocity of the close-support attacks carried out by Galland and his fellow pilots brought grim respect from the enemy. Gen Kutrzeba would recall that:'. … a furious air assault was made on the river crossings near Witkovice – which, for the number of aircraft engaged, the violence of their attack, and the acrobatic daring of their pilots, must have been unprecedented. Every movement, every troop concentration, every line of advance came under pulverising bombardment from the air. It was just hell on earth. The bridges were destroyed, the fords blocked, the waiting columns of men decimated.'

Galland's men had achieved some of the most outstanding performance records of the campaign. By developing the battle tactics which evolved through his experience in Spain into focused close-support for a fast-moving armoured battle, Galland was able to maximise the effectiveness of outdated biplanes and fill a niche no other aircraft or unit could match. (At a more trivial level, one of the unexpected lessons of the fighting was that if held at 1,800rpm the blubbering staccato of the BMW's nine cylinders sounded like amplified heavy machine gun fire, striking absolute terror when broadcast to the enemy from a height of 30ft. Unfortunately the pilots were unable to capitalise on the effect to the full, since at those revolutions the synchronisation mechanism for the twin machine guns was unreliable.)

The end for Poland came soon afterwards, when on 17 September the Russian army invaded its eastern border, as had been arranged with Hitler barely a week before the opening German assault. The line of demarcation between Russian and German forces was established by agreement at the river Bug. Because the Russian army made great strides across Poland, the Luftwaffe was ordered to support as a priority the taking of Warsaw before the scheduled arrival of the Soviets on 1 October. By 24 September the regrouped German armies were ready for the final assault on the capital. The defenders and citizens endured heavy air raids; fires raged out of control, and the defence collapsed, formal capitulation following on 27 September.

For the first time since 1918 the German army had gone onto the offensive, and this time supported by an independent air force practising a totally new form of warfare. It had spectacularly achieved its objectives, and had demonstrated an efficiency which was not lost on foreign observers. The paralysing effect of the air campaign on the movement of men and supplies, and on the exercise of command and control, was particularly noted by the French. Everyone who had participated was taken aback by the sheer pace of the assault, not daring beforehand to imagine that everything would go as planned. In fact it did not, and given their available assets and their many handicaps the Poles had put up a spirited and credible resistance. What was more, many Poles chose to escape abroad to continue the fight; and of the thousands who did so, hundreds would in time fly with the French air force and the RAF. The Luftwaffe had suffered significant losses: 564 aircraft, including 285 written off through damage or training accidents, and 734 casualties – 279 killed, 221 wounded and 234 missing.

* * *

Hitler had begun a process that tumbled a willing and enthusiastic generation into war against the world. On the day Germany invaded Poland the British government had sent Berlin a message warning that it intended to stand by its obligations to that country. Neville Chamberlain's deep reluctance to take an irrevocable step, which he knew would have incalculable consequences, was overcome by the strength of feeling in Parliament. Britain held firm, and sent an ultimatum to Berlin on Sunday 3 September saying that if it had not heard by noon (11.00 London time) that Germany was prepared to withdraw its forces from Poland a state of war would exist between the two countries. That message was delivered by the British ambassador to Dr Paul Schmidt, Hitler's interpreter, at 09.00 (Berlin time). It is reported that after Dr Schmidt had slowly read out the ultimatum Hitler sat transfixed for several seconds before turning to Ribbentrop: 'What now?', he asked, as if searching for an answer. Dr Schmidt withdrew, and quietly informed those gathered in the anteroom. Goering turned to him and, with a grim look on his face, voiced what everyone in the room was probably thinking: 'If we lose this war, then God have mercy on us.' No reply was sent; and at 11.15 on 3 September Chamberlain stood up in the House of Commons and announced that, as a consequence, 'this country is at war with Germany.' By the end of the afternoon France had followed suit.

Word had reached Galland during the early hours of 4 September, and by the end of that day most German servicemen knew that they were now in a war for survival; if they lost again their nation would go down for the second time in less than 50 years. Among Galland's fellow officers there was a feeling of foreboding and tension which outlasted the Polish campaign. They had been focused on that campaign for many months beforehand; now, instead of returning victorious to a country at peace, they had to acustom themselves to the idea of a new and more daunting struggle, whose course and end were quite unpredictable.

As he had done in Spain, Galland drew on his experiences and observations to formulate ideas about the proper use of air power in close-support operations. (Ironically, it was this determination to excel in any assigned task that kept him from his ideal assignment; the better he mastered the challenges facing him, the more he was asked to consolidate experiences among the close-support squadrons from which he longed to escape.) Even as he was organising the movement of his Staffel back to Germany he was formulating conclusions on how the air war had been conducted in Poland, how II.(Sch)/LG2 had performed, and how the latter had contributed to the former. Hours were spent discussing tactics with fellow pilots, talking to ground crew to get their views on flight readiness, and gleaning from them ways in which the administrative control of the squadron could work to their and the common benefit. Galland's creed was that each component of the Staffel must work with the others as a team, and that a Gruppe could only operate effectively if each Staffel bent a little toward a common objective. All this made him an exceptional officer; for the quite lowly rank of Oberleutnant his concerns were ahead of his responsibilities. For the moment, it was satisfaction enough to wrestle answers out of these problems.

To his men he was a demanding commander; leading from the front, but with considerable administrative experience and competence; he had the moral authority to impose upon his men tasks which he was seen to be carrying out himself. To his fellow officers he was sometimes a thorn in the side, driving hard where others would have allowed a slackening of pace. In the air he was a veritable hurricane, and his flying skills were already legendary; what he was able to do with an aeroplane invariably exceeded its documented performance. Of his activity in Poland Galland was self-critical, always believing he could improve his operational tactics or his flying technique. But he was even more critical of the way the Luftwaffe's ground-support assets were being employed.

He noted with concern a tendency to use close-support aircraft for preparing the forward edge of the assault area; notwithstanding the enormous success with which the Blitzkrieg had been conducted, he detected a dangerous tendency to drift away from proven applications in the air-land war. The Luftwaffe had tended to use dive-bombers and close-support aircraft as a battering ram against the enemy's front line. Their proper use, Galland thought, was to close or annihilate assets available to the enemy that would have immediate effect on their ability to continue the fight. By smashing rail and road bridges he would concertina the traffic waiting to get through, thereby making it easier to pick off. What the Luftwaffe had attempted was a duplication of artillery fire. But, said Galland, all that did was to bloody the enemy's nose while leaving his vital organs intact.

For his practical efforts in Poland Adolf Galland was awarded the Iron Cross, Second Class, the citation being dated 13 September; this decoration was awarded for 'conspicuous bravery and outstanding merits in leadership.' From Poland it was back to Germany and the leafy countryside of Braunschweig. On 1 October Galland was promoted to Hauptmann (captain). His ambition to pursue his chosen calling as a fighter pilot was bubbling again. Had he not done enough, in flying more than 360 combat missions in two wars, to deserve his choice of job now? Tentative feelers were put out, through official and unofficial channels alike.

He was advised that this was no time to be switching tracks: his experience was as a ground-attack leader, he was a newly promoted Hauptmann who could perhaps expect his own Gruppe soon, an accomplished tactician and an obvious leader of men; did he not know there was a war on? His country needed all the expertise it could get, and while he would probably make a fine fighter pilot there were tough battles ahead that called for experienced hands. It seemed he was destined to rush about the battlefield in a radial-engined biplane while less experienced pilots got to fly the 300mph Messerschmitts and fight a real war in the sky – a war which everybody thought was imminent, including Galland.

* * *

In fact, the journey toward total war was not to be the headlong dash that Hitler planned. He was loath to let the French and British seize the initiative, although during the first two weeks of October he was still making tentative approaches for a peaceful settlement. He was incredulous over French reactions: just a month after pledging massed air raids on Germany if Poland was attacked, they had stayed put behind their Maginot Line. As for the British, Hitler still could not bring himself to believe that they would make war with Germany; wedded to his belief in a 'common destiny' for both nations, he refused to accept what the British people were already resigned to.

On the very day Warsaw surrendered, 27 September, Hitler called a meeting to explain to his generals that he wanted to deal with the French as quickly as possible – and the British too, if they did not make peace on his terms. He believed the Anglo-French forces were still building up to war readiness and that sound military sense would stop them from attacking before they were ready. The generals – including Goering – were appalled. The Wehrmacht was still recovering from Poland, and was in no respect ready for war on another front against powerful modern armies with strong air power. Adamant, Hitler intimated he would like the assault to begin on 12 November.

The plan of attack, known as 'Case Yellow', was drawn up during October and tracked a succession of Fuehrer Directives to the OKW defining its objectives and the rationale for its implementation. Self-justifying, and apparently intended mainly to convince the generals that he knew what he was doing, they are a useful indication of his personal agenda in the sense that they reveal the dictator 'thinking aloud'. In conference with Hitler on several occasions from late 1940, and during numerous social visits with Goering at his hunting lodges, Galland came to know the broader plan for German actions beyond Poland. He was able to discuss elements of this in retrospect and to piece together the grand vision held by Hitler in 1939 and early 1940.

Unsurprisingly, Hitler's deepest motivation lay in his obsessive hatred and fear of the 'Slav hordes' and of communist Russia in particular. He was also deeply concerned with correct timing: Goering would ramble at great length to Galland about the Fuehrer's preoccupation with sequences, timings and schedules, believing himself to be at the helm of world events which he could direct according to his own programme.

After victory in Poland, Hitler believed that if he waited upon the democracies to take the initiative the relative strength of Germany's armed forces would decline. The broader agenda envisaged an attack on Russia during spring 1940, with his armies conquering France and the Low Countries before that could take place. Unsure about the British, he convinced himself that they could be brought to heel; if not, a swift invasion would finish them off. In fact a series of obvious practical problems during that winter, rather than the expressed opposition of his generals, combined to postpone his scheduled date for the attack several times, and finally until spring 1940.

As it turned out, these postponements worked perfectly to Adolf Galland's advantage. Unable to convince anyone that he should be posted to a fighter squadron, he knew that sooner or later the peace would shatter and his chance would be gone. This 'Sitzkrieg' was unbearably frustrating; he felt trapped by circumstances that until this last year had favoured him. And then something happened which was to change his entire life: Adolf Galland got a touch of marsh rheumatism.

Unwilling to seek medical attention he stuck it out for a while, but the years of flying in open cockpits had taken their toll. He had to do something; the pain was excruciating, and he had difficulty with some of the controls in the cockpit of his Henschel. He was sent to Wiesbaden for a rest and physiotherapy. His back pain had started shortly after he arrived in Spain more than two years earlier; it had got much worse in the damp of Poland; and Galland now feared the verdict of the medical experts as greatly as he had when extricating himself from the grounding after his crash in 1935. But suddenly, it dawned on him that this affliction could be turned to his advantage to accomplish what his badgering of the OKL personnel office had failed to achieve.

Returning to Braunschweig, he minimised the effect of his chronic backache and saw the medical officer as a matter of routine. Yes, he had benefited from the treatment at Wiesbaden; yes, he was feeling much better; and he believed that if he kept away from drafty open cockpits he would be as good as new. Of course, to prevent a recurrence of the malady he would have to be assigned to closed cockpits from now on; didn't medical opinion agree with that conclusion? Of course it did; and Galland was recorded as medically unfit for Henschel Hs123s, but perfectly fit for Messerschmitt Bf109s – the only German single-seat fighters with closed cockpits. His reassignment, to Jagdgeschwader 27 at Krefeld as operations officer, came through with effect from 10 February 1940. To the end, Galland never admitted whether it was in fact open cockpits that brought on the complaint or some other cause; given his performance before the eye specialists, a certain amount of suspicion is reasonable.

Notes to Chapter 7

1 The Bf110, designed as a 'strategic fighter', owed its birth to the Kampfflugzeug (battle aircraft) concept of World War I. As evolved during the 1930s, the Zerstoerer was intended to protect the bombers, carry out offensive sorties deep behind enemy lines, and maintain standing patrols at long range. The concept was a compromise and a designer's nightmare, resisted by many when proposed in 1934. After Messerschmitt's initial Bf110 proposal wiser heads shifted the requirement to that for a high speed medium bomber, or Schnellbomber – a role satisfied by the Junkers Ju88. After delays and indecision both programmes were behind schedule, and the Bf110 was built as a Zerstoerer; 95 were in squadron service by August 1939, along with 18 Ju88s. The twin-engined, two-seat Bf110 was 100-130kph (60-80mph) slower than the Bf109E and had a penetration range of less than 480km (300 miles), making it highly unsuitable for the designed role of heavy escort. It would prove, by summer 1940, quite unable to survive unescorted in daytime fighter combat.

2 The P-11c, powered by a variety of radial engines of between 525hp and 625hp, had a sea-level speed of barely 300kph (185mph) and a top speed of 390kph (242mph) at 18,000ft. It would acquit itself surprisingly well, however, in the hands of determined pilots. Other squadrons had a total of about 30 P-7s, powered by a 527hp Bristol Jupiter engine built by Skoda, and slower than the P-11 by about 45mph at altitude.

CHAPTER 8

February – May 1940

Jagdgeschwader 27 had been formed in October 1939, and its commander, Obstlt Max Ibel, faced the task of building up the unit's infrastructure from scratch. A veteran of World War I and of the Lipetsk school during the 1920s, Ibel knew that he lacked recent experience, and leant heavily on his young operations officer. It seemed that wherever Galland went he was fated to be buried in paperwork. The pressure of activating the Geschwader ahead of the campaign which all felt to be imminent was considerable; JG27 had only received the first of II.Gruppe's aircraft in January, III.Gruppenstab would not be formed until May, and in the meantime there was a constant flow of aircrew and other personnel to administer.

Galland was conscious of his lack of experience on the Bf109E; while he had matured into a pilot of unusual capability, he felt that the fact that he had never yet shot down an aircraft was hampering his ability to shape the operational effectiveness of this new unit. The Geschwader was not operational, and too far from the French border to hope for one of the occasional aerial encounters which took place during the 'Phoney War'; strict limitations were in force to prevent provocation of major engagements until 'Case Yellow' was ripe. To get the experience which he believed he needed, Galland decided to telephone an old friend.

Werner Moelders had come a long way since he had wandered into that Spanish bar carrying a cardboard suitcase. The Condor Legion's leading ace was now a Gruppenkommandeur with JG53 based down at Wiesbaden, less than half an hour's flying time from Krefeld. He welcomed the opportunity to fly with Galland; it gave him the chance to discuss and practice new techniques. One secret Moelders could not share with him, however, was his extraordinary eyesight; the glass fragments from Galland's crash meant that he could never equal his friend's ability to pick out the darting speck of a diving fighter at great distance.

The two men had very different personalities: Moelders was serious, studious, and never deflected from his passion for perfection, while Galland had a debonair attitude, and never took anything too seriously apart from his duties. What they did share was a common love of the chase, the furious tussle for supremacy in the air and the thrill of the deadly encounter. For each it was the ultimate expression of intelligence, ingenuity and skill; and for each the true enemy was not the opponent, but some hidden flaw in himself that would cut him down if he failed to detect it and eliminate it.

When Galland received permission for temporary detachment to JG53, Moelders could offer him a good chance of experiencing air-to-air combat. His Geschwader was patrolling the Franco-German border to intercept French aircraft if they strayed across into German airspace; such incursions were frequent, and JG53 were always ready for a fight[1]. During these sorties Galland several times witnessed a decisive superiority of German tactics and flying techniques. There was much to be learned, and he absorbed it quickly. On one or two occasions Galland got the chance to engage French fighters, but without conclusive results. On the ground, Galland learned much about the organisation of JG53 which he was able to take back to his own Geschwader.

He was particularly impressed by the rudimentary system for fighter control which Moelders had set up. By putting a small spotter unit close to a carefully chosen sector of the border he received advance word of enemy air activity. In the air he continued to receive information by radio, helping him vector on to the targets, which he was always able to pick out visually long before anyone else. This co-ordinated alert system greatly influenced the way Galland thought about fighters, and he came to regard them as elements in an integrated defence structure. Integration and co-operative interaction between Staffel, Gruppe and Geschwader was an essential prerequisite for success; but the individual Staffeln had to be free to operate unhampered within this framework. Defence was a matter of offence; success in air combat was a combination of aggression, surprise, and the free-wheeling tactics of unfettered squadrons. In April 1940 it may have seemed rather academic; but such considerations would loom large in the fortunes of the Luftwaffe within four years.

Galland and Moelders spent hours working out the best way to use fighters and the optimum methods of waging air combat to their advantage. Back at JG27 it all seemed clearer, and Galland threw himself energetically into shaping the new ideas for Obstlt Ibel to implement; the ageing Geschwaderkommodore was glad to have this enthusiastic young 'gunfighter' as operations officer. Galland relieved each Gruppenkommandeur as they took turns to go on leave, and gained further experience running three Staffeln and a staff flight.

The pressures of building up a new fighter Geschwader were compounded by the tension and uncertainty of these weeks when the world was waiting for the shooting war to start, and there was at least one embarrasing episode of triggerhappiness. At Krefeld, some 15 miles from the border with south-east Holland, JG27 faced little aerial opposition; Holland and Belgium had both remained neutral when France and Britain declared war, and their air power was minimal – Holland had only about 125 combat-ready aircraft, while Belgium had 180. The main patrol area extended to the south, however, where the border with France brought sporadic encounters. JG27's three operational Gruppen were based at Krefeld, Moenchen-Gladbach and Duesseldorf, between which staff officers had to commute regularly. A senior staff officer, or 'Jafu' (a derivation from Jagdfliegerfuehrer) was flying in a Fw58 Weihe twin-engined transport from one of these bases to Luftflotte headquarters on the Lower Rhine one morning in March when he was jumped by two Bf109s from another Geschwader and shot down. The 'Jafu' was not at all pleased, and Galland was incensed. The lack of fighter control nagged at him; it was an important moment for someone who would later control the fighter forces of whole Luftflotten.

Having seen a co-ordinated alert and control system at work with JG53, he vowed to implement such a system under operational conditions. However, he knew it was futile to set up an advanced warning and fighter control network unless the individual aircraft could be controlled in their patch of sky, at least to the point of visual identification. Surely, he argued, with the wider formation of a Schwarm spread across almost 600m (2,000ft) of sky, a tight radio link through a central controller would be vital for vectoring and successful interceptions.

* * *

The forces which opposed the Luftwaffe in the West were the French air force reinforced by the British Advanced Air Striking Force, which had flown to France on 2 September 1939. This consisted of ten light bomber squadrons equipped with the Fairey Battle, later supplemented with the Bristol Blenheim, and two fighter squadrons flying the eight-gun Hawker Hurricane. In addition, the British Expeditionary Force had 13 squadrons (four of which flew Hurricanes) in what was termed its Air Component. In total, the British Air Force in France, or BAFF, had approximately 400 aircraft.

As for the French, their position was calamitous. Their air force had been in serious decline since 1933, and their defensive plans relied on Britain sending 240 bombers within 25 days of an attack. The French military still had not come to terms with modern air warfare and still treated their air force as an army co-operation element. They had the Maginot Line, and a theory that said it was impregnable. Although the French government was being presented with figures which showed an air force of 4,862 aircraft, this was a dangerous self-delusion. When aircraft capable of surviving in the front line were counted, France had 523 modern fighters, 37 modern bombers, and 118 reconnaissance machines – a total of 678 aircraft.

Of even greater concern were the primitive methods employed by the French to control and co-ordinate their air forces. For detection the French used observers equipped with a telephone connected to the civilian telephone system. They had very little dedicated AA artillery, and no system of vectoring the few fighters they could put in the air. Moreover, the fighter units were too widely dispersed along the frontier and could not be brought to bear on a specific sector. There was no organised reporting system, which meant there was no factual tally of aircraft, enemy or otherwise, moving in or through various air sectors across the country. Finally, the French adamantly refused to bomb targets in Germany or, if attacked by German forces, to bomb anything beyond the French border, for fear of provoking retaliation.

By April 1940 the Wehrmacht had amassed the assets for a major assault in the West; as a member of the staff of JG27, Galland knew that a far greater effort than that expended on Poland was being prepared. What he would come to know later from his private and informal conversations with Goering and Hitler was that the

Fuehrer had developed, between August 1939 and January 1940, a vision of conquest on if not a global, then at least a hemispherical scale[2].

Before 'Case Yellow' could take place, the first step in the grand plan was to close British access to the Baltic and to secure Scandinavia; as early as 13 December the OKW was ordered by Hitler to begin preparations for such an offensive – the excuse being that increasing British interest in blocking shipments of Swedish ore threatened vital German supplies. Coincidentally the British planned to land four divisions through the Norwegian port of Narvik when the spring thaw set in, moving to airfields from where they could bomb Germany. Unaware of this, Germany flew airborne troops from Schleswig-Holstein to airfields in Denmark and Norway on 9 April. With minimal casualties the airfields were taken over for Luftwaffe use[3]. As the airborne forces were descending upon Norway, units of the Wehrmacht crossed the Danish frontier. When British, French and Free Polish forces did land in Norway – near Namsos on 15 April and in Romsdalsfjord three days later – it was too little, too late: they were expelled from Norway in early May. Although the brief campaign held some ominous lessons for the Kriegsmarine, there was no significant air fighting.

* * *

When the eve of 'Case Yellow' dawned in the second week of May 1940, III.Gruppe of JG27 was just working up to strength, having received its Bf109s over the past few days (II. and III./JG27 were both composite units, formed from I./JG1 and I./JG21). Galland's Geschwader was part of VIII.Fliegerkorps – coincidentally, again commanded by Gen Wolfram von Richthofen; this was one of three Fliegerkorps under Luftflotte 2, commanded by Genobst Kesselring. For the coming campaign Luftflotte 2 was assigned to support Army Group B (Genobst Fedor von Bock) in the north. Army Group A in the centre (Genobst Gerd von Rundstedt), and Army Group C (Genobst Wilhelm von Leeb) to the south, were assigned Luftflotte 3 commanded by Genobst Hugo Sperrle. It was with Army Group A that the primary effort was to be concentrated. Under Genmaj Erich von Manstein's brilliant plan, Army Group A would cut a swathe through the supposedly impenetrable Ardennes south of the Maginot defences, and press on north-west to the Channel coast, dividing the Allied armies, whose northern elements would be sucked forwards into Belgium by Army Group B and thus set up for encirclement and destruction.

In total, the Luftwaffe had approximately 4,000 aircraft on strength for 'Case Yellow' out of a total paper strength of 5,000. Effective strengths at all units provided about 1,120 bombers, including Do17s, He111s and Ju88s; 324 Ju87 Stukas and 42 Hs123s (the latter with II.(Sch)/LG2); 1,016 Bf109s; and 248 Bf110s operating in the Zerstoerer escort role.

Galland had mixed feelings as the campaign opened. He had finally got his posting to a fighter unit; all winter he had anticipated this day; and now his endless administrative tasks were keeping him away from the cockpit. It was his job to support staff operations; to prepare rosters for pilots and ground crews; to process the requests for equipment, stores and ammunition from Gruppe level; to arrange for conferences between the Staffeln and the Geschwaderstab, between the Geschwaderstab and the Gruppen, and between Geschwaderstab and von Richthofen's Stab/VIII.Fliegerkorps. In addition, he had intelligence reports to process, communications to handle, sortie briefings to co-ordinate with the respective Gruppenkommandeure, and movement orders to arrange. When the assault started it would be worse, for the movement of all three Gruppen to forward bases would need a lot of work. Finally, presumably, there would be the victory claims to handle and de-briefings to arrange.

On that first day of the war in the West, 10 May 1940, Galland was preoccupied by these onerous and frustrating duties. Luftwaffe bombers began intense attacks on Dutch, Belgian and French airfields and French railheads and communications. Despite warnings, the British and French were taken completely by surprise. That afternoon the British Expeditionary Force began a preplanned advance toward Antwerp and a defensive position known as the Dyle line.

It would be a day or so before Galland could take to the skies in combat himself, but the information poured out in torrents by the excited pilots helped him to evaluate the opposition – a task at which he excelled. Since early light the Bf109s had been streaming out in Gruppe formations, and returning Staffel by Staffel. Many had not experienced the Blitzkrieg on Poland, and could hardly believe their eyes as the almost unchallenged assault rolled on across the featureless terrain of southern Holland. The magnitude of the land battle dwarfed even the great German offensive of March 1918.

At the end of the first day, as light drained from the reddened skies, Galland leapt into a small liaison aircraft and hopped across to visit the Gruppenkommandeure at Moenchen-Gladbach and Duesseldorf. It was hard to get a sense of how far or how fast the ground forces had succeeded in advancing, but the reports in from each of the nine Staffeln glowed with achievement. The information came in bits and pieces: very few enemy aircraft in the air, but many seen smashed on the ground by lightning Stuka strikes on Dutch and Belgian airfields; consolidation across the Maas and the Albert Canal, where Dutch and Belgian troops were expected to mass. What Galland did not know was that half the Dutch air force had been destroyed without leaving the ground, and that the Belgian air force had been decimated.

For most of the 10th the Gruppen had been assigned to bomber escort duty; and interesting comments were made about the difficulty of keeping down to the speed of their lumbering charges. The pilots had achieved it by operating in Rotten above and below the bombers; with lateral air clearance they could weave from side to side safely. As the day progressed fighter opposition got stiffer, the most active intercepts coming from the Belgians. During their return from bomber escort JG27 pilots had been released to pursue Belgian fighters, observing on the ground the forward movement of British troops towards the Dyle line (which would soon be crossed by faster-moving and more heavily armoured Wehrmacht units).

The Belgian air force had acquired 12 Hawker Hurricane fighters, and Galland was keen to hear reports of how these fared in combat with JG27. By the end of this first day only half the Belgian Hurricanes remained, the rest shot down in combat. There seemed to be little trouble in fighting off the Hurricanes, said the pilots, and the Bf109E was well up to the challenge. (That would change: the Belgian Hurricanes were early Mk Is, all but one with fixed-pitch propellers, and a decidedly inferior performance to the Messerschmitts.)

The RAF had elected to keep its aircraft back on French airfields and to conduct bombing raids on the German ground forces; but they proved unable to destroy vital bridges ahead of the advancing Wehrmacht. Of 32 Fairey Battles sent against German columns only 19 got back, all damaged; of six Bristol Blenheims sent against Wallhaven airfield all but one were shot down by Bf110s. The RAF had a total of six Hurricane squadrons in France, and Fighter Command sent four more without delay in a planned redeployment. The Spitfires were being held back in England. Production had been slow; it was generally considered to be the ultimate fighter for home defence; and the more numerous Hurricanes had a wide track undercarriage, more suitable for rough airstrips. It was notable, however, that the RAF Hurricanes achieved high levels of success against German bombers, which the Luftwaffe often chose to protect with the Bf110, leaving the Bf109s to cover the ground troops against attack from RAF bombers.

The sheer scale of the attack had been numbing; by the end of that first day the Luftwaffe had bombed and seriously affected operations at 72 airfields, destroying between 300 and 400 aircraft on the ground. The Sitzkrieg had erupted into such sudden and massive violence that the Allied forces were unable to check the Wehrmacht's momentum. Next day, 11 May, the situation deteriorated further. While over the frontier at Krefeld the harassed operations officer of JG27 was submerged by an endless tide of communications and briefings, and demands from Stab/VIII.Fliegerkorps for precise damage assessments from pilot reports, the Gruppenkommandeure were already pleading with him for an estimate of when they would have to pack up their units and roll. The progress of the Panzers was now increasing the distance to the front to such an extent that JG27 would soon have to move forward and occupy newly captured airfields.

Further sacrificial attacks by the hopelessly outclassed RAF light bombers had ended in massacre; by the night of 11 May the RAF had lost over half their strength – 75 of the 135 aircraft on the Continent. In total the Dutch, Belgian, British and French air forces had lost almost 1,000 aircraft. (The day had also seen the successful conclusion to a remarkable operation performed by Sturmabteilung Koch when 55 men from the 1st Parachute Regiment took the 'impregnable' Belgian fortress of Eben Emael with only five casualties; JG27 had provided top cover for the Ju52s and gliders bringing them in the previous morning.)

All through the night the mechanics at JG27 worked feverishly. After two days of frantic fighting and aircraft movements spares were needed, and the logistical check sheet was getting cluttered. The Geschwader would soon be on the move to airfields in Belgium and France, and there were continual changes to the daily orders and operations briefings. On this third day, 12 May, JG27 would be covering 6th Army's crossings of the Maas and the Albert Canal, using bridges captured on the first day. Obstlt Ibel could still put 85 Bf109Es into the air; today he ordered a dawn take-off by two Staffeln led by Hptmn Joachim Schlichting. Staffelkapitaen Oblt Walter Adolph and his wingman Ufw Blazytko were the first to spot three flights of RAF Blenheims – nine bombers in tight formation, heading east at relatively low altitude. After reporting the sighting he rolled over and dived to get below and behind the Blenheim he had already picked out. In the next five minutes, Adolph achieved three kills; Oblt Braune, Lt Ortel and Ufw Blazytko each downed another. As the three surviving Blenheims headed for Liege they were spotted by pilots from 3.Staffel; only one survived.

As the morning progressed JG27 was transformed into a frenzied circus of performing aircraft, coming in, turning around and going back out again. Pilots would land, run to the briefing rooms as ground crew fuelled and rearmed the aircraft, get their new patrol sectors and rendezvous positions, and sprint back to their Bf109s for another race to the receding front. If Hurricanes were spotted en route the temptation to divert was resisted as they flew full tilt to their assigned patrol sectors. Generally, sorties were flown with less than an hour between landing and take-off; the pace was crushing.

By now Galland had decided he was going to join a patrol on sector stand-by and sample the action for himself. With Gustav Rodel as his wingman he took off at 11.00 and flew south-west, crossing into Belgium north of Aachen and from there south of Maastricht on a course which, if continued, would have taken them to Brussels. Just five miles west of Liege, at a height of 3650m (12,000ft), Galland spotted eight Hurricanes about 915m (3,000ft) below in tight formation. Diving down, Galland and Rodel set themselves up to attack separate aircraft. Galland remembered thinking, 'Come on, defend yourself!' as he rapidly closed the range. He pressed the button on his control column, and saw his bullets strike. Shocked into action, the Hurricane pilot flung his aircraft over to one side and straight into the fire from Rodel's 109. Turning inside the arcing path of the British fighter, Galland had a second chance from closer range, and fired several brief bursts into the fuselage and wings. Suddenly the rudder fell away and the Hurricane went into an uncontrollable spin.

Galland broke off and went in pursuit of another; by now they had scattered to all points of the compass. Finding his second victim, he closed to 90m (300ft) and gave it a quick burst before it flicked through a half-roll and was gone into cloud. Plunging after it, Galland flew a following pattern for the kind of manoeuvres he thought his adversary would perform. Out into clear sky once more he found to his delight that he was right behind, but even closer. Galland held his nerve until he was sure of a kill, and fired two-second bursts. The Hurricane pulled up in front of him; he copied the manoeuvre, got in another burst, and it stalled right in front of him to plunge straight into the ground from 450m (1,500ft).

Returning to base, Adolf Galland felt no real elation. It had been so sudden, so anticlimactic, that he had not felt the blood-rush that he remembered from so many desperate strafing runs in Spain. It had all been so easy, as though the pilots had willingly accepted their fate. He felt as though he should have had a tougher fight, as though he had an unfair advantage and that it had been preordained. But it still felt good to have won, and to have proved to himself his mastery of the

Bf109 in the only arena that mattered. He knew that the first few kills were crucial to a fighter pilot: success or failure in later flights could hinge on the reaction to that first deadly encounter, and his had gone well, thanks to luck and good equipment.

Back at base he received the congratulations of brother officers, superiors and ground crew; not a bad morning's work – and Rodel came back with one confirmed kill as well. It was not enough, however; and he was back in the sky again before the afternoon was out, over the Tirlemont area about 25 miles east of Brussels. Part of a patrol, Galland came across five Hurricanes and went after them in a flank dive which had him turning on to the tail of one at great speed. Pulling up quickly, he rolled over while discharging a burst into the side of the fuselage. Lazily turning on to its back, it fell away; and Galland had scored his third victory.

By the end of the afternoon of 12 May JG27 had cleared its sector of enemy fighters, and switched back to escorting Stukas. The tally for JG27 was 340 sorties since daybreak, during which four Bf109s had been shot down, but claims totalling 28 enemy aircraft had been placed.

* * *

On 13 May, away to the south, von Rundstedt's troops made a dramatic crossing of the Meuse at Sedan, and the Wehrmacht reached a crucial point in its operations. The full resources of the Luftwaffe were directed toward 'uninterrupted attacks lasting for eight hours' – as 1st Panzer Division recorded – to pulverise the French defences along the Meuse. On Army Group B's front JG27 were busy throughout the day. For the Dutch it was almost the end. Only Rotterdam could block the German armies moving north, which in turn would influence the pace of progress further south. For many Belgians and Frenchmen the intensity of the attacks on 13 May reached a ferocity the like of which they had never imagined. Increasingly, the Allies were being ground down.

On 14 May the RAF mounted the greatest number of daylight bombing sorties of the entire campaign, and came close to complete elimination. Ten squadrons of Blenheims and Battles were hit by wave after wave of Bf109s and Bf110s; the RAF lost 41 out of 71 bombers – 62 per cent – in addition to 16 Hurricanes and 11 other types. On the same day Rotterdam was devastated by a major bombing raid which did nothing to improve Germany's standing in neutral countries, and which would become a symbol of Nazi terror tactics[4]. That evening the Dutch armed forces capitulated, having lost some 25 per cent of their total strength. The following morning, Queen Wilhelmina's family having sailed to England, the government of Holland formally surrendered.

The day that Holland surrendered, 15 May, brought a turning point in Anglo-French relations. Five days in office, the new British coalition government led by Winston Churchill would move rapidly towards acceptance that France was doomed, and that securing the defence of the British Isles was the overriding priority. On the 15th ACM Sir Hugh Dowding, C-in-C of RAF Fighter Command, would forcefully argue against sending more fighters to France; and after a visit to

Paris on the 16th Churchill himself grasped the full scale of the disaster. The Luftwaffe shot down a further 69 aircraft in the area Sedan-Charleville during 15-16 May; and Luftflotte 2 was increasingly committed to attacking the French rail network to the south.

Meanwhile, JG27 had moved up to keep pace with the Wehrmacht, camping briefly at various airfields as close as possible to the front line. Galland was as anxious as ever to get back into the air; and did so, as part of a plan he developed to counter a pattern of French dusk raids. He organised a Gruppe operation, hunting across a wide area of sky. For several evenings the operation brought no result; but on 19 May Galland, flying from Charleville-Mézières with Gustav Rodel as wingman, intercepted a fast-moving Potez.

Galland signalled Rodel to swing round to cover his left wing while he turned on to a converging path with the enemy aircraft – not easy in the failing light. The Potez was no match for a Bf109, although the pilot was clearly experienced; Galland stuck to it like a leach and saw pieces flying off in all directions under his fire, but it was reluctant to go down. By now the light was bad, and they were sweeping low across fields, over hedges, around woods and houses. Suddenly a village appeared dead ahead, and out of the dark a slender church steeple thrust upwards. Galland deftly exploited the sudden change of path forced on his chase; avoiding the steeple brought the Frenchman into position for a final burst, which sent him into the ground on the far side of the village. Pulling back on the stick and wheeling round in a climbing turn to starboard, Galland flung a quick glance over his right shoulder and saw the burning wreckage spread at the end of the furrow the Potez had ploughed as it went in.

But now there was the problem of getting back through a narrow triangle of German-occupied territory to Charleville-Mézières. Fuel was low, the light had gone, and there was little real hope of finding the darkened airfield. After a vain attempt to read the name on a railway station, Rodel radioed Galland that he had to land – right now. Aiming for a gentle upward slope, he neatly hopped across a hedge and set his Bf109 down for a perfect landing. Galland, trying to follow suit, narrowly missed a dry river bed as he rolled to a stop. Not knowing where they were, the two pilots were prepared for a shoot-out with Belgian troops when approached in the dark by men from a German flak battery – who were, they said, guarding a fighter airfield in the valley below: Charleville-Mézières. Enlisting their help, Galland had his 109 pushed back up the hill and swung around; then, taking some of the hedge with him, he half-glided, half-flew down to the airfield, sending a can of fuel back to Rodel at first light.

Galland's fifth victory on 19 May was followed less than 24 hours later by another three; and his eighth brought the award of the Iron Cross First Class, presented by Erhard Milch. Following the fall of Holland the focus of the battle moved south and the advance into France drew the weight of Luftwaffe operations away from the Belgian front. It was a constant strain to keep moving men, materiel and aircraft forward behind the advancing armies while maintaining the ability to get the Bf109s into the air, fuelled and armed, at any time. Galland's new-found success in combat could not distract him from his primary duty as operations officer.

By the evening of 20 May, 2nd Panzer Division had reached Abbeville on the river Somme – just ten miles from the English Channel – effectively cutting off three French armies, the British Expeditionary Force, and surviving Belgian units. The Blitzkrieg concept of the fast, mobile, flexible mechanised offensive had been triumphantly vindicated: Holland, most of Belgium and a huge swathe of France had been captured, and many of France's effective forces destroyed, in just ten days. One by one the coastal towns fell to the Wehrmacht, the tanks surging onward under a guardian shield of Luftwaffe fighters. Boulogne was taken and Calais surrounded by 22 May. Around Dunkirk a pocket was forming, within which were almost half a million men of the British and French armies. Air cover was essential for the German forces; the beleaguered BEF was now well within range of RAF airfields in south-east England. The Stukas of VIII.Fliegerkorps were now operating out of St Quentin, and the Channel ports of Boulogne, Calais and Dunkirk were at the limit of their range. On 24 May I./JG27 was ordered to move forward to St Omer, about 20 miles from Dunkirk. The British had only just evacuated and it would have made an ideal field, close behind the front. However, as Obstlt Ibel arrived overhead with the lead Staffel he saw shellfire being exchanged between British and German units from either side of the airfield; and prudently diverted his unit south-east to the rather more definitively captured St Pol-sur-Ternoise. The main Geschwader staff remained at Charleville-Mézières with elements at St Pol; the Staffeln were divided between a number of smaller airfields including St Ibert. JG27's commander and his operations officer anticipated orders to swing south and support a push for Paris – just 60 miles from the nearest German divisions. The forced surrender of the British and French troops in the pocket north of Gravelines was not expected to take long to achieve.

Since 20 May the Admiralty in London had been assembling a fleet of military and civilian vessels of every size, from warships down to weekend pleasure craft, ready to set sail for France in an attempt to rescue some of the trapped BEF and get them back to England ready for the final stand against the Wehrmacht. What this Operation 'Dynamo' needed was a respite from all-out German attacks on the Dunkirk pocket; and on 24 May that respite was ordered.

On 23 May 1st Panzer Division had advanced to Gravelines, just 12 miles from Dunkirk. In close touch with von Rundstedt, Hitler discussed the possibility of closing the net. The veteran general informed the Fuehrer that the British were proving particularly stubborn, taking heavy casualties rather than surrender. (Despite inevitable defeat, the British commander in Boulogne had refused a demand for surrender with the declaration that it was 'the duty of the British Army to fight.') Further down the chain of command, Gens Guderian and von Kleist told the same story; and it worried Hitler. Von Rundstedt and Goering pressed hard for the job of finishing off the Dunkirk pocket to be entrusted to the Luftwaffe – the former, so that his precious armour would not face the costly task of digging die-hard British units out of what was, in these coastal towns, bad tank country; the latter, for the glory of the Luftwaffe and the continued influence of its commander.

It must be recalled that Dunkirk was only part – arguably, a somewhat peripheral part – of the picture in late May, when a large part of the French army remained to be fought by German forces at the end of what any professional would see as dangerously extended lines of supply and communication. It is well documented that von Rundstedt and Hitler were both concerned about the former's exposed and overstretched southern flank, and anticipated a French counter-offensive. What Hitler approved was the use of air power to smash up the remaining armour, artillery, munitions, supplies and transport in the Dunkirk pocket, leaving the Panzers free to move south while mechanised infantry mopped up at Dunkirk. Accordingly, on 24 May, Hitler Directive No.13 ordered the Luftwaffe to 'break all enemy resistance … to prevent the escape of the English forces across the Channel, and to protect the southern flank of Army Group A.' When Hitler visited his headquarters von Rundstedt applauded the decision, one he had advocated against opposition from the general staff. There has been much debate concerning the rationale for not allowing the Panzers to push on into the encircled British and French positions. The simple fact is that there was no reason for them to do so: as far as Hitler knew there was no way out for the British, and he did order a complete destruction of the materiel with which the British army might long resist infantry attack (or subsequently oppose a possible invasion, already hinted at in Directive No.13 which declared that 'the Luftwaffe is authorised to attack the English homeland in the fullest manner, as soon as sufficient forces become available.'[5])

JG27 received its orders on the morning of 24 May; the Geschwader was to support the bomber attacks by escorting the vulnerable Stukas and Heinkels. For the immediate task pin-point Ju87 attacks were preferred. On 26 May - the day that the British ordered the commencement of Operation 'Dynamo' - the Stukas from StG77 arrived over St Pol to collect their escort for a raid on Calais, where 20,000 Allied troops still held out. RAF Spitfires from across the Channel were now proving dangerous and Luftwaffe fighter pilots were hard pressed to maintain close defence around the slower dive-bombers. That afternoon Calais finally surrendered to the 10th Panzer Division.

On the 27th the first waves of Britain's 'little ships' - hundreds of tugs, river steamers, coastal cargo boats, yachts and seagoing pleasure craft - lifted 7,669 BEF soldiers to safety. During daylight the Dorniers from KG2 and KG3 set fire to the town and parts of the harbour, the huge columns of black smoke serving as markers for the Stukas which came from as far away as the Rhineland. Among the exhausted soldiers the cry often went up, 'Where is the RAF?' The RAF was not far away, cutting down a force of Dornier Do17s; as the rescue vessels ran a gauntlet of gunfire the Spitfires were proving their superiority, destroying bombers which would have made their ordeal even worse. Indeed, the Luftwaffe saw 27 May as a black day: they had 23 aircraft shot down - as many as they had lost in the previous ten days - in encounters which at times saw up to 200 Spitfires and Hurricanes flying cover for the evacuation.

Galland's JG27 settled into a routine of operations from Charleville-Mézières, St Ibert and St Pol, flying from first light until dusk and often jousting with Spitfires. Over the next few days the race to evacuate the BEF accelerated: 17,804 were taken off on the 28th, 47,310 on the 29th, and 58,823 on the 30th. Galland himself managed to get in some more sorties, and it was over Dunkirk that he tangled with Spitfires for the first time; from that moment he rated them highly, and had the greatest respect for the skill and bravery of RAF fighter pilots.

The daily requirement to rendezvous with the bombers and escort them over the Dunkirk area was fraught with difficulty. The bombers were usually late in arriving at their pick-up zone, and frequently the Bf109s had used up so much fuel by the time they arrived that they would be forced to leave the bombers before they completed the mission. The Luftwaffe's bombardment of Dunkirk was also less than an all-out effort; many of the active Luftwaffe units in this sector were committed to covering possible threats to von Runstedt's southern flank, and only on the 27th and the afternoon of the 29th were anything like full-scale attacks launched. Bad weather and stiff opposition from the RAF wore down the fighter units, but more particularly the bombers; during the campaign to rescue the BEF the RAF would claim 200 Luftwaffe aircraft. On 30 May the weather was foul; and on the 31st, when fog and rain prevented the Ju87s from taking off, no less than 68,014 troops were lifted from the beaches and from the extended jetty of Dunkirk harbour where the deeper-draught ships tied up.

Violent air battles continued as RAF Fighter Command strove to cover the evacuation and to prevent the bombers from reaching the lines; British aircraft ranged over a wide area of north-west France and Belgium, and JG27 was frequently in action against Spitfires and Hurricanes. Galland's personal score continued to rise throughout this period. On 29 May he was airborne with the Geschwaderstab Schwarm when they came across a formation of Blenheims several hundred feet below. A general chase ensued, the British bombers turning and weaving in fruitless efforts to evade the faster 109s. Two were shot down into the sea, and Galland went after a third which appeared to be flown by a more experienced pilot. For several minutes he tried to stay on its tail and bring his guns to bear; more than once Galland nearly had him, only for the Blenheim to flick away in a skilful turn. Eventually, low down, Galland got the better of him; pouring oily smoke, the bomber sliced into the sea and broke apart. Back on the ground at St Pol Galland found that his Bf109 was covered in oil.

On 1 June the Luftwaffe began its final attack on the beaches where the British troops were massed, rather than on the shrinking perimeter inland. The intense bombing would last for three days before Dunkirk was overrun. In that period a considerable amount of damage was caused; the strict orders were to concentrate on military materiel rather than wasting time attacking the boats, though in the general melee of war orders are never universally obeyed. Above the huge, stinking pall of smoke the Bf109s from JG27 patrolled all day and every day.

During one of these patrols Galland was flying wingman for Obstlt Ibel when, without warning, a squadron of Spitfires dived on the Geschwaderstab flight. Galland cursed himself as he lost sight of Ibel; the Bavarian veteran did not have the finely tuned reactions of the young men he led. Frustrated at having lost contact, Galland fastened on to a lone Spitfire and blasted it with cannon and machine gun fire before breaking out of the fray to serch for his CO – in vain. When shortage of fuel forced him back to St Pol he feared the worst, and felt sad and guilty over his failure to protect his colonel. Hours later Obstlt Ibel appeared at the door of the mess, having walked back from a crash landing.

On 3 June Galland was up again when the staff flight got mixed up in a furious dogfight with two squadrons of French Morane-Saulnier MS406 fighters. Narrowly avoiding a collision with one, Galland fastened on to another and gave it a brief burst of machine gun fire. Bursting into flames, the Morane suddenly pulled up and across in front of Galland's aircraft. Instinctively hauling the 109 around to avoid a collision, Galland was unable to prevent the tips of his propeller striking the wing of the Morane as it loomed in his windscreen. Severing his antenna as it went, it spun away to starboard and plunged in flames. No sooner had he pulled round to get his bearings than another Morane crossed his path; taking a long broadside, this one also fell away smoking heavily, but it was not counted as a kill because in the confusion of the dogfight no witness could confirm its crash. Galland was credited with the first Morane as his 12th victory.

On 4 June it was all over; at 14.23 the British Admiralty sent the order officially ending Operation 'Dynamo'. In nine days the 'little ships', the Royal Navy and the Royal Air Force had rescued 338,226 British and French soldiers – but without virtually any piece of equipment which a man could not carry with him. Since 10 May the BEF had lost 2,472 artillery pieces; 63,879 vehicles; 76,697 tons of ammunition; 449,000 tons of miscellaneous stores; and 164,929 tons of fuel. Using the Luftwaffe had undoubtedly saved German lives, and released heavy armour for more immediately pressing tasks. The longer-term consequences of the escape of a third of a million British soldiers are not easily calculable.

Hitler believed that an exhausted, defeated and almost naked army returning home with its tail between its legs would spread a fear of inevitable failure more effectively than any German propaganda, making the logical choice of a negotiated peace more attractive. In this, as in so much else, he misunderstood the British character; he saw pride and a regard for dignity, but does not seem to have recognised the equally strong element of instinctive, bloody-minded vengefulness. For the time being, however, he was satisfied that he had turned a rational military decision to the service of his grand political strategy.

* * *

Adolf Galland's experiences in the 26 days of 'Case Yellow' had transformed his flying career. He had tested the ability and the temperament of French, Belgian and British fighter pilots while flying the beloved Bf109. Although he had gained a respect for his British counterparts, he believed that the 109 had the edge over the Spitfire. Whether or not he was right is beside the point; the importance in any finely balanced fighter-on-fighter comparison lies in the level of confidence the respective pilots have in their equipment. Galland was supremely confident in the Bf109E, and because he believed it to be the best he could wring out that extra ounce of performance that was not available to a pilot unconvinced of its superiority.

Galland made a speciality of high speed dives, either to escape from an impossible situation in combat or to acquire some advantage. Very few pilots would stay with Galland in a dive, because the Bf109 had a reputation for shedding its wings in extremely violent manoeuvres and dives at full throttle.

Inexplicable as it is, his contemporaries believed that Galland had a way of putting the aeroplane to the air so that it would survive this, and it never failed him. They also testify to the extraordinary way he could couple together several separate manoeuvres in a sequential flow that gave him the advantage over his adversary – presumably a legacy from his long experience of glider and powered aerobatic flying.

There was more to Galland than his skills as a fighting pilot. Obstlt Ibel remarked more than once that he had been able to achieve his goals for JG27 largely because of Galland's ability to get extra performance from his men. As operations officer, Galland had constant contact with the Gruppe commanders and with other ranks both junior and senior to himself. He was well respected as a rising career officer with considerable leadership potential. He was popular in the mess and the maintenance hangars alike, demanding but also giving ungrudging loyalty. It is true that some found his healthy off-duty appetites for the good things in life a little excessive. He also had a cutting tongue when he encountered arrogance or laziness; and he held to his beliefs without compromise – a quality which would put him in harm's way in years to come.

Galland's obvious qualities made him a strong candidate for promotion; and he would be missed by Obstlt Ibel when, shortly after the battle of Dunkirk, he left JG27 to take up a posting which would launch him on arguably the happiest and most rewarding period of his entire career. On 6 June he arrived on an airfield in the Pas de Calais to take over as Gruppenkommandeur of III./JG26 'Schlageter'.

Notes to Chapter 8

1 Moelders' first victory since Spain had been achieved on 21 September 1939 when he shot down a Curtiss H-75 fighter. By the end of March, when Galland telephoned him, he had seven victories; with his Spanish score these gave Moelders a total of 21 air-to-air victories.

2 Hitler's vision encompassed the occupation of Scandinavia; a quick and decisive victory over France and the Low Countries; the British being starved towards inevitable submission by blockade; with Spain recruited or compelled, the Straits of Gibraltar would be closed, and with Italian help the Mediterranean, North Africa and the Middle East would be neutralised and partially occupied. With his back secure, Hitler could turn on his ultimate prize: Russia, and endless Lebensraum for the Germanic peoples. As Luftwaffe Genlt Andreas Nielsen was to tell his US interrogators in 1945: 'No one in a position of military responsibility was ever informed of the ultimate aims of the Fuehrer, and no-one – not even the members of the OKW – was given access to sufficient information to construct an accurate picture of the overall situation.'

While Hitler's deranged vision could only have been entertained by a man with a highly selective understanding of the world he lived in, the fact that a chain of events placed him at the head of armed forces capable of achieving even the early stages of his project – at such infinite cost – still has the power to appal.

3 A new air fleet, Luftflotte 5, was formed at Hamburg on 15 April to cover Denmark and Norway under Genobst Hans Juergen Stumpff, who set up his headquarters in Oslo.

4 Galland's recollection of events differs. In charge that day of processing assignments to

keep the skies clear above the ground forces advancing on the city, he stated that at 13.25, following the Dutch rejection of a German demand for its surrender, He111s of KG54 took off to bomb the city and its defenders to clear a path for an assault crossing of the river – a matter of straightforward military expediency. Subsequently there was an attempt to radio the formation to the effect that the Dutch were after all seeking terms and the bombers were to return, but the message failed to get through. Contact was established with German units south of the city, who were told to fire red flares at the approaching bombers – KG54 were briefed to divert to secondary targets if they saw this signal. Shortly before reaching the target the formation divided into two, one section approaching from the south and the other from the east. Just after 15.05, as Obstlt Hoehne gave the order to bomb, he saw in the murk below two red lights; he countermanded his order and immediately turned his formation of 33 Heinkels due south. To the east, Obst Lackner did not see the flares; and 57 He111s dropped in total 158 500lb and 1,150 100lb HE bombs, causing major fires due to the contents of wooden-roofed warehouses below. Some 980 people were killed and 78,000 people made homeless. In later life Galland was bemused at the claim that the burning of Rotterdam was on the direct orders of Hitler and Goering: if such an order had been given, incendiaries would have been loaded; the 33 bombers would not have turned back; and there would have been a longer and more concerted effort, as there certainly was on other targets.

5   It has sometimes been claimed that Hitler held back an all-out assault on the Dunkirk perimeter from some desire to limit British casualties, on the grounds that massive losses would make it harder to conclude the subsequent negotiated peace which he still believed possible. However, it seems unlikely that this played any significant part in a rational military decision.

CHAPTER 9

June 1940 – 24 July 1940

Adolf Galland arrived to take over the reins at III./JG26 'Schlageter'[1] on 6 June 1940. Just two days beforehand the Geschwader had arrived at various airfields in the Calais area.

The terrain was not ideally suitable; the dispersed aircraft would have to be protected from prying eyes in the sky by camouflage nets over crude wooden frames – this close to their English bases, the RAF were expected to be active in hunting for the German airfields.

When Galland arrived at III.Gruppe he had an inauspiciously, if unintentionally nonchalant reception. After jumping down from his 109, thirsty and seriously in need of a wash, he strode across, still in his flying kit, to a group of men pulling water from an old well. When he asked if he could have a drink he was brusquely told that if he wanted some water he was welcome to pull it himself – which he did, without comment. Shortly thereafter, a freshly washed and shaved Hptmn Galland stomped into the makeshift shack that doubled as an officer's mess, and introduced himself to the shaken occupants as the new Gruppenkommandeur.

Galland soon learned that JG26 had not achieved a particularly high reputation during the Battle of France; and that III.Gruppe had suffered from poor leadership, which had bred a casual attitude. He set about changing things, forcefully and without delay – not that he blamed the junior officers and men, whom he considered victims of a failure to give them the razor-sharp lead their talents deserved. He arrived with the advantage of his reputation; a 12-victory ace was a welcome novelty, and the younger pilots could hardly wait for their chance to get into the air and shake out with the new Gruppenkommandeur. For the 28-year-old captain, it was his dream come true: a fighting command of his own, and once again the chance to be the first and the best.

Galland's adjutant was a young and highly gifted officer, Lt Joachim Muencheberg. He had a natural aptitude for flying, and Galland completely understood his frustration in his position as adjutant when he really wanted free rein as a fighter pilot. Accepting that, Galland was nevertheless delighted to have Muencheberg in a position to help him work up the three Staffeln - 7./JG26 under Oblt Georg Beyer, 8. under Oblt Kuno Wendt, and 9. under Oblt Gerhard Schoepfel - into the type of fighting units he sought. There was much to teach.

First came the essential disciplines in the air that formed the foundation for success. The pilots needed to know that their leader could put them into battle at the right time and in the right place; and that meant they had to understand what

Galland wanted from them and how they could achieve it. With encouragement they willingly applied themselves, showing a bolder sense of involvement in the fight. Galland was a hard man to keep up with and the pilots had to be good to follow him; he led by example, stimulating better and bolder flying, commitment and aggression.

It was perhaps not the best time to be training up a new Gruppe for a more aggressive and successful combat role, in the middle of the battle for France; but while the French air force still posed a threat, and there was unease about the possibility of some new British initiative, in fact nothing was to seriously impede the southward advance of the Luftwaffe and the Wehrmacht.

The next offensive, 'Case Red', in fact opened the day before he arrived, with a dawn attack on 5 June. Three phases were planned: an advance on Rouen and Le Havre by Army Group B; the main thrust, by Army Group A towards Reims; and later, the reduction of the Maginot Line by Army Group C. The Germans had massed 143 divisions for 'Case Red', seven more than they had had on 10 May. Although many French units – and the small remnant of British forces still left in central France – would fight stubbornly, the political will was draining from the French government, and the Wehrmacht fought its way to a series of breakthroughs on a broad front. On 10 June it was announced that Italy had declared war on France; Galland remembered groaning at the news – both because of its eloquent timing, and because of his limited but vividly remembered experience seven years before.

Galland's III./JG26 was tasked with escorting bombers, dive-bombers and sometimes Bf110s kicking up dust on the roads to the south. He threw himself into the fray at every opportunity, determined from the outset to lead his men both in the air, and from the front. It took a little getting used to; in marked contrast to his predecessor he was a furiously aggressive pilot, and his self-assurance often outstripped that of his Gruppe pilots. Over the first few days there was much furious flying to be had; and every day the fluid nature of the front brought its own headaches.

Having had no time to find his feet in JG26 before being pitched into action, Galland was still trying to find the right balance in his relationships with his Geschwaderkommodore Maj.Witt, his two fellow Gruppenkommandeure, and his three subordinate Staffelkapitaene. They all had their own way of wanting things done; and although Galland had helped set up Jagdgruppe Boeblingen before the war, this was the first time he had been part of such a dynamic operation, with rapidly changing directives and sector responsibilities. One huge bonus, however, was the latest improved model of the Bf109, the E-3^2.

A major responsibility for Galland was to ensure the serviceability rate of his Gruppe. It was becoming harder to keep those levels where they should be; although attrition was not as high as had been expected, the Blitzkrieg was taking its toll. With a nominal establishment of 39 aircraft for the three Staffeln, the Gruppe was sometimes hard put to get two-thirds that number in the air, and on occasion availability was below half the paper strength of the Gruppe. Pilots, too, were a depleted commodity, their numbers rarely matching establishment strength. With the drain on stores and spares from combat and front line wear and tear, routine servicing took second place in the priorities behind keeping aircraft in the air, although failure to look after the aircraft might quickly ground the remainder. It was a delicate game of judgement and luck: judging how to deploy the technical resources to keep the aircraft flying, and trusting to luck that they would come back without needing too many off-base spares or replacements. (It galled Galland to learn that the shortage of E-3s on the squadrons was being aggravated by simultaneous exports to countries whose goodwill was considered politically or economically useful.)

Fortunately the battle for France was nearly over. By 14 June air operations were concentrated in support of 1st Army and its endeavours to break the Maginot Line from the Saar-Pfalz area. Enemy aircraft were encountered less frequently; and the occupation of Paris that day marked an end to all Allied hopes of turning back the tide of Wehrmacht victories. JG26 had moved south with the advancing armies, and Galland's III.Gruppe now operated out of Villacoublay.

Galland was always looking for ways to improve operational efficiency, and decided to experiment with modifications to the Luftwaffe camouflage scheme to improve concealment on the ground and merge into the background during flight. The standard fighter camouflage in spring 1940 consisted of two shades of dull green in a 'splinter' pattern – large, straight-edged areas – on the upper wing and tail surfaces and on the spine of the fuselage, with very light blue undersides and fuselage sides. Concerned about the high visibility of these light blue sides when aircraft were parked, Galland tried extending the green scheme down the fuselage. This meddling was nearly his undoing.

One day during the final stage of the war in France Hptmn Wilhelm Balthasar, the Staffelkapitaen of 7./JG27, was instructing his pilots in attack techniques when he saw Galland's all-over-green Bf109E-3 crossing his path about 915m (3,000ft) below. By chance Galland had his radio tuned to the same frequency, and listened with interest as Balthasar calmly instructed his students to watch as he intercepted the 'RAF fighter'; he then proceeded to count down the closing distance as he swooped to the kill. Suddenly Galland realised that he himself was the target, and shouted over his radio just as Balthasar was about to fire. Waggling his wings to prove the point, Galland flew alongside the embarrassed Staffel leader and grinned from ear to ear. Several bottles of champagne were extracted as a forfeit for sloppy aircraft identification[3].

* * *

The German terms for an armistice were accepted by the new French regime installed under the leadership of the 84-year-old Marshal Petain on 22 June. Hostilities ended on the 25th in *de facto* total surrender of the French home armed forces and the occupation of the northern half of the country. Diplomatic relations with Britain were broken off on 28 June, and Gen Charles de Gaulle was recognised in London as 'the leader of all Free Frenchmen'.

During the six weeks of war in the West the Luftwaffe had performed well, but although casualties had been fewer than expected all units were in need of rest and a degree of re-equipment. During the period 10 May-25 June the Luftwaffe had lost 1,389 aircraft, including 521 bombers, 122 Ju87 Stukas, 367 Bf109s and Bf110s, 213 transports and 166 reconnaissance and liaison aircraft. In the same period the Luftwaffe calculated that it had destroyed more than 4,200 aircraft, of which 1,850 had been caught on the ground. It was at this moment that the Luftwaffe enjoyed its highest reputation among its military peers, its political masters, and its actual and potential adversaries. Replenishment was a priority after the collapse of France[4]; neither the army nor the air force were in any condition to sustain immediate further campaigns. Most Luftwaffe units would take several weeks to make up losses, bring munitions and stores back up to establishment levels, and revitalise the pilots, administrative staff and ground crews ready for the assault on England.

* * *

The whole subject of Hitler's exact intentions towards Britain; of the seriousness with which the plan for invasion was prepared, and how near Hitler came to giving the executive orders; above all, of its military feasibility – all this has been exhaustively analysed and discussed elsewhere. For the purposes of this book only the most simplified summary of this complex and contentious subject is possible or necessary.

It is well documented that Hitler had little faith in the military prospects for a cross-Channel invasion, and that – despite their entirely conventional preparation of detailed contingency plans – his senior army and naval commanders had none. Several detailed prewar staff studies had concluded that landing and sustaining an invasion force without prior command of the sea and air was impossible; and that there was little realistic chance of the Luftwaffe and Kriegsmarine achieving that command, given British naval and air defence resources, and the distances involved.

It is equally well documented that Hitler was convinced that Britain could be induced to make peace after her defeat in France – by the rational consideration of her best interests; by recognition of her natural destiny as an at least passive ally in the crusade against the 'Slav hordes'; and to some extent by the supposed activity of British personalities opposed to war with Germany[5]. Given his long-standing (and justified) belief that the only available military means to weaken Britain fatally was to confine, starve, and disarm her by naval and air blockade and attack, it was rational for Hitler to seek to increase the pressure for a negotiated peace by unleashing the Luftwaffe against her ports, naval and merchant shipping, oil installations, airfields, aircraft factories, and the whole fabric of her defences. On 30 June Goering issued a 'General Directive for the Operation of the Luftwaffe against England' along these lines.

On 2 July the OKW, with Hitler's permission, ordered the armed services to start planning an invasion – but this was, explicitly, contingency planning only. On 11 July Goering's 'General Directive' was refined in an OKL document on 'Intensive Air War against England', envisaging gradual progression towards an all-out air assault during August or September. On 16 July Hitler issued his Directive No.16: 'As England, despite her hopeless military situation, still shows no sign of willingness to come to terms, I have decided to prepare, and if necessary to carry out, a landing operation against her ... The aim of this operation is to eliminate the English motherland as a base from which war against Germany can be continued and if necessary, to occupy the country completely.'

The repetition of 'if necessary' surely characterises this as a warning rather than a statement of final intent. One is faced by the conclusion that a damaging air assault, and initial preparations for and threats of an invasion (which most serious German military opinion actually discounted), were seen essentially as parallel means towards battering Britain into capitulation, rather than the former being pursued as the practical first step towards the latter – though offering that advantage too, should events dictate.

Despite prewar studies concluding that the Luftwaffe could mount a damaging but not a decisive campaign against the British Isles, in the buoyant aftermath of Poland and the Battle of France Goering – seduced, as he later told Galland, by over-optimistic members of his staff – was apparently attracted to one study (by the Luftwaffenfuehrrungsstab, in May 1939) which suggested that a campaign of attrition just might be successful, given time. Ever eager to consolidate his influence with Hitler, and a gambler by nature, perhaps Goering found the prospect of promising his Fuehrer the destruction of Britain's ability and will to fight on (or to repulse invasion, should that ever be seriously contemplated) simply irresistible. At the peak of its prestige, fresh from an astonishingly complete victory, facing a shocked and half-defeated enemy – perhaps his Luftwaffe could make it all come true? Once events were set in train, they acquired their own logic and momentum.

* * *

In the last week of June 1940 Adolf Galland had immediate problems of his own, not the least of which were the administrative arrangements for resting and refurbishing his Gruppe before relocating to the northern coast of France. The French armistice had found III./JG26 at Villacoublay, but the Geschwader was withdrawn to Germany for the overhaul and servicing of its equipment. Other units were similarly withdrawn, and by the end of June only JG51 and III./JG3 were left on the coast facing Britain.

A secondary consideration during JG26's posting back to Muenchen-Gladbach was the provision of aircraft for home defence in case of RAF raids on the Rhineland. Following the Luftwaffe raid on Rotterdam the British War Cabinet had lifted the ban on RAF raids on targets which might endanger German civilian lives. On the night of 15 May a force of 99 Wellingtons, Whitleys, and Hampdens had flown to 16 targets in the Ruhr. The material results were negligible; the long-term significance, for Galland and hundreds of thousands of other Germans, would be incalculable.

Just two days after the armistice was signed, on 24 June, Major Witt was posted away to a staff job with Jagdfliegerfuehrer 2 at Le Touquet. His place as Geshwaderkommodore was taken by Maj Gotthardt Handrick, Galland's old CO from the Condor Legion. Galland was happy to see him; the old guard were being gently moved into desk jobs, making way for the up-and-coming young bloods of the Jagdwaffe, the men with personal experience of modern warfare. At the end of June there was just time for Galland to snatch a visit to his family, and to spend a few precious hours basking in the satisfaction and the pride his success had already brought to them. It gave him immense pleasure to have vindicated his father's hard-won support in his pursuit of a flying career.

Back at Muenchen-Gladbach there was work to do before the call came to return to the Channel coast. Galland knew that before long he would be leading his Gruppe against the RAF, the most formidable opponents the Luftwaffe had yet had to face. He still believed he had the best fighter aircraft at the front,and he was happy with some of the improvements then being retro-fitted to the Bf109E-3[6]; but less happy with some of the discussions about diversifying the 109's combat role.

Emphasis was not only being placed on close escort for bombers, but even upon close-support operations within the Blitzkrieg concept. Studies of operations during the French campaign indicated that the Bf109 was suitable for some fighter-bomber duties, and tests were conducted using a variety of single bombs weighing from 50kg (110lb) to 250kg (550lb), carried on a centreline rack beneath the fuselage. Galland, with his experience of both roles, believed passionately that the job of the fighter was to clear the skies, unconstrained by secondary duties, and that their application in the Jabo (Jagdbomber, or fighter-bomber) role was a pointless dilution of the fighting strength of front line units[7].

Despite misgivings about the role his Staffeln might be asked to perform, Galland felt that he had a better chance of meeting the cross-Channel challenge than at any time before – given time to prepare. Since the fighting stopped in France there had been comparatively little action by either side; but then came the spreading news of Goering's 'General Directive' on 30 June, and of the start of invasion planning from 2 July. At Muenchen-Gladbach on 2 July, Galland telephoned Maj Handrick at Dusseldorf. No redeployment orders had come through, but this sounded like a maximum effort. JG26 was ill-prepared for an immediate continuation of the air war; in all, it could put up 63 aircraft against an authorised strength of 117. Galland's III.Gruppe had 32 aircraft against an establishment of 39, and only 25 of those were serviceable; of 34 pilots on strength, only 30 were available. What was to be the position if they were recalled to France? Maj Handrick did not know.

During the next two weeks JG26 was rapidly brought up to full strength, and Galland got his 39 pilots and 39 aircraft. Meanwhile, OKL was working out a precise order of battle for the coming operation. On the night of 11 July Goering entertained senior Luftwaffe staff officers to a dinner at Karinhall, his great country estate near Berlin, where he outlined his plan. Over the next few days staffs developed the attack plans, and on 16 July were given added tasks when Hitler issued Directive No.16. This required the Luftwaffe to prevent air intervention during the invasion, to support the invasion forces, to destroy the enemy's communications and keep her naval forces at bay – in addition to the tasks defined on 30 June by Goering. The main brunt of the coming operation would be borne by Luftflotten 2 and 3; the former, to be based north of the Seine, was assigned targets south and east of a line between Portsmouth and Liverpool; the latter, from airfields mainly south and west of the Seine, would attack targets west of that line. Targets in the extreme north were to be attacked by Luftflotte 5 units making the long haul from Scandinavia.

During the first three weeks of July the Luftwaffe gradually stepped up operations, from small groups of bombers making tentative trips across the Channel early in the month to sustained attacks on shipping, ports and ground installations.

Although Maj Handrick had been able to report Jagdgeschwader 26 'Schlageter' ready for assignment, there was first to be an unexpected diversion to Doeberitz. On 19 July the honour fell to JG26 to fly honour guard over the Kroll Opera House in Berlin during an investiture of the Third Reich's most distinguished military leaders. Long after the war Galland would smile over the notional consequences of a single bomb on the opera house that day. In a shower of honours unprecedented in German military history, the Fuehrer bound the officer corps more closely to him by presenting three Luftwaffe and nine army generals with the batons of field-marshal. Goering also received two unique honours: appointment to the new supreme rank of Reichsmarschall, and award of the Grand Cross of the Iron Cross. Hitler used this platform to make a speech reminding the world that: 'If this struggle continues it can only end in the annihilation of one of us. Mr Churchill thinks it will be Germany. I know it will be Britain. I am not the vanquished begging for mercy. I speak as a victor. I see no reason why this war must go on. We should like to avert the sacrifices which must claim millions.'

On that same day Adolf Galland was promoted to the rank of Major; and 24 hours later, Jagdgeschwader 26 got orders to move to the Pas de Calais. Within hours of receiving its orders, JG26 played host to a fleet of Ju52s at Muenchen-Gladbach, Dortmund and Boenninghardt; the Bf109s took off in pairs and Galland's three Staffeln formed up and headed west, leaving the tri-motor transports to begin the lift of supplies, munitions, spares, and all the paraphernalia needed for the daily operations of a group of three squadrons. It took less than an hour to fly the 200-odd miles from Germany's Rhine valley to the gently rolling hills of the countryside of north-eastern France – where JG26 was to spend the next four years, and Galland was to fly and fight for almost 18 months.

* * *

In the roughly 80km (50 miles) between Berck at the mouth of the river Authie, and Calais to the east, there were 19 airfields to which seven Jagdgeschwader were assigned; some dated from the Great War, others were new – and rudimentary. JG26 was to be dispersed across three airfields. The Geschwader-stab, with its staff flight of four aircraft, was based with I.Gruppe at Audembert, just a couple of miles south of the tiny coastal hamlet of Wissant, itself just north of Cap Gris Nez. II.Gruppe was based at Marquise, a few miles further south and approximately equidistant from Wissant and Boulogne. Galland's III.Gruppe occupied Caffiers, about seven miles south-east of Wissant.

From their bases the Jagdflieger were just 40km (25 miles) from the coast of England and 145km (90 miles) from London. Their radius of action, however, was curtailed by the limited fuel capacity of their Bf109s (400 litres/ 88 gallons, giving a theoretical 660km/ 412 miles under optimum, but not operational conditions). In practice, only the south-eastern corner of England would be the hunting ground for single-engine Messerschmitts.

The weather was indifferent when Galland arrived. Accommodation on these grass airfields was spartan but would improve, tents and shacks serving as makeshift dormitories while some officers took billets in local towns. The aircraft were parked under trees, or in dispersal pens partly fashioned out of hedgerows left undisturbed when the farmland was cleared, under the additional cover of camouflage nets.

Throughout June and July there had been frequent heavy clashes with British fighters, and the Luftwaffe was already getting a taste of what the months ahead would be like. On 4 July a Bf109 from III./JG27 had fallen to the guns of a Hurricane from No.32 Squadron. On the 8th four Bf109s from JG51 were shot down by Spitfires; on the 9th, two more JG51 aircraft were destroyed by Spitfires over Dover and Ramsgate; on the 10th, one from JG27. No Luftwaffe fighters were lost to enemy action on the 11th or the 12th; but on 13 July four Bf109s from JG51 were destroyed and one damaged, followed by one destroyed and two damaged from JG2 and JG3 on the 14th. The next fighter loss came on the 19th – a Bf109 from JG51 shot down near Chartres; and between them JG51 and JG27 lost five aircraft on the 20th and three on the 21st.

These were the figures Galland wanted to see when he arrived; but they did not tell the whole story, which is best described by the attrition figures for the month of July. In that month Luftflotten 2 and 3 had 2,569 aircraft of which 1,889 were serviceable; Luftflotte 5 in Norway had a strength of 314 with 244 serviceable. Of the total of 2,133 serviceable aircraft, 172 were destroyed by enemy action and 91 were written off in accidents; the subtotals for Bf109s showed 34 and 19 respectively.

Galland knew that a major part of his job would be to put fighters up to protect bombers. In total, Luftflotten 2, 3 and 5 had 1,112 serviceable bombers and dive-bombers and 725 serviceable Bf109s. Experience showed Galland that bombers and fighters were lost in roughly equal numbers. Between 1 September 1939 and 9 May 1940, the day before the attack on the Low Countries and France, the Luftwaffe had lost 491 bombers and 446 fighters; between 10 May and 1 July the losses were 635 bombers and 604 fighters. Ever the analyst, Galland wanted to know how long OKL believed the war of attrition with the RAF would last, because for every bomber now on strength there was only 0.6 of a fighter; the fighters would be depleted long before the bombers whose operations they were supposed to protect – and of whose prospects of survival without heavy escort Galland had so long been dubious. In late July 1940 Galland was not aware of the prewar studies which invalidated any Luftwaffe offensive against the RAF; but he was certain that in the fight ahead they would need all the luck they could muster.

Galland was keen to press on and could not wait for the full Geschwader to arrive before flexing his skills in combat once more – it would be a week yet before the Geschwaderstab set up shop at Audembert, with an operations room co-ordinating all nine Staffeln at Le Colombier. The opportunity for action came when Galland declared his three squadrons ready for operations on the morning of Wednesday 24 July.

Luftwaffe operations over the Channel that morning began with nuisance raids, followed by an attack on a convoy heading out of the Straits of Dover at about 08.00, which led to an inconclusive skirmish. Shortly after 11.00 a second convoy left the Medway; it was spotted by Luftwaffe intelligence, and two Staffeln of 18 Do17s were assigned the target, escorted by the 40 Bf109s from III./JG26 led by Galland. The 109s formated on the bombers and escorted them over the Channel. RAF Fighter Command 'scrambled' Spitfires of No.54 Sqn from Rochford at 11.20, and shortly thereafter they engaged Galland's three squadrons. At around this time Uxbridge called up nine Spitfires from No.610 Sqn based at Biggin Hill. As the Rochford Spitfires gradually drew the 109s away from the bombers, six Spitfires from No. 65Sqn at Hornchurch took their chance to attack the Dorniers, but a tight formation and a blistering defensive crossfire saved them.

Between the 40 Bf109s of III./JG26 and the 12 Spitfires of No.54 Sqn the fight was at close quarters. Galland was dismayed at his Gruppe's ragged attention to tactics, and saw several instances where a keen-eyed fighter pilot should have prevailed. They were kept milling around for more than 30 minutes, and nothing would induce the outnumbered Spitfires to let go. Galland was greatly impressed by their ability to out-manoeuvre the Bf109s at relatively low speed, and their agility at turning on to the Messerschmitts in seemingly little airspace. One by one the little red low-fuel warning lights started to glow at the bottom centre of the instrument panels. The only way out was down, dropping into a split-S and a long curving dive which the Spitfires were unable to follow, then a dash back at low altitude across the Channel. It took 20 minutes to return to the French fields and safety.

When all the claims and counter-claims were resolved, the facts would show that III./JG26 had shot down two aircraft[8]. The RAF claimed two III.Gruppe pilots: Lt Schauff died when his parachute failed after baling out of his Bf109E-1, destroyed by Plt Off Colin Gray[9]; and Oblt Werner Bartels, the III./JG26 technical officer and a former test pilot, who survived a belly landing after being shot down and badly wounded by Plt Off Sawyer, No.65 Squadron. There had been other casualties. To cover III./JG26's retreat III./JG52 came in low over Dover, losing two 109s when they ran into the No.610 Sqn Spitfires from Biggin Hill.

Even as his Messerschmitts were drifting down one by one to the grass and stubble of Caffiers, Galland was composing some harsh words. It had seemed to him that he had been the only one doing any real fighting, the others milling around like windmills. Galland was not prepared to guard his tongue when it was a question of life and death, and gave his pilots a robust dressing-down. He was highly critical of their lack of discipline in the fight, and their inability to keep up with his lead.

JG26 had lost another pilot on 24 July: Hptmn Erich Noack, Kommandeur of II.Gruppe. Assigned to clear the skies ahead of a bomber formation, II./JG26 –

beset by serviceability problems – could only put up ten aircraft at 12.25 that day. Over the English coast Noack apparently miscounted nine Spitfires from No.610 Sqn, as he turned his formation back to France. He was killed when he stalled on landing at Marquise.

Galland's first sortie over England had been a shock. The tenacity of the RAF pilots, despite being heavily outnumbered and relatively inexperienced, had been remarkable. It had shocked him to see how inept his own pilots were; and that would have to change. This was no sudden Blitzkrieg, bundling a disorganised enemy backwards across indefensible plains; this was the real business of hardened air combat, against an enemy who was going to stand and fight.

Notes to Chapter 9

1 The origins of JG26 could be traced through various reorganisations and renumberings back to JG134 'Horst Wessel' in 1935. From November 1938 the Geschwaderkommodore was Obst Eduard Ritter von Schleich, a highly respected former World War I ace (who had gained 35 kills, and the nickname 'the Black Knight'). That December the wing was officially named after Albert Leon Schlageter, an ex-officer and Freikorps fighter who was shot by the French for sabotage in the Rhineland in May 1923. As he had been a devout Catholic the original unit insignia chosen was a cross and initial 'S', but the cross was later deleted. On 1 May 1939 the wing was redesignated Jagdgeschwader 26 under Luftflotte 2. The policy of retiring veterans in favour of younger officers saw von Schleich replaced in December 1939 by Maj Hugo Witt; approaching 40 himself, Witt would go the same way on 24 June 1940. The Geschwader began receiving the Bf109E-3 in winter 1939-40, and saw hard fighting in May-June 1940.

2 The E-3's 1,175hp DB601Aa engine gave it about 22kph (14mph) more than the 1,050hp powerplant of the E-1. With two MG FF 20mm cannon in the wings and twin 7.92mm machine guns in the upper cowling, the Bf109E-3 was harder hitting than the Hurricane and Spitfire; in a three second burst their eight machine guns could put roughly 80lbs weight of metal on target, compared to the Bf109E-3's roughly 56lbs, but the cannon had greater range and heavier, explosive ammunition. The original design feature of a 20mm cannon mounted between the inverted-V rows of engine cylinders and firing through the propeller boss caused serious vibration problems and was usually removed at unit level, if ever supplied; the problem was only cured with the Bf109F.

3 Balthasar had scored seven victories in Spain and became the highest scoring fighter pilot in the Battle of France, where he had 23 confirmed kills. Awarded the Knight's Cross on 14 June 1940 and the Oak Leaves on 2 July 1941, he achieved a total of 40 victories on the Western Front. He became Kommandeur of III./JG2 'Richthofen' and later Geschwaderkommodore before he was killed in action the day after receiving his Oak Leaves.

4 The fall of France gave Germany a considerable supplement to domestic munitions production. Almost the full capacity of the French airframe and engine industry survived to be turned to the requirements of the Luftwaffe; licence production of many types of German aircraft was undertaken, and between 1940 and mid-1944 French factories supplied to the Luftwaffe 3,606 airframes and 11,254 engines.

5 One does not have to be a sentimentalist to believe that Hitler badly misread both

British public opinion, and the operation of British institutions. He commented to Galland – in what must be one of his few jocular exchanges on record – that the British could be made to agree to anything if they kept two things: their dignity and their pride. Galland would remark to the author that the Fuehrer forgot one other thing: the British sense of 'fair play'.

The simplest expression of this is perhaps Winston Churchill's reply to an appeal for a negotiated peace from the King of Sweden: he said that only with 'the restoration of the free and independent life of Czechoslovakia, Poland, Norway, Denmark, Holland, Belgium and, above all, France' could 'such proposals be considered.'

Hitler apparently believed that Churchill could be removed from power by forces inside Britain more open to reason; but the individuals who have been named in this connection are deeply unconvincing, suggesting vulgar fantasies rather than serious intelligence work. The Nazi leadership were themselves conspiratorial personalities; products of their time, class, and country, they lacked any instinctive historical understanding of the workings of mature democracies. Their inability to grasp the distance which separated the trivial figures upon whom they apparently placed their hopes, from the true levers of British wartime power, is still remarkable.

6 Experience during the Battle of France led to several improvements, notably the redesign of the cockpit hood to take the weight of an 8mm armour plate protecting the pilot's head and back, more armour for the seat, and in some aircraft a bulletproof windshield. Such improvements would be standard on the E-4, then coming into service. The E-4 also standardised armament as two MG17 machine guns above the engine and two 20mm MG FF/M cannon, with improved ammunition and rate of fire, in the wings. The E-4/N subvariant had a new high compression engine, the DB601N; burning 96 octane petrol instead of the standard 87 octane, under full boost the DB601N would produce 1,200hp at 2,600rpm or 1,270hp for one minute at 5,000m (16,400ft). Concern expressed by the pilots at the relatively poor range of the Bf109 produced a 300litre (66gal) drop tank; moulded out of a wood pulp compound, it leaked badly, and was simply too unsafe for routine use.

7 A special trials unit, Erprobungsgruppe 210 led by Hptmn Walter Rubensdoerffer, flew Bf109Es and Bf110Cs equipped to carry bombs, and one of the three Staffeln flew the Bf109E-1/B in this role against shipping in the North Sea. Results were so encouraging that Goering decreed that each Jagdgeschwader should incorporate a Jabo Staffel; instructions were given to modify ageing Bf109E-1s into E-1/Bs for fighter-bomber duties. Soon, the E-4 was being modified into an E-4/B variant equipped to carry up to four 50kg (110lb) bombs or one 250kg (550lb) bomb.

8 Spitfire Mk Is N3192 (Sgt Plt G.R.Collett, slightly injured, force-landed); and R6812 (Plt Off J.L.Allen DFC – seven confirmed, five probable kills; damaged by Galland over Margate, stalled attempting landing at Foreness, pilot killed). Galland also badly damaged R6710 (Plt Off H.K.F.Mathews).

9 This was the first of 27 kills and six probables, plus eight shared, by Plt Off, later Wg Cdr Gray DSO, DFC, who retired to New Zealand after the war.

CHAPTER 10

25 July – 12 August 1940

Luftlotte 2 had decided to co-ordinate Channel attacks under a Kanalkamp-fuehrer ('Channel battle leader') – Obst Johannes Fink - who was also in command of the 75 Dornier Do17 bombers of KG2. From headquarters at Cap Blanc Nez just 25 miles across the Channel from Dover and Folkestone, Fink also had control over 65 Ju87 Stukas in two Gruppen and 100 Bf110 in a single Geschwader. Galland was directly linked to the daily orders of the Kanal-kampfuehrer via Maj Handrick, JG26's commanding officer, and Jafu 2 at Wissant.

On 25 July Obst Fink received reports of the movement of convoy CW8 westbound toward the Dover Straits, plotted on the 'Freya' radar system[1]. Throughout the morning a series of co-ordinated attacks involved large formations of Bf109s, Spitfires from No.65 Sqn and Hurricanes from No.32 Squadron. Around noon Hurricanes from Nos.32 and 615 Sqns were embroiled in a running dogfight with almost 50 Bf109s. In the early afternoon Fink ordered a full Gruppe from JG26 to escort each of three waves of 20 Ju87 Stukas against the convoy; timed to coincide with the withdrawal of RAF fighters to refuel and rearm, the Stuka attack met no aerial opposition.

Galland's group was assigned to the first wave, and had to weave back and forth around the much slower dive-bombers in order to maintain close escort. Responding to signals from the convoy, Spitfires from No. 54 Sqn raced to the scene, five British fighters hitting the Stukas just as they were about to peel off into their dive. More than 20 Bf109s ripped into the British fighters from all sides. Meanwhile, vectored to lower altitude, Spitfires from No.64 Sqn at Kenley were waiting at 4,000ft to catch the Stukas as they pulled out of their bombing dive.

Galland's III./JG26 engaged No.54 Sqn, and he fastened on to the tail of a Spitfire Mk I[2]; getting in a full burst of fire, he saw it drift into a lazy, curving descent and slowly catch fire before it plunged into the Channel. A second Spitfire was shot down by the Gruppe, the pilot baling out unhurt. Oblt Georg Beyer took 7. Staffel down with the Stukas to protect them from No.64 Sqn's Spitfires, shooting down two and damaging two more.

More attacks were launched against the convoy later that day, with 60 Stukas hitting the ships as they passed Folkestone, co-ordinated with an attack by nine E-boats – this characterised the intense effort now building up to close Britain's shipping lanes and destroy her lifeline. Next day the British stopped all merchant ship movements through the Straits of Dover by day; on 29 July this was extended to naval forces as well.

JG26 flew a few escort patrols on 26 and 27 July as the Gruppenkommandeure were kept busy with the staff plans for the coming assault in force. On Sunday 28 July III.Gruppe was back in the air again on escort duty. (This was the day that Galland's friend and competitor Maj Werner Moelders flew for the first time as Geschwaderkommodore of JG51; with 25 victories since returning from Spain, he was already a holder of the Knight's Cross. That afternoon he was wounded in the leg in a fight with two Spitfires, only just reaching Wissant in time to crash-land.)

Galland's Gruppe locked horns with Spitfires from No.74 Sqn led by 'Sailor' Malan[3], and with Hurricanes of No.257 Sqn; flying wingman to Galland, his adjutant Oblt Muencheberg forced down one of the latter. Now No.41 Sqn's Spitfires were scrambled from their forward airfield at Manston. In the ensuing wild melee Galland had difficulty overcoming the superior low-speed handling of a Spitfire of No.74, but eventually managed to turn inside it and shoot it down[4]. All in all the day had been a good one for Galland's men, and there was a marked improvement over their performance of four days earlier; but this first week of fierce fighting over the Channel and the Kent coast had given Galland a taste of what was to come in the months and years ahead.

During July the success of the Bf109s in drawing the RAF up to fight showed how best to deploy single-seat fighters of superior performance. These free-wheeling tactics were designed to grind down the enemy fighters by keeping pressure on their rest and refurbishment cycles. The RAF realised what was going on, and stopped playing the game: Fighter Command started to keep the aircraft on the ground until some threat too great to ignore required the Hurricanes and Spitfires to take off and attack[5]. Some attempt was made to deploy bombers to draw the RAF up where massed fighters could cut them down, but with little success; so by the end of July tactics changed again, and the Bf109s were given freedom to go hunting across south-east England in attempts to pull the RAF into the sky. Galland felt that this 'freie Jagd' was the right direction; however, the inherent limitations of the 109's restricted combat radius gave it barely 20 minutes' fighting time over much of the south-east of England. The Channel itself provided a serious obstacle, requiring a sophisticated air-sea rescue service using fast moving boats and seaplanes to pluck downed pilots from the water.

* * *

On 17 July the army's basic plan for the invasion – Operation 'Sealion' – had been unveiled, involving landings by 90,000 men at various points between Ramsgate and Lyme Bay, building to 260,000 by the third day. On 29 July the navy rejected the OKH plan, and indeed any invasion before at least May 1941. Comparison of naval and air achievements in sinking British shipping suggested that U-boat warfare was a better investment than a bombing campaign; and called into question the ability of the air force to achieve the preconditions for invasion by bombing. At the highest level inter-service rivalry, and a determination to avoid being saddled with responsibility for doomed enterprises, played their usual part. Nevertheless, the Luftwaffe held firm to the general principles outlined in Goering's directive of 30 June and the Hitler Directive of 16 July, and by 25 July

Luftflotten 2 and 3 had completed their plans for the main air assault which was to destroy the RAF[6].

Feldmarschall Kesselring's approach was the more cautious, envisaging a dispersed effort that would avoid heavy attrition of his Luftflotte's fighting strength. Fm Sperrle favoured an all-out effort using dive-bombers, bombers and fighter-bombers (including Bf109 Jabos) against the ports to cut Britain's lifelines. The OKL asked Kesselring to modify his plan, selecting a list of key targets rather than dispersing his effort. On 1 August Hitler issued Fuehrer Directive No.17 which outlined how the attack should be conducted. First, the Luftwaffe was to attack 'flying units, their ground installations, and their supply organisations (and) the aircraft industry.' After achieving 'temporary or local air superiority the air war is to be continued against ports, in particular against stores of food, and also against stores of provisions in the interior of the country.' However, there were no defined military objectives and no specific schedules or fixed agenda. The rest would be contingent upon the outcome. Hitler defined the start of this intensified effort by the Luftwaffe as on or after 5 August, and in separate protocols to the memorandum he ruled that all three services should be ready to launch 'Sealion' by 15 September, if a decision was made to proceed[7].

On 1 August Goering received the revised attack plans from the OKL and signed them off for activation. Next day details were issued for Adlerangriff (literally, 'the attack of the eagles'), but with no date set – there was still disagreement between Kesselring and Sperrle about targets, flight paths, altitudes, escorting fighter requirements and a host of separate items that should have been cleared up long before – an inauspicious start to what should have been a precisely defined assault with specified objectives. Goering ordered a conference at Karinhall to resolve matters; this was achieved, in concept, by 6 August. The date was eventually set for 13 August[8].

At the same time, a new tactical control of fighters was introduced – the Jagdfliegerfuehrer or Jafu, one to each Luftflotte. As we have seen, the post had in fact been in existence for some weeks; the brainchild of Gen Wolfgang Martini, it anticipated the future development of an integrated radar and radio control network for fighter operations which did not as yet exist. When Galland attended Gen Martini's briefing he was given a foretaste of how Jagdwaffe operations would be controlled. Each evening the fighter Geschwaderkommodore would assemble at their local Luftflotte co-ordinating centres and receive instructions on the operations for the following day. They would receive information about British aircraft movements of the day just finished, gleaned partly from coastal radio intelligence listening posts, and extrapolated to the following day. The Jafu would thus provide information which would be about eight hours old, and of highly questionable relevance to the next day's operations. Far from receiving timely updates on RAF activity, the fighter commanders would essentially have to make it up as they went along. There would be no radar to warn of Fighter Command activity, and no ground control and co-ordination of the fighters once they were airborne.

They were, in fact, to be tied to the bombers under strict orders to remain with them and protect the formations. From his experience Galland knew that the way the fighters were going to be asked to work was flawed and dangerous. He contested the operational tactics with Maj Handrick, who organised discussions with Jafu 2, but to no avail. As early as 1 August, during a meeting with Theo Osterkamp (by then Jafu 2) at The Hague, Goering had been adamant that, despite the enormous difference in performance, the fighters must escort the bombers during the vulnerable period when they crossed the coast. To Goering – who had been widely criticised by his pilots in 1918 for his tactically rigid style of command at Jagdgeshwader 1 – it was simple; to Galland it was simplistic.

He pointed out to Maj Handrick that the Bf109 was superior to the Spitfire in speed and performance at altitude, above about 6100m (20,000ft). Below that altitude and at slower speeds the remarkable aerodynamic performance of Reginald Mitchell's magnificent fighter allowed it to handle better, turn tighter, and catch the Bf109 on at least equal terms. The Heinkels and Dorniers would usually fly to their targets at optimum heights and speeds for them, not for the fighters. That meant the 109s would have to weave in and out, wasting fuel and flying time, keeping to an average forward speed of around 305-320kph (190-200mph); and would have very little time to fight the RAF before turning for home.

For Adlerangriff the main deployment of forces within Luftflotten 2 and 3 was essentially the same as for the Battle of France. The really significant change was the position of Genmaj von Doering – and subsequently, Genmaj Theo Osterkamp – as Jafu 2, based at Wissant and responsible for five Geschwader and one Gruppe of Bf109s and two Geschwader of Bf110s[9]. It was to Jafu 2 that Galland would report fluctuations in the strength of III.Gruppe, as well as to Maj Handrick at Stab JG26, so that the former could control the balance of escort Gruppen to be assigned operations for the following day.

The disposition of forces to the north-east coast of France and down into the Cherbourg area was a gradual process which was not complete even by the beginning of August. JG51 was soon joined by LG2, and by mid-July III./JG3 had arrived; JG27 followed, then JG26 at the end of the month; then JG52. During August the existing forces were joined by JG54, JG2 and JG53.

Returns showed that Luftflotten 2, 3 and 5 had a total strength of 3,196 aircraft, of which 2,485 – 78 per cent – were serviceable and ready for operations. Assigned to British targets north of the river Humber, Luftflotte 5 had 123 serviceable He111s and Ju88s and 34 operational Bf110s; its Bf109s only had the range for the defence of Luftflotte 5's Norwegian airfields. Luftflotten 2 and 3 could muster 875 serviceable He111s, Do17s and Ju88s, with a further 316 operational Ju87 dive-bombers. Together, the two southern Luftflotten could put 227 Bf110s into the air, and 702 (of 813) serviceable Bf109s.

* * *

Facing them in Britain, RAF Fighter Command had 59 squadrons; squadron establishment, reduced after Dunkirk to 16 aircraft plus two reserves, was restored to 20 on 1 August. The squadrons were assigned to four groups, the most important of which were No.11 Group covering south-east England from

Lowestoft on the east coast to Southampton on the south coast, and including the London area; and No.12 Group to the north, almost as far as the latitude of Lancaster. No.10 Group covered the west up to a line of latitude just south of Coventry; and No.13 Group covered England and Scotland north of Lancaster. Fighter Command had been led by Air Chief Marshal Sir Hugh Dowding since July 1936, when the various Commands were formed. Fighter Command Headquarters was at Bentley Priory, near Stanmore in Middlesex. The three southern groups were sub-divided into sectors, and the group and sector areas each had their own operations rooms and control of operations in their defined regions.

Fighter Command would assign a group to a particular raid if there was doubt about its destination, and would authorise one group to co-operate with another when it was pressed by the enemy. Information came in to Bentley Priory via a chain of reporting stations starting with local radar stations or Royal Observer Corps observation posts, to local centres, and from there to the sectors, the groups, and Fighter Command Operations at Bentley Priory, which was responsible for co-ordination and control of all air raid warnings. Once a decision had been made about how to respond to the threat, the information was passed back down the chain. Usefully, each group and sector had a snapshot view of what was going on across its area because it was through their channels that the information had first been passed. This gave Fighter Command, air defence and the general alert network an enviable efficiency which was central to British success in the months to come.

It would be with No.11 Group, under the command of the energetic New Zealander, AVM Keith Park, that JG26 would tangle in daily attempts to outwit and outfight one another. No.11 Group Operations was at RAF Uxbridge; in early August the group had 21 squadrons (13 of Hurricanes, six of Spitfires, and two of Blenheims) at seven airfields (Debden, North Weald, Hornchurch, Biggin Hill, Kenley, Northolt and Tangmere), but with additional forward airfields near the coast to which squadrons could be deployed if the threat demanded.

With headquarters at Watnall in Nottinghamshire, No.12 Group was commanded by AVM Trafford Leigh-Mallory – a firm believer in assembling several squadrons into large wings before interception, for maximum results. The group had 14 squadrons (six with Hurricanes, five with Spitfires, two with Blenheims and one with Defiants.)

Luftwaffe intelligence on RAF strengths was poor, and remained so. The responsible staff believed more fighters had been destroyed than Fighter Command had in fact lost, although the total strength was overestimated. The information circulated to Luftflotte headquarters during mid-July estimated that the RAF had 675 serviceable Hurricanes and Spitfires and 860 operational bombers, figures between 30 per cent and 100 per cent overestimated: the RAF had fewer than 420 operational bombers. The true state of affairs was that Fighter Command had 492 aircraft classified as fighters, of which 467 were Hurricanes and Spitfires – the only effective types. The Germans were also unaware of crucial changes in British aircraft production and RAF manpower[10].

To Maj Adolf Galland the most significant event of 1 August 1940 was his award of the Knight's Cross of the Iron Cross, presented in person by General-feldmarschall Kesselring, in recognition of his 17th confirmed air victory. It was the supreme acknowledgement of a remarkable three years in three campaigns, and gave Galland a tremendous sense of pride and achievement; it was public recognition that to his Luftwaffe he was, at least, among the first and the best – Werner Moelders was then the only other fighter ace to have received the Ritterkreuz. (The coveted Knight's Cross, worn at the throat, was notionally awarded to fighter pilots for 20 kills, though this was not a rigid figure; and but there was a complex points system which recognised exceptional duty apart from combat victories[11]).

The first week of August was relatively quiet compared to the activity of the preceding few weeks. On 8 August a number of operations coincided (and, quite without reference to German intentions, this date was later selected by some British historians as marking the opening of the Battle of Britain purely on the grounds of intensity of operations).

Convoy CW9, comprising 20 merchant ships and nine Royal Navy escort vessels, attracted interest because clouds at 2,000ft and visibility of no more than eight miles gave good cover to attacking aircraft. CW9 had passed through the Straits of Dover the previous afternoon; shadowed by E-boats, it was heavily attacked during the night. Three ships were lost and the convoy became spread out over a distance of ten miles – easy pickings for the dive-bombers. When Sperrle got word that the convoy was still proceeding westward he ordered a full attack from VIII.Fliegerkorps and, through Jafu 2, arranged for Bf109 support with a 'free hunt' mission over Kent – i.e. a covering fighter mission without close escort duties, to draw the RAF up and away from the Stukas. Despite several attempts to get through to the ships the RAF successfully protected the convoy, which by mid-morning was off Brighton.

Several fighter units were now called upon to co-ordinate a systematic attack. From Angers, Caen and St Malo, 57 Stukas from StG2, 3 and 77 were sent against CW9 off the Isle of Wight just after noon. Some 20 Bf109s from V./LG1 at Caen were to ride shotgun on the Stukas, rendezvousing with a further 30 Bf109s of II. and III./JG27 from Crepon and Carquebet to escort them all the way. Simultaneously, to keep the RAF as distracted as possible, III./JG26 and II. and III./JG51 took off for a 'freie Jagd' over the Kent countryside – the type of assignment Galland liked. Three squadrons of Spitfires rose to the bait, and a bitter air battle broke out.

The first contact came about 11.40 when Oblt Fraunhoefer fastened on to one Spitfire of No.65 Sqn from Hornchurch, shooting it down in flames near Manston. Galland and his wingman, Oblt Muencheberg, got on the tail of another about five minutes later and began a typical chase, one handing the target off to the other. Galland, distracted momentarily by another Spitfire flashing through his line of sight, left it to his wingman to send it down. Galland pulled hard on the stick and climbed just as Obfw Gryzmalla locked on to yet another Spitfire from No.65 Sqn; pulling up into an inverted loop and rolling off to starboard in an attempt to escape the 109, the pilot threw his aircraft into a series of descending twists and turns. Hit but not seriously damaged, he ran for home.

The battle was not to be without loss. Two Spitfires from No.64 Sqn fastened on to Oblt Oehm's Bf109E-4 like terriers. One was piloted by Sqn Ldr A.R.D.MacDonnell, the squadron CO, and the other by Flt Lt 'Jackie' Mann. Oblt Oehm spiralled into the sea to his death about four miles off Dover[13].

It was just after midday that III./JG26 came upon a Blenheim from No.600 Sqn based at Manston. It was Galland who spotted it first and swung his Schwarme round to come from the sun above the slow, twin-engined machine. He signalled Oblt Sprick to move in ahead of him and gave him the chance to put bursts into the fuselage, peeling off to port as he overshot by about 96kph (60mph). Wheeling to starboard, Galland scanned all around the sky for enemy fighters; Oblt Sprick and a second and third 109 came at the Blenheim again. Sprick put cannonshells right in a fuel tank; the flames grew as it fell toward the Channel, transforming the dying aircraft into a flaming torch before it struck the sea off Ramsgate[12]. The Gruppe reformed and spread out, searching the sky.

In the days remaining before 'Adlertag' Galland took advantage of the chance to 'free hunt' over England. This was the last opportunity for such probing flights, which were sanctioned because of the value of any up-to-the-moment intelligence about the state of the RAF before the main assault commenced on 13 August. Several Geschwader had pressed for a relatively free hand in the run-up to Adlerangriff; but such latitude involved a compromise – too much roaming around for sport could cost casualties who would be needed on the big day. Nevertheless, as Galland would recall years later, there was something very special about the anticipated clash, and he felt the benefit of keeping up a tempo before unleashing his Gruppe. As for the Staffel pilots, many of them benefited from his experience and that of other veterans – but there was nothing like getting in amongst a nest of angry Spitfires to build experience and learn the ropes.

Quiet days on 9 and 10 August were followed by a major sweep of the English coastline on the 11th. The morning started bright and attracted several Gruppen of Bf109s. III./JG26 was looking for trouble; Galland had been setting up this little run for two days, and wanted to give his pilots a thorough shake-out, flying and fighting as if the Adlerangriff had started that day. Attacks on the southern ports by the Bf109 and Bf110 Jabos of EGr210 brought No.74 Sqn up from Manston; they failed to intercept EGr210 before it fled, but 'Sailor' Malan led 12 Spitfires headlong into Galland's III.Gruppe. Fire was exchanged and some dogfights developed briefly; one RAF pilot baled out successfully, but then the two formations moved apart as Malan's squadron was vectored south toward Dover and Folkestone.

This pattern – of the RAF appearing to know exactly where and when to send its aircraft to meet the most urgent threat – was unnerving; it was quite evident to Galland that there was a co-ordination and battle control system at work here that put him and his Gruppe at a disadvantage – relatively, they were flying blind. In the cloudy skies over England an attack could come from any quarter; and Galland chose to get as high and as fast as possible, to enjoy, at least, the conditions where the Bf109 was always at its best. One thing was certain: these free hunts were paying off – he was learning things about the RAF.

Back at Caffiers the Messerschmitts were quickly refuelled and rearmed before returning to the Channel and those inviting white cliffs. As he approached the English coastline once more – his wingman to one side and slightly behind, 26 other Bf109s to left and right and stacked up above and behind – he kept his head moving ceaselessly, searching for the tiny, fast-moving specks that would mean another challenge.

In No.11 Group's operations room AVM Park watched as the blips on the radar screens were translated into plots on the table. There was no obvious pattern; something was brewing, but what? Resisting temptation, he held his fighters back, unwilling to release them to battles of attrition that would put them in the wrong place when the main force appeared – which he was sure it would.

As Galland and his three Staffeln crossed the coast, their 109s bumping in the morning up-drafts along the cliffs, they could see swarms of fighters heading south-west toward the Sussex downs; but no significant contact was made until No.74 Sqn once again caught the 109s in a brief, furious fight. 'Sailor' Malan locked on to the Bf109E-1 of 7.Staffel's Lt Buerschgens. Putting several holes in the engine and fuselage, Malan chased the 109 back toward Cap Gris Nez, got in a further burst from his eight 0.303 Brownings, and left the crippled Messerschmitt to pancake in a field near Caffiers.

The main force of the day had been an attack on Portland by 54 Ju88s from two Gruppen of KG54, 20 He111s from KG27 and 61 Bf110s from ZG2: 135 bombers, accompanied by 30 Bf109s from III./JG2 'Richthofen' based at Le Havre. Largely due to the initial free runs over Kent and parts of Sussex, Fighter Command had been drawn into an enormous dogfight which spread across the width of Weymouth bay. In that melee the RAF lost 16 Hurricanes and one Spitfire, with several more damaged; while the Luftwaffe limped home minus six Bf110s, five Ju88s, six Bf109s and one He111.

As the bombers regrouped and withdrew, a further formation of Bf109s from JG27 arrived to fly top cover across the Channel; Jafu 2 and Jafu 3 had integrated their efforts. Back in France intensive efforts were made to repair damaged aircraft, make a log of those which could not be ready for Adlertag, and assign fresh deliveries to weakened Staffeln. Some units had taken a hammering in these past weeks and there was concern about establishment levels; for instance, during its furious confrontations over England JG27 had already lost nine Bf109s, with two damaged awaiting repair, and today they had lost another three. On the day of the Portland bombing Galland's III./JG26 got off lightly, with only one Bf109 written off. The total tally for that Sunday was 27 British fighters lost for 37 German aircraft shot down, of which 14 had been Bf109s and 11 Bf110s – too many for either side to tolerate as an average.

* * *

On Monday 12 August – the day before Adlertag – the weather was fine but misty. From the cliffs at Wissant the Channel lay brooding under a veil, and there was a chill in the air as Galland's Staffelkapitaene stood around discussing the daily orders. With the rising sun the mist would disperse, leaving a perfect day for preparatory attacks. Impressed by the co-ordination of enemy attacks on fighters and bombers alike during the previous day's operations, and at the urgent pleading of Gen Martini, Luftflotten 2 and 3 headquarters had agreed to concentrate on destroying the radar towers around the southern coast. Attacks could then be launched against the inland fighter stations most likely to intercept the raiders in force the following day. Kesselring authorised free hunts just after dawn, and before 07.00 II./JG52 took off and headed west. The Dover Chain Home station picked them up at 07.20 heading fast for the Kent coast between Folkestone and Hastings. At 07.31 the group controller scrambled 12 Spitfires of No.610 Sqn led by Sqn Ldr John Ellis. Within 30 minutes the two formations clashed, and the nine Bf109s tried to gradually suck the British fighters east. One Spitfire was shot down, three more were damaged, and two Bf109s were destroyed.

The main attack on the radar stations was conducted brilliantly by the elite EGr210, which took off from Calais-Marck at 08.40 and headed up the coast parallel to the Chain Home stations. Sections of Bf110 fighter-bombers peeled off in turn to hit the separate radar stations, putting those at Dover, Pevensey and Rye temporarily out of action. While furious efforts were made to repair the damage and get them back into the network, Luftwaffe bombers took advantage of the blackout to hit the airfield at Lympne south-east of Hawkinge; this had only been used as a forward operating base for West Malling, and the raid had little impact on the Biggin Hill sector. Other attacks on radar stations put that at Ventnor out of action for several days. Meanwhile, also taking advantage of the radar blackout in some of the southern stations, Ju88s from II./KG26 struck Hawkinge and did considerable damage, burning out two hangars and destroying four aircraft on the ground.

When the Bf110s of EGr210 returned to base their reports initially indicated that a large part of the Chain Home network was out of action. Seeking advantage from the radar hole, Kesselring immediately ordered two formations of Ju87s to hit two separate convoys off the North Foreland, and Galland received orders to fly escort for the second wave. But No.11 Group was not blinded as Kesselring thought, although certain sections of the south coast were not completely covered. The first wave of Ju87s successfully engaged one of the two convoys before Spitfires from No.65 Sqn arrived; and as these returned to Manston to refuel the second formation of Ju87s was making its way to the second convoy. With the Spitfires on the ground, No.11 Group put up 12 Hurricanes of No.501 Sqn and three from No.151. at 11.30. Galland's III.Gruppe was unable to spot them and warn the Ju87s, which were hit by the 15 fighters before the 109s could protect them. The Stukas were scattered, immediately turning away to run for France, jettisoning their bombs for extra speed. Within seconds of the Hurricanes reaching the Ju87s Galland's men were on to them, tearing through them like scythes and creating a furious battle. Galland had taught his pilots to get in fast and act decisively; now it was all beginning to pay off – what a difference he could see in the Gruppe's tactics.

Galland got a Hurricane in his sights, but the pilot, Sqn Ldr Holland, was good. Following the hunch-backed fighter down, twisting and turning, Galland was able to get in the odd shot but nothing decisive. All the way down from 12,000ft the Gruppenkommandeur hung tenaciously to Holland's tail, sometimes having to slow down to avoid overtaking him. The arch-exponent of the diving attack, Galland got close in several times, and he could see strips of fabric ripping away from the rear fuselage. Still the Hurricane kept diving, twisting and turning through an ever widening arc until he finally got in a good long burst at 1,370m (4,500 feet) altitude. Galland saw the Hurricane nose over and enter what appeared to be a terminal dive; but pulling out again, under control, Sqn Ldr Holland managed to put the smoking Hurricane down just outside Dover, damaged but repairable. This claim was never officially allowed to Galland; but he was not to know that now, as a grin spread over his face. The hunting was good.

Down around 900m (3,000ft) Galland pulled back on the stick, did a 360 degree roll while searching the sky for enemy fighters, but saw none. He regrouped his Staffeln, and while heading home he slowly lit a cigar from the electric lighter – removed from a car, and installed by his mechanics. He took a fistful on every sortie; they were his favourite Havanas, the special brand acquired in Spain three years earlier, and he enjoyed a smoke on the way back to France. (It was difficult to smoke on the way out; they tasted terrible at altitudes above 9,000ft, and he rarely flew to rendezvous with escort formations below that altitude.) His brother officers tormented him mercilessly about the cigar lighter: 'What, no ashtray?... And where's the champagne, Dolfo?'

Back on the ground shortly before 13.00, Galland and his men ate a hurried lunch as the mechanics, fitters and armourers swarmed all over the 109s. Refuelling bowsers were driven up and made ready. Some aircraft were pushed into makeshift repair bays, simple revetments protected by brush from prying RAF eyes; others were wheeled away to be transported back for major surgery. It had been a good morning's work; the Gruppe had got five Hurricanes for no losses.

The day's work was not done yet. Just as III./JG26 had been mauling the Hurricanes, a very large formation of bombers was massing for a raid on Portsmouth. Its flightpath had Nos.10 and 11 Groups guessing. The armada – nearly 100 Ju88s from KG51, 120 Bf110s from ZG2 and ZG76, accompanied by 25 Bf109s from JG53, almost 240 aircraft in all – headed for Brighton from the south, then turned west toward the Isle of Wight. About 58 Hurricanes and Spitfires were scrambled to intercept; the escorting Bf109s formed a large circle off the coast, waiting at altitude for the British fighters to appear. As though making straight up the Solent to attack Southampton, a large formation of about 70 Ju88s suddenly turned to starboard and began a series of runs across Portsmouth docks and town, causing extensive damage and setting many buildings, installations and oil tanks alight. The second formation of Ju88s turned to port and made straight for the Chain Home station on Ventnor. The bombs were well placed and the damage was severe, keeping the already battered station inoperative for some time.

As the raiders withdrew, orbiting 109s at 3,000m (10,000ft) were unable to come to their rescue in time to prevent RAF fighters tearing into them and shooting down ten of their number. As the raid headed back another group of 109s came out to cover them – and was intercepted by 12 Hurricanes from No.615 Squadron. Galland's III.Gruppe had been on standby, but Kesselring decided they would not be needed. He planned late raids by three formations of Do17s to probe the defences around Kent coastal towns; and the efficiency with which they were intercepted left no doubt as to the operability of the British alert and control network.

That day 30 Luftwaffe aircraft were destroyed or damaged beyond repair, including 12 Bf109s. Two casualties from I./JG26 were Lt Regenauer, taken prisoner, and Oblt Butterbeck, shot down and killed by Flt Lt Alan Deere of No.54 Sqn over the Straits of Dover. The RAF had lost 21 fighters with a further ten damaged. On balance the Luftwaffe had had the better day; and when the evening put a halt to operations, it was time to take stock and await the dawn of Adlertag.

It had been a surprise to see how quickly the British had put their radar stations back into operation: of the four hit that day, those at Dover, Pevensey and Rye were back on net by the middle of the afternoon, as witnessed by the Dorniers on their evening probe. Galland knew now that Fighter Command was more than the sum of its aircraft – good as they were – and its pilots. They had a weapon that was superior to the technically more advanced German radar which was, to date, not used for vectoring fighters. Galland was happy to learn from the enemy where he could; but for the time being there was no alternative to the methods in place.

Although he respected his opponents, Galland was in no doubt that in a straight fight he could take on anyone he had yet encountered. He did have misgivings about the way JG26 was run, however. It concerned him that Maj Handrick seemed ineffective at cutting in for the kill, and he asked his CO point blank why he chose not to fly with I.Gruppe, which was based with his Stab at Audembert, but habitually flew behind and above the Staffeln; and I./JG26 had yet to score a single kill. Maj Handrick, reiterating a Luftwaffe training manual from 1935, explained that it was only by doing this that he could get an overall view of the battle and direct his men accordingly. This did not convince Galland, who believed in leadership from the front; he discussed the matter critically with the commanders of I. and II. Gruppen, who agreed with him, while naturally not voicing his feelings any more widely. It was a disturbing prelude to the start of an assault which would call for all the drive and bravery the Geschwader could muster.

Notes to Chapter 10

1   The 'Freya' radar station at Wissant was used primarily – like the whole of this system developed for the Kriegsmarine – for coastal early warning. The Luftwaffe was working on the 'Wurzburg' system for the anti-aircraft Flakartillerie. At this time there was no central co-ordinating network to circulate reports from 'Freya' stations, and no application to fighter control.

2   R6707 (Flt Lt Basil 'Wonky' Way; drowned).

3   The South African Flt Lt A.G.Malan would end the war as Gp Capt, DSO, DFC, with 27 confirmed victories, 7 shared and at least 6 probable.

4   P9547 (Plt Off J.H.R.Young; killed)

5   As is well known, the RAF's ability to select and manage threats was based on the 18 'Chain Home' radar detection stations around the eastern and southern coasts. A sophisticated, efficient and flexible system had been developed to collate radar reports of the size, range, direction and altitude of enemy raids with the availability of RAF fighters in the various sectors, to co-ordinate the commitment of the selected squadrons, and to vector them onto the incoming raids with some accuracy. The Luftwaffe had been generally aware of British work on radar location for some years, and Galland was briefed on the CH network in July 1940; but the way the whole control system worked was not understood; and the apparently flimsy structure of the CH stations proved surprisingly resilient under Stuka attack. It was ironic that while RAF fighters were still routinely flying in outmoded, over-rigid 'vic' tactical formations, the system that controlled their deployment was the best in the world, and would be the crucial mechanism for conserving RAF resources.

6   By eliminating a Ministry of War, and seeking personal domination of the OKW, Hitler denied the armed services the 'committee of conciliation' so ably provided by defence ministries and joint chiefs of staff in other combatant nations.

7   Not long before his death Galland told the author that in his view the RAF had a structure far superior to the Luftwaffe: in arranging duties by Commands – Fighter, Bomber, Coastal, Transport, etc – the RAF focused needs within a common cause right across the board. By separating its assets between individual all-category Air Fleets the Luftwaffe fragmented the effort, and created competing and duplicated structures.

8   Galland had admired Goering, at first simply as a representative of a heroic generation of airmen, and later for achieving the creation of an independent air force. But by mid-1940 Goering's fundamental strategic ignorance, and his inability to give leadership to intelligent men who differed over the exercise of their commands, was becoming obvious. Galland would later learn that at this critical juncture the Reichsmarschall himself was unable to reconcile the conflicting objectives of 'Adlerangriff', and took refuge in pomposity and self-vindication while leaving his Luftflotte commanders to reach some kind of collective concept.

9   In fact, after Moelders was wounded on 28 July, Osterkamp – who had added six victories on the Western Front to his 32 World War I kills – had to remain in his previous command of JG51 while his successor spent a month in hospital. His predecessor as Jafu 2, Genmaj von Doering – another popular former Great War ace – also remained in post for this period.

10 In mid-May 1940 the new Ministry of Aircraft Production was set up under the newspaper magnate Lord Beaverbrook. In April total production was 1,081 aircraft, of which 256 were fighters; comparable figures for July were 1,665 and 496. Progress had also been made in getting more pilots to the squadrons, actually raising by 20 per cent the available number of pilots during the month of July to 1,414. Reacting to these figures, Dowding made a paper increase in the strength of the establishments and gave Fighter Command a notional figure of 1,588 pilots; in theory it looked like a deficiency of 174 pilots, but in fact he had more pilots than he had expected by 1 August, and was setting targets to work toward. As combat attrition took its toll the numbers of adequately trained pilots reaching the squadrons, and of experienced junior leaders surviving, would be a constant worry.

11 Employed on the Western Front only, the points system was misinterpreted after the

war by those who sought to deny the high combat scores of German pilots. Under this system – relevant only for awards, and not for listing numerical 'kills' – a pilot got one point for destroying a single-engined fighter or damaging a twin-engined fighter, two for destroying a twin-engined fighter or damaging a multi-engined aircraft, and three points for destroying a multi-engined aircraft. There were also various credits for destroying an already damaged aircraft, and for forcing a bomber out of its protective formation, a process known as 'Herausschuss'.

12 L8665 (Flg Off D.N.Grice, Sgt F.J.Keast & AC1 J.B.W.Warren, killed)

13 MacDonnell ended his war with nine confirmed kills and one unconfirmed; he ended it early, spending four years as a POW after being shot down by Werner Moelders, but returned to a distinguished postwar career. 'Jackie' Mann ended the war with five confirmed kills and one probable; an airline pilot for many years, he was taken hostage by extremists in Beirut in 1989 and held until September 1991. Made CBE, he died in November 1995.

14 The New Zealand-born 'Al' Deere – later Wg Cdr, DSO, OBE, DFC, AFC – scored a total 17 kills confirmed plus four shared and/or probables. He remained in the RAF postwar.

CHAPTER 11

13 August – 21 August 1940

On this day of all days – Eagle Day – Adolf Galland had hoped to be charging in the forefront of the battle. Instead his lot was to deploy III.Gruppe on Channel patrol, covering the air-sea rescue aircraft and boats which dashed out from the coast of France to save downed airmen.

The weather was generally fine, with some sea mist and a gentle drizzle, as some 74 Dornier bombers of KG2 made ready to begin the assault. Escorted by 60 Bf110s, they were to have proceeded in massed formation to the Isle of Sheppey; but because the weather was not ideal all Adlertag operations were postponed until the afternoon. Astonishingly, the message did not reach the bomber formation; and there was some surprise when the twin-engined Messerschmitts turned round in mid-Channel, leaving the Do17s to drone on alone. This was not the only mission which was not informed of the postponement: I./JG2, a Ju88 Gruppe from KG54, and a Gruppe of Bf110s from ZG2 all proceeded oblivious of the change of orders, the latter taking some casualties from Hurricanes of No.238 Squadron.

The decision was now made to launch Adlerangriff at 15.00; and the operation looked impressive enough on the radar scopes of the Chain Home stations at Worth Matravers and Hawks Tor. The main force comprised 120 Ju88s from KG54 and LG1, escorted by 30 LG1 Bf110s, flanked by 27 Ju87s of II./StG2, the entire formation of 177 aircraft spread out across 40 miles of sky, and preceded by 30 Bf109s of II./JG53 from bases in Guernsey and the Cherbourg peninsula. Another formation of 52 Ju87s protected by JG27 Bf109s completed the first major air assault, an attempt to shatter the fighter defences in No.10 Group's area. Meanwhile, Galland's Gruppe continued their uneventful and thankless Channel patrolling.

The results of that first day would show – had they but known it – that however impressive their aerial photos and maps, Luftwaffe intelligence was poorly informed about the identity of the targets they chose for the bombers[1]. As important would be the extreme optimism of the claims submitted for RAF aircraft destroyed[2]. Although they recorded more than double the figure, in fact the Luftwaffe had destroyed 13 RAF fighters in combat and a further 47 at six airfields during 13 August; they had themselves lost 46 aircraft, including ten Bf109s and 13 Bf110s. The losses did nothing to detract from the determination of the Luftwaffe crews to press home their attacks; but the results had a negligible impact on the ability of Fighter Command to protect English airspace. Between the misunderstanding of where Britain's strategic air assets lay, and the falacious intelligence data, the Luftflotten were sending their men on needless operations.

The following day the OKL had given orders that attacks were to be concentrated on aircraft factories and RAF stations. This time JG26 was out in force, all three Gruppen being briefed to escort Ju87s from II./StG1 and IV./LG1. Maj Handrick and his wingman would take up their usual place above and behind the Gruppen. At the briefing the previous evening Galland had won his argument that one Gruppe – his own – should fly 'detached escort' ahead of the Stukas and slightly higher than any potential threat. Hptmn Fischer's I.Gruppe would be the attached close escort; and Hptmn Ebbighausen's II.Gruppe would be either attached or detached, depending on enemy strength and the developing situation. The Stukas would be going in over the Dover Straits, which gave the Bf109s plenty of combat time should the RAF begin its intercepts over the coast.

Shortly after 11.00 the Bf109s were warmed up and final briefings were given at the dispersal tents – JG26 was still waiting for proper sheds to replace the canvas. As he walked to his Bf109E-3 Galland felt confident that today would make up for the frustration of the 13th; he had a sixth sense for these matters, and commented to his wingman, Oblt Muencheberg, that today was a 'hunter's day'. At about 11.30 the pilots strapped themselves into their cramped cockpits and engines were run up. From their airfields the three Gruppen assembled just south-east of Cap Gris Nez at 10,000ft and, for once, the 80 Stukas arrived right on schedule. For part of the flight across Galland smoked a cigar, dropping 2,000ft to get a better taste on the pretext of 'a quick look around' ahead of the formation. Long before the 160 aircraft set off across the Channel the Dover radar had been logging their progress.

No.11 Group scrambled four squadrons of Hurricanes and Spitfires (Nos.32, 65, 610 and 615) at 11.50 as the formations converged on Dover. Long before they crossed the cliffs Galland's pilots could see the approaching fighters. They collided across a broad front and soon a pitched battle was under way, the three JG26 Gruppen sticking to the agreed plan. Galland swept into the middle of the fight with his usual flair for high speed manoeuvres, locking on to a Hurricane that seemed to be in a sky of its own. The pilot threw his aircraft into a quick half-roll from which he fell away almost to the sea without pulling out. Resisting the temptation to follow him down, Galland let him go, gunned his throttle and roared away from the whirling combatants, gaining 1,000ft to collect his wits and doing his usual 360 degree roll to search for fighters closing on him. He still had his wingman with him, but not for long. Just as he was regrouping with some of his other pilots Muencheberg tore off after a Hurricane and dispatched it within five seconds, shattering the cockpit canopy like a glass bomb.

Pulling back into an inverted loop, Galland saw another Hurricane sighting on a Ju87. Almost defenceless and highly vulnerable, the angular dive-bomber with its prominent wheel spats looked incongruous in the midst of this dazzling high-speed display. Throttle to the gate, Galland tore after the RAF fighter and opened fire at the limit of credible range. At the hammering of gunfire and the flashes in his rear-view mirror the British pilot dived into cloud, and Galland made an instant, educated guess where he would reappear. He was right: suddenly the

Hurricane was right in his Revi gunsight and well within range. A full three-second burst into the fuselage just below the cockpit sent it down out of control.

The fighting raged for about an hour as 200 aircraft wheeled and battled in the skies over Kent. The sheer numbers spread the engagement across a wide area; Galland's victory had been won over the Goodwin lightship, which was then sunk by Ju87s. Hptmn Ebbighausen managed to shoot down a Hurricane, as did Oblt Hans Krug, but a lot of the time it difficult to get into the fight because of the numbers of aircraft involved. So tight was the dogfighting that one Staffel went off and destroyed eight barrage balloons over Dover before returning to orbit the still-raging battle. Galland's Gruppe had a good day's hunting, as he had told them they would. Oblt Georg Beyer, Oblt Gerhard Schoepfel and Lt Gerhard Mueller-Duehe each shot down a Hurricane, the latter for his first confirmed victory; the only Spitfire to be destroyed that day fell to the guns of Lt Joseph Buerschgens. The only JG26 casualty of the day was Fw Gerhard Kemen of I.Gruppe, shot down and captured; he had only been out of training two months and had yet to score a victory.

Overall the operations of 14 August saw little in the way of massed formations of the strength that had attacked southern ports the previous afternoon. The weather was unfavourable, and very few of the planned raids were carried out. In all the British lost seven fighters, three of them on the ground during a raid on Manston, with a further four damaged. The Luftwaffe had flown 489 sorties during the day and lost 21 aircraft, of which four were Bf109s. No one knew it at the time, but the first phase in the battle to annihilate the RAF had only four more days to run.

Galland knew that something big was brewing. For the first time, Reichs-marschall Goering was rumoured to be seething with anger at his Luftwaffe for their apparent lack of success. Maj Handrick got word to attend a high level meeting at Karinhall the following day, 15 August, and when morning came everyone had heard that many senior commanders would be away for a major conference. Increasingly, there was an uneasy feeling that 'the big fat one' was about to meddle in operational matters which were beyond his competence.

* * *

The disappointing weather forecast for 15 August suggested another day on which no concerted effort would be possible. Yet that was all to change by the early afternoon; and 15 August would see the largest attack on England so far – and, as it would turn out, of the entire battle. A ridge of high pressure sat motionless over England, quickly burning off a little haze in the early hours but leaving cloud over the Channel. Goering had called his conference at Karinhall to examine the disappointing results from the first two days of Adlerangriff because only the previous evening the weather forecast gave little hope of improvement. The senior officers who travelled to Goering's estate outside Berlin were not to know that this was the one day they should not have left the front.

A few early morning raids and probing reconnaissance patrols kept the Chain Home stations awake, but by 10.00 the skies were completely clear of enemy aircraft. Gradually the good weather over England pulled the murky curtain from the Pas de Calais. Further north, too, the weather began to improve; and preparations got under way for synchronised raids by Luftflotte 5 from Norway and Denmark. If co-ordinated with Luftflotten 2 and 3, these would represent a systematic attack on British defences along an 800-mile front from the north of Scotland to the south coast of England.

Standing in for Gen Bruno Loerzer, away at the Goering conference, Obst Paul Diechmann took his career in his hands and ordered elements of II.Fliegerkorps to begin their briefed operations. Setting in motion the first raids, he summoned up around 40 Ju87s from LG1 and StG1, escorted by fighters including JG26. On British radar screens the blips grew broader, indicating a large raid assembling over the Pas de Calais. Shortly after 11.00 they began to move away from the coast of France. Hurricanes of No.501 Sqn had been ordered into the air from Hawkinge, as had 12 Spitfires of No.54 Sqn from Hornchurch. Timing was critical; because of the short distance from France the forward line of fighters had to be in the air by the time the Luftwaffe formation left its rendezvous point. Galland was flying detached escort for the Ju87s, which for this raid were flying in a looser formation than previously. Shortly after 11.30 they reached the English coast and clashed with No.54 Squadron. Once again flying with Muencheberg, Galland furiously drove the pair of Messerschmitts among the Spitfires, scattering a formation of six. Pushing the stick forward, he pulled an outside loop – through which his wingman somehow managed to stay with him – and fastened on to a Spitfire taking a long curving dive to starboard. Galland tightened on to the Spitfire's tail, raising his legs and pressing his body forward to counteract the 'G' as the Daimler-Benz engine hauled him round in an ever tighter circle to cut across the Spitfire's path from its starboard side. Taking the longer line round the wider circle, Muencheberg caught up with the Spitfire, behind and slightly to port. But it was Galland who had him right in his sights and sprayed the forward half of the fuselage from roundel to exhausts, watching the bullets splash home as they dug out pieces of flying metal. Perfectly timed and expertly positioned, he did not need a second pass; the Spitfire fell away and went down.

Pulling quickly back toward the Ju87s, Galland caught them as they were reforming. Three had been shot down; but from the air it looked as though they had completely destroyed the airfield at Hawkinge – smoke was billowing from a wrecked hangar and a barrack block. On top of this, peripheral but important damage was caused to the Chain Home radar at Dover and Rye when bombs landing away from the airfield cut their power supplies, not restored before the evening. The rest of the Stukas had done considerable damage to the forward airfield at Lympne.

Galland pulled his Staffeln together and covered the retreat of the Ju87s out over the Channel until he was sure they were safe; then he turned III.Gruppe around and, at an altitude of 4,600m (15,000ft) returned to the blue skies over England for a quick free hunt. Within minutes he had dived on to the back of another Spitfire plucked from a squadron reforming after the fray and, without any protracted contest, he saw chunks of the airframe flying off before it burst into flames. Then he saw a second Spitfire challenging another Bf109 and tore into it, raking the fuselage; it suddenly reared up in a steep climb, its Merlin hauling it to safety – that one lived to fight another day.

Having effectively conducted two sorties in one operation, it was back to Caffiers for refuelling, rearming and minor repairs; there was no damage that would keep an aircraft on the ground, and none had been lost. Galland contacted Maj Handrick at Audembert, who had already been informed that JG26 would be needed for the rest of the day. Luftflotten 2 and 3 were about to launch a series of operations involving raids, feints, decoys and bogus attacks in an attempt to confuse what was assumed to be the tight control of Fighter Command assets through Stanmore[3]. Galland was told that III.Gruppe, accompanied by II.Gruppe, would be involved that afternoon.

A force of 80 Do17s from KG3 would be escorted or accompanied by 130 Bf109s from JG51, JG52 and JG54 and 60 from JG26 – in all, some 270 aircraft including 190 Bf109s would then conduct a massive assault on the airfield at Eastchurch and the Shorts factory at Rochester. As the Dorniers approached from Antwerp the fighter squadrons picked them up and moved out across the Channel: first JG54 under Maj Mettig, then JG51 under Obst Osterkamp and JG52 commanded by Maj Truebenbach. Galland's III.Gruppe joined from Cap Gris Nez, flying the detached escort it had come to perform so well. A total of 40 RAF fighters scrambled from Nos.64, 111 and 151 Sqns and tried unsuccessfully to attack the bombers. Two bomber Gruppen split off and went for Rochester; they caused considerable damage and delayed production of the Short Stirling, the RAF's new four-engined strategic bomber. Turning north-west, Hptmn Rathman meanwhile led III./KG3 directly for the Coastal Command station at Eastchurch. Raised successively by sector control, Nos.3, 234, 249, 601 and 609 Sqns were soon airborne across the south of England as German units diverted to attack Hawkinge airfield and Chain Home stations at Maidstone, Dover, Rye and Foreness.

Fighter Command, seriously stretched by the combined attacks, had around 130 aircraft in the air, but they were making very little impression on the bombers. This was the war of attrition which the Luftwaffe staff study had predicted would be the only way to bring the RAF down; gradually, increasing numbers of Hurricanes and Spitfires were falling to the guns of the Messerschmitts.

Galland failed to get another victory himself, but his Gruppe did well; they escorted the bombers back over the Channel before peeling off to set down again at Caffiers. It was during the return of III.Gruppe from this mission that three pilots of 7.Staffel had a curious encounter with a Spitfire (K9964, flown by Plt Off Ralph Roberts from No.64 Sqn based at Kenley). Just as Lts Mueler-Duehe, Walter Blume and Jupp Buerschgens were closing on the French coast near Cap Gris Nez they spotted a lone aircraft ahead of them, only later realising it was a Spitfire. Instead of engaging the fighter they cut across its path, signalling for it to land. Roberts turned on his adversaries and put up a spirited defence; and as the Bf109s were running out of fuel and ammunition, after a hectic chase through the countryside of the Pas de Calais they were forced to break off one by one. Shortly afterwards Roberts, disorientated and thinking himself over Kent, landed his Spitfire on the beach at Wissant.

Galland ordered a thorough technical examination of the aircraft, claiming that as it was during an engagement with his pilots that the British airman had been brought down, it was within his purview to take charge – always his natural inclination, anyway. The Spitfire's VHF radio set came as a surprise for the mechanics, who were impressed by the advanced nature of the equipment and its workmanship.

The day's work was far from over, however; and while the fitters, armourers and mechanics scurried around the 109s the pilots met for a briefing on their next sortie – the fourth of the day. It was to be a free hunt later that evening, ahead of Dorniers attacking RAF Biggin Hill, the sector station covering the south-eastern area between Lympne and a point midway between Hastings and Hythe. Meanwhile another major raid by Luftflotte 3 hit targets around and inland from Southampton and Portland in mid-afternoon: some 220 Ju87s, Ju88s, Bf109s and Bf110s heavily outnumbered the three squadrons sent up against them, which lost five Hurricanes and two Spitfires. Had all the raids been co-ordinated Fighter Command might well have been overwhelmed; as it was, sector controllers had time to rest their squadrons and regroup aircraft and pilots.

Back on the French side of the Channel, another Spitfire was presented to the Luftwaffe. Plt Off Richard Hardy from No.234 Sqn – a survivor of the battle over the south-west who was wounded, low on fuel, with his radio destroyed and controls damaged – put N3277 down near Cherbourg. Many Luftwaffe officers went to see it first hand; Galland went along with his technical officer, but needless to say his ambition to fly it was thwarted. (He took a keen interest in the later test reports, however.)

Back at Caffiers the afternoon was drawing on, and Galland gathered his Staffelkapitaene for a briefing on the evening sortie. Dorniers were assigned Biggin Hill as a primary target, while 15 Bf110s and eight Bf109 Jabos of EGr210 were to hit Kenley. Galland led III./JG26 on a detached escort and had no luck, although there was plenty of hostile activity. No.151 Sqn lost three Hurricanes and two damaged in as many minutes, bringing their losses for the day to six. The raid was pressed home hard – but on the wrong targets. The crack EGr210 Jabos put their bombs right on the hangars at the airfield they believed to be Kenley; in fact it was Croydon, and in the ensuing running fight six Bf110s and their crews were lost, including the CO, Hptmn Rubensdoerffer. The Dorniers bombed West Malling – a new, only partly operational station – in mistake for Biggin Hill, which got off without a scratch.

The attack on Croydon brought a response from No.54 Sqn and Flt Lt Alan Deere once again found himself tangling with Galland's boys. The New Zealander became attached to a Bf109 Jabo and pursued it clear across the Channel, stirring up a hornet's nest when he blundered over an airfield with Bf109s in the circuit. Galland and Hptmn Muencheberg chased Al Deere right back over the Channel in a running fight, breaking off at the coast just as Deere's engine caught fire; he got clear of the cockpit with some difficulty, and parachuted to safety.

Deere had been lucky; he had survived a meeting with one of the up-and-coming aces of the Jagdwaffe. The engagements logged by Galland in the preceding two weeks had driven his score to 22. He was within three kills of

Moelders, who was still grounded by his wounded knee. Already, people were listening to Galland; his operational tactic of flying a detached escort had been seen to work well. The OKL had agreed to a compromise over the deployment of fighter escorts; instead of tying two Bf109 Gruppen to each bomber Gruppe, only one Gruppe of fighters would stay close to the bombers all the way out and all the way back. The second would rendezvous with the bombers over England and fly above and ahead of the formation, with the freedom to attack RAF fighters as they rose to intercept, or to divert to disperse enemy aircraft in the vicinity. However, it was to be a short respite from a flawed tactic; news was about to come from Karinhall which would once again change the tactics to be practised by the Luftwaffe over England.

Although Galland and his Gruppe had had a good day, by nightfall on 15 August the overall figures were painting a different picture. On this day, which the Luftwaffe would forever remember as 'Black Thursday', the Luftwaffe had flown more than 2,000 sorties and lost 78 aircraft, with an additional 20 damaged. The Luftflotte 5 raid from Norway and Denmark had been a costly disaster, the nearly 20 per cent losses including a massacre of the Bf110s of ZG76. The British casualties were 45 aircraft lost and 13 damaged. The German attrition rate and the lack of visible success now led Goering to try to dictate tactics, from far away and based on flawed theory rather than practical observation. The conference of commanders from which Maj Handrick returned had been subjected to a rambling declaration, rather than being involved in a genuine attempt to redefine strategy. To begin with Goering had examined dive-bombing tactics: 'The fighter escort defences of our Stuka formations must be readjusted, as the enemy is concentrating his fighters against our Stuka operations. It appears necessary to allocate three fighter Gruppen to each Stuka Gruppe, one ... remains with the Stukas and dives with them ... the second flies ahead over the target at medium altitude and engages the fighter defences, the third protects the whole attack from above. It will also be necessary to escort Stukas returning from the attack over the Channel.'

His solution to the undeniable vulnerability of the Bf110s to attacks from single-engined fighters was an order that they should stick to the bombers and allow the Bf109s to form a second screen of defence around the whole formation – thus diverting fighters to escort other fighters, in an air force whose major problem was the lack of fighters relative to bombers.

Goering next reiterated the importance of 'the destruction of the enemy air forces' and ordered that all other targets should be ignored from then on – including the radar sites. He declared that 'It is doubtful if there is any point in continuing the attacks on radar sites, in view of the fact that not one of those attacked has so far been put out of operation.' As to the increasingly vexed problem of faulty navigation and target identification, Goering simply said that Kampfgruppe 100 – a special unit operating a highly accurate radio navigation and blind bombing system – must 'operate against the enemy air force and its aircraft industry'. It is hard to extract any practical military meaning from the remark.

Galland's immediate reaction was one of disbelief. As he saw it, the Jagdwaffe were actually performing excellently against the RAF Hurricanes and Spitfires – when given the freedom to set up the battle to their own advantage. They had destroyed 29 British fighters that day for the loss of 26 twin-engined Bf110s and six single-engined Bf109s. (The balance of the British losses were 16 aircraft, only two of them fighters, destroyed in raids.) However, since most of the British aircraft lost were shot down by Bf109s, the ratio was definitely to the advantage of the Jagdwaffe. For JG26 it had been a very good day: no losses and 22 confirmed kills.

Technically the Bf109 was competing well. It could outrun the Spitfire, and out-perform it at altitude and high speed; it could bunt, dive, and fly inverted without the engine cutting out; it had a good field of view (once you got used to it); its suite of armament gave the option of short range, slow-firing cannon or long range, faster-firing machine guns.

The problems were that the bombers were not performing effectively; and that the hidebound tactics of a Blitzkrieg air force were not coping with the flexible, radar-vectored British defence. In an air force where bombers outnumbered fighters two to one, it stood to reason that Goering's tactics would not work – and that leaving the radar stations unattacked would simply ease the defence. As he sat with his Staffelkapitaene and senior officers that evening, after a day in which he had effectively flown four sorties and had shot down three fighters, Galland felt serious concern not only about the resources which the Luftwaffe took into this battle, but also about the sheer professional competence of the commanders who were sending his men to risk their lives. He found it all the more galling that his Geschwaderkommodore had apparently accepted these mistaken orders with a cool detachment from responsibility, which offended everything Galland believed about leadership.

He believed that a leader looked after his men, the objectives of the day, and the well-being of the unit – in that order. Galland ran his Gruppe on a very tight rein, and insisted on accountability at every level. The pilot who lost his wingman or Rotte leader in combat had to explain exactly how and why it happened, and if any lesson emerged from this inquisition it was applied to the whole Gruppe. In the Luftwaffe more than in the RAF, personal victory scores were considered a legitimate measure of individual prowess, and led directly to tangible rewards. Galland believed that natural competitiveness was positive, and could raise the standards of the unit as a whole as long as it was harnessed by a watchful insistence on teamwork. Galland tried to select the members of his unit, as far as the system allowed; and both the selfish prima donna and the passenger seeking a free ride were anathema to him.

From the pilot to his wingman, from the Rotte to the Schwarm, to the Staffel and the Gruppe, and on up to the overall morale and effectiveness of the Geschwader – Galland compared it to the 'champagne cascade', each level enhancing the next. He believed passionately that this pattern of high personal standards, of mutual accountability both upwards and downwards, of teamwork enforced by strong, involved leadership and inspired by example, was essential for an effective, unified fighting organisation. He was unhappy about some aspects of the way JG26 was being run; but he did what many a soldier has done when in disagreement with his superiors. Although naturally outspoken, he knew his place in the hierarchy of rank. For the time being he governed his tongue, unwilling to do anything to prejudice his chances for command - and the opportunity to make changes. This was to come quicker than he imagined.

* * *

Next day, Friday 16 August, I. and II./JG26 flew escort missions to England but Galland's III.Gruppe was given a rest. The cycle gave pilots a chance to recoup their strength, and mechanics an opportunity to catch up with repairs and carry out some engine changes. In bright but hazy weather the Luftwaffe mounted its second day of intense raids, putting up 1,715 sorties against airfields and installations across southern England. Tangmere airfield took a beating, as did Gosport, Lee-on-Solent and Poling. At Brize Norton the RAF lost 46 training aircraft; West Malling got a return visit, suffering further damage which kept it out of action for four days. Altogether, on 16 August the Luftwaffe lost 45 aircraft, of which 17 were Bf109s (of JG27, JG51, JG53 and JG54); 16 aircraft were damaged including four Bf109s. The only casualty from JG26 was Hptmn Karl Ebbighausen, whose Bf109E-4 was shot down in the sea off Deal; he was replaced as commander of II.Gruppe by Hptmn Erich Bode from 4. Staffel.

Discounting the 46 trainers, the RAF had lost 28 aircraft of which 22 had been fighters; a further 11 had been damaged. Behind these figures the reality was a little more revealing. Of the 22 British fighters lost, 17 had been shot down in combat - a 1:1 ratio with their Jagdwaffe counterparts. (Of the 11 damaged only five resulted from combat, the balance being aircraft caught on the ground by raids.) The following day, Saturday 17 August, saw a lull in the battle. For Galland's Gruppe it was a day to relax and catch up on activity vital to the functioning of the unit but put aside during the recent days of intense action. Many also took the chance to sample the delights of local towns; but Galland - usually only too happy to join in - would not be with them. He had been ordered to Karinhall to attend a conference with Goering. When he left for Berlin on 17 August all he knew was that Werner Moelders would also be there.

As Galland travelled back across Germany he felt as though he had returned through a time tunnel. Everywhere people were happy and relaxed. The weather was beautiful, adding a glow to mundane streets, shops, restaurants and parks. In the evening Berlin was thronged with partygoers and theatre-lovers; it always had been a city apart from the rest of Germany, but now it seemed to Galland like a never-never land where they had not heard there was a war on. It bothered Galland considerably that these people were being kept in their pleasures because men like him were prepared to fight and, if need be, die in a war to expand the restricted borders set by the failures of a past generation. Commonplace enough to any wartime soldier confronted suddenly with carefree civilians, the paradox affected Adolf Galland deeply, and remained with him all his life[4].

From Berlin Galland was driven the 40 miles or so to the palatial estate of the Reichsmarschall. Situated in the Schorfheide, a forest extending far to the north-east beyond the environs of Berlin, Karinhall was immense. Named after

Goering's Swedish-Irish first wife, Karin, who had died in 1931, it had been built in the style of a Swedish hunting lodge, and the estate was stocked with game. Here Goering could express his fantasies and his appetites without restraint or competition. That was a big difference between the two men: Goering hated to compete, and was never happier than when adored and cosseted, stage-managing every luxurious detail and flamboyant effect. Galland could not deny that it was impressive; but it also disturbed him. Karinhall was surreal, a Gothic theatrical set, a place for actors; it was not a place from which great men ran wars.

The walls were covered with hunting trophies. Across marble floors were strewn furs and skins; massive wooden statues represented mythical and historical figures, beneath soaring timbered ceilings; on the walls, tapestries and huge paintings completed the impression of medieval splendour. Down one side of the great reception hall massive carved tables supported exquisite Czechoslovakian crystal. Great decanters, larger than any Galland had ever seen, held fine wines from France and the Rhine. Goering apologised for these with a belly-laugh that seemed to set his whole body rocking: the best cases were still en route, and if the Luftwaffe had not requisitioned so much transport they would be here now for him to serve to his guests – 'fine wine for my bold eagles!' Galland looked at Werner Moelders, who looked back in silence; neither knew how to react. It all seemed so grotesquely decadent that if they had not been in such distinguished company – several senior staff officers were present, together with Milch and Udet – they would have believed they were in a farce. However, their host distracted them soon enough from the vulgarity of the surroundings.

Goering launched into a long diatribe summing up the general situation, as if his guests had no knowledge of the war. Goering's entire future lay within the measure of his success or failure in this one battle, and he knew it. After telling them what they already knew, he attempted to put the battle in the context of the greater scheme of the Third Reich, and shifted hats to play the politician. He then explained how he wanted the battle to be played. In the general discussion among the senior officers that followed, Galland began to believe that he could indeed see the whole picture, and that optimism had a place after all – that his own limited perspective gave too restricted a view for a truly informed opinion. Surely the overwhelming confidence expressed here by senior staff officers must be born of knowledge of the whole war front, and of intelligence analysis beyond the reach of squadron officers like him? Galland, and to a lesser extent the quieter and more inward Werner Moelders, were seduced by the ambience.

There was an interlude during the business when the two pilots were taken aside and each awarded the Pilot's Badge in Gold with Diamonds, a highly prestigious recognition of distinguished service devised and awarded by Goering himself[5]. While reflecting the ostentatious nature of the giver it was, nevertheless, an enormous honour. In the whole reign of the Third Reich there were only 40 recipients, the badge usually being given to foreign heads of state or military leaders as a token of German respect. Both Galland and Moelders were greatly surprised at this award; but Galland at least would live to understand the precise reason why it had been given.

When the presentation ceremony was over Goering took the two aviators aside

At nine months old, the future fighter ace faces the world with a fearless stare. Adolf Galland on Christmas Eve 1912.

Reunited in the peace of Westerholt in the 1950s after Adolf's return to Germany from Argentina; Anna Galland and her second son.

Left: *The clean-shaven 22-year-old Adolf Galland in the uniform of a Deutscher Luftsport-Verband pilot officer after his discharage from army training in late 1934. He had not yet suffered the crash injuries which remodelled his features in October 1935.*

Above and below: *Heinkel He51 biplanes of J88, the Condor Legion fighter squadron, on makeshift Spanish airfields. Note the auxiliary fuel tank between the undercarriage legs; as commander of 3.Staffel, Galland had these modified into incendiary bombs for ground attack missions.* (Courtesy Hans Obert)

Above: *Messerschmitt Bf109B-2 fighter of J88; all Condor Legion Bf109s carried the type number 6 left of the black Nationalist disc insignia, and individual aircraft numbers right of it.* (Courtesy Hans Obert)

Below: *Ground crew of J88 posing with a Bf109B on a Spanish airfield in 1937. Note the seven white victory bars on the fin; the coloured rudder suggests that it might be the Staffel commander's machine.* (Courtesy H. Nowarra)

The Henschel Hs123 biplane dive-bomber, the type which Galland flew with II.(Schlacht) Gruppe of Lehrgeschwader 2 during the Polish campaign, September 1939. (U.S. National Archives)

Above: *Always a keen marksman, Galland tries out a Mauser 98k service rifle on the range at Caffiers, the base of III./JG26 during the summer of 1940.* (Courtesy Kent Battle of Britain Museum)

Right: *Wearing a lifejacket and flying boots over his service dress uniform, Galland clambers into his Bf109E-3 for a mission over south-east England in summer 1940.*

Below: *Goering visits his fighter commanders on the Channel coast to discuss tactics during the Battle of Britain. Galland stands immediately in front of the Reichsmarschall's standard, Werner Moelders at Goering's left shoulder.*

Above: *Galland carries out final cockpit checks, his cigar still clenched in his teeth; note the experimental telescopic sight, the S-shield insignia of JG26 'Schlageter', and Galland's personal insignia under the cockpit, inspired by that of 3./J88 'Mickeymaus' in Spain.*

Left: *Galland's Bf109E was the only Luftwaffe aircraft known to be fitted with a cigar lighter and holder – a luxury he also permitted himself on subsequent aircraft.*

Right: *Uffz Meyer, Galland's crew chief throughout the war, works on the cockpit between missions over England. The telescopic sight modification only lasted for a few operations.*

Above: *Galland is helped into his parachute and lifejacket before a mission late in 1940. He wears the trousers of a captured RAF Bomber Command issue Irvin sheepskin flying suit,* **Right:** *a coveted item in the winter months, though very bulky for the Bf109's narrow, cramped cockpit.*

Left: *In full service dress with decorations, Major Galland poses in front of the Brandenburg Gate in Berlin after receiving the Oak Leaves to his Knight's Cross from Hitler on 25 September 1940.*

Above: *In the classic pose of the fighter pilot discussing his profession, Werner Moelders makes a tactical point watched by Galland and (right) Jafu 2, the World War I ace 'Uncle Theo' Osterkamp.*

Right: *Returning to the Pas de Calais after a Bf109F mission in summer 1941, the Geschwaderkommodore shows the strain of prolonged combat service. Unlike Allied pilots, Luftwaffe aircrew were not rested with occasional non-operational tours of duty; apart from brief and infrequent leave they stayed at the front until they became casualties, or were promoted to senior rank. Here Galland wears the rank insignia of Oberstleutnant, and the Swords to the Knight's Cross, awarded that June.*

Above: *a snatched winter picnic, with (L to R) Luetzow, Schoepfel, Wick, Galland, von Maltzahn and Ebersberger.* **Below:** *Galland frequently organised hunting parties for his pilots as a relaxation from combat.*

Left: *Galland rests between ski runs, winter 1940-41: at the behest of Goering, JG26's pilots got their only vacation of the war at the resort of Zurs in the Voralberg mountains.*

Below: *Bf109F in front of a camouflaged hangar in north-west France, 1941. The F-model was Galland's favourite variant of the whole 109 series.*

Above: *Attended as always by Uffz Meyer, Galland prepares to take off in a Bf109F-2. Losing touch with one another in the chaos of 1945, Galland and Meyer would be reunited in 1983.*

Below: *Galland during a visit by Goering to JG26 in the Pas de Calais in 1941.* (Courtesy H. Nowarra)

Above: *December 1941: JG26 are paraded for farewell speeches led by Goering on Galland's departure to take up the appointment as General der Jagdflieger. One of Galland's two modified Bf109F-2 fighters bears the chevron and bars which he displayed as Geschwaderkommodore. On the rudder is painted his victory tally: 69 up to the award of Swords to his Knight's Cross, and another 25, making 94 kills – a total which would remain almost unchanged until he returned to combat flying in the last months of the war.* **Below:** *One of Galland's most treasured souvenirs to the end of his life was this cartoon, drawn by Ernst Udet, depicting the friendly rivalry of the aces Galland and Moelders in 1940-41.*

and entered into a lengthy discussion about his concerns, openly voicing his dissatisfaction with the Jagdwaffe. It was simply not performing as an aggressive fighter arm should, he said, making some allusion to his days at the head of the Richthofen Geschwader; the fighter wings were not sufficiently dynamic, and were too cautious in their tactics. Their primary role, said Goering, was defending the bombers, and too many of these – Germany's most vital air assets – were being shot down. He accepted that the fighter-versus-fighter kill ratio was in favour of the Luftwaffe, but still insisted that lack of aggression was behind the attrition of the bombers, apparently ignoring the contradictions of this position.

The two pilots responded at length, describing operational difficulties and the restrictive effect of outmoded tactics.

They challenged the failure of high command to recognise the reality of high speed combat in enemy airspace. They explained to Goering their limited ability to affect policy at command level; although Moelders had been promoted to Geschwaderkommodore of JG51 on 27 July, he had only led his men in that capacity for one day before being shot down. Galland only stopped short of reproaching the Reichsmarschall directly when Moelders interrupted him in more diplomatic terms.

What Goering wanted was to inject a fresh and invigorating new force into the Jagdwaffe, which he saw as the only means by which he could achieve his military – and political – aims. As an old fighter pilot himself, he said, he understood the dynamism of youth; and the aggression he sought to inculcate into the men who led his Jagdflieger could only come from a new generation of leaders. It was with some surprise that Galland heard that he was to be a part of that process, as he was to replace Maj Handrick as Geschwaderkommodore of JG26. At the age of 28 he was to command a wing of nine squadrons and order the daily lives of almost 100 pilots. Galland's reaction was predictable: he protested that he was already in the position where he could be of most use, and that command of a Jagdgeschwader would deny him the opportunity to control the fight and lead his pilots. Goering rejected his protests, promising him a free hand to lead his men into battle, and not entombment behind a desk.

Galland's promotion was only one of a major series of personnel changes. Many more senior officers would go, replaced by spirited young pilots who had shown their potential on the Western Front. Moelders already had JG51; and now Johannes Trautloft was to command JG54. Trautloft, a Condor Legion veteran and commander of III./JG51 who was Galland's close contemporary, was one of that rare breed who excel in combat yet also show great abilities as teachers. He became one of the most respected among his peers; and Galland would find in Hannes Trautloft a good friend when darker times threatened even the most loyal combat officers. Other names coming to the fore in this quiet 'purge' of the old guard included Wolfgang Schellman, a year older than Galland, who would assume command of JG2 'Richthofen', and in the coming winter of JG27. Guenther Luetzow, at 27 years old, was already named to take over JG3 'Udet', which he would lead with real dash and flair. That October Guenther Freiherr von Maltzahn would take command of JG53; he was to see much action, not only on the Western Front but in the Mediterranean and North Africa.

Added to this concentration of talent in leadership roles, the Jagdgeschwader from Luftflotte 3 were now to move from the Cherbourg region and join Luftflotte 2 in the Pas de Calais, from where the next phase in the struggle against the RAF was to be controlled. JG2, JG27 and JG53 joined JG3, JG26, JG51, JG52 and JG54 – on paper, at least, a concentrated force of more than 450 Bf109s operating from the closest piece of mainland Europe to British airfields. On 19 August Goering had yet more to say about how the war against England was to be conducted.

He declared that 'the main task of Luftflotten 2 and 3 will be to inflict the utmost damage possible on the enemy fighter forces.' It is clear that by this he did not mean primarily the destruction of fighters in air combat, but the destruction of their airfields and other infrastructure by bombing. Therefore, in stressing the protection of the bombers Goering believed that he was following a strictly rational approach. He was unable to see that by shackling the fighters to the bombers he was seriously restricting their ability to achieve his goal by shooting down RAF fighters and killing their pilots.

Goering not only wanted to knock out the airfields; he also put increasing emphasis on the elimination of 'material supplies of the enemy air force, by the destruction of the relatively small number of aircraft engine and aluminium plants.' He ordered raids on these targets to take place at night, if possible, and the allocation of specific units to specific areas for the sake of familiarity with enemy territory. 'Within this area a list of target priorities should be drawn up, so that each sortie will produce some valuable result... To myself I reserve only the right to order attacks on London and Liverpool.'

When Galland and Moelders left Karinhall they were whisked to the RLM in Berlin, where there was much for Galland to do setting up the organisational links that he wanted for JG26. There were to be changes in the Geschwader; Galland had made it plain that in accepting command he was assuming a free hand to hire and fire as he saw fit. Goering had assured him that he would not put restrictions in his way and that, indeed, strong leadership from the front – in the air as well as on the ground – was exactly what he hoped for in appointing him to the position.

Despite these assurances, Galland moaned to Moelders about the pitfalls of the job all the way back to Berlin in the staff car. Moelders was a visionary leader, who saw no great clash of interests between combat leadership and all the other aspects of commanding such a large unit; he relished the opportunities it opened to him. Galland wanted above all to fly and to hunt out the enemy, to pit his skill against theirs. Jokingly, he told his friend that if Moelders saw himself as the Oswald Boelcke of this war – setting new standards in tactics and combat control – then he, Galland, would take on the mantle of Manfred von Richthofen – the tenacious hunter, offering and expecting no quarter. Moelders replied that as long as he kept that approach for the enemy, he would probably survive.

For all his confident and outspoken nature Galland had misgivings about this radical promotion. While his authority would be unquestioned, the large number of senior and staff officers at the RLM, at Luftflotte level and at Jagdfliegerfuehrer headquarters – most of them old enough to be Galland's father – might not look kindly on a group of young officers demanding to transform the way the fighter war was run.

Notes to Chapter 11

1 Examples included the belief that Supermarine's Spitfire factory at Woolston – a vital production centre – was an Avro bomber factory; and that airfields such as Eastchurch and Upavon were front-line fighter bases, when they had not been used as such since the 1920s.

2 The claims for RAF aircraft destroyed – and consequently comparative attrition ratios of British and German air strength – were often erroneous. A cumulative loss ratio for the four heaviest days' activity to date (8 and 11-13 August) was reckoned at 3:1 in the Luftwaffe's favour. It was claimed that the RAF had lost 15 per cent of its fighter strength compared to 3 per cent of Luftwaffe bombers and fighters. Official Luftwaffe figures for 13 August show 134 British aircraft destroyed; in fact the RAF lost 60. The problem – experienced by every combatant air force – lay simply in the difficulty of confirming and reconciling claims made by pilots in the confusion of a fast-moving air battle, where in good faith men could easily report as destroyed aircraft which escaped damaged, and where pilots often duplicated claims for the same kill. (This last was a particular problem in the Luftwaffe, which did not recognise the concept of 'shared' kills by more than one pilot.)

The procedure a German pilot had to complete in order to get a claim recognised was painstaking and bureaucratic. The first step was immediate: if he thought he had just shot down an opponent the pilot shouted 'Horrido!' into his R/T, which alerted others to look for a flamer or falling wreckage and thus to serve as witnesses. If there was neither witness nor tangible evidence, it did not count as a kill; if there was, an accumulating dossier began its lengthy journey through channels. By 1944 the RLM had a staff of several hundred civilian clerks doing nothing but checking claims and gathering evidence for final decisions about specific kills.

3 The Luftwaffe still did not know how RAF squadrons were controlled; attempts to probe the radar stations and listening-in to British R/T traffic failed to reveal the secret. There was an almost total lack of information about the reporting system, and about the way Fighter Command stations were separated between active and rest status.

4 In Galland's words: '... this Second World War seemed to be like a pyramid turned upside down, balancing on its apex ... And for the moment the whole burden of war rested on a few hundred German fighter pilots on the Channel coast. Did not their number pale into insignificance, like a speck, in comparison with the millions of men under arms in Germany? ... Naturally, neither the Army divisions which led a peaceful life in occupied territories or in garrison at home, nor those happy and carefree crowds bent on amusement, could have been of any help to us in the fight against the RAF. And yet this contrast had a deeply depressing effect on me.'

5 The standard Pilot-Observer Badge, the qualification worn on the left breast of the tunic, comprised an oval wreath half of oak and half of laurel leaves, over which was superimposed an eagle with spread wings clutching a swastika in its talons; the wreath was in gold-plated, the eagle in silver-plated metal. The Pilot-Observer Badge in Gold with Diamonds instituted by Goering varied slightly in design details, and was much more massive; the wreath was in gold, the eagle and swastika in silver, and it incorporated 104 rose-cut diamonds. Because of its value Galland had a replica made, in gold-plated silver mounted with blue sapphires, for everyday wear.

CHAPTER 12

22 August – 14 September 1940

When Galland arrived back in the Pas de Calais on Thursday 22 August to take up his new post at Audembert, it was to reports of continued frustration with a fragmented performance and steady attrition. On the 18th StG77 had lost 16 Stukas in five minutes – this was the last time Ju87s would venture over England in any numbers. Fighter losses had also been considerable: 15 destroyed and nine significantly damaged, out of total Luftwaffe figures of 60 and 37. Two pilots from III./JG26 had been killed by Spitires of No.54 Sqn: Lts Blume and Mueller-Duehe. On the other side, the RAF had lost 43 fighters with seven damaged.

There had been one extraordinary success for JG26 that day, when Oblt Gerhard Schoepfel, standing in for Galland as III.Gruppe's acting CO, shot down four Hurricanes. The Gruppe was on detached escort duty, flying about 25 miles ahead of a bomber formation, when Schoepfel spotted eight Hurricanes from No.501 Sqn, which he realised would pass him still climbing and put their backs to the sun. Ordering his Gruppe to stay out of the way he trailed them, working his way round to an up-sun position. He closed in from below and behind the 'tail end weaver' until he was within 300ft before opening fire, shattering the Hurricane so severely that bits of metal and burning debris flew past all round his Bf109. Hardly believing his luck when the rest of the formation failed to react, he moved up to the next rear aircraft and did the same thing, again almost demolishing the Hurricane at point blank range. With mounting incredulity he continued to ride his luck, sliding into the blind spot behind two more Hurricanes from up-sun; but he was so close to his fourth that his canopy was covered with oil and he had to break away.

Sunday 18 August brought an end to the first phase of the Battle of Britain. The losses so far had been too high to sustain for any length of time: in the past six days the Luftwaffe had lost 350 aircraft and the RAF had lost 250, of which 170 were from Fighter Command. For the next five days the Luftflotten would regroup, and re-equip in an attempt to restore failing numbers.

For the Luftflotte staffs it was a nightmare. The Bf110s were clearly a liability rather than an asset; and because of the added burden placed on the single-seat fighters JG77 would now have to be transferred from Scandinavia to the Channel coast. Goering had not really addressed the vulnerability of the so-called 'Destroyers', and Galland was quite certain that the entire inventory should have been either withdrawn or redirected to other duties (as they would be later in the war).

Fighter Command too was rethinking tactics; and on 19 August – while

Goering was pronouncing abstractions at Karinhall – AVM Keith Park issued new directives for No.11 Group sector controllers. Noting that the Luftwaffe had been partially effective in luring fighters back towards France, Park ordered that, if possible, fighters should not fly over the sea, to avoid their loss if forced to ditch in the Channel. He advised that controllers should scramble only the minimum forces necessary to repel escorting fighters, preserving the bulk of the fighters for attacking the bombers. He also wanted squadrons placed just beneath the cloud layer over critical airfields if heavy attacks on these places were imminent. There was little activity on either side of the Channel on the 19th; in accordance with Park's warning No.11 Group failed to take the bait of an overflight by some 100 Bf109s organised by Jafu 2.

On 20 August a heavy raid up the Thames Estuary in the afternoon met 40 fighters in a fierce confrontation that fanned out all along the north Kent coast. In all, the Luftwaffe lost eight aircraft with five limping home damaged, three of the losses being Bf109s; the RAF lost three aircraft. Reorganisation of the Jagdwaffe and bad weather kept the pace of operations low for the second day running on the 21st; but in raids against several targets across the south and west the Luftwaffe still lost 13 bombers, and five aircraft were damaged, four of them fighters. The RAF lost four fighters, all but one on the ground, with nine aircraft damaged, four of them on the ground.

* * *

It was against this relatively bleak background that Galland took up his new position at Audembert and began to prepare for the next phase of the battle. First of all he was going to wield an axe; he gave himself two days to reorganise JG26. The first thing he did was to promote Oblt Schoepfel to command III.Gruppe, Schoepfel's place at the head of 9.Staffel going to Oblt Heinz Eberling. Hptmn Rolf Pingel, a rising star from JG53 who had fought in Spain with J88, replaced Hptmn Kurt Fischer in command of I.Gruppe. Galland's wingman Oblt Muencheberg was given command of 7.Staffel, swapping the post of adjutant on the Geschwaderstab with Oblt Georg Beyer, another veteran of Spain. In a couple of weeks 1.Staffel would go to Oblt Eberhard Henrici.

These were not the only changes. Gathering his Gruppenkommandeure together at the mansion at Audembert where he had his headquarters, Galland explained the way JG26 would be organised and run. First, he wanted it known that he was not about to ask any of them to do anything he could not be seen doing himself. The wing should understand that his own tactics in the air were an example of what he wanted other pilots to aim for. He did not want any superficial formality, and his men should feel that they could approach him at any time; but he expected a strong sense of discipline. There was to be no time-wasting criticism of policy or chafing at unpopular jobs; they were to focus their energies on the tasks they were ordered to perform, and leave the head-scratching to Berlin. Above all, he regarded them all as colleagues; they were all in it together, regardless of rank or position, and they had his word that arrogant prima donnas and free-loaders would both be weeded out and posted.

As to operational matters, he expected the Stab flight, of four pilots led by himself, to be active on every major sortie involving at least two Gruppen. The technical officer, Oblt Horten, would fly as Galland's regular wingman – an exciting prospect for Horten, since his two previous bosses had been somewhat lackadaisical about combat flying. From time to time, however, Galland would select experienced enlisted pilots from the Staffeln to fly on his wing, for personal evaluation and tuition. He let it be known that he supported the well-tried method of flying the Rotte as a fixed pair in combat, which would only work in practice if the two men could stay together, sometimes exchanging roles as leader in the chase but almost invariably flying with the Rotte leader directing the combat. He emphasised that his role as Geschwaderkommodore was a job for the ground; his place in the air was at the head of his men, and his subordinate commanders had better get used to the fact that he would be seeing a lot of them up there – and watching their performance. He wanted JG26 to be the best fighter wing in the Luftwaffe, and anyone who did not share that ambition had no place under his command.

He then visited every airfield where a JG26 Staffel was located, and met the fitters, mechanics, armourers, cooks, clerks, medical personnel, signallers, intelligence officers, and the truck drivers who brought up the supplies. To every group, at their own level, he conveyed the message that he had given to his officers, trying to get across that there was going to be a new atmosphere throughout the wing. Sitting on oil drums or sand bags, he would gather men around him and talk with them about their problems, about what they needed and how he could help them do their jobs for the good of the Geschwader. After his high-speed tour he sat down with his new adjutant to go over detailed operational planning for the next few days.

On 22 August there was little activity over England. Bf110s from EGr210 escorted by 27 Bf109s attacked shipping, and returned again in the evening to a raid on Manston. Only handfuls of aircraft were lost on either side. Next day, isolated attacks were made against Tangmere, Portsmouth, Cromer and Harwich; and after dark Luftflotte 3 sent 18 He111s from KGr100 against Cardiff Docks and Pembroke Dock as well as the Dunlop factory at Birmingham[1]. Flying from Vannes in the Brest peninsula, these aircraft used the efficient X-Geraet radio navigation system – involving transecting radio beams transmitted from Continental stations – for blind bombing. Once again, small numbers of aircraft were lost or damaged on both sides in operations throughout the day.

The major reorganisation of Luftflotten 2 and 3 would produce results: Saturday 24 August saw a return to full scale operations in what the Luftwaffe hoped would be the final punch prior to the complete neutralisation of the RAF. Although Luftwaffe intelligence had little accurate information on the state of Fighter Command, its situation was beginning to deteriorate. In the week ahead attacks on factories and airfields and the loss of British fighters in combat would deplete reserves. More immediately worrying, because more difficult to solve, was the attrition of experienced pilots, the increasing fatigue among those who were left, and the reduction of training standards in order to get replacements quickly onto the squadrons – sometimes with only 20 hours' on Hurricanes and Spitfires.

The 22nd saw the Luftwaffe mount 1,030 daytime sorties, beginning with a build-up of formations early in the morning followed by a raid involving 40 Dorniers and Ju88s escorted by 66 Bf109s from several units including Oblt Schoepfel's III./JG26. Once again the Galland tactic of a detached forward screen worked, protecting most of the bombers from attack. Late that morning another raid hit the area around Dover and Manston; during the afternoon a large formation of Heinkels and Dorniers accurately dropped more than 200 bombs on North Weald airfield, and Hornchurch was hit again. There was a major raid on Portsmouth. The most significant event, in the longer term, took place that night; more than 100 bombers made their way to London unimpeded, lighting up the sky for the first time since 1918 with fires in the City and East End. JG26 was launching escorts virtually all day, and Galland flew his Stab flight with some of these. The day cost the Jagdwaffe 19 fighters, all but one of them Bf109s, and five damaged; 15 bombers were lost with three damaged. The RAF lost 25 fighters with a further seven damaged.

Next day, 25 August, there was very little activity for JG26 until the afternoon. Luftflotte 2 had mounted what it called demoralisation formations over the Channel before noon, designed to intimidate the RAF – an odd idea, which predictably failed. However, a number of new techniques were tried out for exploitation later in the day. Because of the previous day's losses there had been a call for the fighters to remain closely grouped around the bombers, and another edict from on high ordered the abandonment of the detached escort policy. Galland was forced to comply: he had told his Geschwader that orders were orders. That afternoon there were attacks on Portland and Warmwell, the latter turned back by Hurricanes from No.17 Sqn; they and the Spitfires of No.609 inflicted heavy losses on the Bf110s of ZG2 and V./LG1.

Just as Luftflotte 3's raid was turning away another mass formation was assembling over the Pas de Calais. Escorted by Galland's JG26, a formation of Dorniers crossed the Channel to Dover at about 18.00; an over-stretched No.32 Sqn pounced on them, only to receive a severe mauling and lose two Hurricanes. In all the day cost the destruction or serious damage of 13 Bf110s and 11 Bf109s, and six bombers were shot down. The RAF lost 17 Spitfires and Hurricanes with three damaged.

When the Staffeln from JG26 got back to the Pas de Calais that evening there was some discussion about the bombing of targets in greater London the previous night. In truth the raids on London had been a mistake due to poor navigation resulting in Luftwaffe bombers missing strategic targets on the outskirts. It was an error that would have major consequences for both air forces. On the 25th the British War Cabinet authorised the first bombing raid on Berlin; and that night 103 aircraft were sent out.

About half bombed through cloud cover, doing infinitesimal damage as most bombs fell on farmland south of the capital. The effect was electrifying, however. For more than three hours flak guns barked, searchlights probed the sky and sirens wailed. This was the first time bombs had ever fallen on Berlin; civilians were dazed, uncertain of what to make of it. Leaflets dropped along with the bombs warned that the war would last as long as Hitler did. The Germans had erected anti-aircraft defences against a day they were convinced would never come; now that it seemed that it had, they were bemused. RAF Bomber Command returned on the night of 28-29 August, and for the first time people were killed in the city itself (the official count was ten dead and 29 wounded). The entire Nazi propaganda machine went into overdrive: 'British air pirates over Berlin!' screamed the headlines. On 4 September Hitler would address his people from the Sportpalast in Berlin. What he would have to say would change the nature of the air campaign.

Galland had time to implement further plans for the restructuring of JG26 and time, too, for meetings about the allocation of fighter escorts for the bombers now that the detached tactics were forbidden. For two days the Geschwader was not called upon to fly sorties, and preparations for a major effort on Wednesday 28 August were advanced. In the interim, on 26 August morning raids were conducted against Kenley and Biggin Hill airfields; later raids were less successful, a few Dorniers reaching RAF Debden and others being turned back from Hornchurch. In all 24 Luftwaffe bombers and 23 fighters were destroyed or damaged for 32 RAF fighters lost or damaged.

On 27 August the weather prevented much activity, but sporadic raids did produce some engagements and a few stray German bombers were shot down at the cost of one British fighter. In the Pas de Calais intensive discussion about close escort tactics kept the adjutants of the fighter and bomber wings busy. All three Gruppen at JG26 were occupied for most of the day with preparations for the next series of raids and the revised rendezvous points. Despite the loads they were carrying the bombers generally had greater range, and were scheduled to converge above the fighter bases rather than expecting the fighters to fly to distant rendezvous points.

One of the problems forced upon Galland's attention now that he was responsible for a Geschwader was that of casualties and replacements. Unlike the RAF, most German pilots taking to their parachutes were lost as prisoners of war. The story for the Jagdwaffe as a whole, seen over the period since the start of the offensive in the West on 10 May, gave food for thought. On 1 May the single-seat squadrons had 1,010 operational pilots; during that month 76 Jagdflieger were lost – 6.8 per cent of the total. By 1 June the available number of pilots had fallen to 839, an attrition rate of 7.8 per cent. On 1 July, responding to an increased flow of personnel from operational training units, there were 906 Bf109 pilots; but losses during the month amounted to 124, or 11 per cent of the total. During August increased attrition took its toll; despite further increases in supply during the month the starting base of 869 pilots was reduced by a further 168, or 15 per cent of the total. As a result, there were only 735 operational Bf109 pilots by the end of August – 27 per cent less than available three and a half months earlier.

* * *

Wednesday 28 August brought the first opportunity to exploit fully the combined resources of Luftflotten 2 and 3 fighter units in one series of attacks on the south-east. Now that Luftflotte 3 had transferred its fighter Geschwader to Kesselring's

Luftflotte 2 there could be a greater concentration of fighter protection, at least in theory, for the bombers. A co-ordinated assault on No.11 Group would give no respite to AVM Park's beleaguered squadrons and would focus almost the whole Jagdwaffe on one corner of England. Luftflotte 3's bombers had stood down from daylight raids and would, for the time being at least, confine themselves to night operations. To some extent Galland's continual plea for greater concentration of fighter power had been heeded; and now it was time to test it.

At about 08.45 local time (07.45 in England) 50 bombers began converging on the Pas de Calais. III./JG26 was ready to share the escort duty with two Gruppen from Moelder's JG51, and this time Galland was flying low cover. RAF Fighter Command alerted 32 Hurricanes of Nos.79, 501 and 615 Sqns, and the 12 Boulton-Paul Defiants of No.264 Squadron[2]. As the bombers approached England they separated into two formations; escorted by III./JG26 led by Galland and the Stabschwarme, 27 Heinkels of KG53 headed for Rochford while the Dorniers of KG3, with their own escort, made for Eastchurch. Flying low cover was a thankless task and Galland had reserved it for his Stabschwarme, leaving the three Staffeln of III. Gruppe trailing and flying at a slightly higher altitude. Hurricanes of No.79 Sqn spotted the bombers, and passed a sighting report before they swept into the attack.

The upper Schwarme of III./JG26 split into Rotten and swept round from opposite sides of the approaching Hurricanes to catch them in a crossfire, hoping to split them up for specific targeting. The Heinkels maintained tight formation while one Staffel of 109s fanned around the threatened arc. Arriving on the scene, the 12 Defiants tore straight into the Heinkels from below, only to be set upon by Stab/JG26. Galland threw his 109 into a sweeping turn to starboard, Oblt Horten hardly having time to react before his CO was pulling away. Within seconds his wingman had caught up, and the Geschwaderkommodore led both Rotten full tilt for the ragged cluster of Defiants. Opening fire at one aircraft, he found himself rapidly overtaking it; he throttled back but not before sliding alongside the incongruous-looking two-seater. For perhaps two seconds he caught a glimpse of the pilot and gunner both looking at him incredulously as the Defiant hung alongside Galland's aircraft; then it gradually pitched over to port, sliding into Horten's Revi gunsight as he flew behind and slightly above Galland's port tail. In another three seconds Horten had instinctively calculated deflection, positioned his aircraft and fired; the Defiant erupted into flames and fell like a Roman candle.

Galland pulled up sharply to kill his excess speed, pressed firmly into his seat by 3G as he came up on a second aircraft which appeared to be going much slower. With no chance to get his gunsight on it, Galland transferred his attention to another Defiant and dived hard after it, firing from a range of 300ft all the way in to just 60ft from his target. Out of 20mm cannon ammunition, he put his two 7.92mm nose machine guns to good use. Bobbing and weaving, ducking under the protection of its tail whenever possible, Galland raked the Defiant. The rear gunner put holes in the 109 as he fought fiercely for his life; but suddenly the Defiant's fuel tank boiled into flames. With fire spreading along the fuselage both of the crew climbed out and took to their parachutes[3]. Galland broke hard to starboard as the Defiant rolled lazily over on to its back, one of four destroyed and five disabled that day.

Galland gathered his squadrons and ran for home, the red fuel warning lights glowing in several cockpits. It was too late for five JG26 pilots, who had to put down in the Channel with empty tanks; but the air-sea rescue network – notably better organised and resourced than its British counterpart – picked them all up safely. When Galland got back to Audembert he learned that two of the Stabschwarme were not coming back at all, both shot down by Spitfires of No.610 Sqn and taken prisoner: Oblt Beyer, Galland's adjutant, and Fw K.Straub, an enlisted pilot borrowed from 7.Staffel.

The day had been one of heavy activity for Luftflotte 2 with raids taking place throughout daylight hours. The second major formation attack of the day came shortly after noon when KG3 conducted a raid on Rochford. Later in the afternoon a massed free hunt over south Kent drew up No.11 Group fighters, resulting in just the sort of engagement the RAF had been trying to avoid – eight Spitfires and Hurricanes were lost, bringing to 18 the total destroyed during the day, with a further four damaged. Of the 42 Luftwaffe aircraft destroyed or damaged 22 were Bf109s, most of them lost because of the added task of defending the Bf110s and flying close formation on the bombers.   .

With the Bf109 squadrons concentrated in the Pas de Calais Kesselring had an opportunity to step up his attacks on No.11 Group's airfields, still considered to be the primary target for defeating the RAF. With such large forces at his disposal Kesselring could increase the frequency of bombing raids; and every raid required Bf109 escorts. Until now he had phased daily raids at intervals of approximately two to three hours, but from 30 August he scheduled them closer together to increase the pressure on Fighter Command. This, in turn, had repercussions for the Jagdwaffe. Daily raids were planned the preceding evening, but events would invariably result in plans being changed. When raids were reported not to have achieved their objectives reserve Gruppen would be alerted to conduct a repeat less than two hours later, forcing the fighter wings to scramble together escort squadrons on demand. Subordinated in this way to the bomber effort, the Jagdflieger were at times under almost as frenzied pressure to get off the ground at short notice as were their counterparts across the Channel.

In one typical plan, implemented on Friday 30 August, Kesselring ordered three transecting raids across Kent at intervals of 30 minutes. First, three Gruppen of about 60 Bf109s came in low at 10.30 to excite the Fighter Command stations at Biggin Hill, Kenley, Northolt, Croydon, North Weald, Rochford and Hornchurch. The fighters were already over England when 70 Heinkels and Dorniers streamed across the Channel at 11.00 accompanied by another 60 Bf109s and 30 Bf110s; and a third wave came across at 11.30, comprising Ju88s, Bf109s and Bf110s. While such saturation attacks were effective at confusing No.11 Group about who was where in the skies above south-east England, virtually every Bf109 available was tied up.

The first series of raids was followed from 13.30 by successive waves of fighters and fighter-bombers at 20-minute intervals until 16.00, when the third sequence got under way – again calling for large numbers of Bf109s. Over the next two hours Luftflotte 2 threw 19 Gruppen of bombers and fighters into the skies over England, eclipsing all previous raids on a single day. RAF Fighter Command was pushed hard to mount 1,054 sorties, with almost all the 22 squadrons involved flying at least twice and some four times during the day. For its part the Luftwaffe flew 1,345 sorties, involving a lot of careful scheduling from the Bf109 wings involved.

It usually took about 40 minutes to get each 109 back into the air. With a combat turnaround taking a minimum two hours (80 minutes flying time plus the 40 minutes on the ground), three echelons of Bf109s were in flow at any one moment during Kesselring's new compressed raid schedules: one returning from a mission, one turning around from the previous mission, and one working up for take-off. Because of this, if 120 Bf109s were involved in each of three successive waves, 360 aircraft were committed. In reality a further 60 aircraft were needed, because the attrition rate was running at 15 per cent. On a day when three major raids were planned, more than 400 Bf109s were tied up at any one time.

The big raids of 30 August meant that each Jagdgeschwader could only put up one Gruppe to each bomber wave. Fortunately, there were fewer losses than there had been two days before. On the day Kesselring tried his experiment only 13 Bf109s were lost, of which three were from JG26. Only one had been lost in combat, the other two ditching in the sea when they ran out of fuel. This was becoming a serious problem; the driving imperatives to achieve combat victories and to stay close to the bombers all the way were forcing pilots beyond the safety margins.

The Jagdwaffe was beginning to feel real pressure from the attrition. Galland was particularly concerned that he was being starved of the men he needed to carry the battle to the enemy. During these days when it seemed that the fight was getting ever harder he was finding that he could not rely on the training schools to give him the calibre of pilots he needed. He was not interested in turning JG26 into a conversion unit, and would resist the temptation to place inexperienced men in combat squadrons in the hope that they would live long enough to learn from the experts on the job.

On 31 August the pressure continued. Airfield attacks were to predominate, together with the free hunts which these days often failed to tempt Fighter Command into costly battle. Still living out of makeshift facilities, the Staffeln spread out around the farmland of the Pas de Calais were linked by telephone to the feverish activity at Geschwader headquarters. There Galland tried to match available aircraft to calls from Luftflotte 2. At first light the planned raids called for three JG26 support operations during the day, two on bomber escort and a third on free hunt. The first raid involved around 200 aircraft and reached the coast just before 09.00. One stream of Dorniers made for North Weald, and JG26 was soon engaging 12 Hurricanes from No.56 Sqn; in the ensuing scrap the Bf109s shot down four fighters within five minutes, and the Dorniers severely damaged the airfield buildings.

Galland's judicious planning managed to get another escort operation up for the early afternoon when Dorniers and Heinkels were sent to raid Biggin Hill and

Hornchurch. Shortly after noon the raid assembled with a massive escort of Bf109s and Bf110s; from 12,000ft the Heinkels bombed Biggin Hill, hitting several key buildings including the sector control room, but met stiff resistance from seven Hurricanes of No.253 Sqn, which shot down one Heinkel in return for one fighter.

Later that day Galland got a call from Genmaj Theo Osterkamp at Jafu 2 in Wissant asking for escort of a previously unscheduled operation; Kesselring's headquarters had decided to mount a return raid on Hornchurch with Dorniers from KG76. I. and II./JG26 would fly close escort, III.Gruppe a detached escort for this operation. Shortly after 18.00 the bombers met up with the three Gruppen and moved west. The raid was supported by Bf110 Jabos with their own protective screen of Bf109s. Over the Channel III.Gruppe climbed high above the Dorniers, gaining 10,000ft on the bombers before they crossed the coast. Just before they reached London the RAF fighters came up in swarms, their climb veiled by cloud; during the bombers' run in Spitfires of No.222 Sqn attacked, and the fight was soon joined by others from No.202. The advantage of height allowed the Staffeln of III./JG26 to swoop on selected flights of attackers, and within minutes two Spitfires of No.222 Sqn had been sent out of the battle. With some damage to Hornchurch, the raid was not a failure; but the intended obliteration of the fighter field had not been achieved. On the way back another Spitfire was sent down. The bombers limped along, stragglers trying hard to catch up, while fighters bobbed and weaved to keep in contact; the RAF's instructions to stay on their own side of the Channel had not been copied to the Luftwaffe.

Although many JG26 pilots had seen bombers falling on the way back out of the target area, in fact only one of 'their' Dorniers was lost that evening. There were victories to celebrate, and in the usual fashion that was a process which went on long into the night. Galland made a visit to several Staffeln that evening; he congratulated Oblt Muencheberg on a victory, and gave Oblt Eberling very special recognition for shooting down two Spitfires. Losses during the day had been particularly heavy for the Jagdflieger, with 22 Bf109s lost and seven in various states of damage. JG26 had lost four Bf109s and three pilots, only one of whom was plucked from the Channel. The Bf110s, despite their protection, had lost 12 either destroyed or seriously damaged. The RAF lost 34 fighters destroyed and three damaged.

The following day, 1 September, JG26 flew only one escort operation, but this led to furious fighting; the Geschwader claimed 11 kills for the loss of one pilot, Oblt Jupp Buerschgens from 7.Staffel. The following day the wing stood down, using the time for the usual mix of rest and administration.

The time was approaching when Hitler had to make up his mind about invasion. The OKW had released the final draft of its military plan for securing a foothold in southern England, and on 1 September the Kriegsmarine began to move its invasion shipping from North Sea ports to the embarkation points in north and west France. Two days later Hitler approved a directive from Keitel advising all senior staff that 'The earliest day for the sailing of the invasion fleet has been fixed as 20 September, and that of the landing for 21 September. Orders for the launching of the attack will be given on D-20, presumably, therefore, on 11

September.' Hitler still had very justified misgivings over 'Sealion', and was still prevaricating.

The relentless effort to destroy Fighter Command continued on 3 September, and JG26 flew an escort for 54 Dorniers returning from a raid on Essex, Kent and the Thames Estuary. The raiders were late in assembling, delayed by the 80 or so escorting Bf110s; by the time they arrived over south-east England an hour had passed, and some 122 RAF fighters were forming a defensive screen from north-east of London to the south-east coast. One group of Dorniers hit North Weald from 15,000ft, bombing just about every building on the airfield and cratering the runways. Frustrated by gun stoppages on their newly cannon-armed Spitfires, No.19 Sqn had to disengage and leave the returning bombers to Hurricanes from six other squadrons and Spitfires from No.603.

By this time II./JG26 were over Essex and the Thames Estuary to cover the bombers' return, and tangled with the RAF interceptors. Fresh on the scene, the Bf109s tore in and gave a good account of themselves, although only two kills were credited, both to Hptmn Erich Bode[4]. Galland's tactic of launching escorts to cover returning bombers was not common practice, but it was one way of getting round the Bf109's limited combat radius. Escorts covering the outbound leg were being covered by Bf110s with longer range, which were themselves covered by Bf109s flying straight to the fight from France. The net effect was to give the Bf109s an improved combat endurance where it mattered, although it increased the number of aircraft needed for each raid.

For their exertions JG26 were ill rewarded over the next two days. Despite numerous escorts and a couple of free hunts Galland's boys were unable to find the RAF. Unknown to them the battle was about to take a new turn, and the decisions taken would finally doom Goering's hopes.

* * *

The salvation of Dowding's fighter airfields can be traced directly to the second RAF bomber raid on Berlin on the night of 28-29 August. Although militarily insignificant, it infuriated Hitler and affronted Goering, calling into public question his boasts about inviolate air space. On the morning of 31 August Hitler had given permission to extend the air war to British cities; two days later he sanctioned an increase in the production of 1,000kg (2,200lb) high explosive bombs specifically designed for use against buildings. The public declaration came during a surprise visit to the Sportpalast in Berlin-Schoeneberg on 4 September (the day after another night visit by the RAF). Ridiculing Churchill and vilifying his 'night pirates', Hitler threatened: 'If the British air force drops two, three or four thousand kilos of bombs, then we will drop 150,000, 180,000, 230,000, 300,000 or 400,000 kilos, or more, in one night!'

It took time to reorganise the air campaign, and Goering was reluctant to have his primary objective changed by a political whim. He decided to take a more direct hand in the air assault on Britain, to hasten the success which he felt was only a matter of time. There had been conflicting intelligence, and Goering had not used the best sources for an objective overview of the battle.

At his insistence, the initial claims logged by the Jagdflieger returning from sorties were teletyped to Berlin within hours so that he could have immediate kill figures and preliminary information about the raids. Early, unqualified estimates of kills and raid damage were routinely optimistic. Galland had warned against sending these unchecked figures to Berlin, and twice tried to hold them back for verification by claiming a communications failure, but was quietly warned by Osterkamp that Berlin interpreted the absence of the evening figures as a sign that little or no fighting had taken place. Galland pointed out in vain, to Jafu 2 and to the RLM, that they could not expect to fight a war successfully if these analyses were flawed. Because the figures Goering seized upon were in excess of the real losses suffered by Fighter Command, he came to believe that the claims were fraudulent. As tempers frayed in communications back and forth between the RLM, Luftflotten headquarters in Belgium and the Jafu office at Wissant, Goering's frustration was vented in rage at the fighter squadrons in the Pas de Calais. Believing, like all inept leaders, that he was betrayed by incompetent subordinates, he decided to move his headquarters to The Hague and take direct control of the air war. On 6 September Goering's great war train pulled into Holland and 'Fatty', as Moelders called him, bore down upon his Jagdflieger – a prospect which pleased no one.

Goering had resisted the redirection of effort outlined by Hitler, believing that the RAF must surely succumb soon, a view endorsed by several senior staff members. Yet others, such as Jeschonnek, had campaigned for a major assault on London from the outset. Over the next few days the OKL would restructure the allocation of units and give Luftflotte 2 the task of hitting military and other strategic targets in the area of greater London, while Luftflotte 3 would concentrate on the City, government buildings and the docks. A militarily sterile emphasis on reprisal raids on civilian targets would divert priority from the destruction of the RAF, although Goering still believed that Fighter Command might be tempted into unwise battle if the very capital were threatened. In practice, it would spread the bombers over a wider range of targets and deplete reserves which could otherwise have been thrown against the airfields. This would prove crucial to the survival of Fighter Command.

Before the Blitz on London began Kesselring mounted a series of phased air raids on south-eastern England from early on 6 September. Schoepfel's III./JG26 accompanied the first bombers, which left the Pas de Calais shortly after 09.00 and headed for airfield targets. The Dorniers brought Hurricanes of No.73 Sqn ripping into the close escort over Kenley; within a few moments three pilots from Muencheberg's 7.Staffel were shot down and a fourth Bf109 from 9.Staffel was damaged. Losses overall were high that day, with 21 Bf109s destroyed and six damaged – JG26 and JG53 lost six each and JG27 nine. The RAF lost 23 fighters with three damaged. The Kampfgeschwader lost ten bombers, seven of them to flak. The numbers were running against the RAF, however; had Luftwaffe intelligence known the truth, raid policy would almost certainly not have been changed.

* * *

On Saturday 7 September, the day after Goering arrived in The Hague, the Luftwaffe opened its major assault on London; personally stage-managed by the Reichsmarschall, it was the biggest raid to date. The morning was quiet enough as Goering's personal train conveyed him and his retinue to the Pas de Calais, where he was to witness the armada of almost 1,000 aircraft thundering overhead on their way to bomb the capital of the British Empire. After a long lunch on his train, during which he proffered his views on how Britain was to be subjugated, he drove by car to the coast. Close by the lighthouse at Cap Gris Blanc he stood looking across at the white cliffs of Dover – clearly visible in the bright sunlight – with Kesselring and a knot of other senior officers.

JG26 was one of seven Jagdgeschwader assigned to escort massed formations of 348 Dorniers, Heinkels and Junkers. Just about every bomber in the sector was up and operating. In addition Bf110 and Bf109 escorts numbering an additional 617 fighters were vectored on to the bomber streams – almost the whole of Germany's fighter strength on the Western Front. Galland's wing was buried well back, protecting the Ju88s.

In England the sector controllers put fighters up until, one by one, all 21 squadrons within a 112km (70 mile) radius of London were in the air. Advancing on them across the south-eastern tip of England was a massed formation stepped up from 4270m to 7300m (14,000ft to 24,000ft), extending 64km (40 miles) across and 32km (20 miles) in depth; when the first raiders were crossing the white cliffs the rear groups were just falling into formation over the Pas de Calais, an endless carpet of bombers.

It was about 16.30 local time when this daunting mass of nearly 1,000 aircraft was sighted by the RAF fighters over Sheppey. The first bombs to fall hit the Ford works at Dagenham, followed by the gas works at Beckton. The afternoon was bright and the skies were largely clear with only scattered cloud. The great reaches of the Thames, probing like fingers into the Woolwich basin, made for easy identification of targets in the docks and the East End. Factories and warehouses from Woolwich to the Tower of London were set alight in a conflagration similar to those of Warsaw and Rotterdam. The fires spreading out of control gave a strange glow in the east of the late afternoon sky as the lead formations turned in a huge circle for the return home.

Up above, great battles of 30 to 50 aircraft developed all across the greater London area. Adolf Galland never forgot the sight of London burning beneath the evening sky, and admitted to a pang of horror at the thought that such punishment could ever be meted out to a German city. By 18.00 the huge air fleet, now split up and no longer in precise formations, had returned across the Channel, leaving the fires to rage behind them. There were few fighters to hunt them home; out of ammunition and fuel, their pilots exhausted, they had landed as the bombers turned for France. Less than two hours later it began again, as 318 Heinkels and Dorniers from 11 Gruppen stoked up the fires and extended the conflagration into one continuous inferno stretching for nine miles. The scenes on the ground were beyond all previous imagination; the very Thames itself caught fire. The raids continued until first light; and would go on for the next 69 nights, every night without fail, and then on again after a tiny respite until May 1941.

Luftwaffe losses for that first great London raid of 7 September were not as high as they might have been: just 15 Bf109s and eight Bf110s destroyed, with four and two damaged. The bombers, too, got off relatively lightly considering the numbers involved, with 13 destroyed and 14 damaged. The RAF lost 31 Spitfires and Hurricanes and 11 were damaged.

At the end of the first day of the raids on London Galland had grave misgivings about the redirection of effort; he had already guessed that to abandon the destruction of the RAF at this stage in an attempt to break British morale was futile. Revenge and frustation were no substitute for clear-headed strategy. The change of policy would be enshrined in an OKL directive on 9 September, to the effect that 'The destruction of London will be accompanied wherever possible by raids upon the armament areas and harbour facilities throughout England as hitherto.' In other words, the terror-bombing of the British people was to assume priority over the strategic assault on Britain's war-fighting potential. There was no mention any more of destroying the RAF.

Although he still resisted the delays inherent in No.12 Group's 'big wing' policy, AVM Park now switched to using paired squadrons whenever warning time allowed. This worked well against the Geschwader formations on escort or free hunt operations. Fighter Command remained resilient despite the attrition it was suffering; the respite from attacks on its own bases was put to good use. Galland sensed that the change in No.11 Group's tactics meant increased availability of aircraft and pilots. He would always remain convinced that it had been a close-run thing.

With Goering in the Pas de Calais it was inevitable that the Reichsmarschall would visit his fighter wings, and so it was that one day he arrived in his train to meet Moelders and Galland, to inspect aircraft and discuss the air war. Predictably, Goering was looking for a reason why the Jagdflieger had not yet managed to annihilate Fighter Command, and predictably, the fighter leaders repeated their perplexity over the ability of the RAF to vector fighters on to the Luftwaffe formations. Then Goering said something which truly stunned both Galland and Moelders: he asked them for their views about shooting at baled-out British pilots on their parachutes. Both men forcefully rejected such barbarity; and after a few uncomfortable seconds of silence Goering put his hand on Galland's shoulder and said that this was what he had thought he would say. He did not say he disapproved, but nothing more was ever said on the matter.

It was during this meeting that Moelders and Galland were able to present their shared concerns about the way the close escort mission sapped the capability of the Bf109 by tying it too closely to the slow bomber formations. Again, Goering would have none of it, insisting that the duty of the fighters was to support the bombers, and that fighters were essentially subordinate, whether in tactical or strategic operations. Goering was somewhat aroused at what he considered an impertinence from his young wing commander; he admired Galland's flair for combat, but suggested that his personal victory log was of secondary importance to the overall offensive against Britain.

At this point Goering turned away dismissively and pointedly asked Moelders what he needed to get the job done. Ever the diplomat, Moelders bent forward slightly in deference and said that he would like a ready supply of the Bf109E-4/N variant with the new DB601N high compression engine; that would help widen the gap between the performance of the British fighters and an already superior German aircraft. Turning back, Goering looked at Galland: 'And you?' Galland looked him straight in the eye: 'I'd like some Spitfires for my Geschwader,' he replied. Goering returned his look, his cheeks growing redder; slapped his baton into his left palm; drew a single long, deep breath; then turned on his heels and walked away.

What Galland had meant was that he would really like an aircraft that could turn in peak performance for the operational tasks the Jagdflieger were being asked to perform. He liked the Bf109 as an interceptor operating at full bore, but not as a defensive aircraft lazing around the sky at two-thirds throttle. It was a simple fact that the Spitfire had the edge in manoeuvrability at the height and speed of the bomber formations where close escort duty now confined his pilots; and he resented his men having to attempt a task mismatched to their equipment.

During their brief discussions Goering had said nothing about the possible invasion. Hitler, unconvinced as ever that the Luftwaffe would be able to destroy the RAF, seems by now to have virtually abandoned any thought of it. Three days before the OKL formalised the redirection of the bombing effort, Adm Raeder noted in his diary: 'The Fuehrer's decision to land in England is still by no means settled, as he is firmly convinced that Britain's defeat will be achieved even without the landing.' On 10 September – the day before the deadline for giving a ten-day notification to implement 'Sealion' – Hitler decided to postpone the decision until the 14th, the day before what history records as the pivotal date in the Battle of Britain. On the 12th Hitler notified his service chiefs that he wanted to meet them over lunch on the 13th and at a full war conference the following day; he wanted concise and accurate information for a final assessment of the 'Sealion' question.

On the evening of the 12th Goering demanded as much information as possible about the status of the air war; Kesselring, Sperrle and Stumpff were ordered to send in situation reports covering the last six days. I. and II.Fliegerkorps provided estimates of bomb damage; from Wissant Osterkamp asked his wing commanders for detailed loss and claim records in order to refine the figures sent each evening to Berlin. Galland spent that evening going over the returns for the past five days of operations.

The rate of claims had slowed considerably since the close escort of bombers achieved unchallenged priority. Since beginning this phase on 7 September JG26 had not lost a single Bf109 in combat, but its claims in fact still outstripped those of the other Jagdgeschwader. This was an achievement, especially since experience was teaching the bomber pilots a dislike for the flak batteries and they were flying at higher altitude to escape the less powerful guns. This had the effect of reducing their optimum fuel-management cruising speed, which made it harder still for the Bf109s to maintain close escort position.

Instrumental to the pending tri-service discussions was a report from HQ Naval Group West on 12 September that British naval activity had 'assumed major significance. The harbours at Ostend, Dunkirk, Calais and Boulogne cannot be used as night anchorages for shipping because of the danger of English bombings. Units of the British Fleet are now able to operate almost unmolested in the Channel.' When Hitler had lunch with his commanders the following day he announced that he was on the verge of abandoning 'Sealion'.

At the meeting on the 14th Adm Raeder passed him a memorandum to the effect that 'the present air situation does not provide conditions for carrying out the operation.' Among his reasons for hesitation Hitler made the frank admission that 'Our own reports of successes do not give a completely reliable picture.' When he mentioned the prospect of breaking the will of the British people through air attacks inducing 'mass hysteria', Jeschonnek and Raeder urged all-out terror-bombing of British cities; Hitler emphasised the importance of hitting military targets, however, and wanted 'bombing with the object of causing a mass panic ... left to the last.' At the end of the Fuehrer conference a directive was issued postponing a decision for a further three days. The German Naval War Diary for 17 September states, almost as a resigned afterthought: 'The Fuehrer ... decides to postpone Sealion indefinitely.'

The real loser in this game of charades was Goering, who became increasingly bitter about the inability of his Luftwaffe to carry out his demands. The survival of Fighter Command and Hitler's reference to 'unreliable reports' cut Goering to the quick. In his view the Jagdflieger had failed doubly: to destroy Fighter Command in the air, and to defend the bombers. He broke faith with good men who had done his bidding and who had suffered because of it; the consequent recriminations were deep and wounding, and destroyed a loyalty to which Goering had been blind.

Among the junior front line commanders no one had known any details about 'Sealion'; Galland and his men would frequently fly over the massed barges and ships, but knew nothing of the timing. Galland had been informed at length about these plans only when a special commission had visited JG26 and informed him that his Geschwader had been singled out to make the first landing in England after a successful invasion. Given minute instructions on how to prepare all his equipment and supplies for the trip across the Channel, he admits to having been sceptical: every day he faced RAF fighters whose behaviour gave him no reason to believe in any imminent invasion. He went through the motions of preparation, but did nothing which would reduce his wing's immediate operational capabilities. He found coping with the strain on his men and machines of three or four operations a day over southern England a sufficient preoccupation.

Notes to Chapter 12

1 Goering recalled to Galland later in the war that a member of the RLM planning staff had worked out a scheme to completely ground the RAF within five days by bombing every rubber factory in Britain, and dropping delayed action fragmentation mines all across Britain's airfields to strip the tyres from fighters' landing gear. Goering added that he had placed the man under psychiatric care.

2 The Defiant, like the Bf110, was the product of a mistaken prewar concept which saw a

tactical role for relatively slow but heavily armed two-seat fighters. It mounted a manned four-gun power-operated turret immediately behind the pilot. When it first went into action in May 1940 its superficial similarity to the Hurricane allowed it some success against confused enemy pilots; as soon as it was recognised, however, the Defiant was doomed. The two squadrons deployed during the Battle of Britain suffered crippling losses, and the Defiant was relegated to night patrols.

3 L7021 (Sqn Ldr G.Garvin survived; Flt Lt R.Ash struck tail baling out, killed).

4 One was X4277 flown by Plt Off Richard Hillary, No.603 Sqn, who baled out severely burned; he wrote a famous account, *The Last Enemy*, before dying in a crash in January 1943.

CHAPTER 13

15 September–5 December 1940

In the week after the first big raid on London the bombers were hard pressed to maintain the pace of the attack. Weather conditions were often unacceptable. Raids were put together from smaller groups given specific targets: aircraft factories on the 9th, London factories and warehouses on the 11th, and radar stations on the 14th. JG26's period without losses ended on 14 September when both Oblt Daehne, Stab/I.Gruppe adjutant, and a pilot from 9.Staffel failed to return. An improvement in the weather allowed the resumption of massed raids on 15 September – the day which, with the hindsight which is the luxury of historians, would be recorded as the pivotal point of the Battle of Britain. The reduced level of Luftwaffe activity over the preceding week had given Dowding the opportunity to re-deploy his squadrons and some of his most experienced pilots, and for all of them to get some desperately needed rest.

Sunday 15 September dawned bright and clear over the Pas de Calais and southern England. The assembly began around mid-morning, as the Dornier Do17s trundled down from their bases to designated rendezvous points. Some bombers missed their rendezvous, and others were not aware of how tight they should hold formation for the ascending fighters, and in the confusion it took time to get the formations in order. The usual practice had been for the fighters to formate upon the bombers during the Channel crossing, converging into their appropriate positions by the time the bombers entered the Thames estuary or crossed the coast; today the masses of fighters formed up behind the Pas de Calais, and it was only after 11.00 that about 100 Dorniers from KG3, accompanied by large numbers of Bf109s, crossed the English coast.

No fewer than nine squadrons of Hurricanes and Spitfires hurled themselves upon the escorts with such force that they broke right through to the bombers. Within minutes more than 160 RAF fighters were mauling the Dorniers, breaking up their tight formation, sending some down in flames and others weaving off in desperate efforts to shake off interceptors. The Bf109s scattered, reformed, and hit back hard. Led by the legless Sqn Ldr Douglas Bader, the two Spitfire and three Hurricane squadrons of the Duxford Wing swung round to hit the flank of the ragged bomber formations and carved out individual aircraft at will. The force of the attack dispersed the bombers across the sky; the shepherding Messerschmitts lost their flock; and the battle quickly broke up into a series of separate fights between small groups of aircraft. The disorganised bombers dropped their bombs all over London, from Lewisham to Westminster; ten of them were shot down or crashed later in France. The wall of fighters put up by AVM Park had prevented a concentrated attack on selected targets, and the weight of Bader's wing had, on this occasion, achieved decisive results.

Park was ready for a repeat raid which, even as the first formations were returning, was already building up across the Channel. By 13.45 the RAF was back in the air and within 30 minutes Fighter Command had 170 Hurricanes and Spitfires stacked up across Kent and the Thames Estuary. This time more than 150 Dorniers and Heinkels from KG2, KG53 and KG76, escorted by 150 Bf109s from Galland's JG26 and Trautloft's JG54, approached London across ten miles of sky. For about ten minutes, as they approached the East End, RAF fighters harried the three massed formations without seriously disrupting them. Then Bader's five Duxford squadrons hit, joined moments later by six more from No.11 Group and two from No.10 Group. Once again, more than 600 aircraft were caught in a whirling maelstrom in the sky.

Galland fastened on to a squadron of Hurricanes about 760m (2,500ft) below him and pushed hard forward on the stick, bunting to a steep dive as the screaming engine dragged him down with ever increasing speed. Selecting the left-hand flight of three aircraft he began firing at 245m (800ft), and kept firing until he was almost inside the cockpit of the Hurricane. Such had been his speed that the Hurricane pilot did not have time to react before his aircraft began to shed large chunks of metal in all directions. Flicking the 109 to starboard, Galland shot past his quarry and immediately found himself in the midst of the other Hurricanes, stepped down in flights. In a split second he selected the right-hand fighter and spent the remaining energy of the dive to gain rapidly on it from above and behind, shattering it with his cannon and spraying the fuselage with machine gun fire until it burst into flames and nosed over. Hauling back on the stick in a 4G pull-up, Galland rammed forward the throttle and at the top of a brief climb did a 190-degree wing-over. He could see two parachutes drifting in the sky almost 600m (2,000ft) below – a double kill within ten seconds.

Pulling away from the rest of the squadron Galland found himself in relatively free air; he looked around, inverted for a good view below, turned heads-up again and made for the stream of Dorniers flying irregular patterns away from London. Gaining altitude above the bombers, he had a brief moment of contact when a Spitfire shot past him and dived for home. Far below, streaming in across the patchwork of the English countryside, were Bf109s and Bf110s sent to fend off enemy fighters attacking stragglers. The flight back to Audembert was a shambles of fighters and bombers clawing their way into ragged formations, the 109s gathering with the twin-engined Dorniers and Heinkels in some attempt at a defensive formation. This time 19 bombers failed to return, a further seven limping home trailing smoke. As they returned to their cornfields in the Pas de Calais the fighter pilots knew that the end of this battle was nowhere near. The defence put up against these major raids was as vigorous as anything they had experienced before. But there was more to come before the day was out. Around 15.00 that afternoon, 27 Heinkels from III./KG55 set course toward Southampton before veering off to hit Portland's naval installations, where they tangled with Spitfires from No.152 Squadron. Just after they withdrew the radar plotted

18 Bf110 fighter-bombers from EGr210 making for the vital Supermarine works at Woolston where Spitfires were produced; they were turned back by flak from the Solent, and the factory was spared. As they turned for home the last of the day raiders had done their worst. In all, the Luftwaffe had lost 58 aircraft of which 23 had been Bf109s; a further 22 had been damaged, three of them single-seaters. RAF Fighter Command had lost 27 aircraft that day, with a further eight damaged. It was demoralising and unnerving, especially for the bomber crews. The Heinkels and Dorniers limped home across the hungry sea carrying dead and wounded, with engines coughing, smoke coiling from electrical shorts, guns jammed, gaping holes letting in the freezing air. For the Jagdflieger it was dispiriting to know that every time they were tasked with flying close escort for the bombers they would be met by a hundred, perhaps two hundred fighters; and that after giving of their best they would return to the recriminations and accusations of their supreme leader in his gilded railway coach. (To keep abreast of events and control operations planning, Goering had moved his train down to Ronce in Belgium and then to Boulogne; on the 18th he would move to Coudraix near Bordeaux[1].)

There had been nothing to set 15 September dramatically apart as the peak of Britain's fight for survival; but in the Pas de Calais there was no shred of belief in Goering's stubborn insistence that the RAF would be a force no more within four or five days. At Luftflotte 2 headquarters in Brussels on the 16th he once more expressed his faith in the bombers, railing against the Jagdwaffe for their lack of aggression. General Osterkamp, with the moral authority of a distinguished Great War veteran who nevertheless enjoyed the trust of the new young generation of pilots, protested at this simplistic condemnation. He tried to make the Reichsmarschall understand that the complexities of modern aerial combat were not a matter simply of guts, but of logical planning and good intelligence in the service of sound strategy and realistic tactics. The Reichsmarschall simply walked angrily away.

Back on the Channel front, JG26 was holding up well. On 15 September not one 'Schlageter' fighter had gone down or been damaged; on the 16th, when rain and cloud over England kept the bombers back, one Bf109E-1 from 7.Staffel was lost and Uffz Bock became a prisoner of war. The next day JG26 was stood down; there were few losses to either side on the 17th. The nature of the campaign now shifted from massed bomber raids to individual formations of bombers combined with high altitude sweeps by massed formations of Bf109s. Again, the RAF was selective and went for the bombers, all the while conserving and building its resources. By the third week of September, when deteriorating weather anyway prevented the possibility of mass raids, the pattern had become entrenched. A distance between the perceptions of the high command and the squadron officers is suggested by the OKW war diary for 23 September: 'Our forces feel greatly superior to the enemy as before, and there reigns complete confidence in the successful continuation of the air war.'

Nevertheless, there were days when it seemed the fighters could enjoy an Indian summer. When the bombers were grounded and the Bf109s were given free rein, Galland took full advantage of the opportunity to range back and forth over England – and to increase his personal score, gaining on Werner Moelders as the primacy of close escort sorties diminished. Such a free hunt took place on 23 September, when a morning sortie over the Thames Estuary and Kent brought fierce resistance from Spitfires of No.92 Sqn; in the ensuing dogfight a large number of hits were made, one Spitfire pilot being forced down wounded and two Bf109s from 8.Staffel falling[2].

On 20 September Werner Moelders had shot down his 39th and 40th kills – two Spitfires over Dungeness – which qualified him to become the first member of the Luftwaffe to be awarded the coveted Oak Leaves to the Knight's Cross of the Iron Cross. When Galland heard the news he had a case of champagne delivered to JG51 with a curt note to the effect that he was on Werner's tail and his Revi gunsight was switched on! He would only have to wait four days to reach the same number himself.

Tuesday 24 September dawned clear, with coastal haze; the weather forecast prophesied cloud over the Channel but good visibility over south-eastern England. Jafu 2 had received orders the previous afternoon to organise escorts for about 150 bombers in five separate formations across a ten-mile front. Galland led the escort to rendezvous with the bombers behind the Pas de Calais at 09.20 local time, then headed directly for London. The British radar picked them up, and again it was Biggin Hill's No.92 Sqn which took off first; brought forward from its base at Debden, No.17 Sqn was also airborne and heading south. During the fight which followed, Galland was flying high up above the stacks looking for enemy fighters when he saw an incoming squadron of Hurricanes flying in three 'vics' of three aircraft each.

Using his altitude advantage for maximum effect, he bunted the Bf109 and went into a near-vertical dive, gaining speed fast before flattening out dramatically and hauling round on to the tail of one Hurricane (P3878 of No.17 Sqn, flown by Plt Off Harold Bird-Wilson). His opponent was a determined fighter, throwing his aircraft about in violent evasive manoeuvres; he had the knack of seemingly dragging it round by its propeller. He got the advantage of Galland for brief moments, skidding into high-G turns and thrashing the engine until it howled. But within 30 seconds Galland had him under fire and saw strikes on the rear fuselage, machine gun bullets ripping open the taut canvas skin to expose the cage of thin stringers beneath. Unstitching the side of the Hurricane, he saw sparks come off the cowling, and then a wisp of smoke leaking back. Slowly at first, fire glowed under the engine cowling; then the flames spread. Keeping his head, the British pilot kicked his rudder bar and slewed the tail to port, fanning the flames away from the cockpit as he struggled to get out. The long 'glasshouse' canopy came away as the Hurricane flipped on to its back; with flames already coming up under the instrument panel, the pilot unfastened his straps and kicked himself free. He had the presence of mind not to pull the ripcord until he had fallen well clear of the blazing Hurricane; but after a long delay his parachute blossomed and Bird-Wilson drifted into the sea off the Kent coast, to be rescued by a motor torpedo boat[3].

Before Galland arrived back at Audembert he radioed the good news ahead, and when he landed a large group of officers, NCOs and men flocked round his

Bf109E-4. With its familiar yellow nose, 'Schlageter' shield on the forward fuselage, and heavily armed, cigar-chewing mouse painted beneath the canopy, the fighter served as a fitting backdrop to the celebration. Within minutes Oblt Rotenberg, Galland's adjutant, had produced Hptmn Causin bearing a special bottle of champagne; and very soon about 50 men were gathered round him as more bottles were popped. Right there with him as well was his mechanic, Uffz Meyer, who had been with him since he joined JG26 and would remain with him throughout the war. It was a very special party, a spontaneous gathering of men who looked up to their leader and knew that he was bringing credit to them all. Now he would receive the Oak Leaves to the Knight's Cross, reflecting distinction on the 'Schlageter' Geschwader and attracting publicity which they could all share. The serious party took place later that evening, and duly separated the men from the boys.

Galland's score, at 40 aerial victories, now equalled that of the legendary leader Oswald Boelcke of World War I – and, rather more immediately, that of Werner Moelders. Moelders was in Berlin, having been summoned on 22 September to receive his Oak Leaves, and now Galland would be following suit. After telephoning Theo Osterkamp at Jafu 2 he received a telegram that afternoon telling him to report to the RLM in Berlin the following day, whence he would be taken to the Reichskanzlei for a meeting with Hitler.

Although Galland now shared with Moelders the honour of being the highest scoring Luftwaffe pilot, there were challengers coming up fast. Some pilots in his own wing were rising stars; Galland's example had taken root, and like Manfred von Richthofen he watched out for the best pilots in other units and spirited them away to his own Geschwader whenever he could. Less than two weeks earlier Hptmn Gerhard Schoepfel of III./JG26 had been awarded the Knight's Cross for achieving 20 kills, followed three days later by Oblt Muencheberg commanding 7.Staffel and Hptmn Rolf Pingel commanding I.Gruppe[4].

* * *

Early on the morning of 25 September Galland left Audembert for Berlin, flying his own staff aircraft. From the airport he was whisked at high speed to the RLM where he was given his schedule for the day: straight to the Reichskanzlei where he was to be invested, a brief interview with the Fuehrer, and from there to meet with Goering at the Reichsjaegerhof in the Rominterheide – a great East Prussian hunting lodge. When Galland arrived at the Reichskanzlei he was greeted by administrative staff and a photographer; the propaganda machine dearly loved fighter aces, whose pictures often appeared in the newspapers with their respective scores as their fame grew among the population at large. Galland accepted the inevitable with some irritation; he had a natural hunger for the respect of his fellow pilots, but he was embarrassed and resentful when he had to put up with the public adulation of those outside the brotherhood. However, this meeting with Hitler would be no meaningless formality to endure and put behind him.

His brief previous encounters with the Fuehrer had been anti-climactic; but this first genuinely personal interview would help Galland come to terms with his uncertainties about the German leadership, aroused by the handling of the Luftwaffe in the Battle of Britain. When he left this meeting he would feel that a mutual respect had been forged – a respect that on a later date would save his life.

After the investiture Hitler led Galland to a reception room where, with officials and photographer dismissed, they could be alone to talk. Galland had expected the Fuehrer to be rigid and self-opinionated, but the first thing Hitler did once they were alone was to ask about the fighting over Britain. He urged Galland to be frank, and said that he wanted to know how things really were on the Western Front. Disarmed by this calm and friendly approach, Galland told him the truth as he saw it: about the problems they were facing with the escort patrols, about the quality of the fighting airmen they were up against – even about his distaste for the way the German press sneered at the RAF. Galland spoke for several minutes without pause while Hitler sat attentively, watching him with his piercing eyes, every now and then nodding in acknowledgement of his points. Galland had not expected this, and was frankly seduced. After all the recriminations from senior Luftwaffe staff officers and the pontifications of the Reichsmarschall, Hitler alone seemed to completely understand; and not only that, but actually to agree with him.

Then Hitler began to talk, as though admitting the young pilot to secrets, expressing his opinions, hopes and fears. He agreed with Galland's respect for the British, saying how he longed for a peace with England, explaining that his choice of war had been a hard one to make. Galland recalled being surprised that Hitler spoke openly about having contrived to 'make war' rather than having it thrust upon him – the usual form in public statements. He gained an impression of a deeply etched fatalism, of Hitler's belief that he could not escape the burdensome destiny of saving the Germanic race. For Galland it was a bewildering revelation: rather than a politician talking of reversing unjust treaties forced on his country within living memory, here was a man who apparently thought in terms of centuries-long historical imperatives.

It was almost with shock that Galland heard Hitler say that he thought the English were 'a hundred years ahead of Germany', that they had created a great nation-state which would withstand challenges under which other countries would crumble. He told Galland that if this war with England continued it would be a war to the death for one or the other nation: the British, he said, would never give in.

For the rest of his life Adolf Galland would remember how on that Wednesday afternoon he had been drawn under the intensely focused spell of Hitler's personality. All the accumulated bitterness and cynicism fell away. Hitler told him that he and the other young pilots in positions of leadership were part of a great historical movement, born to fulfill the legacy bequeathed by all the great German leaders before them. As for his fears about the problems on the Western Front, Hitler told him to continue his good work, to rise above the trivial everyday irritations and concentrate instead on the broader accomplishments. He told Galland – with complete conviction – how much he respected the dedication of his young fighter pilots.

For an averagely unreflective young man of 28 from an authoritarian background, most of whose experience had been confined to the intense but fairly narrow channels of a life of action, this was, inevitably, a mesmerising encounter. When Hitler finally brought the conversation to a close it seemed to Galland that he had been in that quiet room for an extraordinarily long time.

* * *

Galland left for the short drive to the Ministry of Propaganda in the Wilhelmsplatz, where he met the press in the Theatersaal. Facing a large group of correspondents, some Americans among them, he told them what he had said to Hitler about his respect for the British and his disgust at the way the German press maligned the RAF. Galland hated the press, and it showed; but the newspaper men liked the forthright young major. The ministry taped Galland's brief speech and his answers to questions from the press; it liked him too, despite his opinions about anti-British propaganda, and Goebbels would find reason to have his reporters procure Galland's services for German radio.

Next it was on to the Brandenburg Gate where, resplendent in his best dress uniform and Knight's Cross with silver Oak Leaves, he was photographed once again. Over the next few weeks there would be additional demands; the award apparently required that an official portrait be painted, by the well-known artist Leo Poeten – the first of several.

The following day Galland flew to attend on Goering at the Reichsjaegerhof in East Prussia; and as he approached the impressive doors he met Werner Moelders coming out. Hurrying to his car, Moelders threw a comment to the effect that 'Fatty promised to detain you as long as possible!' With competition between these two now keener than ever, this unavoidable absence from the Western Front denied him any immediate chance to advance his score. Within minutes the Reichsmarschall appeared, dressed for the part in silk blouse, green suede hunting jacket and a long medieval-style hunting knife attached to a broad belt; on his feet were long dark brown hunting boots, and on his head a hunting cap complete with feather. Goering seemed to be in a different world, to have assumed a different personality from the one that had argued with Theo Osterkamp just ten days before.

Goering had a prize for Galland which he knew he would appreciate – a stag of regal proportions, which Galland was to hunt on the morrow. Goering found Galland easy to talk to through their common love of hunting and the countryside. It was a strange relationship: despite their utter difference of character and the gulf which separated their circumstances, Galland found that on these occasions they could get on together well enough at a personal level. (Even his prosecutors at Nuremberg would acknowledge the odd attraction of Goering's personality.) That evening Galland was entertained royally, and subjected to a non-stop flow of verbosity. The Reichsmarschall was not even averse to sharing the confidentialities of his position under Hitler, such as the Nazis' Machiavellian dealings with Gen Franco's Spain and the French Vichy leadership.

The next morning Galland was up at dawn, dressed in considerably less flamboyant hunting attire than his host of the previous evening. He wanted to make an early start back to France, but had been told by Goering that he could not leave the Reichsjaegerhof until he had shot the royal stag; as an added spur, he learned that Moelders had been challenged to accomplish this feat and failed. In any other circumstances Galland would have been delighted to take his time over stalking this fine beast, diverging from the scent to bag the occasional trophy on the way. But this was a race against Moelders, who even now would be back at the head of his Geschwader. As Galland set off into the forest he knew he had to execute this particular kill without delay, and by 10.00 he had bagged his own very special stag. He returned quickly to the great lodge to proclaim his success and take his leave – only to be told that Goering had promised Moelders to keep Galland at the lodge for as long as he himself had been detained! There was nothing for it but to comply, so Galland had another few hours to enjoy the scents and the peaceful sounds of the surrounding woods. He was soon to be dragged back to real life with some brutality.

Late that afternoon of 27 September Goering received the telegrams showing the results of the day's air activity over England. It had been a disastrous sequence of events, and Goering insisted that Galland go over them with him. The daylight raids had begun at around 06.00 British time when reconnaissance aircraft and fighters tried to tempt up Nos.10 and 11 Groups, without success. Little more than two hours later a large raiding party of Jabo Bf110s and Bf109s swept across Kent in a wedge 80km (50 miles) wide, crossing the coast between Dover and Brighton. Some Bf109s had belly tanks fitted, and the dispersed formations remained over southern England for almost an hour, taunting the fighters that came up to hit them. This operation was only a feint: when the Spitfires and Hurricanes landed to refuel and rearm the main raid would cross.

It all went badly wrong: when 55 Ju88s of KG77 arrived over England Nos.10 and 11 Groups had been able to muster around 120 fighters, which quickly knocked out 12 of the bombers and seriously mauled the escorting Bf109s. Further west, 19 Jabo Bf110s and 30 He111s escorted towards Bristol by 27 Bf110 fighters ran headlong into five RAF squadrons at serious cost, although the Parnall aircraft factory nine miles outside the city was bombed. In all, no less than 54 Luftwaffe aircraft had been destroyed and a further 13 damaged; JG52 alone had lost seven of the 18 Bf109s destroyed during the day. RAF Fighter Command had lost 26 with 13 damaged.

What Goering saw in the telegrams from France confused and appalled him. He failed to comprehend the reason for the losses and completely misunderstood the way Fighter Command was responding to the threat. Dimly, Goering began to see that the claims made by the Jagdflieger and the actual kills achieved were not incompatible. The Gruppe intelligence officers needed detailed information about specific combats; when an enemy aircraft fell down the sky from 3,600m (12,000ft), it was impossible to know whether it had recovered or crashed. The process of confirmation took days, sometimes weeks, and in the meantime it was impossible to get an accurate picture of the air war.

Although Goering involved Galland in lengthy conversation about this, the

Reichsmarschall did not want to hear the sober truth: that the RAF was holding out and had passed the peak of its vulnerability. Galland asked if he could leave immediately for the front, and a dispirited Goering agreed.

Packing up the stag's head, Galland began the long flight back to Audembert; but engine trouble forced him to make an emergency landing in fields near a railway station. Bundling his bags and his all-important trophy into a train for the cross-country journey, he found himself distinctly unpopular with his fellow passengers, who protested at the stench from the freshly severed stag's head.

*   *   *

On the day when Galland had been to the Reichskanzlei to receive his Oak Leaves the fighter units from Luftflotte 3 had returned to their original bases in the north-west, the reason for their concentration on the Pas de Calais having disappeared along with the massed daylight bombing raids and the preparations for Operation 'Sealion'. Jagdgeschwader 26 had suffered no losses in the past few days, but on 28 September two pilots from I.Gruppe went down over the Channel in combat with Hurricanes of No.249 Sqn and Spitfires of No.72. There were no casualties on the 29th; but on 30 September Kesselring and Sperrle once again mounted heavy daylight raids. Galland returned and went straight to work.

Activity began in the morning with 200 aircraft raiding London and the south-east. Later that morning Sperrle sent a force of Bf109s from JG2 and JG53 and Bf110s from ZG26 on a free hunt from the Cherbourg peninsula. During the afternoon Kesselring sent across another 300 aircraft, while a large raid during late afternoon hit the Westland works at Yeovil. During the day Galland was involved in a violent clash with Spitfires but was unable to score on his first sortie. For this flight Galland had taken Hptmn Walter Kienzle as his wingman so that he could assess his capabilities. Kienzle was under consideration as a Gruppenkommandeur; unfortunately, he was jumped by a Spitfire of No.222 Sqn and forced to take to his parachute.

Galland was unable to increase his score until the third sortie of the day. Returning from a free hunt, he ran into several Hurricanes and was quickly able to pick out a vulnerable quarry below. Exploiting height and speed advantage, he dived fast and hit the Hurricane from close range, rupturing its oil tank and sending it down in flames. His aircraft covered in grimy oil, Galland dashed for the Channel and was away to Audembert with another victory to his credit. On landing, his mechanics wheeled the Bf109 into a tented area between trees and set about the arduous task of cleaning it up. His aircraft, an E-4 (WNr 5819) had been especially nursed by Meyer and his team of mechanics. With its yellow cowling Galland's 109 sported a black and white spinner, and on the fuselage sides the chevron and two horizontal bars denoting a Geschwaderkommodore.

During 30 September a total of 46 German aircraft were destroyed and 13 damaged, of which 34 were Bf109s; and JG26 had suffered badly. Five Bf109s had been lost and two extensively damaged: in addition to Kienzle, Uffz Perez was missing, Gefr Ziemenz and Gefr Hornatschet were dead, and a wounded pilot had crash-landed his badly shot-up Bf109 at Caffiers. There was much work to organise from Audembert, and the mechanics and fitters were unable to carry out routine servicing for two days. This was the last time the Luftwaffe sent such large raids across the Channel in daylight.

For the Jagdwaffe pilots September had been a disaster. They started the month with a base of 735 pilots available for the 740 operational Bf109s on strength; by the end of the month they had lost 229 men, a staggering 31 per cent. The monthly attrition rate had now reached 23.1 per cent, up from 15 per cent during August and 11 per cent in July. For Galland this began to look like the situation that had faced the fighter units at the end of the Battle of France. There were simply more aircraft being lost than could be immediately replaced from reserve, and too few pilots coming through the training schools. (Had Galland known it, the RAF's attrition rate was even worse: 26 per cent of fighter pilots had been lost in August and 28 per cent in September.)

The wear and tear on aircraft and equipment had been equally bad. Losses during the months of July, August and September for the Luftwaffe as a whole totalled 1,636 aircraft, or 37 per cent of the initial strength three months earlier. Of those 518 were Bf109s, a staggering 47 per cent; when the 185 Bf109s damaged in the same period were included the total reached 64 per cent of initial strength. The total number of aircraft lost since Germany attacked in the West on 10 May had reached 3,064, or 57 per cent of initial strength; the total for Bf109s had reached 775, also 57 per cent. As telling was the availability figure, which by the end of September had dropped to 68 per cent for the fighters and 52 per cent for the bombers.

Galland had made special efforts to maintain a high rate of serviceability, and at JG26 the percentage of available aircraft had gone up from a disappointing 52 per cent at the end of June to 67 per cent at the end of September. Moreover, JG26's attrition was lower, with fewer aircraft shot down and damaged than in other combat units.

As to the impact on the RAF, Fighter Command had lost 847 Hurricanes, Spitfires, Defiants and Blenheim fighters in the three months to the end of September; but these numbers were not relevant to a direct comparison with the Luftwaffe. In addition to the 518 Bf109s lost, the RAF had also destroyed 235 Bf110s and 709 bombers and dive-bombers, a real total of 1,462 Luftwaffe losses against the 847 losses to Fighter Command. As a reflection of how British production matched the loss rate, the number of aircraft available to Fighter Command went up from 871 at the beginning of July to 1,061 at the beginning of August, 1,181 at the end of August and 1,048 at the end of that month. Luftwaffe intelligence knew none of this, and grossly understated the RAF's estimated strength – thus the Jagdfliegers' ironic groans whenever they heard some official boast about 'the last fifty Spitfires'.

For the German fighter pilots the strain of the past three months had been gruelling. Every sortie was a test of human strength, nerves and endurance, and it was taking its toll. Galland felt the pressure bearing down upon him in a way he had not experienced before; and October brought little or no respite in the pace of operations, only in their nature. The longer-range bombers were to strike more distant targets on unescorted night raids. The day fighters would escort Junkers

Ju88s on raids over south-east England; this medium bomber was to serve the Luftwaffe exceptionally well throughout the war, and Galland preferred escorting aircraft of this type to the Dorniers and Heinkels, which were about 80km/h (50mph) slower.

While the hectic pace of combat operations that summer had taken its toll it had also forged relationships. Around him Galland had men who were loyal, committed, and dedicated to seeing that he got the best aircraft, the best engine and the best guns. One such was Uffz Olemotz, Galland's armourer, who personally examined every machine gun cartridge and cannon shell for signs of imperfection before it was loaded into Galland's aircraft. Olemotz was a gentle, sensitive person who lived for his work. He would get very upset if something was wrong with the armament of Galland's aircraft, and would puzzle for hours over minor problems with gun settings or the electrically operated gunsight.

Olemotz was always suggesting ways the major could get the best out of his equipment; and he worked with Galland to procure a small telescopic sight which, he thought, might be an improvement. Olemotz fitted the telescopic sight to the right of the Revi gunsight, mounted so that the front one-third of the tubular housing projected beyond the armoured windscreen. Galland flew it on about five operations, but found it useless and had it removed[5].

Galland encouraged hard play as well as hard work, and whenever opportunity allowed he organised hunting parties. He remained convinced that an eye conditioned to firing at moving game and an instinct for the chase would help develop the necessary skills of the fighter pilot. These outings usually ended with a sizzling barbecue over camp fires in a wooded clearing; they helped relieve the pressure of operations, but Galland knew that what his men really needed was withdrawal from the front for a proper rest.

Early in October Galland had cause to send Werner Moelders a note of commiseration when, on the 6th, his brother Viktor was shot down over England, belly-landing near Hastings and being taken prisoner. (He had some difficulty convincing the RAF interrogators at Cockfosters that he was not his famous brother[6].) Viktor Moelders, Staffelkapitaen of 1./JG51, was flying top cover on that occasion for 2.Staffel operating in the Jabo role. Increasingly during October the Jagdwaffe employed bomb-carrying Bf109E-7 fighters on high altitude Jabo operations across southern England. The policy was that each Geschwader was to include a fixed number of such fighter-bombers, but it was left to individual wings whether to assign an entire Gruppe or one Staffel within each Gruppe. (Perhaps predictably, JG26 would be among the last to comply.)

By the end of the first week in October Galland noticed that the RAF were beginning to put priority on attacking these aircraft; and Jafu 2 stepped up the pace, assigning large numbers of Bf109s to Jabo missions. Ever keen to get height advantage, the Spitfires were pushing higher and higher in an attempt to get above the raiders. AVM Park issued specific instructions that Spitfire squadrons were to ride guard on other squadrons climbing to their maximum altitude. Already, in that first week of the month, some Bf109 Jabo Staffeln were up around 8,500m (28,000ft), and Galland issued orders that when covering the Jabos his fighters were to patrol at 9,750m (32,000ft).

Over the following weeks the Jabo raiders did very little real damage, but they increased the stress on Fighter Command. While daylight raids on London persisted they were not in the numbers seen previously; but the Jabos were coming at such extreme altitude that the long periods on oxygen put the RAF pilots under a new pressure. The call for increasing numbers of Jabo operations brought demands upon JG26 for escort runs.

Each Jabo was equipped to carry either one 250kg (550lb) SC250 bomb, four 50kg (110lb) SC50 bombs or a 250kg (550lb) incendiary. The Jabo Staffel broke down into three Ketten of three aircraft each, which usually flew at altitudes in excess of 7,600m (25,000ft) with their escorts up to 1,800m (6,000ft) higher. Shortly before the target the leader would select the aiming point, and push over into a 45-degree dive with his wingmen on either side. All three would release their loads at around 915m (3,000ft), pull up and turn away. Accuracy was negligible, but the raiders had considerable nuisance value. Most escaped without interception, but the escorting Bf109s worked hard to keep the Spitfires and Hurricanes away. If interceptions did take place they occurred at great altitude, and there was little chance to get confirmation of a kill.

So concerned were the RAF about these raiders that AVM Park instituted a special flight of modified Spitfire Mk.IIs to get up above the Jabo flights and spot for the intercepting squadrons coming up from lower altitude. A new form of fighter control evolved, with observant pilots high above reporting high-flying Bf109s in time for better vectoring. The Bf109E-4/N had the edge over Spitfire and Hurricane variants available during October 1940, and the pressure placed on sector controllers was considerable.

This was a very different kind of air war. It had fewer casualties – JG26 lost only seven pilots during the month of October – but it seemed to the Jagdflieger to be a punishment for the failure of the bombers to complete their task. Galland was furious over the imposition of the fighter-bomber role, and held out for several weeks before he too was forced to incorporate Jabos into JG26 in November. For the pilots these missions had a demoralising effect; they had nothing but contempt for the task, and were unable to see that it could have any material effect on the enemy. In fact it did tie up considerable RAF assets, but these operations were abandoned before they achieved any measurable results.

On 25 October Galland lost three aircraft and three pilots to fighters over the Thames Estuary and Kent, and had two crash-land at Boulogne and Marquise after combat over England. After more than three months of sustained fighting, daily returns were often showing more aircraft lost or badly damaged in accidents than to enemy action. (The Bf109 was not an easy aircraft to handle at take-off and landing, its vicious torque making it notoriously prone to ground-loops and consequently, on rough grass strips, to collapsed landing gear.) On the 27th there were 18 Luftwaffe aircraft damaged, most of them bombers – 16 during taxying, take-off or landing. On the following day 13 out of 21 incidents were engine failures, taxying collisions or damage caused on landing; total losses for the 28th included 14 Luftwaffe aircraft and one RAF fighter.

Despite the growing fatigue of the pilots the combination of high-altitude Jabo runs, occasional free hunts in strength across southern England at relatively low altitude, and escorted raids by medium bombers was continuing to cause the RAF problems. On 27 October Fighter Command mounted 1,007 sorties to cope with these various intrusions, but such were the tactics now used by the Luftwaffe that fewer than 12 German aircraft were destroyed.

The last day of October called to mind the picture of two exhausted, punch-drunk boxers pawing the air. During daylight hours there was little activity; poor weather and a brisk response from Fighter Command deterred Luftwaffe fighters and bombers. However, one RAF Hurricane from No.219 Sqn at Redhill crashed during a night landing in bad weather, and another from No.601 Sqn was damaged in a rough landing at Exeter. As for the Luftwaffe, two Dornier Do17s were lost when they ran out of fuel and crashed; a Junkers Ju88 stalled on take-off at Laon, and a Henschel Hs126 wrote off its undercarriage in a similarly bad take-off at Theville.

Now bomber formations would no longer challenge Fighter Command during daylight, confining their operations to the night-time Blitz on British cities. With the onset of winter bad weather would soon bring a halt to Jabo runs. The British would step up their convoys through the Channel; the Ju87s would resume hit-and-run attacks on them; the RAF would turn its attention to the Stukas; and that, in turn, took the Bf109s back to escorting Stukas, just as in the first days of the Battle of Britain. For the Stuka pilots, too, it was a thankless task, although the short distance they were required to fly did ensure some degree of protection; even with their radar, the British were unable to respond as quickly to Channel raids as they had to the massed bomber formations of August and September.

On 1 November Adolf Galland received another accolade when he was promoted to lieutenant-colonel while still only 28 years of age. This called for another celebration, one more fitting the dignity of an Oberstleutnant – in fact, a double celebration, for on the same day Galland achieved his 50th kill, a Spitfire downed after a furious battle. The German public were given blow-by-blow accounts of his victory, with a commentary on his race with Moelders for the honour of leading ace. Moelders had scored his 54th victory only three days earlier; Galland knew he had to beat him – knew he would beat him. Jagdgeschwader 26 were now flying a mixed bag of missions, but mostly anti-shipping runs. The pilots took little satisfaction from it, and longed for the return of one-to-one combat with Spitfires and Hurricanes. For JG26 the Jabo operations – so long avoided, by every means Galland could devise, and very short-lived due to the weather – began on 7 November when the Geschwader reluctantly received its first E-7s equipped with the drop tank and bomb shackle facility.

* * *

Despite the much changed character of operations JG26 continued to produce pilots of distinction, and Galland had the satisfaction of seeing several reach the 20 kills which qualified them for the Knight's Cross. Oblt Gustav Sprick achieved his twentieth on 1 October; next was Hptmn Walter Adolph, a veteran of the Spanish war. Galland too got a chance to increase his score on 17 November.

Jafu 2 had been requested to put up a detached escort for the special unit

EGr210 and its Bf110 Jabos, scheduled to carry out a raid on Martlesham Heath airfield near Ipswich. As the formation of Bf110s and the Bf109s of JG26 came across the Channel the radar warning brought up Hurricanes from Nos.17 and 257 Squadrons. The pilots from No.17 waded in first; Galland fixed on to the tail of one and soon had it firmly in range, but the first burst from his machine guns sent the British fighter twisting and turning out of the 109's gunsight. It dived away and Galland did not follow, pulling round and catching sight of another Hurricane at his 5 o'clock position. Pushing the stick forward and to the right he banked to starboard, kicked the rudder hard over and turned in a tight, high-speed 5G turn which got him onto the starboard wing of the Hurricane for a traversing shot. Galland was not keen on these extreme defelection angles, but fired as he overshot the British fighter and hauled up into a full turning loop which put him exactly where he wanted to be: 180m (600ft) behind, slightly below and gaining fast. With a three-second burst he caught the canopy dead centre, and his next burst hit the engine. He could see the propeller winding down as he throttled back and left the Hurricane alone to nose gently over, its pilot taking to the silk almost immediately. In this battle, of which his was only one engagement, Galland had the grim disappointment of seeing three enemy fighters shoot down a Bf110 apiece.

As they turned back No.257 Sqn were upon them less than two minutes later. In a furious free-for-all Bf109s and Hurricanes twisted and rolled, each fighting for the advantage in a tight corner of sky too crowded for comfort. Going for the escorting Bf109s, the Hurricanes tore in as the Jagdflieger tried desperately to form a defensive screen for the Bf110s. Galland found another Hurricane cutting right across his Revi sight; he pulled round, got on its tail and shot it down all in a moment, immediately twisting and craning to look for others. Flashing a quick glance at the falling Hurricane he saw the pilot scramble free and bale out; but then another caught his attention, a lone machine making fast for a patch of cloud. Aiming for the spot where he thought it would reappear he found himself almost within range but held his nerve, closed that crucial extra distance, and fired when he was sure of it. Debris started breaking away immediately as he pressed home his attack. The pilot was injured, he could tell that, and Galland's machine guns put him out of his pain when the Hurricane's cowling tore off and smashed into the canopy. On the return home to the Pas de Calais the Hurricanes pursued the fleeing Bf109s, several of which were out of ammunition; one of their number – Oblt Eberhard Henrici, Staffelkapitaen of 1./JG26 – was shot down into the sea.

Back at Audembert it was time to reckon up the victories and the cost; time for a maintenance man to paint three more bars on the rudder of Galland's aircraft; and time, sadly, to find a replacement for 1.Staffel's lost leader. Galland kept a file in his office drawer which contained the names and units of men he had seen in action, or about whom he had heard good things in conversation with his fellow commanders. They always knew what 'Dolfo' Galland was up to, and always waited with baited breath to see where he would strike next. In this case he was to secure the services of Oblt Josef 'Pips' Priller, who only the previous month had been awarded the Knight's Cross (and who one day would take over the mantle of command himself).

As autumn gave way to winter on the Channel coast, fog and rain rolled in across the cliff tops and the muddied turf where once rich cornfields had waved under an azure sky. Usually these days JG26 were called upon to escort, or to fly, the dreaded and militarily pointless Jabo runs to London. Always the Spitfires were waiting for them, hanging high above the Thames. Always the Bf109s would stick close above their bomb-burdened charges, defying the British fighters to attack – which they always did. But even now the occasional chance for a free hunt made it all worthwhile; and such an opportunity came during the late morning of 5 December 1940.

At around midday that Thursday the Geschwader challenged the suspect weather and turned out in force. Galland had cleared the operation with Jafu 2 at Wissant, which had received approval from Brussels for an offensive sweep over southern England by all three Gruppen. The Geschwader made a fast run across the Channel, and caught the Hurricanes of No.253 Sqn up from Kenley. Two III.Gruppe pilots had unsuccessful fights, but a third shot down a Hurricane, and another managed to force one down damaged. Meanwhile the other two Gruppen were being followed by sector control, who had alerted No.64 Sqn at Hornchurch and Nos.74 and 92 at Biggin Hill. All three Spitfire squadrons came upon the intruders in successive waves.

In the first attack the Spitfires pulled round the Bf109s and attacked from the flank, groups of three or four picking out Schwaerme of German fighters. Galland pulled up and over, diving on one Spitfire with which he only narrowly missed colliding, hurtling down and under his wingman to come back up behind a third. Firing from close range he managed to get a row of direct hits on the fuselage, and from the crazy way the aircraft fell he knew he had killed or severely injured the pilot. Another Bf109 was in the process of knocking down a second Spitfire. After a fierce contest with more waves of attacking Spitfires Galland pulled round and gathered up a group of stray Bf109s to head back in the general direction of Folkestone, where one of his men was shot down. Crossing the Channel another 109 damaged in combat had difficulty staying airborne, but the wounded pilot, Ofw Robert Menge, finally managed to nurse it back to base. Yet another Bf109 had to belly-land at Wissant.

In this combat Galland had achieved his 57th confirmed victory, which made him the highest scoring pilot in the Luftwaffe – and of all combatant powers at this date in war. It was no longer just with Werner Moelders that he was competing. Maj Helmut Wick of JG2 'Richthofen' had reached a score of 56 on 28 November, only minutes before falling to the guns of Flt Lt John Dundas. At 25 the youngest major in the Luftwaffe, Wick had scored 37 victories in the three months prior to his death, and had been recognised with the Oak Leaves to his Knight's Cross on 6 October. Moelders now had 54 kills to his credit; but Adolf Galland was, at last, the first and the best among his distinguished peers.

Notes to Chapter 13

1 As much as anything else, Goering's movements seem to have had the aim of allowing him to conveniently transport additions to his collection of art looted from the

occupied countries. With remarkable insensitivity, Goering would later show Galland around a gallery of treasures gathered during his meddling in the Pas de Calais; remembering the bloody battles over Kent, Galland had to listen while Goering fondled and cooed over these statuettes and paintings.

2 Ofw Grzymalla and Fw Kuepper, shot down by Flt Lt C.B.F. Kingcombe and Flg Off J.F.Drummond.

At this stage the RAF was beginning to receive the Spitfire Mk.II, with a more powerful Merlin XII engine delivering 1,175hp, pressurised water-glycol cooling and cartridge starter. With a top speed of 600kph (375mph), about 25kph (15mph) faster than the Mk.I, it was still only just the match of the Bf109E.

Just a few weeks earlier the Bf109E-7 had begun reaching the Staffeln, although the variant would not see service with JG26 before early November. The E-7 was essentially equivalent to the DB601N-powered E-4/N, but with fuselage shackles for either a 300-litre (66gal) fuel tank or 300kg (550lb) of bombs. The light metal tanks were a great improvement on the compressed wood pulp type; but they did cut performance, and pilots jettisoned them if combat threatened.

3 Awarded the DFC that same day, Bird-Wilson was a prewar RAF regular officer who continued to serve with distinction until 1974. By 1984 he had flown 213 aircraft types, including the F-15 Eagle. By coincidence, he too had badly damaged his face in a training accident in 1938, being Sir Archibald McIndoe's second 'guinea-pig' patient at East Grinstead hospital.

4 Outside JG26, the most famous fighter pilot of summer 1940 was Oblt Helmut Wick, Staffelkapitaen of 3./JG2 'Richthofen', who had been awarded the Knight's Cross on 27 August for 20 kills. Hptmn Walter Oesau, JG51, was awarded the Knight's Cross on 20 August for achieving 20 kills; Hptmn Guenther Luetzow, JG3 'Udet', on 18 September, for 15; and Oblt Hans 'Assi' Hahn, 4./JG2 'Richthofen', on 24 September, for 20.

5 Many photographs were coincidentally taken of Galland in his Bf109 during the brief period when the telescopic sight was fitted, leading to the myth that he used it for a considerable time; neither is it true that it was transferred to his Bf109F-0 when he received that variant in April 1941.

6 Not long afterwards, on 25 October, the British again thought they had captured Werner Moelders when Hptmn H. Asmus was shot down while flying Moelders' aircraft marked with the Geschwaderkommodore insignia.

CHAPTER 14

December 1940 – November 1941

By the end of November the only single-seater units left in the Pas de Calais were JG2 'Richthofen', JG3 'Udet', and JG26 'Schlageter'. The incessant rain, and the imprisoning quagmire of mud on the ill-drained airfields which had so recently been farmland, made it difficult to keep the Gruppen at operational readiness. Planks were laid across muddy patches for the aircraft wheels, and duckboards laid end to end made precarious paths between makeshift buildings and hangars. There was diminishing activity and fewer operational sorties for several months. On 7 December JG26 packed itself up and moved lock, stock and barrel about 80km (50 miles) south to Abbeville-Drucat near the mouth of the Somme, recently vacated by JG53 and ZG26. It was here that over the months to come Jagdgeschwader 'Schlageter' would establish a reputation, on both sides of the Channel, as the 'Abbeville Boys'.

The winter months dragged slowly by at JG26, with little opportunity for sport or hunting – in the air or on the ground – except in the bars and cafes of Boulogne, Calais, Lille and, occasionally, Paris. As his rank and fame increased, so too did Galland's circle of friends; and inevitably, he sometimes became the target for those who wanted to turn the contact to personal advantage, or to bathe in the reflected glory of Germany's leading ace. His close colleagues tried to keep these hangers-on at arm's length; and an administrative officer assigned to Stab/JG26, 'Papi' Causin, helped guard his freedom to continue to live a discreet private life.

At 28 Adolf Galland was single, darkly attractive, a national celebrity, and a dedicated admirer of beautiful women; and although reluctant to involve himself in a permanent relationship which might clash with his responsibilities and commitment, he did have a number of girlfriends. He could often be seen dining with attractive companions at one of his favourite haunts, the Club Scheherezade in Paris; one particularly stunning actress named Joshy would contact him discreetly through 'Papi' Causin whenever she was visiting the Pas de Calais region. In the course of his frequent dealings with Luftflotte 2 headquarters in Brussels Galland also found excuses to visit Monique, a beautiful Belgian who had been introduced to him in Paris.

For Galland these normal pleasures were an important release from the extraordinary pressures of combat and command. He had never imagined that fatigue could go so deep; and after he scored his last victory of the year on 5 December he felt more than ever the need for a complete rest. He knew that his Geschwader needed it too, and he began to make arrangements to get it for them; he pressed for his men to be allowed to rotate home on leave, and for his officers to be given a holiday in the Austrian Alps. Beyond that – being Galland – he also argued for a chance to receive the latest variant of the Bf109, which Messerschmitt had been working on for some months; and to be granted permanent assignment to the Western Front (the feared alternative at that stage of the war being a staff desk at the RLM).

Christmas was coming up, which would bring some relief from the drudgery of relocating to Abbeville. As preparations got under way Galland received word at short notice that the Geschwader was to receive a personal visit from the Fuehrer; Hitler's secretary would tell Galland after the war that his obvious concern for his men during their meeting had touched Hitler, who expressed the wish to visit them to bolster morale and to thank them for their efforts. When he arrived at Abbeville on Christmas Eve Galland had arranged a tea party; there could be no alcohol and, for once, Galland had to put away his cigars. Sprigs of fir and holly decorated the white tablecloth, fine bone china was brought in for the occasion, and tea and cakes were served by candlelight. As Hitler sat with them, Galland to his left, Rolf Pingel to his right, he told them how highly he regarded their dedication and service to the nation. Then he gave a half-hour speech to the unit; and Galland saw not the man who had sat quietly with him in that room at the Reichskanzlei, but the Hitler that the German public saw – confident of victory, glorying in military successes, and intent on final subjugation of the British. He told them that new investment in armaments would expand the Luftwaffe and fund development of new generations of aircraft. Expanded production of U-boats would seal the fate of the British, and with the spring would come a renewed offensive against the RAF. Galland was, nevertheless, wary about over-enthusiasm and knew the danger for Germany of a war on two fronts – something that was becoming a possibility.

Italian adventures in Africa were already going sadly awry, and German troops would probably be needed to save the Italian army from being expelled from North Africa and perhaps from the Mediterranean islands by the British. Moreover, Galland was by now perfectly aware of Hitler's short-term view of the Ribbentrop-Molotov non-aggression pact with Soviet Russia. Galland was a straightforward patriot and his political views, as has been said, were inevitably somewhat simplistic. A product of his time and his national and social background, he had been raised to fear and distrust the looming Bolshevist threat so relatively close in the East. He instinctively supported the idea of a major offensive against Russia; but he was convinced that the fight against Britain should take precedence, and that only when that was decided could the armed services turn to other objectives.

As the fury of the Battle of Britain receded and Luftwaffe operations settled into a war of night raids and attacks on shipping, the fighter wing commanders in northern France had petitioned – on Galland's initiative – for rotational leave for their men, which Goering granted and paid for from government funds. As part of the revitalisation of the Jagdwaffe, units were rotated back to their home bases for repairs, re-equipment and familiarisation training with new aircraft. Early in the new year JG26 withdrew to their former German airfields of Duesseldorf, Boenninghardt and Muenchen-Gladbach. From there Galland took a short home leave, followed by the special vacation in the Austrian Tyrol.

Goering had set up a small Alpine retreat for Luftwaffe officers at Zurs in the Voralberg mountains. Here they could ski, hike, eat, drink, enjoy the company of other vacationing Germans, or simply sleep. For most pilots from JG26 and the other Geschwader this was the first time they had spent out of uniform for more than 16 months; and it was to be their last vacation until the end of the war. It was at Zurs that Galland formed one of his most enduring friendships, with a divorcee named Monica who was vacationing with her four-year old son. She and Galland quickly became attached to one another, although in many ways it was an attraction of opposites. Monica had many friends in the world of films, theatre and the arts; this was a liberal milieu, deeply critical of the Nazi regime, and Monica herself hated the very idea of war. But in the unfathomable way of human affections Galland found in Monica some special quality, and she was to become a devoted friend and confidante. Four years hence, in the most critical moments of his life, even when her very association with Galland would bring him closer to death, she would become the instrument of his survival.

In the meantime, Galland's thoughts often strayed back to the central question of how best to combat the RAF when the weather picked up. Hitler had said greater resources would be poured into the Luftwaffe for a revitalised assault in the spring; there would therefore be a need for tactical decisions. Galland knew the RAF had been able to vector their fighters on to the Bf109s because they could plot the direction, strength and altitude of the intruders. He decided to find out what technical developments might be in the offing to benefit German fighters in a similar way. Stimulated by the increased number of RAF bomber raids into Germany at the beginning of May 1941, German radar defences would improve markedly thereafter; but at the end of 1940 Galland learned to his consternation that very little progress had so far been made, because the emphasis in Luftwaffe research and development had been on offensive systems.

For the first time it occurred to Galland that RAF Fighter Command might increase its strength to the point where it could go on to the offensive, carrying the fight back into French and Belgian skies. Remembering the effectiveness of the primitive experiments set up by Werner Moelders on the Luxembourg border during the 'Phoney War', Galland believed that some sort of fighter control from the ground – vectoring information passed through the R/T link – was essential; but he was instinctively resistant to anything that would restrict the freedom of the Rotte or the Schwarm to act independently in combat[1].

* * *

During January 1941 the situation in the Mediterranean worsened as the British consolidated their positions on Malta and along the North African coast. The Italians were totally outclassed by the numerically inferior British forces, and

Hitler agreed to send Luftwaffe elements to help attack British shipping in the Mediterranean. X.Fliegerkorps was sent from Norway to Italy, and from there to Sicily on 8 January 1941. The Germans had an immediate success on 10 January when a convoy for Malta whose escort included the carrier HMS *Ark Royal*, and a British force including the carrier HMS *Illustrious* which had sailed from Alexandria to meet the convoy, were both attacked by Ju87s. The Luftwaffe increased its deployments to this theatre; and on 22 January Galland organised the transfer of about 40 ground personnel of his 7./JG26 to Rome by Ju52 transport; the pilots were already in Italy with their new Bf109E-7s. The pilots and ground crew of the 'Red Heart' Staffel under Oblt Joachim Muencheberg moved to Gela airfield, Sicily, on 9 February, and were in action three days later against Hurricanes of No.261 Sqn based on Malta, shooting down three of them. The RAF pilots had perhaps become complacent through facing only Italian opposition; certainly the Hurricane Mk.I was outclassed, particularly at altitude, by the Bf109E-7. As the battle for Malta intensified Oblt Muencheberg's squadron continued to score well without loss. The Hurricanes were reinforced at great risk from HMS *Ark Royal*, but it was an indomitable spirit rather than adequate equipment which saved Malta.

In April 7./JG26 moved briefly to Taranto to support Wehrmacht operations in the Balkans; and at the end of May X.Fliegerkorps supported the invasion of Crete, with 7./JG26 operating out of airfields in Greece. Within days they had been transferred to Ain-el-Gazala on the Libyan coast of North Africa where they were to reinforce the sole German fighter unit, I./JG27. By mid-June the Staffel was scoring victories over the desert. Joachim Muencheberg received orders in August 1941 to pull his pilots out and return to III.Gruppe in north-west France. During the period they had been away the Staffel had achieved 52 kills without a single loss, Oblt Muencheberg increasing his personal score to 48.

Although operating as an independent unit in a faraway theatre of operations, letters home and to comrades in France show that the Staffel never lost its sense of identity as part of III.Gruppe and of JG26. This *esprit de corps* was common in the Luftwaffe at the level of the Gruppe, which was perhaps the natural size of unit to serve as a focus of loyalty. The sense of unity and common purpose that Galland forged throughout his Jagdgeschwader, in its determination to be the best fighting unit in the Luftwaffe, was not so common.

* * *

Back in France, fresh and tanned from the Tyrol, the bulk of the 'Schlageter' pilots faced new challenges in March 1941. JG26 were to fly from airfields in Brittany in defence of warships operating out of Brest; with all possibility of an invasion now firmly postponed the economic blockade of Britain came to the fore, and naval operations consequently gathered pace. In the same month the Geschwader at last began receiving the new Bf109F series fighter.

Its appearance was immediately striking. The nose section was completely remodelled into a beautifully symmetrical profile, and the wingtips were improved and rounded. The new aircraft incorporated several modifications progressively fitted to late E-series variants, and many would argue that the F-series was the finest Bf109 of them all. With the DB601N engine now standard pending availability of the more powerful DB601E, the Bf109F had reduced drag from a much improved radiator, rounded-off cowling and enlarged spinner which gave the entire front end the appearance of a bullet. The cleaned-up tail assembly had lost the 'Emil's' ugly external bracing struts.

More controversially, wing armament was eliminated from the Bf109F series in favour of a single engine-mounted cannon firing through the propeller boss in addition to the twin MG17 cowling machine guns. The F-1 had the MG FF/M cannon, which had taken so long in development that it had been eliminated from earlier E-series variants. The F-2 had the MG151/15 Mauser of 15mm calibre, and the F-4 the MG151/20 of 20mm calibre. With a rate of fire of 650rpm and a muzzle velocity of 300m/sec (1,040ft/sec), compared with 520rpm and 200m/sec (700ft/sec) for the MG FF/M, the MG151 was in a different league. Standard ammunition load was 200 rounds for the 15mm Mauser and 150 rounds for the 20mm version.

Galland considered the 'Friedrich' drastically undergunned, and later in the year he would acquire three specially modified F-series aircraft, two of which came from the armament experimental factory. One, a Bf109F-2 which he designated F-6/U^2, would be fitted with an extra 20mm MG FF cannon in each wing, necessitating a small bulged plate in the underside of each wing to accommodate the magazines; this would be the only F-series to fly with wing guns. Access to the non-standard wing guns was via undersurface panels, but there were no significant changes to the internal wing structure. The other two modified aircraft, designated F-2/U in his combat reports, retained the engine-mounted cannon but carried two 13mm MG131 heavy machine guns in place of the standard MG17 cowling guns. This modification was performed at Audembert, and necessitated small bulged plates standing proud each side of the rear of the cowling to accommodate the bigger breech. (This would be adopted by Messerschmitt as the standard cowling gun configuration for the Bf109G-5 and all subsequent variants, the bulges earning the aircraft the nickname 'Beulen' – 'boils').

Apart from its armament Galland was pleased with the Bf109F and was keen to try out its air-fighting qualities. The F was about 40kph (25mph) faster than the E-4/N thanks to its aerodynamic refinements, with greatly improved manoeuvrability; its wing loading was very little different so its handling was as good. A full circle turn at 1,000m (3,280ft) could be completed in 18sec, a full 7sec faster than the E-4/N. Climb rate had been improved by almost 10 per cent; its time to 5,000m (16,400ft) – 5min 12sec – was nearly a full minute faster. All three Gruppen of JG2 and I. and III.Gruppen of JG26 were equipped with the type, II./JG26 retaining its Bf109Es until the new Focke-Wulf Fw190s arrived in July.

The restructuring of unit assignments within the Luftflotten had shown Galland the new order of priorities. Only JG2 and JG26 remained with Sperrle's Luftflotte 3, with JG51, JG52 and JG53 operating under Kesselring's Luftflotte 2. More telling in the long run would be the position of Luftwaffen-Befehlshaber Mitte (Luftwaffe Command Central), set up in March to co-ordinate operations for the remaining units committed to defending Reich skies. (In time, under bombardment that in 1941 could hardly be imagined, this organisation would become Luftflotte Reich.)

For the time being Jagdgeschwader 'Schlageter' would set up camp in Brittany, with I.Gruppe and Stab at Guipavas near Brest, II.Gruppe at Morlaix and III.Gruppe at Lannion. They would fly patrols to protect the U-boat pens and surface anchorages of the German fleet, including the battleships *Scharnhorst* and *Gneisenau*.

The tempo of Luftwaffe bomber operations over Britain picked up again with better weather; in December 1940 there had been 3,844 sorties over Britain, in February only 1,400, but in March 4,365, rising to 5,448 in April. Almost all were flown at night; and sustained bomber operations against Britain would wane in mid-May, to almost cease by the end of the month as the Kampfgeschwader began a massive shift from West to East in fulfilment of Hitler's grand strategy. The ebb and flow of the Kampfgeschwader would be of little concern to JG26 now, however; already more attention was being paid to the reversal to RAF tactics. Now it was the British who were beginning to send their fighters across the Channel to look for trouble. Enthralled at the prospect of rejoining the battle in the skies with a new and more effective aircraft, Galland flew to Le Touquet on 1 April, with wingman Ofw Robert Menge, en route to Guipavas in his old Bf109E-4. Both aircraft had been fitted with the 'plumbing' for the new 300-litre (66gal) metal belly tank. While there they visited friends at JG53; and three days later, almost exactly four months after he had shot down his 57th aircraft, Galland and Menge flew on to Guipavas – via southern England....

Determined to add to their scores, the two Jagdflieger excited a response from Fighter Command, which sent up a flight of Spitfires from No.91 Sqn at Hawkinge. Those piloted by Sgt Spears and Sgt Mann were spotted climbing fast; the two Messerschmitts positioned themselves up-sun, and executed a perfect diving attack. At an altitude of 900m (3,000ft) Galland peppered his selected target with machine gun and cannon fire, ripping holes in wings and fuselage. Within seconds it had burst into flames and was spiralling down out of control as Sgt Mann took to his parachute. Meanwhile, Menge had got the better of Sgt Spears and sent him down damaged for a forced landing. Reassured that none of the old skill had evaporated, and with kill number 58 in the bag, Galland called to Menge that enough was enough. They gunned their 109s at high speed toward Guipavas, where they would exchange their 'Emils' for sleek new Bf109F-0 fighters.

The title of Germany's leading air ace, won by Galland on 5 December 1940 with his 57th combat victory, swung back to Moelders on 20 February 1941 when a double kill took Galland's arch-rival to 58. By the time Galland equalled that, with Menge over England on 4 April, Moelders had 62; but there was little opportunity to chase his score over the next ten days. They were working up with the new Bf109Fs; and the mission of defending the naval installations offered few opportunities for combat beyond chasing away reconnaissance aircraft, and generally giving the RAF the impression that these were dangerous skies.

Refusing to accept this lack of activity, Galland decided that if the enemy was not going to come to him then he was going to go to the enemy. The perfect chance occurred on 15 April when Galland accepted an invitation from 'Uncle Theo' to drop in on his 49th birthday party at Jafu 2's new headquarters at Le Touquet. Into the small space beneath the fixed rear section of the cockpit canopy behind his head Galland wedged and strapped a basket packed with lobsters and champagne; with the hinged section of the canopy closed, the armour plate closed off this compartment. With Ofw Hans-Juergen Westphal as his wingman, Galland took off and headed for Le Touquet – with a little diversion to southern England en route. Over the Channel off Dover he identified a lone Spitfire moving fast toward the coast. Galland and Westphal were spotted as they manoeuvred for position, and a wild chase began. Galland managed to close the distance and get on the Spitfire's tail; a short burst sent the RAF fighter into a wild gyration out of the line of fire. For several minutes the Spitfire successfully avoided staying in Galland's gunsight; but the Bf109 finally had him, and he went down into a village close to Dover. Looking about for other aircraft, the two Jagdflieger turned for the Pas de Calais, satisfied that they had a suitable present for 'Uncle'.

They were not at the party yet, however: as they made a hasty exit from English skies they spotted a squadron of Spitfires climbing fast ahead of them. Without breaking radio silence, Galland signalled manoeuvres designed to put them in position behind a trailing straggler. Minutes later they were on the British squadron's trail and closing unnoticed. Holding his breath, edging ever closer to the unsuspecting aircraft, Galland got close enough to do real damage and opened fire – victory number 60, and apparently without alerting the other Spitfires. With luck on their side, the two pilots stalked closer to the main formation; getting in a good burst at very close range, Galland nearly rammed his third victim of the day, who fell away without trace (and was therefore not confirmed as a victory). Westphal also missed his opportunity to get a kill when his guns jammed.

The rest of the Spitfires had scattered, but were now coming back for them as the two Bf109s rocketed for the coast of France. True to form, the Spitfires chased the two Jagdflieger far out across the Channel, but the Messerschmitts outran them. Galland's aircraft was losing ground to Westphal, who pulled gradually ahead. Scanning his instruments, Galland wondered whether he had been hit; but nothing appeared to be wrong, although his engine might be losing power. It would be farcical to come all this way only to dump 'Uncle's' lobsters in the English Channel. The Messerschmitt seemed fine in every other respect; it handled a little sluggishly, but perhaps that was from some minor damage.

Coming in to land at Le Touquet, Galland hit the undercarriage button and lined up for touchdown – only to see red flares shooting into the sky, and ground crew rushing about signalling to him: 'Wheels up, don't land!' Galland went round again; when he pushed the undercarriage lower/retract button once more the wheels came down and locked, and he landed without further drama. So that was why the aircraft felt slow and sluggish: at some point during combat he must have unintentionally hit the button and lowered his wheels... Theo Osterkamp greatly appreciated his lobsters and fizz – probably the only bottles of champagne ever to have survived the high-G gyrations of an air-to-air dogfight.

* * *

To the young wing commanders in western France the prospect of all-out battle with Britain dominated the arrival of spring 1941; but from Berlin all eyes were looking East.

As early as 21 July 1940 Hitler had ordered Halder at OKH to quietly begin the planning for an invasion of Russia. Ten days later the Fuehrer informed his generals of that momentous decision; and Halder's diary seems to dismiss the age-old nightmare of German strategists – simultaneous war on two fronts – with the windy formula that 'Britain's hope lies in Russia and America. If that hope is destroyed then it will be destroyed for America too, because elimination of Russia will enormously increase Japan's power in the Far East … if Russia is smashed, Britain's hopes will be shattered… .Decision: in view of these considerations Russia must be liquidated. Spring 1941.' On 18 December Hitler issued a directive giving detailed instructions for 'Barbarossa'; it was explicit on the merciless harshness to be employed against the population, and the goal of permanent subjugation of the Slavic peoples as a race of helots in a new Germanic empire.

While the military preparations moved towards completion, Hermann Goering – secretly given by Hitler vast powers for the economic exploitation of the new Eastern territories to be captured by the Wehrmacht – crushed his misgivings about the wisdom of this almost limitless commitment. During a special conference called in April 1941, to which many Luftwaffe combat commanders down to Geschwader level were invited, Goering explained that the coming months would see a focused commitment to the destruction of the RAF and the elimination of Britain from the war. Galland listened intently; this was exactly what Hitler had told him a few months before. After his speech Goering took Galland and Moelders aside, and told them the truth – which was the exact opposite of what he had said in public only minutes earlier.

The two young commanders were stunned. Each had immediate questions arising from their amazement at the folly of the idea, let alone the sheer scale of what Goering implied. What about Britain – would this not constitute the second front that Hitler had himself condemned as disastrous? Goering dismissed Britain with a sweep of his hand, and got down to the reason why he was letting them in on what was, at the time, the most sensitive state secret in the Third Reich. The Russian campaign would involve two, possibly three months of Blitzkrieg war. During that period Moelders would lead his JG51 on the Eastern Front. JG2 'Richthofen', under the command of Wilhelm Balthasar (Walter Oesau after Balthasar was killed on 3 July), and Galland's JG26 'Schlageter' would remain on the Western Front to defend the back gates of Germany from the RAF.

When Galland and Moelders returned to their respective headquarters they were filled with dismay. Deeply shocked, Galland was under oath to remain silent; there was no one with whom he could talk out his worries – giving way to his instinct to telephone Monica would be disastrous. Once again he had been reminded that despite the public rewards and the moments of apparent intimacy with the leaders of his country he was, after all, only a very small player with a very limited perspective. Even so, he could only apply military logic to the situation; and military logic argued that this decision would lead to catastrophe. At the same time – being the man he was – part of him disliked the notion of being left behind to stand guard at the back gate.

Only a matter of days afterwards Goering was to present Galland with another profound, almost surreal shock. Early in the evening of Saturday 10 May, as Galland was working at his desk at Guipavas, the Reichsmarschall telephoned him in person and ordered him to put the entire Geschwader into the air at once. He was to intercept and if necessary shoot down a Bf110 flying in a north-westerly direction toward England. At first he could not believe his ears; the identity of the caller and the bizarre nature of the order reduced him to confusion. Screaming down the telephone as if his very life depended upon it, Goering then told him that Rudolf Hess, the Second Deputy Fuehrer, had gone mad and was escaping to England; he had stolen a Bf110 from Augsburg and was piloting himself. Goering did not elaborate on Hess's reasons for fleeing the country, repeating only that he had to be brought down.

Galland's huge reservations about this implausible order were both practical and personal. It would be dark in another ten minutes. Goering could give him no details about markings or identification codes for the aircraft; there were several aircraft in the vicinity at that time, and some were being tested prior to raid assignments for the night – there must be upwards of a score of Bf110s somewhere above north-western Europe at that very moment. Moreover, alerted to such extreme inconsistencies among the Nazi hierarchy, Galland had no wish to be bundled into aligning himself with some cause he did not remotely understand.

Erring on the side of caution, he decided to send up one or two aircraft from each Gruppe; that way he could not be accused either of disobeying a direct order from the Reichsmarschall, or of being too eager to shoot down the Second Deputy Fuehrer. For more than a fleeting second he actually wondered whether the voice on the telephone could be that of an impostor. Galland gave instructions that his pilots should not remain long in the air or risk wrecking their aircraft attempting night landings – there was no airfield guidance system for these day fighters, and the Bf109 was notoriously unsuited to landing on unprepared fields. After a decent interval he ordered his pilots down, and called Goering to tell him that they could find no trace of the Bf110. Goering was concerned whether Hess could reach England from Augsburg in a Bf110; Galland did a quick calculation, and said it would be marginal.

As is well known, thanks to long range fuel tanks Hess reached Lanarkshire in Scotland, baling out near the estate of the Duke of Hamilton, whom he had met during the 1936 Olympic Games. The background to this bizarre adventure clearly lay in Hess's obsession with the idea that a direct appeal to certain circles in Britain might bring about a negotiated peace. The timing of his flight was presumably dictated by the wish to establish such an understanding before the invasion of Russia – although by now a marginalised figure, Hess would certainly have been privy to Hitler's intentions, even if not the exact timetable. Again, Goering's anxiety that he should be shot down presumably stemmed from fears that Hess would compromise Operation 'Barbarossa'. (Galland would later be the recipient of many elaborate embellishments to this tale, both during hunting trips with Goering and in Argentina in the 1950s. The essential flaws in Hess's plan have already been touched upon at sufficient length.)

* * *

The affair was a fleeting, dreamlike distraction from events nearer to the world of a combat wing commander. On 1 May JG26 had been congratulated by Generalfeldmarschall Sperrle on gaining its 500th air combat victory, and opportunities to increase that total should not have been long in coming. Aware of the reduction in German forces in France as the Wehrmacht juggernaut redeployed eastwards for 'Barbarossa', the RAF began to probe the coastal regions of the occupied countries more often, more aggressively, and in larger numbers. This shift to a newly offensive posture was clearly detectable; so it was to Galland's disgust that time was spent incorporating the Jabo tactic into Geschwader training, and pilots were rostered to practise hurling concrete bomb shapes at rocks near the beaches.

On 27 May JG26 was given a mission which would connect Galland – not for the last time – with the Kriegsmarine's capital ships. On 18 May 1941 the *Bismarck*, newest and most prestigious of Germany's great battleships, sailed from Danzig with the battle-cruiser *Prinz Eugen* to add the weight of her guns to the naval war against Britain in the Atlantic. Spotted by the RAF, and damaged by the Royal Navy in a battle on the 24th which cost Britain the mighty HMS *Hood* and all but three of her crew of more than 1,400, the *Bismarck* was limping for the shelter of Brest on 26 May when her steering gear was damaged by a Swordfish biplane torpedo-bomber from the carrier HMS *Ark Royal*. On the 27th Galland received instructions to send Bf109s out to meet the *Bismarck* and cover her approach to Brest. I.Gruppe took off, fitted with the new auxiliary fuel tanks, and flew west in a desperate attempt to reach the crippled battleship. They were about 160km (100 miles) out over the Atlantic, and still some 750km (460 miles) short of the *Bismarck*, when they were recalled: torpedoes from HMS *Dorsetshire* had finally sent her sliding beneath the waves, with some 2,100 of her crew.

Four days later, on 31 May, Galland received orders to move the Geschwader from the area around Brest back to the Pas de Calais. There had been very little chance to raise significantly the wing's victory tally during this posting, but it had not been without value. Encounters with the latest Mk.V variant of the Spitfire showed it to be the equal of the Bf109F series. The primary difference lay in the Merlin 45 engine rated at 1,315hp, giving the type a maximum speed of 595km/h (369mph) at 5,945m (19,500ft) and a climb time to 6,100m (20,000ft) of less than seven minutes, compared to nine minutes for the earlier versions. The Mk.VB, by far the most common model, was armed with four machine guns and two 20mm cannon. So it would be with new and upgraded fighters that Fighter Command and the Jagdwaffe would clash once more over the narrow seas during the coming summer.

On 1 June 1941 the entire Geschwader moved. Galland took the staff flight and set up headquarters in the palatial surroundings of the converted mansion at Audembert. I.Gruppe flew in to Clairmairas, not far from St Omer; II.Gruppe took up position at Maldegem just over the border in western Belgium, and III.Gruppe was based at Liegescourt close to Abbeville. All the airfields were rough strips only suitable for use during spring and summer, and needed some work as soon as they arrived. (At the same time JG2 'Richthofen' moved to occupy the area vacated by Galland's groups.) It took a couple of weeks for JG26 to settle in, and very little action was seen before the middle of June.

Since January the RAF had been flying daytime 'Circuses', formations of medium bombers escorted by fighters, attacking targets on the Continent without any obvious strategic or tactical pattern. Before the summer the Jagdflieger still encountered earlier marks of Spitfire, definitely inferior to the Bf109F, and successes were easier to achieve. But Galland knew that the Mk.V was being produced in large numbers and would soon equip all Fighter Command Spitfire squadrons; and that the Spitfire was increasingly replacing the slower Hurricane, which had born the main burden of the fighting in 1940.

Committed to developing the fighting potential of all three Gruppen, Galland re-established the policy of guiding the flying and fighting skills of each Staffel in turn. He would rotate each Staffel through Audembert every two or three weeks, watching, evaluating, correcting and advising. The presence of this rotating so-called 'Fuehrungsverband' or 'lead unit' at Audembert made things crowded, but manageable; and the extra training paid off.

On 16 June Galland was flying with Oblt Pingel's I.Gruppe when it bounced an inviting formation of six Blenheims and ten Hurricanes from No.11 Group making for Boulogne. As the bombers climbed away from their targets in different directions to split the flak they became easy pickings for the Bf109s. Now the boot was on the other foot; it was the RAF who had ventured across the Channel, and the Jagdflieger who were fighting on their own doorstep. In the ensuing battle the Luftwaffe shot down two Blenheims and destroyed or damaged several of their escort. Galland quickly fastened on to a Hurricane and sent it into the Channel; but four JG26 pilots were either shot down or sent limping back to Clairmairas with damaged aircraft. As usual the claims by both sides were out of all proportion to the actual losses, the RAF returning to claim 11 Bf109s destroyed and a further nine either destroyed or damaged.

Over the next months these raids would build into large formations involving groups of fighters operating effectively, but virtually independently of the bombers they were there to protect; and Galland developed a respect for the way Fighter Command allowed its pilots freedom to fly escort patterns. Instead of clustering the escort and bunching up the bombers, the formation would comprise several different elements each with its own operational task.

In one example, a formation of bombers would be preceded by three target support wings each consisting of three fighter squadrons, one flying ahead and one at some distance to either flank. The obvious disadvantages of tying the fighters to the bombers, experienced with excruciating frequency by the Jagdflieger over England, were avoided; these support wings operated, in effect, as an outer perimeter defensive screen. To synchronise the different speeds of the fighters and the bombers the forward support wing started after the bombers had departed their holding pattern for the cross-Channel trip, to overtake them just before reaching enemy airspace. The flank support wings would converge on their holding positions some distance out from the bombers by flying tangentially to the main stream, thus dissipating the extra speed by the time they arrived over target.

The escort itself would be divided into four fighter squadrons, one each for close-in and medium range escort and two for top and bottom cover. High above the top cover would be another squadron flying the so-called cover wing; and far to the rear of the entire formation there would be two squadrons flying additional support wings. It would be their job to dive in and mop up straggling Jagdflieger after the target support wings that preceded the attack had withdrawn. These three target support wings, consisting of nine squadrons in all, would separate into flights of four aircraft each – the 'finger four' had now replaced the outdated 'vic', in direct imitation of the Luftwaffe – to form an outer defence over the target area. These highly sophisticated 'Circuses' could involve upwards of 200 aircraft across a very large piece of sky; they were the optimum formation for shooting the bombers through to the target, without shackling the Spitfires to slower aircraft, and giving them plenty of flying room to use their capabilities.

Over the summer these RAF tactics would be refined further; Galland obtained as much information as he could about these tactical formations, grilling his pilots for details after every encounter. He needed to know how they formed up, where they converged, whether anything could be done to separate them, how best to break the support wings away from the escorts. Clearly, such complex and well-timed operations involving so many aircraft in two distinct performance categories could not have been developed without the months of practice in fighter control techniques through sector operations during the Battle of Britain.

There was seldom an opportunity to throw the entire Geschwader into a head-on clash with such large formations, and tactics were developed which put Gruppen, even individual Staffeln on alert for reaction at short notice to an encroaching threat. It was then up to the individual Schwaerme or Rotten to seize the initiative and attack at the discretion of individual pilot pairs. In general, following the principles worked out between Galland, Oesau from JG2 and Osterkamp, the preferred tactic was to go for the escorts and expose the bombers to the 'Experten' – the aces, who could dash in and knock down the bombers. The priority was to inflict maximum damage on the RAF and not to measure success wholly by individual victory scores.

'Circuses' could be of any size and any combination of aircraft. It was a medium-sized force that drew Adolf Galland into action on 21 June 1941, one of the more memorable days of his life on the Pas de Calais. Throughout that fine, sunny morning Galland had been busy checking out some re-equipment needs for II.Gruppe. Shortly after noon the radar station on the coast provided warning of an approaching force of bombers, which turned out to be Blenheims, and approximately 50 escorting fighters. Radar indicated that they were going for airfields near St Omer, close to II.Gruppe. When Galland received the alert warning he scrambled all three Gruppen, and ran for his own Bf109. Airborne at precisely 12.24, he gained altitude rapidly and, passing through 3,050m (10,000ft), the JG26 pilots could see the British bombs falling on Arques, one of the St Omer landing fields. With height in his favour, wingman Ufw Hegenauer alongside and the Fuehrungsverband close on his tail, Galland signalled the accompanying Staffel to go for the escort fighters while he took his Rotte down in a steep dive straight for the Blenheims.

In the first pass Galland sliced straight between two bombers, getting a three-second burst at one that sent it straight down in a spiralling turn toward the ground. It was 12.32. Hauling round to come back at the second from behind he manoeuvred in close, got in two long bursts, and saw smoke starting to pour from one of the engines before it too fell, flames licking along the wing. He had left the fighters behind on his lightning dive through their midst, but he now came under attention from a couple of Spitfires who had diverted to follow him and his wingman. Glancing down, Galland could see two parachutes plop open. Then, without warning, there was the deep thud of cannon shells and machine gun bullets hitting his aircraft, and glowing tracers were zinging past his canopy and into his engine cowling. He was hit and going down. The engine howled in protest, and Galland saw that the temperature gauge was boiling off the scale. With streams of white smoke pouring from the smashed radiator he throttled back and dived to gain air speed. Seconds later the engine seized completely, and he was back to being a glider pilot. Fortunately he was close to the Calais-Marcke airstrip, and managed to manoeuvre his dead Bf109 into a reasonable approach, bracing himself for the stunning jolt and noise of a belly landing. When it finally slithered to a stop he clambered rather shakily out into the sudden silence and walked slowly round the crumpled 109. It would be a long time before this one flew again; but it wasn't the only Messerschmitt in France.

Less than an hour later he was back at his Audembert headquarters, after being collected by the adjutant in his Me108 Taifun communications aircraft. During that afternoon Galland had his second Bf109 readied and stood by for the further raids which Jafu 2 had warned him to expect. Late in the afternoon, at around 16.00, the alert went again and all serviceable aircraft were scrambled. This time Galland was without his Rottenflieger, who had been shot down during the morning and had yet to be ferried back to Audembert. Climbing fast toward the attacking bombers over Boulogne, Galland caught up with I.Gruppe just as they spotted a formation of Spitfires across to port. Gating the throttle, he thundered after the British fighters and positioned himself for a high-speed run on to the tail of a straggler. A single quick burst from his machine guns and the Spitfire flamed, falling almost vertically toward the Channel. Without a wingman to stand witness for his victory Galland wanted to be sure it did not recover, and tipped his 109 to watch it.

Without warning, for the second time that day, he heard and felt the bone-jarring thudding of bullets on metal, followed in fractions of a second by hammer blows to his arm and his head. He could feel warm, wet blood flowing, and suddenly he was fighting to stay conscious. Cannon shells gouged holes in his wings; then a second burst literally tore out the side of his fuselage along the cockpit, leaving him exposed to the blast of cold air. Fuel and cooling fluid came streaming in through the ragged metal, and past him in a long white trail behind his 109. The engine was dead; but the controls still seemed to be answering, and Galland fought against waves of pain and sickness for the energy to bring this crippled thing down to the second crash landing of the day. Suddenly a violent 'Whoompf!' rippled through the fuselage as petrol vapour ignited, in a flash that ran through the full length of his aircraft. Flames licked and grew from behind him as ruptured fuel lines from the L-shaped tank embracing his seat threatened to roast him alive.

He tugged furiously at the canopy jettison lever in the front left corner of the cockpit – and again – nothing! The latch or hinges must have been distorted by the shells that ripped open the fuselage. Quickly unbuckling his seat harness so that he could get both hands to it, he wrenched at the lever with all his strength. He could feel the flames now. But by a miracle he wasn't spinning, the falling aircraft was still relatively stable. Jamming a leg in front of the control stick to keep the nose up he crouched forward, coiled his body like a spring, raised his back against the canopy, braced his feet – and straightened until his spine and eyeballs popped. Brain swimming, he willed the twisted metal to relent, to let him out of this flaming coffin. And it flew open. And as the freezing airstream hit his burned face he was still trapped: half way out, his parachute somehow caught by the fixed section of the canopy.

The 109 was now a wind-blasted mass of flames, petrol from the torn fuel lines spraying in to feed the inferno. These were the most terrifying moments of his life. So this was what it felt like... This was what it had all been for, all the years of striving, all the luck? But behind all the racing thoughts there was still something he could hold on to and use – the iron determination not to give in, to fight, to overcome. He wrapped his arm round the slender aerial mast behind the cockpit, and pulled as if he was trying to burst his heart. And without knowing how, he was in free-fall, tumbling away from the burning hulk, breath torn away by the rush of air.

As he fell Galland reached down and fumbled for the cord to release his canopy. Why wouldn't it open? Surely – not a dud parachute? Tearing at what he thought was the ripcord, he realised with a sickening twist of his stomach that he was pulling at the release which opened the harness itelf. Concentrating, forcing himself to pause and be sure, he pulled hard on the real ripcord and the canopy went billowing up, to check his fall at last with a sickening jerk. He hung in the huge silence in the firm grip of his harness, dazed, alive ... safe. Down far below him smoke rose from the shattered debris of his aircraft. Then the earth rushed up to meet him, and his parachute snagged on a row of trees in the Foret de Boulogne, and collapsed, leaving him to gravity – and the relief of a landing in the soft boggy ground at the edge of the forest. To the pain of his torn arm and injured face was now added a twisted ankle, which immediately started to swell up.

He lay for several minutes, totally exhausted, his panting breath slowing, his mind gradually coming back under command. He could not even get up, let alone walk. In a while a friendly farming couple, a man and his wife, arrived on the scene. They picked him up and carried him back to their farmhouse, and someone ran to fetch some men from the Todt Organisation working on a nearby construction site. They fetched a car and drove him back to Audembert, to the happy relief of his men. He soon found himself in the naval hospital at Hardinghem, under the expert attention of Surgeon-Dr Heim, well known for his skill at patching up the fliers of JG26. As a special concession Galland was allowed to puff away at his cigar on the operating table – after all, he would recall 50 years later, they had to keep him happy: 'otherwise I might not have brought them my business in future!'

* * *

After Galland had been patched up and returned to Audembert, Theo Osterkamp drove across to congratulate him on his escape, and to bring him some good news. In recognition of his bravery, and his 70th victory, he had received a special message from Adolf Hitler congratulating him and awarding him the Swords to his Oak Leaves of the Knight's Cross. This was the first ever award of this coveted decoration, of which only 159 would ever be given. Such an honour gave legitimate excuse for liberal quantities of champagne to flow long into the night. The message, however, contained a bitter postscript: an order from Hitler forbidding him to continue flying. It was an order Galland was determined to get around somehow.

Next morning, 22 June 1941, the Wehrmacht crossed the borders of the Soviet Union in the greatest mechanised assault in the history of warfare.

The attack on Russia involved 3,855 front-line aircraft including 2,770 combat types, and 3.2 million men in 152 divisions along a 1,000-mile front from the Baltic to the Black Sea. The Soviet air force, an integral part of the army equipped with large numbers of tactical aircraft, had in the western part of the USSR some 7,500 combat machines, but mostly of outdated types and with low serviceability. The Germans caught the Russians completely by surprise, and by noon on the first day had destroyed about 800 Soviet aircraft on the ground; by midnight on the 22nd some 322 aircraft had been destroyed in combat and a total of 1,489 on the ground at 66 airfields. By the end of the second day a total of around 3,000 Soviet aircraft had been destroyed; and by the third night the Soviet air force in the west had been all but eliminated. By 29 June the Soviets had lost more than 4,000 aircraft, against German losses in combat of only 150 aircraft[3].

On the next day JG51 became the first Jagdgeschwader to score 1,000 confirmed victories when pilots from this group shot down 96 Soviet aircraft and Moelders scored a phenomenal 11 kills in one day. When he left for the Eastern Front Moelders' victory log had stood at 68; within days it exceeded 80 – the total reached by Manfred von Richthofen in World War I and the greatest number of air combat victories by any pilot up to that date. On 15 July he shot down two aircraft, becoming the first fighter pilot to reach and exceed 100 kills. The next day he was awarded the Diamonds to the Swords and Oak Leaves of his Knight's Cross – the first of just nine airmen in that most exclusive of military brotherhoods.

Confined at first to a chair, and allowed after a few days to hobble around

Audembert on a stick, Adolf Galland marvelled with his men as the reports of almost incredible Wehrmacht successes came flooding back from Russia. Nobody was interested in JG2 and JG26, the lonely guardians of Germany's western gates. But in early July Britain signed a mutual co-operation agreement with Moscow; the RAF began to press harder on the Luftwaffe along the Channel coast, hoping to draw back some of the elite Jagdflieger and take the pressure off the Russians. On 9 July the RAF redirected Bomber Command's efforts to concentrate on strategic targets.

Soon Galland was back in the air testing out his two new aircraft, the Bf109Fs with new armament arrangements (he assumed that the order grounding him applied to combat operations only). After his near-fatal encounter with a Spitfire on 21 June his trusty crew chief, Uffz Meyer, devised additional protection, and welded a flat armour plate forward from the top of the standard back and neck plate, the entire assembly moving with the hinged section of the canopy. Galland discovered this when he took off for a test flight on 2 July: no sooner had he strapped in than the canopy was slammed shut, the new armour striking him painfully on the top of his injured head. A torrent of obscenities at poor Meyer drifted back out of the open side panel as Galland taxied away for take-off.

A new and dramatic entrant on the 'Circus' scene was the Short Stirling, Britain's first four-engined bomber of the war. The first examples of these were used to add punch to the increasing number and size of daylight formations; with their 6,350 kilo (14,000lb) bomb load they provided a dramatic increase in the tonnage dropped. In fact the Stirling had been used first in March against the battleships *Scharnhorst* and *Gneisenau* in Brest harbour, and JG26 had seen them, but not yet fought them. In July the first two Stirling squadrons were active over the French coast, and on the 10th they sent three aircraft to Boulogne. JG26 tested the Stirling's respectable defences – eight machine guns in power-operated nose, mid-upper and tail turrets – and probed for weak spots and optimum lines of attack.

During July, too, Messerschmitt introduced an improved version of the Bf109F. The F-3 and F-4 had the new 1,350hp DB601E engine, giving them 30km/h (20mph) edge over the new Spitfire Mk.V. Remarkably, the more powerful engine was designed for standard 87 octane B4 fuel instead of the 96 octane C3 type, which was much harder to come by. The F-3, with the 15mm MG151 engine cannon, was rapidly supplanted by the F-4 with a 20mm MG151, and it was one of these that Galland began to use when he resumed operational flying. (Only a few examples of the F-3, which was virtually identical to the F-1 with the exception of the new octane rating, were operated by JG26 and JG2.)

An opportunity to try out the Bf109F-4 came on 23 July when Galland scrambled late in the afternoon to attack a fighter sweep – known as a 'Rodeo' – with the full Geschwader. Hurtling into the fray he quickly shot down two Spitfires, and was setting about a third when another Spitfire attacked him from behind – and put a cannon shell squarely on the new cockpit roof plate welded in by Meyer. Without the plate Galland's career would have ended right there; as it was the damage was considerable, wounding him in the head yet again. He managed to keep control of the aircraft and get it back down to the tight landing field at Audembert – where he stalked across to Meyer and gave him a grateful slap on the back.

Flying with him that day – to score his first, though officially unconfirmed kill – was his younger brother Wilhelm-Ferdinand, 'Wutz' as he was always affectionately known. Wilhelm had joined the Luftwaffe Flakartillerie, but yearned for the life of a fighter pilot; towards the end of the Battle of Britain he transferred to fighter training school, and in due course his famous brother secured his assignment to JG26. Paul Galland, too, had aspirations to follow in Adolf's footsteps, and in March 1941 he completed his accelerated training course, to join III./JG26. Adolf's protective feelings for his two younger brothers made him want them close by, to ensure their very best chance of surviving this war. He even went some way towards a reconciliation with his elder brother Fritz, and eventually had him taken up by a fast-track training school from where he passed out to serve in reconnaissance and later in fighter units.

Galland's position gave him the freedom to set up a comfortable, homely environment in his requisitioned mansion at Audembert. It was not merely well stocked with cigars, fine wine, excellent food and other comforts; he tried to provide a semblance of the happy and carefree life the boys had known at Westerholt, which now seemed so very long ago. In one of the protected outbuildings he even had installed a magnificent model railway layout, where from time to time the three brothers would gather and settle down for a session, much as they had done in their childhood home. Galland tried to teach and advise his brothers how to fly, how to fight and, more important, how to survive. His was an unenviable position: with two brothers under his orders as members of a combat unit on active service, he felt a deep sense of personal responsibility for them, and yet could not shelter them from any of the risks faced by their brother pilots. Whenever anything happened to delay the return of Paul or 'Wutz' from a flight he had to sit in stoical pain while he waited to discover their fate.

Galland had been at war for almost two years now, and in that time he had risen to greater responsibility than he had ever imagined possible. The remorseless necessity to fly and to fight was beginning to extract its price. He had been jumped and shot up badly twice in four weeks; he had been shot down twice in a day, escaping with his life by the narrowest margin. Now his body, as well as his mind, knew that being the first and the best did not grant immortality. Despite the outward control inseparable from his whole creed of leadership he inwardly questioned his own ability to carry on. The burden of command was heavy enough; but now it was as nothing compared to the sheer terror that gripped him every time he walked out to his aircraft, strapped himself in, and began to rumble across the hard soil for take-off. Once airborne, the sweat and the fear fell away and he was as alert and ready for the fight as he had ever been; but when he returned the stress and fatigue were showing more visibly than ever before. Life against the 'Circuses' was no turkey-shoot; every day the mental pressure became more acute.

After he was wounded for the second time on 23 July, and Surgeon-Dr Heim had attended to him again, Galland was granted a brief respite and sent to receive his Swords to the Oak Leaves of the Knight's Cross from Hitler. This time he was to meet the Fuehrer at Rastenberg in East Prussia – the Wolf's Lair. Deep in the dark pine forest he was driven at speed past barbed wire barriers, armed sentry positions, machine gun towers and numerous checkpoints, through gatehouses and past guardrooms, until he was finally admitted to the Fuehrer's quarters. He had prepared himself for what he wanted to say. He had decided to express his concern that all the attention rivetted on the monumental advances in the East had deflected a proper concern for the efforts of two fighter wings who, with fewer than 250 aircraft between them, were staving off the full attentions of the RAF.

When he was received by Hitler he was immediately forestalled by the Fuehrer's concern for his personal safety. There were no recriminations for having thrown himself back into action directly against orders; there were only words of gratitude and appreciation for his continued loyalty and outstanding contribution to the war effort. Instead of gloating over victories in the East Hitler spent his time with Galland seeking information about conditions in France, about the performance of the RAF fighters, about the morale of Galland's men. He wanted to know about the increasing delivery of American aircraft to the British, and asked whether Galland had encountered any yet. He commiserated with the plight of the few fighter pilots left in the Pas de Calais, and asked that Galland convey to them his belief that the war in Russia would soon be over and that the Red Army would be destroyed by the winter. Then, he explained, he would attack British positions in the Near East, accelerate production of U-boats and aircraft, and turn again to a decisive blow against England.

The spell worked again. Despite himself Galland left feeling revitalised, his hopes at least partially restored, surprised at how quickly this man could make everything seem as though it was going to plan when deep and unanswered questions remained. Yet he was convinced more than ever before that the war must end soon. A protracted fight with Russia would sap Germany's strength and destroy her ability to fight on what were now three active fronts: Western, Eastern and Mediterranean.

* * *

In the meantime there was the impending arrival of a radically different new single-engine fighter to look forward to: the Focke-Wulf Fw190. Designed in 1937 and first flown in 1939, the new fighter was built as an interceptor to supplement the Bf109. When it appeared in 1941 it was arguably the world's finest radial-engined fighter, and would set the standard by which others were measured. Like any new aircraft it had already had its teething troubles, and would encounter problems as it entered squadron service; but Galland's JG26 had been selected as the logical choice for service tests and shakedown trials. Accordingly, a special unit of 30 selected personnel under Oblt Karl Borris, Staffelkapitaen 6./JG26, and Oblt Otto Behrens, the technical officer, had been sent in March 1941 to Rechlin-Roggenthin to work with six Fw190A-0 pre-production aircraft as Erprobungs-staffel 190. The Geschwader's II.Gruppe had been selected as the first unit to re-equip with the new fighter, and in late July they duly handed in their Bf109E-7s for brand new Fw190A-1s. The first pilot to receive the new aircraft – nicknamed the 'Wuerger', or Butcher Bird – was the CO of II./JG26, Hptmn Walter Adolph.

Between August and October the three squadrons of II.Gruppe worked up on the Fw190. As they got used to its capabilities the pilots were quickly able to establish its superiority over the Spitfire Mk.V: it was found to be 30-50km/h (20-30mph) faster at all altitudes, superior in the climb, markedly faster in the dive, more manoeuvrable except for tight turning circles (where the Spitfire excelled), and superior in rate of roll. As II./JG26 were re-equipping with their Focke-Wulfs, Galland found further opportunities to prove the qualities of the faithful Bf109.

On 9 August Galland got the chance to increase his score again by knocking down two Spitfires; but that evening the wing had a more intriguing reason to celebrate. Hptmn Rolf Pingel, Gruppenkommandeur I./JG26, contacted Galland and told him that his Gruppe had just shot down the famous legless British air ace Wg Cdr Douglas Bader – credited with 20 confirmed kills, six probables, five shared and 11 damaged. Bader had been in combat when the tail of his Spitfire was shorn off. Managing to extricate himself only by leaving one of his 'tin' legs jammed in the cockpit, Bader had parachuted to safety and been taken to the hospital at St Omer. When Hptmn Pingel told Galland the story he ordered a search to be made for the wrecked Spitfire so that Bader's false leg could be retrieved for him. Bader was visited in hospital by several officers from JG26; and on one occasion, after his second leg had been retrieved, repaired by one of the fitters, and returned to him, a certain amount of champagne had flowed. Before weaving off the Luftwaffe officers passed along an invitation to visit Audembert and enjoy Obstlt Galland's hospitality.

Bader enquired about getting his replacement tin leg flown over, perhaps by the Red Cross? The message was passed along and Galland said he would do what he could but made no promises. (Eventually the RAF flew Bader's spare legs over, but rather than accept the offered safe passage they dropped them during a routine bombing run.)

Galland arranged for his staff car, a splendid Horch, to collect Bader and bring him the 15 miles to Audembert. When Galland introduced himself Bader noticed the burn marks above his eyes from his recent adventures. Neither could speak the other's language, but through an interpreter they framed an amiable conversation – surprisingly, perhaps, since the often cantankerous Bader had little respect for the enemy. Through it all, however, Bader sensed a common bond that made them more akin than their uniforms would suggest. Galland walked Bader across to his famous train set; with a gleam in his eye he started it up and the entire display came alive, with little trains recklessly careering around the miniature track, points clicking and signals dropping.

As Bader relaxed Galland took him on a tour of the airfield and the Englishman was genuinely impressed, congratulating his host on the attention to detail. As they walked, pausing frequently to rest, they got into a long conversation about their respective aircraft, neither giving away secrets but each engaging in the common talk of airmen the world over. Enthusiasm took over and, proud of his new fighter, Galland allowed Bader to sit in his Bf109F while he explained all the instruments and controls. Enthusing over the German fighter, Bader leaned over the side of the cockpit and asked Galland for a special favour. Would he allow him to get the feel of this wonderful aircraft? Just a couple of circuits of the airfield? Galland smiled: 'If I grant your wish I'm afraid you'll escape and I should be forced to chase after you. Now we have met, we don't want to shoot at each other again, do we?' As he departed, Bader was given a tin of English tobacco.

* * *

During the autumn of 1941 Galland spent some time at one of Goering's hunting lodges at Elchwald in East Prussia. There had been many changes, and his old friend and arch-competitor Werner Moelders had excelled himself. With 115 victories he had been promoted to Oberst – full colonel – and withdrawn from the front to a staff job in Berlin. During September Moelders had been appointed Inspekteur der Jagdflieger, and from that date he was constantly on the move, visiting the fighter units on all fronts.

While Galland was at Elchwald Ernst Udet joined the group. There was much Galland wanted to talk about, but the great Word War I ace seemed morose and withdrawn, declining to take part in the sport on offer. As the Luftwaffe chief of supply and procurement, Udet was being held responsible by Goering – who had himself been blamed by Hitler – for the apparent lack of progress in expanding the air force to meet its wartime needs. Delayed for several reasons, the attack on Russia still began with the Luftwaffe no bigger than it had been in May 1940; Udet had managed no more than to keep up with the attrition rates. Udet was completely the wrong man for an administrative job which he had probably never wanted. He had been persuaded by Goering to join the Luftwaffe to reflect the lustre of his fame on the young service. An honourable and generous-hearted man, he felt his public failure and his false position keenly; now he had become the victim of a powerplay by Erhard Milch, assigned by Goering the task of quadrupling aircraft production, and determined to shift Udet to the sidelines.

Udet left Elchwald and went to a sanatorium to rest and to brood. While he was there Milch visited him, and brought up the issue of inadequate production levels. It was the final humiliation; on the morning of 17 November he put a gun to his head and shot himself. The propaganda machine would claim that he had died test-flying a new aircraft.

Galland had a deep regard for Udet and was stunned by his death. Paradoxically, for all his ineptness at mobilising production and delivery, he was a staunch advocate of increased emphasis on fighters in the overall production plan, worrying himself ill over the inability of the Luftwaffe to regain the offensive and act decisively in the West – passions close to Galland's heart. Now, with black irony, Udet's death would directly shape Adolf Galland's future.

The day after Ernst Udet took what he had been brought up to regard as the gentleman's way out, Galland achieved his 94th and, as it transpired, his last officially confirmed victory when he shot down a Spitfire 12 miles west of Boulogne at a height of 3,600m (12,000ft), flying his Bf109F-6/U carrying wing cannon in addition to the standard armament. His detailed combat report notes the use of just 98 rounds of ammunition.

The state funeral was to be held for Udet on 22 November. As distressed as Galland at the old hero's death, Werner Moelders signalled his intention to attend as a pall-bearer. Galland was there in full dress uniform; but Moelders did not after all attend. On the way to Berlin the Heinkel He111 carrying Moelders to his appointment crashed, killing Germany's most highly decorated flying ace. On 28 November 1941 Obstlt Adolf Galland stood pall-bearer for an admired comrade for the second time in a week. With solemn military honours the body of Obst Werner Moelders was carried through the streets of Berlin to the Invaliden Cemetery, where he joined Manfred von Richthofen and Ernst Udet. With what Galland considered appallingly bad taste, Goering called him over as he stood with the honour guard, sword drawn, by the side of the grave. Not quite knowing what to do with his sword, or what the protocol was under such circumstances, Galland stalked across to the Reichsmarschall. He would be next, said Goering; and officially appointed Adolf Galland Inspekteur der Jagdflieger at the graveside of his friend[4].

Notes to Chapter 14

1 One intriguing initiative during the Battle of Britain for providing pilots with information about their opponents had sprung from the linguistic skills of Sonderfuehrer Horst Barth, who made an art out of studying the informal chatter of RAF fighter pilots from his radio listening post on Cap Gris Nez. Over time he came to understand the coded references; from this he could tell where they were, and even started recognising individuals by their verbal mannerisms. Osterkamp incorporated the intelligence into Jafu 2 operations planning; Galland was highly sceptical, and resisted attempts at using this information to control the movement of his fighters. This activity inevitably came to Goering's attention and, seizing on anything that might bring an advantage, he formalised it into a specific unit under a senior officer; but it failed to mature into an especially useful tool. It was also resented by Luftwaffe fighter pilots, since it involved the simultaneous 'plotting' of their own R/T traffic; the Jagdflieger were known for their chattering over the radio, a habit which infuriated Galland.

2 This was an informal designation adopted by Galland with the approval of Jafu 2. Despite original intentions Messerschmitt never actually produced the Bf109F-5, F-6 and F-8; the response to Galland's request for a specific type designation was therefore one which would never conflict with a production aircraft.

3 Soviet re-equipment with more modern types had just begun, and the Luftwaffe was to get some surprises in the months to come. The ease of their victories and their contempt for the Russians betrayed the Germans into optimistic interpretations of the data. They ignored visible signs of a strengthening Soviet air industry; they underestimated the almost unlimited resilience which its vast size gave the Russian state; and they ignored evidence of massive factories being relocated from the western USSR to safety east of the Urals – a programme which in fact began before 'Barbarossa', not after.

4. Confusingly, though he held it in the rank of Oberst, the appointment carried the courtesy title 'General der Jagdflieger' – the sense of this perhaps translates as 'Chief of Fighter Pilots'.

CHAPTER 15

December 1941 – February 1942

To all intents and purposes Galland had scored his last victory when he downed a Spitfire on 18 November 1941. Appointed now as Inspector of Fighters, he was forbidden to fly combat missions, and would leave Jagdgeschwader 26 'Schlageter' forever. On 5 December Goering kept a promise to attend the farewell parade at Audembert, during which it was announced that Galland had been promoted Oberst. Maj Gerhard Schoepfel took over JG26 and Hptmn Josef Priller replaced him at the head of III.Gruppe; in his turn, Priller would replace Schoepfel just over two years later, maintaining Galland's legacy. Goering had combined this visit with one to the grave of his nephew Peter, shot down on 13 October when he had been flying as Galland's wingman; his untimely death came little more than three weeks after his leaving the Wiener-Neustadt training school, where he had been a close friend of Paul Galland.

The onset of winter 1941 was a miserable and disorienting time for Galland. Friends and colleagues were falling all around him. Udet, a man whom he respected and liked enormously, had shot himself; Werner Moelders, the friend against whom he had measured himself and with whom he could share many thoughts, was dead in a meaningless accidental crash. Now he was to lose his command – the wing he had devoted himself to shaping and leading – and had to go and play staff officer in Berlin. Galland felt the fighting soldier's normal contempt for staff officers, despising their comfortable arrogance; now he was to join their ranks himself.

As he stood in his full dress uniform, a black leather greatcoat shielding him against the bitter wind, he was only half-listening to the banalities of the Reichsmarschall at the rostrum. He would never leave JG26, not in his heart: this was where he really wanted to be, flying and fighting alongside his own men – not in Berlin, among staff officers who knew nothing of the real war. As his thoughts came back to the present Goering was finishing his speech; he wanted to look over Galland's aircraft before departing the Pas de Calais with the new Inspekteur der Jagdflieger.

The office of Inspector of Fighters had been set up in 1935, but was still evolving. His predecessors had included Udet, von Greim, Loerzer, Raithel, von Massow, von Doering and Moelders but none had lasted more than a year, or had

had time to make a great impression. None had produced any real strategy for the fighter forces; the appointment existed in a sort of bureaucratic limbo, without real responsibility, accountability, or influence over policy. Galland was inheriting the post at a time when increasing pressure was beginning to bear upon not only the fighter forces but the entire Luftwaffe.

Effectively an element in the Fuehrungsstab – the Luftwaffe operations staff – Galland would now have contact with Goering on a day-to-day basis. Indeed, he had been dismayed to realise that he would, in fact, have no authority to conduct operational activities except by special order from Goering. However, the fact that his remit was so nebulous could be turned to his advantage. He was determined to develop this into a real job, with real authority over fighter operations. He could have accepted an easy life as a bemedalled figurehead; he was an honest man, and he chose not to. It would be a hard path for an officer who was politically naive, unschooled in the machinations of the Fuehrungsstab, and totally inept when it came to dealing with Nazi Party members.

With his position came a house in a fashionable part of Berlin and a generous salary. He would now enjoy access to places denied to all but the powerful and the favoured. His fame and public popularity had risen to great heights: soon Galland would be given the freedom of the city, and all those incidental prizes – the parties, the glittering social functions, the public admiration from the famous – which can so easily trap a man and make him forget his real work.

Much of December was spent settling in, but before Christmas he travelled to Hitler's staff headquarters at Goldap in East Prussia to meet the Fuehrungsstab aboard Goering's train. There he met Genobst Hans Jeschonnek, chief of the Luftwaffe general staff; but he was given no indication of what his duties should be – it became clear that in Jeschonnek's eyes his appointment was primarily a matter of propaganda. Hitler liked to have around him decorated young warriors, and Goering saw to it that he got them. Galland was considered a splendid fighter pilot but nothing more, and his elevation was not popular among the older generation who still held on to the power to make operational decisions.

Jeschonnek himself had been promoted at a younger age than his subordinates: a colonel-general at 43 – the rank senior to full general, and thus junior only to marshals – Jeschonnek was a politically reliable general whom Hitler admired and trusted. It must be remembered, however, that among the leadership of the Third Reich – as in any dictatorship – the conventional chains of command were distorted. Power did not flow down predictable channels, but was diverted through various patterns of relationships. Jeschonnek tried to please everyone, and some older commanders patronised him. In assembling his air fleets for 'Barbarossa' Kesselring managed to acquire units which Jeschonnek had not sanctioned, and the opinionated Wolfram von Richthofen almost openly defied his authority.

As chief of staff Jeschonnek was in an invidious position. A Prussian, he had little in common with what he regarded as Goering's Bavarian frivolity; and he was on acrimonious terms with Milch, whose aide he had once been. Goering kept close to him a coterie of World War I veterans, a 'Karinhall set' including Genobst Bruno Loerzer, State Secretary Paul Koerner, and Gen Karl Bodenschatz, liaison officer between Goering's train and the RLM in Berlin. Jeschonnek found it difficult to maintain his authority when, typically, Goering disappeared to one of his hunting lodges, and issued through various adjutants orders which were at variance with those of his chief of staff.

When he first met Jeschonnek Galland hoped that the chief of staff would be sympathetic to his views and that they could work together. He was not so sure about other members of the Fuehrungsstab; he found the politics and the factional conflict irritating and confusing. In this new world unseen complexities and hidden agendas could snare a man unwilling to play games of intrigue. The problem was not only a clash of personalities, but also of cultures. Jeschonnek's loyalty to Hitler and his single-minded commitment to the Fuehrer's orders put him at variance with his own general staff, who wanted in his post a detached advocate of objective military planning rather than a stubborn defender of basically political edicts.

Conflict within the general staff was aggravated by Jeschonnek's appointment of his friend Gen Hoffman von Waldau as chief of operations planning. No sycophant, von Waldau increasingly questioned the illogical and unsound basis of many decisions; he fell out of favour with both the chief of staff and Goering, and was transferred to a front line post in early 1942. Galland saw that no true independence of thought was tolerated from the general staff, who had no power to act on conclusions drawn from detached consideration of the objective facts.

It was with a heavy heart and strong feelings of nostalgia that he returned to Audembert to spend Christmas 1941 with his comrades of JG26. It had been a hard year, and the successes of 1940 seemed a long time ago. There had been mixed feelings at JG26 about Galland's promotion. Some had believed that he would be in a position to benefit the pilots by influencing the decisions so crucial to their daily lives; others believed he could never be replaced, and that his dynamism and loyalty to the Geschwader were unique. He had chosen his successor well, however, and Maj Schoepfel would continue to follow the tradition he had created.

At least, in his so far ill-defined new role, Galland would have the time and the statistics to stand back from the battle and analyse just what 1941 had meant for the Jagdwaffe, and what the future promised -or threatened.

* * *

As a Geschwaderkommodore, Galland had been aware of the changing situation in the air war and had developed suitable tactics to counter the 'Circus' and 'Rhubarb' operations of an RAF increasingly determined to carry the fight back to the enemy. When the bomber element of these operations increased during April 1941 there was alarm among senior staff at Jafu 2, at Luftflotten headquarters in Paris and at the RLM in Berlin. The RAF were resuming daylight raids for the first time since they had been abandoned as too costly for the results in 1940; now they were back, hitting railways, airfields and industrial targets. In the initial stages of these operations the RAF paid a predictably heavy price. In the first six months of 1941 the RAF lost 51 pilots to 44 German aircraft; in the six months from 14 June they lost 411 fighters and destroyed only 103 Luftwaffe fighters over the Continent, although a further 51 had been lost in accidents and 11 had been shot down over England. Nevertheless, the RAF persisted.

Galland had long been worried that the lack of an adequate radar warning system was hampering the ability of the Geschwader to perform as it should. Although Jafu 2 at Le Touquet had access to radar equipment it lacked the operations network to put the system to work as effectively as it could have done. An audio-listening service had done useful work in alerting JG26 of imminent raids as the British equivalent had in 1940, when the raiders had crossed the Channel and the Chain Home stations were of no further use. Nevertheless, the two operational Geschwader on the French coast had to operate an 'alarm start' system, with pilots kept at readiness in their aircraft until scrambled with barely minutes to spare before the raiders arrived. This was costly in pilots and equipment because it tied them up for long periods. The weather also frequently militated against successful and timely interception of raids. All in all, the entire warning system was flawed.

When alerted to raids individual Gruppen, sometimes even individual Staffeln would usually operate independently. At the time of scrambling the pilots were given details of the position, course and, if they were lucky, the altitude of enemy formations. There was no grid like the British system upon which the fighters could be vectored to the bombers. Throughout 1941 the Jagdflieger relied on eyesight as the only credible means of finding the RAF. Galland was particularly disgusted by an early raid on Cologne, when bombs were falling on the city before JG26 was alerted, only just in time to get some of the bombers on their way home. Ground stations would use code-names for geographical features to which the Jagdflieger could be directed as way points, but it was all very vague and, in Galland's view, a bit like a party paperchase; and if cloud obscured the ground it was well nigh impossible to locate the raiders.

On average, during the 1941 'Circus' season, the RAF had sent over 25 bombers escorted by 75 fighters; but sometimes there were up to 80 bombers and 250 fighters. From early in the year the entire Jagdwaffe in the West could put up not many more than 200 aircraft, and tactics had to accommodate this unfavourable ratio. Their freedom of action was limited at first to the Continental side of the English coastline and later in the year to a line mid-Channel. The bombers usually came across at an altitude of about 6,500m (21,000ft), and the interceptors would try to get above and behind them before diving at high speed, in Schwaerme, through the escort to the bombers – JG2 and JG26 had been ordered to go for the bombers first. Galland disagreed that this was the best tactic and had managed to get some latitude for attempting innovations. Some of the high escorts would often peel off to follow the Bf109s down as they dived through, and on recovering from his first pass at the bombers the Jagdflieger could find a devastatingly effective cannon-armed Spitfire Mk.VB on his tail.

As 1941 wore on and the relative size of the 'Circuses' increased Galland adopted a daring tactic which few would emulate, and which would have little general application. His Stabschwarme would use cloud cover to approach the British escorts unseen, and then furtively attach themselves as though they were a component of the formation. It worked most of the time, the RAF pilots seeming oblivious to the differences of shape, camouflage and markings if the stalk was gradual and masked. At such close range the Bf109s would wreak havoc when they gunned their throttles and hit the firing buttons before diving away.

On other occasions Galland would use cloud to infiltrate the bombers themselves, matching his speed to theirs in a position close beneath and slightly behind his target while the escorts were distracted by other units. He would then tip up the nose and fire into the vulnerable underside of the bomber before bunting away into a high speed dive. He would usually be watching for suitable clouds to cover his escape; and once into a cloud he would often execute an extreme 5G pull-out, climbing fast from an unexpected point of reappearance.

Tactics could be tried out, adopted, taught or discarded; but aircraft availability was a key issue throughout the year. The RAF was losing two to four times as many fighters as the Luftwaffe. The losses to Bomber Command were even grimmer: during 1941 the RAF lost 701 bombers on night and 213 on daytime operations. But despite these figures the overall picture reflected a massive increase in British aircraft production. In September 1939 the RAF had fewer than 2,000 front-line combat aircraft. By August 1940, when the Battle of Britain was almost at its height, there were about 3,000. By the end of 1941 the RAF had 4,300 front-line aircraft – considerably more than twice the number just over two years before.

This compared to an increase of only 25 per cent in German front-line aircraft. The Luftwaffe had been unable to increase appreciably the number of operational aircraft on hand for 'Barbarossa' – 4,882 – over those available for the attack in the West 13 months before – 4,782 aircraft. Single-engined fighter strength had barely changed, going from 1,356 to 1,440. Production then increased to compensate for greater losses and by the end of 1941 first-line strength would be almost 5,200 aircraft, both production and losses reflecting the added burden of the campaign in Russia. During 1941 2,852 single-engined fighters, about 24 per cent of total output, were built, compared to 1,870 fighters in 1940, or 17 per cent of output for that year. Production of fighters had risen by 52 per cent while its share of total aircraft production went up by 41 per cent.

Behind these figures lay a grim truth which Galland had seen at the sharp end during his term at JG26, and which he would try, but apparently fail, to get across in Berlin: Germany was already losing the air war, because it was incapable of meeting requirements for machines and pilots from factories and training schools.

Taking aircraft first, Galland examined the loss levels and found them appalling. Out of 11,776 aircraft produced in 1941 the Luftwaffe lost 5,002, with a further 3,552 damaged, leaving a net gain of 3,222 aircraft. Of the 5,002 aircraft written off from all causes, 2,153 were due to accidents, many of them preventable. Of the 3,552 damaged, 2,685 were not in any way associated with combat. On closer examination Galland discovered that, for the Luftwaffe as a whole, 1,193 aircraft were damaged too badly to be repaired at unit level, taking them out of service for considerable periods. The inescapable conclusion was that the Luftwaffe was writing off in a year the number of aircraft equal to its entire first-line strength for that period.

As Inspekteur der Jagdflieger Galland was obviously concerned primarily with single- and twin-engined fighters. What he discovered was a revelation (though a testimony to the standard achieved by JG26). Of the 1,327 fighters written off during 1941, a total of 705, or 53 per cent, had not been in any way associated with enemy action. Monthly fighter losses began the year quite modestly, a mere 2-3 per cent rising to around 6-7 per cent with enhanced RAF activity and the Balkan campaign in April and May. During June, with the attack on Russia, they increased to 14 per cent, and to a staggering 23 per cent in July. Thereafter they oscillated around 10-13 per cent.

The task of getting supplies to the front lines along fast and efficient logistical routes became a nightmare as the Luftwaffe stretched its requirements outside Germany's territorial boundaries (a maximum distance of 400 miles east to west and 500 miles north to south). By the end of 1941 Luftwaffe supplies had to travel across a distance of 1,500 miles east to west and 2,000 miles north to south. Where once Galland had been concerned with routing supplies from western Germany to eastern France, he must now think in terms of intercontinental distances. He read reports that several hundred aircraft in Russia were idle awaiting spares and replacement parts. The supply and maintenance operations were so separated from the Luftwaffe's operational units that co-ordination to keep the appropriate stores moving to where they were needed was quite inadequate. By the end of 1941 Germany was fighting on three fronts, stretching beyond tolerance the fragile logistic lifelines.

When Galland explored the serviceability figures he saw a frightening magnification of the problems he had suffered in microcosm at JG26. Serviceability rates at the beginning of 1941 were respectably high, at 62-66 per cent; bombers had the lowest rate at around 55 per cent, and fighters the highest at about 70 per cent. As the year dragged on with increased commitments and ever greater territorial expansion, the serviceability rate suffered; by the end of 1941, of an authorised strength of 1,950 bombers, the Luftwaffe had only 468 that it could fly operationally. Fighter serviceability was running at 52 per cent of aircraft assigned to units. There were simply neither enough aircraft being built, nor an effective logistic chain to maintain the aircraft there were.

In addition to production and serviceability, there was a third statistic which was even more important: availability of operational pilots. At the beginning of 1941 fighter stations could rely on 75 per cent of authorised strength. After another year of war, pilot strength ran at barely 55 per cent of establishment.

When Galland went over the figures he knew that if Hitler had been correct in his assertion that the war with Russia would last a few weeks, a couple of months at most, then the Luftwaffe could survive. But six months on the war with Russia was not over. In reality, when offensive ground operations came to a halt on the Eastern Front on 30 October 1941, the Luftwaffe was so over-extended that, on paper, it would wither away to nothing within a measurable future without any further military action whatsoever.

There were at least two new operational threats facing or threatening the Luftwaffe. Galland's remit would now cover an area to which he had hitherto given little thought: nighttime interception. The first stirring of the RAF's night bombing offensive in July 1940 had led to the formation of the first of three Nachtjagddivisionen; and the extension of that offensive in 1941 (when in August the RAF bombed targets east of Berlin for the first time) required the expansion of the night fighter force, commanded by Generalleutnant Josef Kammhuber. Resources were applied to building up the ground capability for bigger and better acquisition and tracking radars, a technology that would offer collateral benefits for the day fighters. By February 1942 the night fighter force had increased from 195 to 367 aircraft in seven Gruppen: a motley collection of Bf110s, Ju88s, a few Do17s and some Do215s. All information about Nachtjaeger operations would pass through Galland's office in Berlin. Indeed, an immediate effect of his taking up the appointment was his requirement for a precise and detailed catalogue of reports and operational data on every aspect of life involving fighter forces; this enabled him to have as clear an overall view as anyone in the Luftwaffe.

The other new threat, in the longer term more dangerous than the RAF's area bombing, followed Japan's stunning attack on Pearl Harbor on 7 December 1941: Hitler's declaration of war on the United States four days later. The consequences were as yet unquantifiable; but America's vast capacity for industrial production was already legendary, and the part played in Germany's last national catastrophe by the AEF's arrival in France in 1918 was rather more than a historical footnote.

* * *

Galland's first hint of an opportunity to establish himself in his new appointment, and to give some public definition to his role, came early in January 1942 when he was called to a conference at the Wolfsschanze. He would always remember the subsequent operation as one of the most challenging and exciting tasks he performed throughout his service.

Jeschonnek briefed him beforehand: Hitler was concerned about a possible attack on Germany from the north, perhaps orchestrated by the new Triple Alliance of Britain, Russia and the USA. He therefore planned to move the battleships *Scharnhorst* and *Gneisenau*, and the heavy cruiser *Prinz Eugen*, from their berths in Brest on the Atlantic coast of France to Norwegian waters where they could play a part in resisting any such attempt. The only possible routes were the short but perilous English Channel; or west into the Atlantic and far north around Ireland and Scotland, running the gauntlet of the British fleet at Scapa Flow. The short Channel route had been selected; and Galland was to organise fighter cover to protect the warships from the RAF as well as the Royal Navy.

Jeschonnek was candid. He made it clear that the Kriegsmarine did not want to move the ships; that the Luftwaffe did not want the responsibility of their protection; that Goering had distanced himself from the operation; and that no one else in the Luftwaffe wanted command of the organisation and execution of the air cover. Remarkably, Galland would always declare that at the time it did not occur to him – new as he was to the staff world – that he was being groomed for the role of scapegoat. This was a job for a combat commander; he accepted the challenge with relish, and went to the conference on 12 January convinced that he could make it work.

Present with Hitler and Keitel were Adm Raeder of the Kriegsmarine with Adm Ruge and Adm Ciliax, the commander of the battleship force; Genobst Jeschonnek and Obst Galland represented the Luftwaffe. The admirals argued that the crews of the two warships were in no condition to fight a running battle: they had been in port for almost a year and needed a shake-down cruise. Just their presence had seriously interfered with the operations of the Royal Navy's 'Force H' which protected convoys to North Africa and Malta. Moreover, with American naval resources concentrated in the Pacific and the Royal Navy now having to protect British interests in the Far East as well, what better time than now to increase the pressure on Britain's maritime lifeline with North America?

In the end the Kriegsmarine deferred to Hitler, who remained adamant that the risks of a Norwegian campaign were too great to ignore; and Adm Ruge was offered as the naval planning officer for Operation 'Cerberus'.

Hitler emphasised the importance of the Luftwaffe's role, and appeared to welcome the employment of Galland; Jeschonnek was apprehensive about making claims for the Luftwaffe's ability to carry out the job. The vital importance of absolute secrecy about the planned sailing was discussed, and extraordinary measures would be taken by both services to limit the spread of sensitive information. The Kriegsmarine's preparations would include sweeping mines from a course which would allow the maximum speed and a minimum depth of 15 fathoms right through the Channel close to the French coast; and setting up marker boats which would come out from shore at various points to cut the time necessary for exact shipboard navigation.

From the time the conference broke up until after the operation had been performed, Galland had a free hand: he alone would mastermind the entire air operation and implement its phases without its participants knowing completely what was going on. First, it was necessary to secure the communications channels and specialists from the Generalluftzeugmeister, to work with radar and radio technicians to come up with an evasion and deception plan to keep the British guessing. In this work Gen Martini was of great help and applied innovative methods of interference designed to veil the radio traffic. Martini and Obst Max Ibel were the only people in whom Galland confided.

Total resources for air cover would include JG2, JG26, and 12 Bf109s from a fighter training school which were moved up to Le Havre for the air operation, codenamed 'Thunderbolt'. As he reviewed the aircraft necessary to protect the warships Galland decided that these assets fell short of minimum requirements so, on the pretext of organising a series of escort formations for a particularly large daylight bombing raid on England, he had JG1 based in north-west Germany committed to supporting the operation during the morning hours, when it was planned that the ships – after a night sailing – would reach the German Bight. With the 60 Bf109s from JG1 he would have a maximum of 252 aircraft, plus a further 30 Bf110s for dawn and dusk patrols.

These resources would have to be assigned specific sectors along the route and timed to interconnect as the ships moved north. It would be impossible to provide full fighter cover continuously at both high and low levels, so Galland arranged for 16 fighters at a time to remain over the ships for approximately 35 minutes; relief patrols would engage ten minutes before the previous patrol was due to leave, so the cover would increase to 32 aircraft for at least 20 minutes in every 70 minutes. To achieve this mechanics would have to turn the fighters around between sorties in no more than 30 minutes – a major challenge.

To control all these patrols Galland set up four sectors. The first, designated IA, covered the coast from Cherbourg to Le Havre with headquarters at Caen; this would provide the dawn patrols. Sector I had its headquarters with Jafu 2 at Le Touquet and covered the area from south of Abbeville up through Calais to a point just north of Dunkirk. Sector II, headquartered at Schipol, covered the area from the Scheldt through the Rhine and Zuider Zee to north of Amsterdam. Sector III, with headquarters at Jever, covered the area around Wilhelmshaven and Hamburg.

To make it all work the ships had to be between Cherbourg and Le Havre at dawn, and time their transit with such accuracy that the fighters from Sector II could return and refuel at 15.00 for a second sortie to supplement the standing patrol. Each airfield in each sector had a special radio link and, in addition to an ultra-short wave radio which Galland would use to communicate with his units, he would use a long-wave set for maintaining contact with the ships. He could fine-tune schedules to maintain full cover all the way if he could keep track of the actual pace of the warships; if he could not, the intricate plan would collapse. Taking as his inspiration the forward air controllers used by Moelders almost two years before, Galland decided to have airmen on each ship through whom he could communicate[2].

Throughout the preparations for 'Cerberus' the British intercepted the relevant Enigma traffic, which was so detailed that by 1 February the British knew that *Scharnhorst* gun crews aboard the *Prinz Eugen* were moving back to the flagship in preparation for sailing. Although they evaded air reconnaissance, Enigma traffic revealed that the capital ships were slipping berth at night and returning by dawn in an effort to give the crews a concentrated working-up period. Admiral of the Fleet Sir Dudley Pound received intelligence that there was a concentration of fighters in north-west France which might be linked to an imminent departure of the three warships. It is to the credit of the German security system that while they were able to read all the Enigma messages, the British never had a direct indication that 'Cerberus' was planned, or that a dash through the Channel was the objective. Nevertheless, in the light of subsequent events the Germans were fortunate that the staff performance of the RAF and Royal Navy did not match the remarkable job done by the intelligence services.

By 3 February Galland received word that the naval forces were in place; reinforcements between Brest and the Hook of Holland included destroyers, torpedo boats, minesweepers, E-boats and smaller support craft. In London the Admiralty also passed this information to RAF Coastal, Bomber and Fighter Commands. In anticipation of a breakout the British had prepared plans for attack known as Operation 'Fuller', with aircraft and ships on standby.

On 4 February Adm Ciliax raised his flag on *Scharnhorst* and issued sealed orders, to be opened only on receipt of the code word 'Ganges' – chosen to give a fictitious flavour of joint German-Japanese operations. The date and time for departure was set for 11 February at 19.45, chosen for maximum advantages of tide, moon and weather. Since intelligence reports to London from French agents about activity in Brest were automatically assumed, the commanding officers of the entire squadron were very publicly invited to dine with the Admiral Commanding, Western Group at his headquarters in Paris at 20.00 on 11 February; the invitations were then cancelled through coded channels.

On the afternoon tide of 11 February the submarine HMS *Sealion* slipped into Brest roads on orders to watch for any movement. A British air raid began at about 19.00, and the battleships' planned sailing time was put back by three hours; at 20.35, none the wiser, *Sealion* withdrew to recharge batteries. An RAF Hudson, patrolling off the peninsula, turned back for base when its radar failed at 19.30. A second Hudson arrived on station at around 21.30; just as it turned for home at 22.45 the German warships sailed. Its replacement arrived after midnight, but only for a few minutes during the next three hours was the aircraft in radar range of the flotilla, whose movement went unreported.

By shortly after midnight *Scharnhorst, Gneisenau* and *Prinz Eugen* were rounding Ushant at 29 knots, and had already made up some of the time lost to the air raid. At Jafu 2 Galland began to receive regular reports from the radar stations (there was, of course, complete radio silence). With the three-hour delay Galland was convinced he would have to move the fighters in the Pas de Calais down to the Le Havre area, but as the night progressed and he followed the radar blips he was relieved to see the warships making up more time.

At 05.15 on 12 February the flotilla was north-west of Alderney, and turned abruptly east to hug the coast across the top of the Cherbourg peninsula. For weeks, under a plan worked out with Galland, Gen Martini's men had been using a primitive form of radar jamming which created a response on the receiving set simulating natural atmospheric interference. Introduced gradually, at first for a few seconds a day and then, with an oscillating frequency, for several minutes, the jamming signal gave the impression that early morning atmospherics were disrupting the radar returns. Long before dawn, on Galland's orders, two Heinkel He111s took off and began to fly parallel with the English coast; they carried radar distortion equipment which gave the appearance of a larger circling formation.

At 08.50 the first Bf110 night fighters arrived for the dawn patrol over the ships; they were flying too high, and were caught by British shore radar. Flying under a 460m (1,500ft) cloud ceiling, they would have been clearly visible to any aircraft vectored to inspect them; but the radar station at Beachy Head which spotted them chose to ignore their presence. Some time later the same radar 'saw' the Heinkels, and reported that aircraft were circling over ships moving through the Channel at 25 knots. Nobody reacted.

When dawn broke at 08.00 the flotilla had been on schedule to pass Dieppe at around 09.30; the weather was misty with light rain. Adm Ciliax was pleased with progress so far, having snatched back the lost time from the night before. Almost ten hours and 250 miles along their route, the flotilla of two battleships, one cruiser and 16 destroyers would soon grow to a force of almost 60 vessels when the E-boats and other light units from Western Naval Command rendezvoused off Cap Gris Nez.

At 08.25 Wg Cdr M. Jarvis, senior controller at RAF Fighter Command, Stanmore, decided that the reported radar blips were in fact bunches of 20 or so aircraft escorting shipping in the Channel. He informed No.11 Group; and noticed some familiar interference similar to atmospherics. This information, and another radar sighting from Swingate showing aircraft circling ships in the Channel, was believed to indicate a German air-sea rescue operation, and was ignored.

At 08.45 Fighter Command sent out a standard 'Jim Crow' patrol of two Spitfires from No.91 Sqn at Hawkinge, one of which sighted E-boat activity off Boulogne and Berck; the second sighted several small craft east of Zeebrugge. Since radio silence was mandatory, these were reported verbally on the pilot's return.

At 09.25 Wg Cdr Jarvis at Stanmore told the duty air commodore that plots from Newhaven radar appeared to show two or three aircraft circling over the Channel, and that he had calculated that they were migrating up Channel at in excess of 20 knots. The duty air commodore and No.11 Group duty controller decided that radar interference was distorting the plot.

At Le Touquet Galland could hardly believe his luck. Hitler had been right after all: he had said the British would dither, and would never get a strike force together in time. But it was still early in the day, and the perilously narrow Straits of Dover still lay ahead.

By now the flotilla was approaching Dieppe. At 09.41, 09.47 and 09.59 British radar reports indicated the same progression northward of a small group of ships with escort circling overhead. Technical experts were brought in, and decided that the interference was too bad to rely on the spasmodic returns. At 10.00 Wg Cdr Jarvis reported these cumulative reports once again; but Fighter Command had already decided, on the basis of the verbal reports from the 'Jim Crow' pilots, to mount a shipping strike against the small vessels off Berck and Zeebrugge. Again, the radar plots were dismissed as nothing to worry about. At about 10.16 the Beachy Head radar picked up a return indicating two ships off Boulogne; they tried to ring Dover, but all the telephones were down.

Meanwhile, the Bf110 Nachtjaeger had returned to airfields in Holland, there to wait until dusk when once again they would pick up the flotilla moving toward Wilhelmshaven. By now the ships were off the mouth of the Somme and had been racing up the Channel for two hours without anyone having realised they were there.

From his control station at Le Touquet Galland monitored the weather, the progress of the ships, the movement in and out of the escort patrols, and serviceability on his airfields. The only sound in the control room was the hissing from a large loudspeaker on the wall; it was connected to a radio receiver tuned to the frequency the flotilla would use if its cover was blown and its location plotted by the RAF.

At 10.20 two more 'Jim Crow' Spitfires took off to perform a second sweep; this time Sqn Ldr Oxspring, commanding No.91 Sqn, was making a positive attempt to confirm whether there really was something going on in the Channel. Sqn Ldr Igoe, senior flight controller at Biggin Hill, had rung to ask him to make this second sweep because he was very concerned that no one at No.11 Group was taking the reports seriously. Wg Cdr Jarvis at Stanmore was also frustratingly unable to get anyone to react. At 10.30 he suggested that the 'atmospheric interference' might be deliberate jamming; scientists were again called in, but could reach no firm conclusion. Jarvis suggested to No.11 Group that a special reconnaissance should be mounted, but that was turned down on the grounds that Oxspring and his wingman Sgt Beaumont were already airborne and would return soon with further information. At about this time telephone discussions between Flag Officer Dover, Adm Sir Bertram Ramsay, and the Admiralty and RAF produced the conclusion that there was no danger of a breakout from Brest that day; Operation 'Fuller' was stood down until the next routine alert at 04.00 next morning.

For all the scores of people who had been peering at suspect radar blips and phantom shapes on cathode ray tubes, it fell to a maverick Spitfire pilot to uncover the truth. Gp Capt Victor Beamish, senior staff officer to C-in-C No.11 Group, was a Battle of Britain veteran with nine confirmed and 11 probable kills. Officially forbidden to fly, he was given a limited ration of flying hours to keep him quiet. He took off from Kenley that morning on one of his 'specials' – jaunts over the Channel on the lookout for trouble – accompanied by Wg Cdr Finlay Boyd in the thankless role of nursemaid. It was 10.33 when they chanced upon a hornet's nest of Bf109s, almost at the same time as did Oxspring and Beaumont. The two pairs of Spitfires were tearing into the Messerschmitts before they suddenly saw the warships.

As both pairs made for home, it was Sqn Ldr Oxspring who decided that this was no time to follow orders blindly; he broke radio silence to report the warships, placing them 50 miles off the mouth of the Somme and 15 miles from Le Touquet. German listening posts close by picked up the report and brought it to Galland within seconds. Unknown to Oxspring or Galland, the Spitfire had been too low for his radio message to be picked up in England. Galland knew that if he broke radio silence by sending the command 'Open Visor' he would unleash a babble of radio traffic from ships, aircraft and shore command posts that would tell the British where they were and what they were doing. He kept his gambler's nerve and maintained radio silence, buying extra time and miles up the Channel.

When Sqn Ldr Oxspring and Sgt Beaumont landed back at Hawkinge at 10.50 they raced for a telephone to back up the radio call which they believed had got through. They were unable to get anyone to accept what they had seen; the best that Oxspring could get was a commitment to enlarge the previously authorised strike against the small vessels reported by the first patrol almost two hours earlier.

At 11.09 Gp Capt Beamish landed at Kenley; and at long last, thanks to his rank and his forceful personality, the report was finally taken seriously. Warnings went out to all three RAF Commands.

At Le Touquet, Galland was still not convinced that radio silence should be broken yet. By now the warships were approaching the most vulnerable stage of their voyage, and were navigating their way through the marker boats around Cap Gris Nez. The cloud layer had descended to around 180-250m (600-800ft); it was raining, but visibility was reasonable. Opposite Boulogne the additional E-boats joined up with the flotilla, and Galland began to change the levels of aircraft availability. He had used none of his reserves, and the fighters sent up so far had not yet been in combat. He had not really believed that they could get this far without detection; their chances looked good. It all depended on how quickly the British could react.

North of the Channel difficult decisions were being made quickly. In an hour or so the warships would be off the Scheldt, the range increasing rapidly. Organised in haste, an attack would take place at 12.45 by the only immediately available force: Lt Cdr E. Esmonde's No.825 Sqn, Fleet Air Arm, based at Manston with 165kph (90-knot) Swordfish biplane torpedo-bombers. Five squadrons of fighters were to meet the Swordfish at 12.25 and escort them in. No one was under any illusions: this would be a sacrificial mission against a heavily defended target with substantial fighter cover.

Shortly after noon the flotilla passed Cap Gris Nez and the E-boats swung into position. Dover coastal artillery fired a few dozen rounds, the nearest falling a mile from an escort destroyer. Esmonde's Swordfish were to have rendezvoused with their five escort squadrons over Manston at 12.25, but only one squadron turned up on time; and at 12.28 they were ordered to move against the warships. The six Swordfish and ten Spitfires flew out to a point approximately 16km (10 miles) north of Calais, where the flotilla was calculated to be. There was still radio silence between the Jagdflieger, and no one aboard ship saw or reported the approaching biplanes. The first to spot them were the 40 or so Bf109s flying low around the massive warships; Galland had been able to increase the fighter escort because of the proximity of the flotilla to many Luftwaffe airfields.

While the Bf109s engaged the Spitfires the Swordfish laboured on, looking for their targets. Fighter control aboard the ships now broke radio silence, as was their prerogative, and directed the fighters visually. The first Bf109s to attack the confusingly slow biplanes were successfully driven off by the Spitfires. The first Swordfish flight to attack was led by Lt Cdr Esmonde in the face of a hail of flak from the destroyer screen. A shell tore off Esmonde's port lower mainplane and the fuselage began trailing smoke; still the aircraft held its course. Flying at 150kph (80 knots), Esmonde lined up on the *Scharnhorst*, now less than a mile ahead, and dropped his one torpedo at 900m (3,000ft), just seconds before the Swordfish erupted in a ball of flame.

The second pilot, Sub-Lt B.W. Rose, was hit in the spine by shrapnel. Bf109s were carrying out slash attacks, but with the Swordfish a mere 15m (50ft) above the water there was not much room for them to manoeuvre. Releasing his torpedo, Rose turned his burning aircraft away and flew it well clear of the escort destroyers before ditching.

The third aircraft endured the wall of fire long enough to drop its torpedo just 450m (1,500ft) from the *Scharnhorst*; with all three crew wounded and two cylinders shot out of the engine Sub-Lt C.M. Kingsmill ditched his Swordfish – he and one other were saved but Ldg Amn A.L. Johnson died.

The three aircraft of the second flight also pressed home their attacks, but were lost in the massive crossfire; nothing was ever found of their crews. Esmonde's body was later washed ashore; he was posthumously awarded the Victoria Cross. At the end of the day the Luftwaffe diary would note of the extraordinary attack by the six Swordfish that they were 'piloted by men whose bravery surpasses any other action by either side that day.'

There was now no need to maintain a universal communications blackout, and Galland gave the order 'Open Visor'. The fighters were released from their low altitude ceiling, there no longer being any reason to remain below the radar, and different formations were ordered up. A babble of unco-ordinated chatter broke across the air waves as orders flew from Le Touquet to the ships, and pilots talked to each other for the first time that day.

Two hours on from the first admitted sighting, the British response had been limited to a flurry of shells thrown into the Channel and 13 extraordinarily brave naval airmen sent to their deaths. Motor torpedo boats from Dover attacked the German warships at about 12.30, but released their torpedoes outside range. The progress of the flotilla up Channel had reached the point where the distance from England would rapidly increase. As the English coastline fell away the flight time separating the ships from their potential attackers increased, allowing a longer warning; and now that radio silence had been broken the German coastal radar stations could advise the ships and aircraft of impending attack.

Galland was now distanced from the action and it was impossible to keep moment-by-moment control. That was exactly the way he had planned it. Ever the lone decision-maker, Galland wanted a set of procedures and operating protocols that enabled each Staffel or Gruppe to operate without consultation. Tired of the bungled micro-management of large formations during the Battle of Britain, he wanted the fighters unleashed to exploit their full potential. Coming so shortly after his appointment as Inspekteur der Jagdflieger, Operation 'Thunderbolt' was the perfect opportunity to demonstrate what he had been arguing to Goering and his senior staff for more than two years: that the fighters were a valuable and independent arm capable of controlling events in their own right.

In England, the first reports of something happening in the Channel reached Bomber Command Headquarters at High Wycombe at 11.27. Motivated to an all-out effort which made nonsense of the more leisurely and cautious standing orders for Operation 'Fuller', Bomber Command readied approximately 240 aircraft out of the 310 theoretically available that morning. The weather was far from ideal, with almost total cloud cover, a cloud base of no more than 600m (2,000ft) and visibility down in places to as low as 200m (700ft). It was agreed to get the first attack force in the air at 14.30 with a second wave at 16.00.

Meanwhile, after the Swordfish attack, Galland telephoned Sector I and Sector II headquarters at Le Touquet and Schipol for aircraft availability up-dates. He believed that a major attack by a force capable of inflicting real damage must be imminent. Not one German fighter had been lost so far; with his margins unexpectedly intact, and the flotilla moving up the Belgian coast, he could afford to consolidate his forces.

At 14.31 the *Scharnhorst* struck a mine and came to a stop as all electrical power was lost for 20 minutes; overtaken by *Gneisenau*, the flagship was not in fact seriously damaged, and resumed her escape at 25 knots. The first wave of 73 aircraft from Bomber Command reached the target area at various times between 14.55 and 15.58. In the low cloud and drizzle only ten crews reported sightings; not one bomb hit any of the primary targets or their escorts. During this period five British destroyers found the flotilla and fired torpedoes from a range of 2.75-3.3km (3,000-3,500 yards); one of them was severely damaged by fire from *Prinz Eugen*; and none of the torpedoes found their mark. At some time after 15.35 nine Beauforts of No.42 Sqn finally located the target; they all launched torpedoes against the *Gneisenau*, without achieving hits or suffering casualties. Two lost Hudson bombers were shot down by escort ships when they ventured below the clouds.

The second wave of 134 aircraft from Bomber Command arrived in the general area at times between 16.00 and 17.06, but poor visibility and lack of training against naval targets prevented any more than 20 crews from delivering attacks, without result. The final motley collection of 35 aircraft reached the target area between 17.50 and 18.15; only nine aircraft attacked and again, not one bomb hit anything solid. A mixed force of Beauforts from Nos.86 and 217 Sqns blundered onto some escort ships in the dusk; two were lost and one severely damaged for no result.

This unco-ordinated succession of RAF attacks, in bad weather and low visibility, were handicapped by haste, muddled orders, communications failures and simple human error; but the situation was frequently confused for the Germans, too. Had it not been for the air controllers put aboard the three warships by Galland the operation would have been chaotic. Even so, some mistakes did happen; one Dornier attacked a Kriegsmarine destroyer. The fighters had been hard pressed at times to fend off some of the patrolling British escort fighters – of which there were at one point 15 squadrons over the Channel – and several furious battles had developed above the clouds while the bombers tried to find their targets.

By dusk the main flotilla was closing on the Friesian Islands. Galland had good reason to be pleased with himself and proud of the Luftwaffe. The British had nothing to show for their losses; but all could still be lost if the Luftwaffe failed to maintain a total 'umbrella' over the warships. As the late afternoon gave way to evening the weather to the north worsened and the clouds were almost down to ground level. Still Galland wanted to maintain the strongest force possible; he decided to have fighters from the Pas de Calais sector fly north to conduct escort patrols over the ships, and then divert to airfields in Holland – some of their home airfields were 120 miles away from the northern bases, and the pilots had already flown four sorties since dawn. By moving up Channel to carry out their patrols they were, in effect, performing a sweep which would encounter RAF aircraft going to or from the target area, providing further opportunity for combat.

Many of the Jagdwaffe pilots decided to extend their operational schedules and put in more flying than had been required by plan. As the afternoon wore on and it became apparent that boldness had paid off, they took off on their own initiative and reported in to their sector controllers that they were available for assignment. This attitude was a remarkable testimony to Galland's inspirational leadership.

During the 'Channel Dash' the RAF and RN lost 43 aircraft: Fighter Command lost 17, Coastal Command five, Bomber Command 15, and the Fleet Air Arm six. The Luftwaffe lost 17 aircraft and 11 men; the Kriegsmarine lost one advance boat, a fishing vessel, and eight other ships suffered relatively minor damage. Ironically, the greatest threat to the capital ships turned out to be mines: the *Scharnhorst* struck a second that night, and limped into Wilhelmshaven on the 13th. The *Gneisenau* struck two that evening and night, but without serious damage, sailing safely into Kiel with the *Prinz Eugen*.

During 13 February Galland flew up to Wilhelmshaven to attend a very thorough and analytical post-operation conference aboard the *Scharnhorst* involving all those who had figured in the planning and operations. He would later conduct his own full investigation into every aspect of the operation when he returned to Berlin; but first he wanted to celebrate this astonishing success, and to reward those who had done most to make it happen. Galland believed his faith in the potential of a well trained and disciplined fighter force to operate effectively without detailed external constraints had been vindicated.

It had been a personal victory, too. There had been many opportunities for Galland to fail in this, his first operational assignment involving all the day and night fighter forces on the Western Front. Both Goering and Jeschonnek had expected his wings to be clipped; his triumph was instead to bring him more widespread respect, and it went a long way to compensate for his lack of years and of a formal staff training. In some respects, Galland had reached the apogee of his career.

* * *

During the planning for 'Thunderbolt' Galland enjoyed two brief but pleasant distractions.

On 28 January 1942 he was invested by Hitler at Rastenburg with the Diamonds to his Swords and Oak Leaves of the Knight's Cross – then the supreme class of Germany's highest decoration for valour and service, which would be awarded to just 27 officers, and surpassed by only one[3]. Several other leading fighter aces were also decorated with classes of the Knight's Cross at the same investiture, including Luetzow, Trautloft and Priller[4].

On the day of Galland's investiture a Spitfire crash-landed on the outskirts of Boulogne with severe flak damage. The pilot was the leader of the Biggin Hill Wing, Wg Cdr Robert Stanford Tuck DSO, DFC, formerly of Nos.92 and 257 Sqns, and a Battle of Britain ace with at least 27 kills to his name. Learning during a visit to JG26 that Tuck was being held locally awaiting transport to a POW camp, Galland sent for him and extended the hospitality of the mess, which he accepted with enthusiasm. The quintessential image of the acquiline, pencil-moustached 'Ronald Colman' type, Bob Tuck carried himself with composure in what might have been humiliating circumstances.

There were about eight officers at table, each of whom stood to introduce himself with a click of the heels. Galland reminded Tuck that he had nearly shot him down on a previous occasion; Tuck reminded Galland that he had not just escaped by the skin of his teeth, but had actually shot down Galland's wingman. They both laughed; and Galland had the steward bring a bottle of White Label scotch and a packet of Gold Flake cigarettes. Conversation turned pleasantly to wine, food and girls. Someone asked Tuck why he wore Polish pilot's wings in addition to his RAF brevet; he explained that they had been presented to him by a Polish comrade. When the Luftwaffe officer remarked that he distrusted Poles, Tuck dryly replied that he would rather have Poles for friends than Italians or Japanese, and Galland roared with laughter. When it was over Galland said that he hoped they would meet again after the war. They did; and became firm and lifelong friends until Tuck's death.

Notes to Chapter 15

1 The *Scharnhorst* and *Gneisenau*, launched in 1936, each had a loaded displacement of 39,500 tonnes and a maximum design speed of 30 knots; each carried 9x11in guns, 12x6in and 14x4in, plus 16x twin 37mm AA guns, six torpedo tubes and four recce aircraft; and each had a complement of some 1,900 men. The two warships had parallel careers to some extent, seeing service off Norway in 1940 and in the Atlantic during 1941. Among *Scharnhorst's* victims were the carrier HMS *Glorious* in June 1940, while *Gneisenau* sent 22 ships to the bottom in two months beginning 22 January 1941. Both arrived in Brest, which was manned from Wilhelmshaven Navy Yard, on 22 March 1941; they were a prestige RAF target, and on 24 July *Scharnhorst* was damaged.

2 Obst Max Ibel was to be stationed on the *Scharnhorst* as 'Fighter Command Afloat', reconciling what was happening at sea with what was needed from the Jagdflieger and directly controlling the air activity. In addition, another officer in charge of fighter operations and interceptions would talk to the aircraft, two more officers on board would co-ordinate interception intelligence, and Obstlt Elle would command the essential wireless personnel keeping a broad picture of operations involving both Luftwaffe and RAF aircraft.

3 The single award of the Golden Oak Leaves, Swords and Diamonds to Oberst Hans-Ulrich Rudel, the outstanding Stuka pilot, on 1 January 1945.

4 There was a long-running sequel. Galland was dining with Goering shortly afterwards when the Reichsmarschall, peering at the decoration, asked Galland to hand it to him. This was mildly embarrassing since Galland, like other fighter pilots, used a lady's garter concealed under his collar to support the heavy cross – in this case one given him by Monica. Goering, however, was more interested in the cluster of small diamonds set into the silver oak leaves and sword hilts, declaring them on inspection to be virtually worthless, and far inferior to the stones commissioned from the government-appointed Berlin jeweller. He later told Hitler of this apparent fraud; and had his own jeweller prepare a suitable replacement, which he subsequently presented to Galland. Unaware of this, Hitler also had a replacement set made by a different jeweller; when Galland visited Rastenburg some time later Hitler proudly announced his discovery of the fraud as if it were a revelation, and presented him with these, comparing them with the fine-quality Goering set that Galland was already wearing with a beaming smile and the words, 'There! Now you can see the difference.' Galland naturally had to play along, with graceful thanks and mock amazement at Hitler's knowledge of diamonds. The story did not even end there. During a furious argument with Goering in 1943 Galland tore the decoration from his neck, refusing to wear it any

longer; and thereafter kept it in his office draped round the neck of a stuffed bird. In November 1943 his building was bombed, and the stuffed bird and third set of diamonds were lost. Hearing of this, Hitler had yet a fourth set made....

CHAPTER 16

February – December 1942

For Galland Operation 'Thunderbolt' did not end once the battleships had reached German ports; his orders had been to protect them until they reached Norway. The RAF made continued attempts to destroy them while they were in Kiel (where *Scharnhorst* joined *Gneisenau* on 15 February); to co-ordinate the necessary fighter cover with the navy and Luflotten 3 and 5 Galland and a small operations staff briefly moved first to Jever on the German Bight, then to Esbjerg in Denmark, and finally to Stavanger in Norway. (In fact it was to be March 1943 before *Scharnhorst* finally reached Alten Fjord; and *Gneisenau*, which ran onto a submerged wreck, never went to war again.)

To perfect 'Thunderbolt', Galland had worked with Karl Koller at Luftflotte 3 and with Jafu 2 at Le Touquet. Galland's lack of a staff background actually helped him gain the confidence of the staff officers he had to deal with. In the modern phrase, he was 'out of the loop' of the entrenched rivalries of the professional staffs; they respected his combat experience, accepted his opinions as objective rather than political, and found his frankness and honesty refreshing. All these attributes would help him in the next theatre of operations to which his attention was directed in early 1942: the Mediterranean.

Hitler's grand plan to seal the Mediterranean at Gibraltar had been shelved through the intransigence of Franco, who – although he owed much to the fascist powers – remained unwilling to drag his ruined Spain into a world war. Hitler still believed that the Middle East was crucial to his war in Russia, commanding as it did access to the southern sector of the Eastern Front through Syria, Iraq and Iran (the route by which the Allies would indeed supply aid to Stalin, though never the actual armies which Hitler feared).

The war in North Africa, started so ineptly in 1940 by the Italians, who had been virtually crushed by small British forces from Egypt, had by early 1942 become a considerable drain on Wehrmacht resources. The second half of 1941 had seen increasing difficulty in getting supplies through to the theatre; apart from Royal Navy submarines the main obstacle was the RAF presence on Malta. An island just 26km by 13km (16 miles by 8 miles), only 96km (60 miles) from Sicily but over 1,600km (1,000 miles) from Gibraltar, Malta was at the strategic centre of the Mediterranean; and its resources had been boosted by the safe arrival in late 1941 of three large Allied convoys. From its baking, rocky airfields bombers and torpedo-bombers haunted the shipping lanes, while Hurricanes provided fighter defence.

Gen Rommel's Deutsches Afrikakorps was entirely dependent logistically on

Mediterranean convoys, and during the second half of 1941 some 280,000 tons of his supplies had been sent to the bottom, largely by aircraft from Malta – in October 1941 60 per cent of supplies assigned to Rommel were lost, and in November 75 per cent. During the British counter-offensive in the desert of November 1941 to January 1942 the effect of this stranglehold on Rommel's supply routes was substantial.

In an attempt to improve the situation, valuable air assets were taken from the Eastern Front in December 1941; Kesselring brought elements of Luftflotte 2 from Russia to Sicily, and Loerzer's II.Fliegerkorps was also transferred south. This raised to 650 the number of operational aircraft available in theatre, almost doubling the striking power of the Luftwaffe. The entire Mediterranean theatre now came under the control of Kesselring, with X.Fliegerkorps in the eastern sector and the central sector under II.Fliegerkorps. It was also decided that the air threat from Malta should be eliminated. In this theatre Galland had JG27 based in North Africa[1], and JG53 and II./JG3 in Sicily.

During the first two months of 1942 Luftwaffe attention focused on crushing Malta by a massive commitment of airpower. But to Kesselring's frustrated fury Malta, like Britain in 1940, refused to collapse under the rain of German bombs. Operations began quite modestly during mid-January; but from 65 sorties a day involving bombers, fighters and Stukas the offensive built up steam until, in February, more than 1,000 tons of bombs had been dropped on the tiny island. II.Fliegerkorps had increased its presence in Sicily to approximately 190 Ju88A bombers and 115 operational Bf109Fs.

The priority in February was to destroy Malta's defences and its harbour and dockyard facilities. The Stukas of III./StG3 were withdrawn and carpet bombing of these objectives began. Galland was involved in discussions about how best to destroy the island's fighter defences. It was agreed that a massive surprise raid on the air base at Ta'Qali to destroy the RAF fighters on the ground should be followed by raids on the bomber and torpedo-bomber bases at Luqa, Hal Far and Kalafrana. The raid on Ta'Qali took place on the night of 20 March when 2,000lb rocket-assisted penetration bombs blasted semi-underground hangars and storage facilities before sustained air bombardment the following day. The raids were extended on the 22nd to Malta's other airfields, and by the end of that month air superiority was firmly in the hands of the Jagdwaffe.

The Luftwaffe fighters continued to support high levels of escort and attack operations, flying an average 1,000 sorties in each of the five weeks after 20 March. By the end of April the bombers had flown 5,800 sorties in that period and dropped 6,500 tons of bombs[2]. Against that, on 7 March HMS *Eagle* delivered 15 Spitfire Mk.VCs to Malta, followed by a further 16 by the end of the month – that the RAF's newest fighter was being delivered first to Malta reflected the importance attached to this island base. However, Luftwaffe command of the air would be emphatically driven home during three days in April. On the 20th the air defence capability received a huge boost when 47 Spitfires flew in from the US carrier *Wasp*; but Luftwaffe reconnaissance aircraft had watched the operation, and subsequent air raids rendered 30 unserviceable by nightfall. By the evening of the 23rd only six remained in flying condition.

The bombardment and the fighter action over Malta was seen as a prelude to its invasion under the code name Operation 'Herkules'.

Kesselring's plan involved 500 gliders, 500 Ju52s, 3,000 German air-landing troops, a massed paratroop drop, and six Italian divisions (70,000 men) landed from the sea. The first plans from the OKW on 11 March were optimistic about the prospect, despite the successful operation against Crete in May 1941 having cost Germany 170 Ju52s and 6,650 troop casualties. The unconvinced Italians demanded a delay until at least August; Hitler, too, was sceptical – mostly about the Italians' part in the operation; but Kesselring's planning went forward. He asked Galland to prepare a report on how the fighter forces could be split between supporting North African operations and the invasion of Malta. Subsequently Kesselring decided to support Rommel's drive toward the Egyptian frontier before redeploying his forces for 'Herkules', and a Fuehrer conference on 29 April fixed the invasion for 18 July. Luckily – one can only believe – for the Transportgeschwader, Fallschirmjaeger and Luftlande-Sturm-Regiment, the invasion would never take place.

After a series of brilliant battles, Rommel took Tobruk on 21 June. Instead of halting to reconsolidate and allow 'Herkules' to be executed he swept on eastwards toward Egypt. Hitler, pleased to have an excuse to refuse his generals' demands for the risky invasion of Malta, claimed that Rommel's obviously imminent advance to the Nile would obviate the strategic need for 'Herkules'.

Meanwhile a dramatic reversal took place. On 9 May 1942 the USS *Wasp* flew another 60 Spitfires on to Malta; and this time, instead of being wiped out on arrival, they were refuelled and put back into the air to repulse a Luftwaffe raid – some were turned around in six minutes, and they flew 74 sorties before nightfall. Nine days later a further 17 Spitfires flew in; and the RAF regained the initiative, which they were never again to lose. Pressure from other fronts pulled Luftwaffe fighters away from Sicily; by the end of May 1942 II.Fliegerkorps had just 36 serviceable fighters on the island, with a consequent fall in their ability to sustain a bombing campaign.

* * *

Far more ominous than the problems in the Mediterranean was the transformation of RAF Bomber Command. During February 1942 AM Sir Richard Peirse was replaced at its head by AM Sir Arthur Harris, with a mandate to 'destroy the foundations upon which the German war machine runs: the economy which feeds it, the morale which sustains it, the supplies which nourish it and the hopes of victory which inspire it', through 'bombing on a scale undreamt of in the last war'. Shaped by ACM Sir Charles Portal, chief of the air staff, and approved by Winston Churchill, the emphasis on Bomber Command as the only means by which Britain could open a strategic offensive in the West was emphatically endorsed in a memorandum dated one week before Harris arrived: 'The primary objective of your operations should now be focused on the morale of the enemy civil population and in particular of the industrial workers'.

On 1 March 1942 Bomber Command had 547 aircraft, of which 78 were twin-engined Blenheims and Bostons capable only of short range daylight operations. Of the rest there were 221 twin-engined Wellingtons, 112 Hampdens, 54 Whitleys, and 20 Manchesters; and of four-engined types 29 Stirlings, 29 Halifaxes, and the first four Lancasters. The transformation to heavy, long range strategic bombers had begun. The tools for a new offensive were being forged, and in the first five months of 1942 Harris worked relentlessly towards a demonstration of the fact.

The visible sign of this commitment to the destruction of German morale was area bombing. Much had been learned from Luftwaffe raids on Britain and, latterly, from RAF raids; they showed that the effects of bomb loads increased significantly if they were concentrated in time and space. An incendiary attack on Luebeck during the night of 28 March had shown that to be true, and Harris now wanted to go further. He had to satisfy three criteria: concentrate the bombers close together in time and space to maximise the effect; raise the tonnage dropped by increasing the number of aircraft involved; and increase accuracy at the target. A relatively new navigation aid called 'Gee' would keep the bombers close together and improve accuracy, and a force of 1,000 bombers would enhance the effect and improve the concentration. Where previously up to four hours had been allowed over the target for a force of 100 aircraft, 1,000 aircraft would drop their loads within 90 minutes.

On the night of 30 May, by dint of risking aircraft, instructors and students from operational training units alongside his squadrons, Harris sent 1,047 aircraft to Cologne; of these about 870 dropped almost 1.5 million kg (1,500 tons) of bombs. The raid destroyed 3,330 buildings, seriously damaged 2,090, halted production in 36 large firms, caused 150,000 people to flee the city, killed 480, injured 5,000, and made 45,000 homeless. The RAF lost 41 aircraft of which 22 were brought down over or near Cologne; the Nachtjagdflieger shot down four bombers. The raid had delivered almost as many bomb loads as had been dropped on the city in the preceding nine months; but the net effect was more concentrated and much more damaging. Harris was determined to work for a 1,000-bomber raid policy. For the rest of 1942 he did not have the necessary forces; but the sustained saturation bombing of German targets was to begin in 1943.

Galland, who never forgot the sight of London burning beneath him on 7 September 1940, had long warned about the consequences of inadequate provision for the defence of the Reich. Now a turning-point in the RAF's war fighting strategy had been signalled. The Cologne raid infuriated Hitler, and Goering once again found it difficult to respond to the Fuehrer's anger. Increasingly the Reichsmarschall was distancing himself from the day-to-day responsibilities of running the air force of which he was nominally the commander, and from the atmosphere of concern that was gathering around the senior Luftwaffe operations staff. Corrupted and debauched by his lifestyle, Goering now sometimes presented the aspect of a buffoon; when he had visited Rome in January 1942 the feline Count Ciano noted that 'he wore some beautiful rings ... [and] a great sable coat ... what a high class prostitute wears to the opera'.

When the bombing campaign over Malta was visibly failing Goering took out his rage, frustration and fear on his fighter leaders – once again. He ordered them to a conference in Naples; and they were obliged to leave their combat responsibilities on the Mediterranean and African fronts in order to hear 'Fatty' attack their professional competence and bravery. As representative of the Jagdflieger, Galland listened until he could stomach it no longer and then leapt to his feet with a vehement rebuttal of what he termed an outrageous and unjustified attack. Galland knew that the Luftwaffe was going through the same agonies it had endured over England almost two years earlier. Goering's rant about lack of aggressiveness was not only monstrously unfair, but irrelevant. In the face of an efficient reporting and ground control system, at the service of a determined force of point-defence interceptors, an inadequate number of single-engined fighters were simply unable either to protect the bombers by close escort, or to leave them unprotected in order to sweep the skies by following the freer tactics which were the only method which had previously produced results.

Nevertheless, Goering insisted that something be done, and ordered Galland to fly to Sicily and see for himself how best the situation could be rectified. It served Goering well in the eyes of Hitler that he had appointed Galland Inspekteur der Jagdflieger; now he could point a finger at his appointee if anything fell short of the Fuehrer's expectations.

Galland would later record that it was during 1942 that he came to fully understand the consequences of Hitler's mesmerising effect on the German people; and that daily contact with the working practices at the pinnacle of the Third Reich stripped away his delusions, revealing a terrifying emptiness that promised nothing but national disaster. Goering, although nominally Deputy Fuehrer, was unable to cope with Hitler's condition or to assume more of the responsibilities of command, while various opportunists were manoeuvring to seize control of their separate sections of the autocracy. Galland felt the cold chill of reality as he came to understand not only that many of the policies were flawed, but that those who had the ultimate power of decision were persistently irrational, if not actually going insane. Beset by these fears, he would find in Monica a confidante to whom he could look for rationality and stability; her presence close by in Berlin was an anchor which he could find nowhere else.

* * *

Galland made use of his visit to Sicily to appoint Guenther Luetzow of JG3 as his personal field liaison officer - 'Inspector of Fighters (South)' - on 17 May. Widely admired and respected, Luetzow was a dedicated career officer who would become Galland's loyal friend, standing by his side in difficult times when the SS took a hand in affairs during late 1944. Luetzow would act on Galland's behalf on the southern front and, while not being his deputy, would convey his views regarding policy and tactics. Galland would come to regard Luetzow as 'the outstanding leader in the Luftwaffe', a man he would 'place above all others'. Their first meeting in Sicily was with Kesselring at his Taormina headquarters.

Galland knew that the British had set up radar stations on Malta and that their fighter operations against the Luftwaffe bombers had achieved the same level of operational efficiency as they had demonstrated in the Battle for Britain. Kesselring had little appreciation of how best to allocate fighter forces to the operational duties demanded of them, and had spread the limited fighter strength too thinly. Clearly, there was need for a new strategy and code of operational practice. Galland returned to Berlin with a wealth of knowledge about why things had gone so badly in the fight for Malta. Once more, the emphasis on offensive warfare had given the bomber units pre-eminence, with the fighters still regarded as subordinate. Once more, the fighters had been shackled by close escort missions and, in the densely packed formations, had been unable to defend either themselves or their charges properly. On top of this, serviceability levels were abysmal. JG27 and JG53 had been in combat for months and were far below strength; they had received few replacement aircraft, and morale was low. At II.Fliegerkorps, Bruno Loerzer seemed incapable of doing anything other than deplore the situation and wring his hands ineffectually. How easy it had been, thought Galland, for these veterans of the previous war to inherit automatically the mantle of command; and how easily some of them collapsed in the face of challenge.

The tactical guidelines written down by Galland required a greater commitment to fighter forces than the OKL was prepared to consider. Drawing upon his experience of fighting the 'Circuses' of 1941, they called for three supporting elements: close escorts, operating in Rotten or Schwaerme, flying in formation with the bombers; Staffeln of 12 aircraft each in positions above, below, in front, behind and either side of the bombers as a cover escort; and free hunting patrols of Gruppe strength (36 aircraft) sweeping ahead of the bombers. The ratio between fighters and bombers would have been 3:1, an almost impossible balance given the production and delivery figures – there were simply not enough fighters being built[4]. Galland's guidelines were optimised for an ideal situation and would be modified according to the available numbers of aircraft. Galland's report ran into stiff opposition throughout the RLM, but he refused to budge on his central point – that there must be adequate fighter production for the tasks assigned by the OKL. The consequences of failure against this elementary criterion were soon about to be demonstrated in North Africa.

Denied the supplies essential to keep units at establishment strength, the Jagdwaffe units in Africa were unable to exploit the opportunities open to them, although they did manage to carry out some strafing missions and to limit British air attacks on Rommel's troops. They received some extra aircraft in the aftermath of Rommel's drive to the Egyptian frontier when aircraft were transferred from Sicily after 'Herkules' was abandoned. After Galland's meeting with Kesselring in May the latter moved down to North Africa and co-ordinated air support for Rommel's capture of Tobruk. Galland thought the Jagdwaffe held the key to clearing the skies and protecting the Afrika Korps' limited materiel from RAF attacks. However, with Malta still a thorn in the side and Rommel's lines of supply stretching as his forces moved east, the task was almost impossible. Fuel supplies for the aircraft, as for the Panzers, were cut by tanker sinkings. Rommel blamed the Luftwaffe, and Kesselring himself; there was little love lost between these two, which hampered their necessary co-operation.

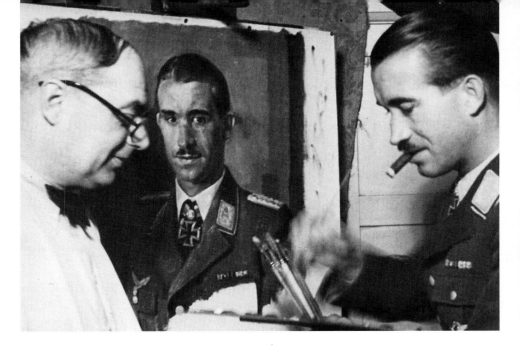

Above: *The painter Leo Poeten receives advice from Obstlt Galland on how to finish off his portrait ...*

Left: *The second of two portraits commissioned by Hitler in 1941, with the familiar cigar removed from between the fingers of the right hand on the Fuehrer's orders; he believed it set a corrupting example to German youth.*

Above: *Focke-Wulf Fw190A-3 fighters of I./JG26 on a French airfield in the Abbeville/ St Omer complex. (U.S. National Archives)*

Below: *Galland's younger brothers Wilhelm-Ferdinand (left) and Paul at JG26 in mid-1941, with one of the newly delivered Fw190As. Paul would be killed on 31 October 1942, followed by 'Wutz' on 17 August 1943.*

Above, left: *Publicity photograph taken in early 1942 for Luftwaffe files, showing Galland in the rank of Generalmajor, wearing a uniform undecorated apart from his Knight's Cross with Oak Leaves and Swords.*

Above, right: *The impressive gold-tooled award document presented with the Oak Leaves, Swords and Diamonds to the Knight's Cross. One of only 27 awarded, the decoration was presented to Galland by Hitler at the Fuehrer's headquarters near Rastenburg on 28 January 1942.*

Right: *Using a Siebel Si204 as a personal transport (note his insignia on the nacelle), Generalmajor Galland arrives to inspect a fighter unit in France, 1942. Over the next two years the aircraft would acquire the insignia of every fighter group he visited.*

Above: *Galland bags a new trophy on Goering's hunting estate near his headquarters at Elchwald in East Prussia.*

Below: *Galland – oddly, wearing flying boots – attending a concert during 1942.*

Right: *Accompanied by 'Franzl' Luetzow – whom he would appoint Inspector of Day Fighters/ South – Galland arrives in Sicily in spring 1943 to discuss the evacuation of Tunisia.*

Below: *Oberst Mettig briefs the General der Jagdflieger on the worsening situation in Italy, where JG53 and JG77 are bearing the brunt of the fighting in August 1943.*

Above: *1943: Hitler presents Galland with the third set of Diamonds to his Knight's Cross, unaware that Goering had already replaced the original set of poor quality stones. At right: Peltz, Luetzow, Wilke and Oesau.*

Right: *Galland was not an enthusiast for the Eastern Front, where his responsibilities took him on periodic inspections of fighter units. Here he is briefed by Oberst von Beck of JG51.*

Left: *Production planning became a vital aspect of Galland's liaison work with industry and other government agencies; he had many discussions with munitions minister Albert Speer, and with Karl-Otto Sauer (right).*

Below: *Flights to familiarise himself with all types of combat aircraft were naturally an important and welcome part of Galland's duties. Here he chats to staff officers after a flight in a Fw190A, during which he shot down an American four-engined bomber.*

Above: *The unceasing search for tactics and weapons to swing the daylight battle of home defence in favour of the outnumbered Jagdwaffe produced a number of unconventional solutions. Some Bf109G-6 fighters of JG3, JG11 and JG26 were fitted with a 21cm rocket launching tube under each wing, instead of the usual 20mm cannon in streamlined 'gondolas'. These 'stovepipes' carried a single projectile, impossible to aim accurately, which was fired into bomber formations.* (Courtesy F. Selinger)

Below: *Heavily armoured Fw190A-8 'assault fighter' of 4.Staffel, II./JG4, autumn 1944; JG1 and JG3 also formed Sturmgruppen. With various underwing cannon pods, and protected from Allied fighters by conventional aircraft, the 'assault fighters' pressed home their runs against the bombers at all costs. The typical 1944 'Reich defence bands' - here black and white - were for quick identification.* (Courtesy F. Selinger)

Above: *Long-nosed Fw190D-9, powered by the 1,7760hp Junkers Jumo 213A-1 engine and armed with four 20mm cannon and two 13mm machine guns. The 'Dora' had a sea level top speed of 357mph and in theory could reach 426mph at 21,650ft. The first of these excellent fighters reached III./JG54 in late summer 1944 and I./JG26 that October. Co-located long-nose Fw190s were used to protect Me262 jets during their vulnerable take-off and landing runs.* (Courtesy F. Selinger)

Below: *The extraordinary Heinkel He162 'People's Fighter', designed for simple, dispersed manufacture partly out of wood, and powered by a single BMW 003 axial flow turbojet. This He162A-2, armed with two 20mm cannon, was evaluated in the USA after the war. Although I. and II./JG1 nominally became operational with the Volksjaeger in mid-April 1945, it is not thought that this dangerously immature aircraft ever saw action.* (Courtesy W. Liss)

Above: *From the first time he flew the jet-powered Me262, capable of 540 mph at 19,686ft, Galland worked hard to convince Speer and Milch that it should be developed as a fighter. Although Hitler's intervention saw it begin its service life as a bomber, that interference did not in fact have much effect on its arrival with the fighter units.*
Below: *One of the camouflaged Me262 assembly lines in a pine forest near Augsburg. The first fighters reached operational status in September 1944.* (Courtesy F. Selinger)

Above: *The Me262A-1a 'Swallow' fighter was armed with four 30mm cannon. This aircraft of 2.Staffel, I./JG7 was photographed at Perleberg on 15 April 1945; the first elements of JG7 – led by Oberst Johannes Steinhoff until he was dismissed for 'insubordination' – became operational in November 1944.* (Courtesy Hans Obert)
Below: *Me262A-1a, thought to be a machine of Galland's Jagdverband 44, being readied for a sortie from Muenchen-Riem in April 1945. The unit – which numbered ten Knight's Cross holders among its pilots – had an average serviceability of about 15 machines.* (Courtesy F. Selinger)

Opposite, top: *Adolf Galland with Kurt Tank, the brilliant aircraft designer from Focke-Wulf, in Argentina. Commissioned respectively to design a new jet fighter and to train a competent group of pilots to fly it, they found that while enthusiasm was high the local resources were a far cry from those they had been accustomed to, even in the last months of the Reich.*

Opposite, below left: *Argentina at least gave Galland plenty of opportunity for hunting; his love of dogs was a lifelong devotion.*

Opposite, below right: *Back in a revitalised Germany in the late 1950s, Galland had to adjust to life as an aviation consultant and lecturer.*

Right: *Galland relaxes between flights at an air rally, one of many he continued to support and compete in during the postwar years. In 1962 a lifelong dream came true when he was able to buy an aircraft of his own - a Beechcraft Bonanza - for his 50th birthday.*

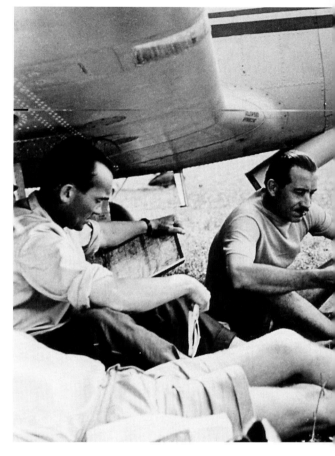

Below: *Representing many companies inside and outside Germany, Galland played the unfamiliar role of businessman with the same tenacity he had brought to air combat.*

Left: *His unparalleled experience of air combat, from the biplane to the jet, made Galland a sought-after speaker to the next generation of military pilots at many seminars; here he addresses the USAF 49th Fighter Wing at their Spangdahlem base.*

Below: *A gathering of eagles: this group meeting at Galland's Oberwinter home are credited with a total of 1,156 air-to-air victories. (L to R:) Steinhoff (176), Hartmann (352 - the most successful fighter pilot in history), Barkhorn (301), Falck (7), Stanford-Tuck (RAF - 29), Hrabak (125), Powell (-), Lindemann (15), Galland (104), Andres (7), and Schoepfel (40).*

Above: *Old adversaries who became firm friends for life: Galland with Wing Commander Bob Stanford-Tuck, DSO, DFC, whom he first met when he extended the hospitality of a Luftwaffe mess to Tuck after he was shot down over France in January 1942.*

Below: *Galland's son Andreas was born in November 1966; in this 1980s snapshot his father enjoys Andreas's musical talent - a gift for which he himself always wished.*

Right: *Galland with his daughter Alexandra, born in July 1969.*

Below: *Early in 1984 Galland married fellow aviator and businesswoman Heidi Horn; they are seen here at a book-signing session, behind them some of the many aviation art prints which he was called upon to autograph in the last years of his life.*

When Rommel crossed the frontier into Egypt on 23 June it looked as if these problems might be rendered academic by a German victory. Appearances, however, were deceptive. After pushing hard for 380 miles the German forces were over-extended: there were only 80 serviceable tanks left, and aircraft attrition was such that some units had only 40 per cent availability. The advance had called for superhuman efforts by the Jagdflieger, with concentrated attacks involving up to 350 sorties a day; in the extreme heat of the desert, with constant problems from the abrasive sand, the result was predictable. By the time that Rommel tried to strike for the Nile Delta on 30 June by circling south around the end of the El Alamein line, air support was minimal. Heavy losses caused Rommel to abandon his plan and dig in along a line between the Mediterranean and the Qattara Depression, some 60 miles from Alexandria.

The situation in North Africa had been causing concern in Berlin for some time, and in the aftermath of this battle of Alam-el-Halfa Galland was despatched to investigate and report. When he researched the background he found contrasting stories of incredible mismanagement, and remarkable bravery and aggression from the Jagdflieger typified by the aces Hptmn Hans-Joachim Marseille[5], Hans-Arnold Stahlschmidt[6] and Guenther Steinhausen[7], all of whom were killed during September. Whatever the skill and aggression of individual pilots, Galland felt that the position of the fighter force in North Africa was almost impossible: the numerical superiority of the British Desert Air Force was now 3:1. The overstretched I./JG27, whose morale was suffering from a combination of exhaustion and the loss of these aces, was withdrawn to Sicily, where it would stay until 27 October. Galland flew to Egypt to see the situation for himself.

Arriving at Fuka, located on the coast between Mersa Matruh and the El Alamein line, Galland first met Gen von Waldau, the Fliegerfuehrer Afrika, who for all his inability to get on with Goering or Jeschonnek was juggling operational requirements with some effectiveness. Placed in the unenviable position of acting on Kesselring's orders while having to placate Rommel, von Waldau had kept his formations relatively tight, ignoring DAK requests for a uniform distribution of air power across the theatre which would have dispersed the concentrations vital for survival and combat effectiveness.

When Galland got to grips with the real situation on the ground, as opposed to the optimistic reports from Kesselring's office, he began to see how low the supplies, spares and munitions really were, and that over-optimistic assurances were masking a potential shortfall of such proportions that it seemed the air war was already lost. Galland was appalled to see the same unrealistic expectations which had been placed upon his own pilots during the Battle of Britain now imposed upon the handful of war-weary desert fighter pilots. Inadequate resources and force levels combined with a willingness to engage in fantasy at staff level were betraying brave men to give their lives for an impossible mission. When he returned to Berlin Galland wrote a frank appraisal of the situation, unembellished by the usual courtesies. He laid down in plain language the reality that if resources were not massively improved the campaign was already lost and there would be no hope of holding North Africa.

The report exploded like a grenade. Resenting this 'interference', Kesselring thundered his disapproval; Rommel was indifferent, having already lost all faith in the Luftflotte 2 commander. A key part of Galland's report revealed from intelligence and reconnaissance information that the Allies were massing offensive air capacity which outnumbered the Jagdwaffe in theatre by almost 7:1. Galland provided evidence that there were more than 800 British and American aircraft in theatre, while only 125 Luftwaffe fighters were operational. Goering simply refused to believe this, demanding the background detail and working papers for Galland's report before he would release it for the RLM files. When these were provided the Reichsmarschall personally examined the reconnaissance photographs and the analysis from Luftwaffe intelligence. He then pronounced that roughly half the 800 Allied aircraft were decoys, and that the revised ratio was within tolerable limits. Sanitised and rewritten on the orders of Goering, the report was then made available, and effectively ignored.

The rest is history: at the end of October, committed beyond reasonable support, Rommel fell back in the face of Gen Bernard Montgomery's sustained attacks at El Alamein, using fuel that should have gone to the Luftwaffe. In response 50 fighters were moved from Sicily to the Alamein front, but it was a fruitless reinforcement: by early November the scale of the enemy offensive had so weakened the supply lines that the Jagdflieger were virtually impotent. By 15 November 1942 the dive-bomber strength had fallen to just 30 aircraft, and there were fewer than 100 Bf109Fs.

Responding to intelligence reports that a massive Allied seaborne force was preparing to support operations in North Africa, four Gruppen of bombers were moved from Norway to Catania and Comiso in Sicily and Grosseto in Italy, from where they were supposed to attack shipping in the Mediterranean. Two more Gruppen of twin-engined fighters were moved from Greece and Crete to Sicily, while other units were moved down when word came that the expected Allied invasion force had landed along the coastline of French Morocco and Algeria. The purpose of Operation 'Torch' was not, as the Luftwaffe had thought, to re-equip and expand Montgomery's 8th Army, but to put ashore a separate army behind the Axis forces. To stiffen resistance to this closing vice, more aircraft were moved to North Africa; and on 15 November Genmaj Harlinghausen was named Fliegerfuehrer Tunisia to co-ordinate operations with the new Panzer-Armee-oberkommando 5 commanded by Gen Jurgen von Arnim.

For a brief period the Luftwaffe held its own against the Allied air power in the theatre, but by the end of the year the Jagdwaffe had been reduced to a fraction of the number necessary to turn the tide. On 1 January 1943 Gen von Waldau had about 150 aircraft of which only 70 were operational fighters, while Harlinghausen had about 100 fighters. By the end of 1942 Hitler's ambitions in the Middle East were in tatters, with no credible way forward.

* * *

Although summer 1942 had seen the arrival at the front of a new variant of the Bf109 with several improvements - the Bf109G[8] - Galland was increasingly concerned about the apparent lack of initiative in providing the Jagdwaffe with new equipment. He began examining the entire issue of fighter production; but before he did, Galland had to know that he could get his suggestions moving forward through the tortuous system of Nazi control: he was beginning to understand how the political game worked. To begin the process he had several meetings with Generalluftzeugmeister Erhard Milch, and established cordial relations. He knew that Milch was a hard, dedicated worker and a master of administration; even before Goering had begun to drift, Milch had been the practical driving force behind the creation and running of the RLM and the fledgling Luftwaffe. Baldly, what Galland now wanted to know was whether Milch could deliver a miracle: massive increases in fighter production, and the right balance between aircraft types. For what 1942 revealed was that Germany would be fighting a long war for supremacy or survival, and not orchestrating a continuing sequence of Blitzkrieg attacks on minor powers.

Examining the probable threats to be faced in the year ahead, Galland favoured extended production of both the latest variants of the ageing Bf109 and developed variants of the highly successful Fw190[9], and felt that they would keep pace with the increased demands placed upon the Jagdwaffe. Later he would admit that this was complacent; but in autumn 1942, when the US 8th Army Air Force was making only modest daylight raids over occupied France, he could not have envisaged the two-year, round-the-clock Allied strategic bombing campaign which would soon face him – let alone the development of escort fighters with the range to accompany the bombers deep into Germany. All he then had to measure the 109 and 190 against was the latest Spitfire variant, which had first seen action in July.

The Spitfire Mk.IX went some way towards closing the performance gap opened by the Fw190A; generally it was marginally faster than the Focke-Wulf at all altitudes, marginally better in the climb to 6,700m (22,000ft), and markedly superior above that height. With better acceleration and faster in a dive, the Fw190 was more manoeuvrable except in tight turns, where the Spitfire was definitely better. However, with a superior roll rate the Fw190 could flick over to a diving turn which the Spitfire had difficulty following, especially if it had a float carburettor.

Galland was relieved that at last an effective and reliable 20mm cannon could be fitted universally to Bf109G and Fw190A types. Development of more powerful cannon was proceeding swiftly; in 1942 the 30mm Rheinmetall-Borsig MK108 engine-mounted cannon began to enter production, some 120 a month being delivered that year. With a load of 60 rounds, one of which was enough to destroy a fighter, the MK108 did not reach production levels necessary to equip the forthcoming Bf109G-6 as planned, and some examples of this next variant of the Messerschmitt fighter retained the less effective 20mm MG151. Another advantage of the G-6 over earlier models, and one close to Galland's heart, was standardisation on the 13mm MG131 for the cowling machine guns, with their familiar bulbous breech blisters. The G-6 would also have the methanol water injection DB605AM engine giving 1,800hp for take-off or 1,700hp at 4,100m (13,500ft); and hardpoints for the attachment of bombs, self-contained cannon pods, or more exotic weapons. Examples of the Bf109G-6 would begin to reach front-line units in February 1943.

All in all, anticipating an increase in daylight bombing but with only his past experience of the vulnerability of bombers to judge by, Galland felt the existing fighter types could more than hold their own if there were only enough of them – and there was always the promise of exotic aircraft like the jet-propelled Me262, albeit a long way from production reality.

With these factors in mind Galland turned again to fighter production, matching type production to the threat. To match requirements with capacity required a commitment from Milch and an allocation of resources based on tactical needs. Examining with Milch the history of production under Udet, and seeing the detailed breakdowns for the first time, was something of a shock. Galland noted that between April and November 1941 production of single- and twin-engined fighters had actually halved, from around 470 to 230 a month. With the absorption of production control into a more streamlined service under Milch improvements had been achieved, and between December 1941 and July 1942 fighter production climbed back to around 470 a month. Galland worked out a production pattern with Milch for raising fighter production to around 1,000 a month by mid-1943, the justification in materials being partly the growing Allied strategic bombing threat, partly a visible change in the pattern of combat in Russia, and partly the generally damaging consequences of an imbalance in favour of the Allied fighter forces such as Galland had seen in the Mediterranean. Intrinsically hostile to the idea of diverting resources from offence to defence, Goering and Jeschonnek were side-stepped to some extent when both Galland and Milch justified increased fighter production as necessary for an increase in offensive operations by the Luftwaffe. Nothing of the sort was planned on any great scale; but given Hitler's attitude, how could they refuse resources presented as being necessary to provide escorts for expanded reprisal raids on Britain?[10]

During 1942 vital changes took place in fighter production and allocation; acceptances – signed-off acceptance by the unit of delivered aircraft as satisfactory – went from a mere 122 Bf109s in January to 306 by December. Galland set up a production programme for Bf109s and Fw190s that would have the units fully ready for any anticipated onslaught by American bombers in 1943. Although, at 2,664, the production of Bf109s in 1942 remained almost the same as it had been the year before (2,628), production of the Fw190 increased from 224 in 1941 to 1,878 in 1942. Total production of single-seat fighters in 1942, at 4,542, was 60 per cent up on the previous year. That such production would continue to make dramatic advances for the remainder of the war was thanks largely to Galland for defining the needs and Milch for mobilising the effort.

* * *

Selection of aircraft types and mobilising production was only one, albeit vital aspect of Galland's attempt to put the Jagdwaffe in a position to combat the threats it now faced. He set about inspecting all the major fighter units and examining the credentials and the training of staff officers. He knew that good pilots were essential to the operation of a good unit, but also that good officers were vital if the units were to weld together as part of a unified force. He found, as suspected, that the bad relations between the Kriegsakademie, the Luftwaffe staff college, and the Jagdwaffe had left the fighter arm short of trained staff officers; he had, after all, been a victim of that prejudice himself. He, like other Jagdflieger, had insulated themselves from the attitude that prevailed throughout each Luftflotte: the fighters were there to support the bombers, the dive-bombers and the Schlachtflieger, but they were not there to think for themselves or to write policy. In any other air force this would have been anathema, but there was very little he could do about it.

In the West Galland found that the Jagdgeschwader were increasingly stretched by British and American operations. The US 8th Army Air Force had begun its involvement in the European war slowly – the first raid in August had involved a mere 12 Boeing B-17 Fortresses flying to a French target, and many had been surprised at the almost casual build-up to an offensive capability. But air action on the Western Front was steadily tilting in favour of the Allies, and the simultaneous need for high-value fighter Gruppen in the Mediterranean and on the Eastern Front leached strength from the Atlantic Wall. One of the first examples of the kind of battle which the Jagdflieger would increasingly face occurred on 9 October, when 108 USAAF B-17s and B-24 Liberators attacked steel works at Lille. Two German fighters and four bombers were shot down, including one by Oblt Stammberger of III./JG26, one of whose comments would prove significant: '... We attacked the enemy bombers in Rotten, going in with great bravado: closing in fast from behind with throttles wide open, then letting fly. But at first the attacks were all broken off much too early – as those great barns grew larger and larger our people were afraid of colliding with them. I wondered why I had scored no hits... The next time I went in I thought: get in much closer, keep going, keep going.' The sheer physical difficulty of shooting down heavy bombers would exercise Galland and his pilots continually over the next two and a half years.

On the Russian Front, which he visited in summer 1942, Galland found a different mood. Morale was higher despite the greater numerical level of air opposition, largely due to the general inferiority of Russian equipment and the poor level of training of their pilots, which had allowed Jagdflieger to build up large victory scores. This was clearly not going to last much longer: the lessons of the last six months of 1941 had taken root, and the Russian fighter units would develop throughout 1942 and 1943 into formidable opponents. Galland was concerned as much about the way the Jagdflieger were being attacked as he was about the equipment they had and the operational tactics employed. He spent a lot of time discussing intelligence reports and reading analyses produced by the various Luftwaffe units on the pace and shape of the air war in the East.

In one graphic report, General von Buest described how the respite of the severe winter of 1941 had allowed the Russians, with their massive production capacity safe beyond the Urals, to build up their fighter forces to numerical parity with the Luftwaffe fighters. Thus rehabilitated, they posed an increasing threat throughout 1942, apparently eliminating the inadequacies of 1941 – insufficient and over-rigid training, lack of technical know-how, poor command structures and defficient staff methods. Von Buest predicted that the weight of Russian fighter forces, quite capable of replacing losses and expanding their numerical strength, would play a decisive part in eroding effective Luftwaffe support for the army. Much has been said about the 'easy pickings' on the Eastern Front; in later years Galland would remind those who too easily dismissed the extraordinarily high combat claims of Jagdflieger in Russia that the 'cannon-fodder' mentality of Soviet air assaults had disappeared by mid-1942.

While on the Russian Front Galland sought advice from leading fliers as to their preferences for equipment and armament. One of them was Hptmn Guenther Rall of JG52, who would end the war as Germany's third scoring ace with 275 confirmed kills in the East. Rall described how Russian fighter tactics were changing. At first, in 1941, they would form defensive circles and avoid one-on-one combat; they were positively discouraged from breaking free to seek the initiative. By spring 1942 they were more aggressive; and by that autumn they began to accept individual challenges if broken from the circle. It seemed to Rall that pilots from the Guards regiments were the most likely to exercise initiative, beginning to seek out Luftwaffe fighter units in tight formations. As British and American aircraft shipped to the Soviet Union came into operational use they caused, it seemed to Rall, uncertainty through unfamiliarity. The Russians could not simply jump into these foreign types and fly them to the maximum. (Rather surprisingly, the Russians had great success with the Bell P-39 Airacobra but never got the hang of flying the Spitfire.)

It was clear that by 1943 the Russian pilots would be on the offensive and actively seeking out Luftwaffe pilots. Galland was particularly interested in the shifting balance between attacks on Luftwaffe bombers and transports and attacks on fighters. With greater confidence came more spirited assaults on the Bf109Gs and the Fw109A-3s. Moreover, the increasing tendency to attack any German aircraft encountered rather than waiting defensively to be attacked led to a division of responsibilities for the hard-pressed Jagdflieger. By 1943 it became necessary to allocate fighter escorts for transport aircraft such as the Ju52.

Increasingly, the need for the Jagdflieger to carry out several separate functions dissipated the strength of the Geschwader; and Galland knew that dissipated forces get cut to pieces. So he began trying to work out a way to increase the strength of each Jagdgeschwader – achieved in practice only when production levels had risen appreciably above attrition rates. In examining the options it became clear to Galland that it would be administratively easier and more economic to do this than to form additional Geschwader.

By 1943 the qualitative equivalence of Russian aircraft was also becoming a serious concern. Instead of the old I-16s the Luftwaffe was confronted by increasingly effective fighters such as the Lavochkin La-5, the Yakovlev Yak-7B and the Yak-9. The LaGG-3 and the Yak-9 were the equal of the Bf109G and the Fw190A in both speed and armament, while the La-5, operational during 1942, was faster and quicker in the turn. At altitudes below 5,000m (16,400ft) these Russian types had the advantage – and most combats in the East took place below that altitude. These trends were already evident in 1942 when Galland visited all the Luftwaffe fighter forces on that Front, and he returned more determined than ever to revolutionise the Jagdwaffe.

A change of organisation started in 1942 but was not effectively completed before 1943. This was the Jagddivision, which comprised elements of day fighter, night fighter, signals and observer corps units bound together and operating as a single entity. Increased day and night air activity over Europe demanded a more generally co-ordinated structure holding together through operational and non-operational periods. By grouping together the separate functional branches into one organisation considerable manpower, paperwork and time-consuming communications tasks were saved. The first, Jagddivision 2, was formed in July 1942, followed at intervals by a further seven up to June 1944[11]. During 1943 further consolidation of command became possible with the establishment of Jagdkorps, the first of which formed in September 1943 from elements of XIII.Fliegerkorps, hitherto exclusively responsible for controlling night operations and which contributed the best signals units.

To control the interlocking networks of the day and night fighter elements effectively, massive underground command and control bunkers would be set up from 1943; the first, at Arnhem-Deelen, was followed by four more at Doeberitz, Stade, Metz and Schleissheim. Ironically enough, the lead in fighter command and control came via the Nachtjagdflieger, because it was to that branch that Hitler gave permission to create a defensive system[12].

Many of Galland's innovations were responses to the activities of special units that had outgrown their usefulness or simply became top-heavy through increased bureaucracy. As commander of JG26 Galland had set up an integral operational training unit; these became standard throughout the Jagdgeschwader. By 1942-43 they were absorbing unrealistic amounts of resources and personnel. The idea was right but the structure was inappropriate; Galland transformed it by abolishing these Ergaenzungsstaffeln and consolidating them into three centralised Ergaenzungsjagdgruppen, one each for East, South and West. Instead of each Geschwader working out its own operational training programme, Galland imposed an optimised system common throughout the Jagdwaffe. In this way he saved the resources equivalent to five fighter Gruppen; men and materiel saved were transferred into Jagdgeschwader 11, based in Holland to reinforce the defence of the West.

Although Galland's duties would be focused more on fighter operations towards the end of the war, the post of Inspekteur der Jagdflieger seemed, in 1942-43, to carry responsibility for many activities demanded of fighters but not central to their function. Just as Jabo tactics in late 1940 had transformed high performance fighters into indifferent ground-attack aircraft, so now did the later marks of Bf109 and the Fw190 assume these tasks at Goering's demand after the 'Baedecker' raids of 1942. To some extent responsibility for bringing this about rests with Oblt Schroder of JG2, who pioneered attacks on Channel shipping during late 1941 and was so successful that he applied Fw190s to this task in 1942. Increasingly, and with the encouragement of Goering, the fighter-bomber role intruded into fighter interception tasks. The Fw190's radial engine gave it a better chance of survival at low level; with its excellent low altitude handling it made a superb aircraft for this purpose.

During 1942 and into 1943 Galland became increasingly frustrated with these activities. He knew – who better? – that under particular military circumstances the ground-attack aircraft had a real contribution to make on the battlefield; but he saw the Jabo role as one wholly unsuited to fighters and fighter pilots and a diversion from their true purpose. In December 1942 Schnellkampfgruppe 10 (SKGr10) was formed at Caen with the specific purpose of carrying out Jabo raids and performing experiments with low level bombing. The OKL even had the idea that specially modified variants of the Fw190 could replace the Henschel Hs123 and Junkers Ju87 dive-bombers; and throughout 1942, much to the annoyance of Galland, Focke-Wulf worked intensively to produce a completely new series of Fw190F Schlachtflugzeug. Galland tried to block this; but the RLM sided with the OKL in wanting to find a more up-to-date ground-attack and dive-bombing aircraft, and issued an order for a design study to achieve this.

During late 1942 two distinct roles had been defined for the fighter-bomber Fw190: the Fw190F would be modified for ground-support operations while the Fw190G would be developed for dive-bombing. By May 1943 some 270 Fw190F-2s had been built, all with reduced armament and greatly compromised performance. From then until the end of the war an astonishing array of weapons – some advanced, some exotic, some quite useless – were hung under the fuselage and wings of the Butcher Bird in its modified form. There were even night fighter and torpedo-bomber versions; and the never-ending diversification of roles and applications bled the Jagdgeschwader of aircraft ostensibly produced, and desperately needed, as interceptors[13].

It was in this that Galland found the most insidious combination of attrition and dispersion: attrition through aircraft officially authorised as fighters but used as bombers, and dispersion because there were fewer interceptors and escort fighters available from the production lines. Moreover, he argued, the ground-attack and dive-bomber roles added to the escort burden by calling upon others of their kind to protect them on these operations. In attacks on shipping in the Channel or the Mediterranean, for instance, the Fw190Fs or Gs operating at low level below the radar were frequently protected by shoals of fighters high above to ward off the enemy fighters.

Ground-attack duties took his pilots away from air-to-air combat and mixed roles too thoroughly; Galland believed that having to learn very specific tactics and operational techniques associated with these other duties would dull the edge of a man trained expressly to fight in the air. Some pilots did welcome the diversion, however, and these low-level 'grass-cutters' showed great dash and courage. But there was no disguising that – despite tying up some British resources – the cross-Channel Jabo raids were militarily insignificant.

Autumn 1942 would give the Inspekteur der Jagdflieger a bitterly personal reason for resenting the wasteful Jabo policy: on 31 October his beloved younger brother Paul Galland was killed while flying escort for a fighter-bomber mission. His Staffel, 8./JG26, provided some of the 62 escorts led by Hptmn Priller to defend 49 Jabo Fw190As of I. and II./JG26 carrying out an evening hit-and-run raid on the cathedral city of Canterbury in Kent. Spitfires followed the Focke-Wulfs out over the Channel under low cloud. Separated from his unit, 'PG' – a well-liked pilot, who had scored his own 17th kill that day – went to the help of another lone Fw190, and was shot down in flames over Calais.

Notes to Chapter 16

1   On 20 December the British advance on Derna and Marada forced elements of JG27 to evacuate to Magrun and Got Bersis. Painted on the door of the flight shack they left a message in English: 'We will be back. Happy Christmas.' The British arrived on Christmas Eve, a day when the operational strength of JG27 was reduced to six aircraft due to an acute shortage of fuel.

2   In the first four months of 1942 the Luftwaffe dropped half the tonnage of bombs on Malta that it dropped on London between August 1940 and June 1941. However, despite air raids on average every two and a half hours day and night throughout April, there were relatively few casualties – 300 dead and 330 seriously injured – as the deep rock caves provided good shelters. The Luftwaffe dropped 10 tonnes of bombs for each casualty; compare this to 1.25 tonnes for each person killed during the German Blitz on Britain between August 1940 and June 1941; 5 tonnes during RAF air raids in 1940 and 1941; and 3.1 tonnes in the first 1,000 bomber RAF raid on Cologne, 30 May 1942.

3   It was during spring 1942 that various eyewitnesses began to note the first serious signs of physical and mental deterioration in Hitler, among them Goebbels and Dr Morrell, Hitler's physician. Gen Halder recorded the succinct opinion that 'Hitler's decisions had ceased to have anything in common with the principles of strategy and operations as they have been recognised for generations past. They were the product of a violent nature following its momentary impulses, which recognised no limits to possibility and which made its wish-dreams the father of its acts...' When Hitler dismissed Halder as army chief of staff in September 1942 he was to explain that what Germany needed was 'National Socialist ardour and not professional ability.'

4   Between September 1939 and the end of 1941 Germany produced almost 7,000 bombers and about 8,300 fighters; but establishment strength for bombers rose steadily to around 1,900 while that for single-seat fighters remained just below 1,500. The net difference in fighters was due entirely to the heavier losses they suffered. Actual combat strength fell far short of establishment quotas – although higher rates of availability put fighters numerically on a par with bombers. The number of serviceable fighters had increased steadily during 1941 from around 700 to about 900, while serviceable bombers rose from 480 at the start of the year to 850 in September 1941 and fell to 740 by year's end. These figures represented the entire Luftwaffe: a surprisingly low strength for air forces in at least three theatres of war (four, if one counts Reich defence as a separate front at this date).

5   Posted to North Africa with I./JG27 in April 1941, Marseille had keen eyes, an aptitude for deflection shooting, and a taste for high speed diving attacks from high altitude. He received the Knight's Cross after his 50th victory on 22 February 1942, followed by the Oak Leaves with his 97th on 6 June, the Swords four victories later on 18 June, and the Diamonds (as only the fourth Jagdflieger to receive them) with victory 126 on 2 September. On 3 June he shot down six aircraft in 11 minutes; two weeks later he repeated the performance in just seven minutes; and during three sorties on 1 September he achieved an astonishing 17 confirmed kills, eight within 10

minutes. With 158 victories in just 382 sorties he was unrivalled anywhere but on the Eastern Front – where the quality of the opposition in 1941-42 was simply not comparable. Marseille was killed on 30 September as he struck the tailplane of his Bf109G-2 after baling out.

6   Killed on 7 September south of El Alamein, Stahlschmidt had 59 victories in little more than 400 sorties since joining JG27 in spring 1941; in a celebrated episode he had walked back to his unit having escaped from the British after landing behind their lines on 26 February 1942.

7   Guenther Steinhausen, with 40 victories over Africa, had been killed the day before Stahlschmidt went missing.

8   During June 1942 the Bf109G-1 entered service with 1./JG2. With the exception of a pressurised cockpit it was similar to the Bf109F, but with the Daimler-Benz DB605A engine producing 1,475hp at take-off or 1,250hp at 8,500m (27,800ft) and permanent installation for GM-1 nitrous oxide boost. The unpressurised Bf109G-2, which JG27 in Africa first received in July, had no such boost but provided a top speed at sea level of 510kph (317mph) progressively increasing to 640kph (398mph) at 20,670ft (6,300m), dropping off to 616kph (383mph) at 8,700m (28,500ft). Armament comprised a single 20mm MG151 engine cannon and two 7.9mm MG17s in the cowling. The Bf109 had finally reached its peak in development, and only the Fw190 series would continue to match the latest Allied fighters from 1943 on.

9   Teething troubles with the Fw190's engine did little to diminish its high reputation. By March 1942 the Fw190A-3 had become the standard production variant, powered by the 1,700hp BMW 801D-2 engine; it had two MG151/20 and two MGFF 20mm cannon and two MG17 machine guns; 8mm and 14mm pilot armour; and a high, jettisonable, almost 'bubble' cockpit canopy.

10   There was some apparent plausibility in this excuse. Increasingly preoccupied with such unmilitary concepts as revenge, Hitler, enraged by RAF Bomber Command raids on Luebeck and Rostock, had intimated on 26 April 1942 that a new offensive operation was to be mounted against the British. Dr Goebbels announced the following day that Germany must 'respond to the attempted destruction of German cities of culture by razing English cultural shrines to the ground. This is now to be done on the biggest scale possible.' What followed were the so-called 'Baedecker' raids, hitting every British city with three stars in that familiar German guidebook. In a series of raids between April and June 1942 the Luftwaffe bombed Bath, Canterbury, Exeter, Norwich and York.

11   Jagddivision 1 covered the central region of Germany and Berlin; Nr.2, the region of the Heligoland Bight; Nr.3 covered Holland and the western Ruhr; Nr.7, southern Germany to the Alps and the Swiss border; and Nr.8 protected the area to the east of Germany.

12   These bunkers were linked with the growing network of radar stations in an air defence line that was to form the core of a Reich defence infrastructure. Spotters, listening posts and radar sites across Germany provided information which fed directly into these centres by telephone and teletype links. All air movements were plotted on giant frosted-glass panels carrying moving illuminated indicators with details on altitude, strength and course of each enemy raid. The five main bunkers were interconnected by communications links. Responses to enemy intrusions were ordered through communications personnel linked to fighter stations in their sector.

13   Some Fw190s were modified to carry 1,800kg (4,000lb) of bombs or torpedoes – a load equal to that carried by early marks of B-17; and the influential Kampfgeschwader

'establishment' were already talking of further modifications to turn it into a medium bomber. Galland could see the usefulness of some operations conducted by SKGr10 and its affiliate SKGr20, but as these were embraced within the fighter inventory it detracted from his resources for escort and interception work. In spring 1943 SKGr10 was sent to the Mediterranean, while SKGr20 went to IX.Fliegerkorps for night flying. Some work was conducted on adapting the F and the G variants of the Fw190 for air-to-air bombing, but this proved impossibly difficult. It would be with relief that in October 1943 Galland would divest his office of responsibility for such sideshows.

CHAPTER 17

December 1942 – September 1943

Almost exactly one year after being appointed Inspekteur der Jagdflieger Adolf Galland was promoted from Oberst to Generalmajor, effective from 19 December 1942. Once again, he was the first and the best: at 30 years of age he was the youngest officer of general rank in the German armed forces, and his promotion reflected not only credit upon him personally, but a new authority on his office, and prestige on his branch of service[1]. It had taken that year for him to settle into the job; but he learned fast, and had already acquired the skill of holding to his principles while 'ducking and weaving' with the dexterity necessary to accomplish his aims.

A few days after his promotion, as he had done the previous year, he left his office in Berlin's Lindenstrasse and flew to visit JG26 for Christmas, at the airfield at Lille-Vendeville. It was, as always, a time for reflection, for renewing old friendships, and for gathering strength from the fellowship of his brother pilots for the start of a new year. That fourth Christmas of the war Galland took time to visit friends across the Pas de Calais, meeting up with Dr Heim, the Navy surgeon who had patched up so many of his men and who had tended to him when he was shot down eighteeen months before. Despite his promotion Christmas 1942 was tinged with sadness, and the weary realisation that things were going to get a lot worse in the year ahead. This mood was not only the result of Paul Galland's death in action. He had recently felt the first contaminating touch of Nazi oppression, in an unusual but direct way.

During the sustained Nazi purge on religious schools and monasteries his mother had signed a letter petitioning for her childhood Catholic school to remain open. In the paranoid atmosphere of the Third Reich this insignificant and obviously innocent act found its way to the centre of the web of tyranny – to Reichsfuehrer-SS Heinrich Himmler himself. Himmler raised the matter with Goering – no doubt as a pleasing pinprick in the constant rivalry between the leading Nazi personalities. What was the family of Goering's protégé doing, causing trouble with such anti-Nazi sentiments? Why did Galland's mother have to involve herself in such matters? Did she not realise this could jeopardise her son's future at best, implicate the entire family at worst? Galland was able to convince Goering that his mother's gesture had been a matter of simple piety, utterly apolitical; but the incident would surface again two years hence.

When Galland visited JG26 for Christmas 1942 he had more to give than greetings. He was putting together a major study of the new threat from the US 8th Army Air Force, whose daylight raids had become heavier and more effective during the past few months. While the B-17s and B-24s had suffered significant losses, the Americans had made their own impression on the Jagdflieger. They felt serious respect for the heavily defended bombers, which were already penetrating German airspace to ranges which limited the Spitfires to escorting them for only the first and last stages of their raids. When they began to appear over occupied Europe in force that past autumn there were only three fighter wings on the Western Front: JG1, JG2 and JG26. The emphasis on Jabo operations and the escorts they required had effectively cut the number of aircraft available to protect German airspace from attack; and Galland was determined to find a way of increasing the kill rate per flying hour.

He analysed where the Jagdflieger were going wrong. They were cautious – perhaps over-cautious – in attacking the B-17, believing its firepower of ten .50 machine guns to be more effective than it actually was. The fighter pilots were simply not getting in close enough, even in their traditional slashing high speed dive attacks through the boxed squadron formations of 18 bombers. Both sides juggled for advantage, the USAAF armourers and gunners devising field modifications to increase the effectiveness of their armament, and the Jagdflieger experimenting with attack formations and tactics. One fighter leader, Maj Egon Mayer[2] of III./JG2, thought he had found the answer, and his Gruppe's success in shooting down four B-17s over St Nazaire on 23 November 1942 suggested that he was right. When he read the report Galland went up and tried it out himself; he liked it so much that he circulated it as the standard method for attacking boxes of B-17s and B-24s.

The Mayer method required the fighter unit to fly parallel to, but out of range of the bomber boxes until they were about three miles ahead. They then turned in to face the formation, flying towards the bombers in successive Schwarme fours at full throttle. Flying level with the bombers and head-on for the last 1,000m (3,500ft), they opened fire at 800m (2,700ft), ideally using the cockpit as the aiming point, and escaped by pulling up slightly and flying immediately across the top of the formation seconds before collision. There was little time to score hits, and accuracy was paramount[3]; but the combined closing speed of up to 880kph (550mph) gave a good chance of escaping unscathed, as the bombers' upper turrets had great difficulty in tracking the fighters – particularly flashing past in successive lines of fours. Some pilots, fearful of a collision and of the consequences of flying right across the top of the bombers with so many turrets blazing away, performed a split-S and rolled away; but this made them vulnerable to belly and tail gunners, and actually reduced their chances of survival.

Those who could carry out the 'flat exit' immediately over the bombers usually scored hits and lived to tell the tale; it had the additional advantage that by remaining at the same altitude as the bombers the Jagdflieger could turn and maul any damaged aircraft falling away from the formation. When Galland took the concept to JG26 for trial, Maj Karl Borris found that a shallow 10-degree dive from head-on was an improvement. The technique became standard; and so was born the cry 'Twelve o'clock high!' from USAAF crews warning of an incoming attack. Its drawback was that it took even greater courage to flatten out in time and streak across the top of the bombers.

An alternative was for the Schwaerme to come in at full throttle from behind, either slightly above or slightly below. When the fighters attacked singly or in Rotte pairs the tail gunners had time to aim. This familiar form of attack, long practised against smaller formations or single aircraft with much lighter armament, now led to heavy losses; but when conducted in fours, streaming in like broadsides one behind the other, the gunners were hard pressed to mark all incoming targets. The closing speed was of course greatly reduced, to perhaps 360kph (225mph), giving the Jagdflieger longer to fire; but this overtaking attack made maximum possible speed essential, and a shallow dive at close on 650kph (400mph) was necessary if the fighters were to get away straight across the top of the bomber boxes. By flying straight across the mid-fuselage line of a single aircraft the waist and nose gunners were compromised, although gunners in other aircraft of the box could get a good fix on the fleeing fighters. During 1943 Galland flew several sorties himself to see how well these tactics worked; he shot down three four-engined bombers this way, and escaped with few hits in his aircraft.

On Galland's Christmas 1942 visit to JG26 he brought an order for all Jagdgeschwader commanders to report to a conference at Hottengrund in Berlin immediately after the New Year. During eight days they were to report on the activities in their wings, and discuss tactics, strategy and requirements. After a year in office Galland wanted as broad and as detailed a picture as possible of the situation on all fronts and in all units. Commanders came from 11 fighter wings: JG1, JG2 'Richthofen', JG3 'Udet', JG5 'Eismeer', JG26 'Schlageter', JG27 'Afrika', JG51 'Moelders', JG52, JG53 'Pikas', JG54 'Gruenherz' and JG77 'Herzas'[4]. Each man made a speech lasting an hour during which tactics, unit performance and activities were described. Galland found this exercise very useful and had all the individual presentations transcribed, printed and bound, the respective Geschwader receiving a copy for reference by all officers.

Galland was concerned that the units of the Jagdwaffe were not interchangeable for purposes of deployment; and, in response to a plea from JG26, he agreed that the wing should rotate one Staffel at a time in exchange with Hannes Trautloft's JG54 in Russia. (It was at this time also that he appointed the Kommodore of JG2, Gerhard Schoepfel, as operations officer for Jafu 2 at Rennes in Brittany; Schoepfel was replaced at JG2 by Obstlt Josef 'Pips' Priller.) As the rotation of JG26 and JG54 Staffeln progressed the pressure of the Allied strategic air offensive increased; and Galland became aware of the diminished reserves on the Western Front. Conditions and tactics were so different between the two fronts that it did not make a lot of sense for JG54 to have pilots in the West or JG26 in the East; by the middle of 1943 the experiment was abandoned and all 'Schlageter' and 'Green Heart' pilots were back where they belonged. There had, however, been enthusiasm for the high scores achievable on the Eastern Front, which were still seen as a quick path to promotion and laurels.

Galland was very aware that after three and a half years of relentless attrition some fighter units were now led by men with less training and experience than he himself – at the age of 30 he was becoming part of an 'older generation'. His views on character and leadership are perhaps expressed best in a letter of 11 January 1943 to his surviving younger brother, Hptmn Wilhelm-Ferdinand Galland, shortly after 'Wutz' had been promoted from Staffelkapitaen of 5./JG26 to Gruppenkommandeur of II.Gruppe:

'Dear Wutz:

Thank you for your letter; your promotion and your attitude toward your new responsibilities brought me great pleasure. I congratulate you.

Continuing our last discussion, here are extra comments: clearly you will be watched during the beginning of your service as a Kommandeur. It is easy to follow a leader who does nothing, by simply doing a little; but I remind you once again that my advice is that you should fight for your Gruppe like a lion. Everyone, down to the most junior ranking member, must believe you are a strong leader who sincerely cares about each of them; then they will go through hell and high water for you. You must remain in complete control because new and serious challenges will face you. Nothing happens of its own accord, and nothing can correct itself without applied effort. Every detail must be rehearsed a thousand times over and every success has to be earned. You will not believe the amount of work a single human being can accomplish. You cannot allow yourself to tolerate a single mistake that you could avoid through proper planning, clear orders or efficient operation.

You must not be too familiar with your brother officers; nevertheless, they can be your best friends. Care and consideration for the junior officers and enlisted men will reward you a thousand-fold. The most important principle is always to make sure that subordinates feel their Kommandeur understands their individual concerns and worries; that as their Kommandeur you can be approached at any time by anyone in the Gruppe; that what each one needs from the Gruppe is important; and that you are never going to demand of them more than you demand of yourself.

On the Eastern Front in particular, these aspects will be of supreme importance. Individual victory scores must never take precedence over the overall success of the Gruppe. Enough of this will rub off on you anyway. It may very well be that the main success of the Gruppe will be achieved when serving as a unit far removed from the rest of your Geschwader. In this case particularly, careful and detailed preparation is vital. All this will be very new for you, but the entire Gruppe must be dedicated totally to the goals set before you because to do otherwise would result in disaster.

Finally, a few words about your Kommodore. You must adopt only one attitude – absolute loyalty and discipline. Without these all the rest will be impossible to achieve. This is the only attitude you must permit yourself to have; there can be no alternative. Your Kommodore carries the responsibility for the entire Geschwader, and can only carry out his tasks successfully if he knows he can rely unconditionally on his subordinate Kommandeure. If that is not there, then the whole thing will fail. The idea of consensus decision-making, with carefree and relaxed compromise, no longer exists. Only one person makes the rules and that is the Kommodore, and his decisions must be unquestioned by the entire wing. I would never tolerate dissent in my own wing.

So now, Wutz, you know what I and the family expect of you. I am always available for you to give help and advice if you feel you need it. I wish you every success in one of the finest commands any officer can receive, and I know that you will do it well. Hals und Beinbruch![5]

Your brother Adolf'

* * *

The first half of 1943 saw three highly significant developments from the Allied air forces: the full scale strategic bombardment of Germany was agreed at the Casablanca conference during January; a combined Allied bomber offensive, implicit in the Casablanca decision, was agreed in June to precede the planned invasion of occupied Europe in spring 1944; and the USAAF introduced P-47[6] escort fighters capable of protecting their heavy bombers over Europe.

Escort fighters had not figured largely in 8th AAF planning for the daylight operations which began in August 1942; the Americans believed in their bombers' ability to fight their own way to and from the target unescorted, despite the scepticism of the RAF. For most of the first six months of the daylight bombing experiment there was little or no indication to the Germans that this was about to change. On 24 January 1943, however, Gen Hunter had ordered the Air Technical Section of 8th Fighter Command to investigate the possibility of fitting long-range drop tanks to the P-47 Thunderbolts; and 900 litre (200gal) tanks made from a resin-impregnated paper compound were produced. From July these gave an additional 75 miles to the aircraft's radius of action; later metal tanks would be found more suitable and further extend the range. On 28 July bombers returning from a raid on Kassel and Oschersleben - their deepest penetration yet - were met over the German/Dutch border by P-47s, which claimed nine kills for the loss of one Thunderbolt (though Luftaffe sources do not confirm this number).

Facing the average total of some 350 Fw190s and Bf109s from the combined forces of JG1, JG2, JG11 and JG26, Thunderbolt pilots fresh to combat were at first apprehensive about flying to war in this monster. By June the number of German fighters facing the 8th AAF had risen to around 600 as units were moved from the Eastern Front and the Mediterranean. Ever the advocate of concentrated firepower, Galland was determined to throw as much weight as possible into the defence of the West. The first Thunderbolt missions were not without incident, and the lack of aircraft recognition training among American aircrew led to a Spitfire being shot down during an early escort mission. Preferring to fly in flights of four aircraft, each American fighter squadron had 18 aircraft but this was soon raised to 25.

The Jagdflieger had been given specific instructions to attack the enemy bombers, and not to tangle with the fighters until they had hit the bombers first. In the first two months of operations, P-47s flew 2,279 sorties for the loss of 18 against the destruction of only 10 German fighters. In these early months of 1943 the battle-proven Jagdflieger were more than capable of matching the American escorts; but instead of slicing into the P-47s and seizing the initiative, they were ordered instead, on Goering's express instructions, to attack the bombers. He was unable to understand that the fighters would be the key not only to exposing the bombers but also to destroying the confidence of a new and uncertain force.

Hitler had been goaded into paying serious attention to the daylight bombing offensive back in January 1943. Following a raid on 27 January when 55 unescorted bombers dropped 137 tons of bombs on the naval base at Wilhelmshaven and lost only three aircraft the Fuehrer, outraged, ordered Galland to Rastenburg. When he demanded of his General der Jagdflieger what could be done to turn the tide of Anglo-American raids, Galland told him that the only solution was a major expansion of the day fighter force. Hitler wanted specifics: How many fighters? Galland told him he would have to consult his staff if he wanted definitive figures. He went away and was advised that at least three German fighters would be needed for every unescorted American bomber penetrating German airspace. Intelligence information from a wide variety of sources suggested that the Americans would soon field a force of escort fighters. This contradicted a declaration by Goering that the concept of the long-range escort fighter was flawed by technical limitations. Hitler was getting mixed messages, and questioned Galland in even greater detail; he had an instinctive trust in Galland's professionalism, even if he often disregarded his opinions. Galland told Hitler that there was no technical reason why Germany would not soon face large formations of heavily armed aircraft protecting the bombers all the way to Berlin. When those escort fighters appeared he would need an additional fighter for every escort aircraft that accompanied the bombers. On a one-to-one basis he could handle the escorts, but overall a ratio of 4:1 for German fighters against Allied aircraft per raid was necessary. Only that way could Galland guarantee 80 per cent of Allied aircraft brought down – a kill rate guaranteed to halt the strategic bombing offensive.

Galland was loath to give hostages to fortune in this way by making any kind of quantified promise; but he encouraged Hitler to accept the staff calculations, with the caveat that the figures could not be relied upon should fuel, pilot training or technical developments fall short. What Galland was not to know was the level of deterioration in all three.

It was when he returned to his headquarters from this meeting that the burden of the past several months seemed to weigh heaviest. Galland longed for two different worlds at once: to be back at the front, fighting the enemy at the head of his men; yet also to have real influence, to have the practical power to change things which the office of General der Jagdflieger so signally lacked. The frustrations of office were legion; the satisfactions were elusive.

On such nights Monica was a great help. She was surrounded by her friends from the Berlin nightlife - artists, actors, theatricals, musicians, and a host of others far removed from the world Galland occupied. Most of these people were vehemently opposed to the regime, but held their tongues. They accepted Galland into their midst because they liked him; and that took courage and generosity, because they knew he would drag behind him, unwillingly and unseen, a Gestapo tail – Himmler had dossiers kept on everyone of any importance in Germany. About this period Galland had mixed feelings, wishing he could have given more to both of the worlds he occupied. Others would say of him, years later and when they had no need to comment, that he was a bright light of reason in the middle ground between the fear of total defeat to a vengeful enemy, and the harsh reality of a totalitarian state. Galland never allowed himself to question the regime's legitimacy openly, only to argue against irrationality and the fraudulent use of power in whatever form – which was a political statement in itself, in the environment of the Third Reich.

It was at this time that Galland was brought face to face with the turning point in Germany's war against the world. On 31 January 1943 the newly promoted Generalfeldmarschall von Paulus surrendered the starving remnant of the 6th Army trapped at Stalingrad. Only the previous week at a Fuehrer conference in Berlin Galland had predicted that the Mediterranean would be the pivotal front for the Luftwaffe that year; but he had reckoned without the appalling loss of men and aircraft at Stalingrad, which Goering had boasted he could keep supplied by air[7]. In all some 850 aircraft were involved in the attempt, and in two months the Luftwaffe lost 285 of them. This sapped the strength of the Luftwaffe and prevented the consolidation essential to supporting simultaneous operations in North Africa and the Mediterranean.

* * *

During April 1943 Galland flew down to Tunisia to assess for himself the North African situation. The reports he had already received were shocking: once again, overwhelming Allied air superiority was grinding down the Jagdflieger, who were deployed in too small numbers to have any real impact on the inevitable retreat from Africa. On 1 January the Luftwaffe officially had 210 single-engined fighters, out of an estimated 800 aircraft in theatre, of which 70 were in Tripoli, 90 were in Tunisia, 35 were spread around Italy, Sardinia and Sicily, and 15 were in Greece and the Aegean.

Air operations in this theatre were concentrated around two tactical groupings relying heavily on single-engined fighters, with a smattering of dive-bombers (20 each), in Tripolitania and Tunisia. German sea traffic was protected by twin-engined fighters – eloquently, based in Sicily, since the forces in Africa were obviously considered unable to influence matters from their own resources. The air war in North Africa was considered to be of secondary importance to the situation in Sicily and the rest of the Mediterranean. In the face of repeated air raids on German airfields, the quota of fighter replacements went up from 150 a month in December 1942 to 260 a month by April 1943 when Galland flew to Tunisia.

It was clear to Galland from the minute he set foot on Tunisian soil that the war in North Africa was lost; but he was helpless against a 'Fuehrerbefehl' forbidding a sensible military withdrawal. Fighting had been intense; after attacking the enemy at every opportunity the Jagdwaffe was, nevertheless, withdrawing from North Africa in the interests of preserving Sicily. Although Rommel still seemed to have no feel for the value he could extract from integrated air support, his Heeresgruppe Afrika enjoyed strong backing during the bloody fighting round Kasserine Pass on 14-23 February from elements of JG77 assigned to cover his flank at El Hamma. On 23 March, just a month before Galland arrived, his old comrade Maj Joachim Muencheberg, leading his JG77 against vastly superior US fighter strength over Tunisia, was engaged in a fierce dogfight when the wings on his Bf109 sheared off and the wreck arrowed to the ground. With 135 kills in exactly 500 missions, the former Gruppenkommandeur of III./ JG26 was buried in a Tunis cemetery along with 500 other Luftwaffe men.

As the Allied offensive grew towards its climax the movement of aircraft to Sicily was described as a military redirection of effort – not a withdrawal. By mid-April the problems of spares and supplies were compounded when the remaining fighters were thrown together on a few airfields around Bizerta and Tunis. Standing Allied fighter patrols inhibited the aircraft from taking off and constant air attacks made it difficult, if not impossible, to service them properly. Throughout the first week of May the withdrawals continued, and several Bf109s and Fw190s fled North Africa for bases in Sicily with mechanics or ground crew crammed inside the rear fuselage, or in the cockpit with the pilot sitting on their laps. There was no doubt that when the final collapse came the Allies would not be content with North Africa alone, although considerable effort was put into keeping German intelligence guessing about where they would strike next. Galland was given the unenviable task of taking charge of the fighter defence of Sicily. On 7 May 1943 the final exhausted remnants of the Jagdwaffe in North Africa pulled out, and the Wehrmacht capitulated to the Allies six days later.

There were few facilities on Sicily, and when Galland flew in he was greeted by Theo Osterkamp, commander of fighter forces in Italy, and told just how bad the situation was going to be. First, there was the usual tirade of abuse from the Reichsmarschall who blamed the Jagdflieger not only for losing control of the skies but for causing the defeat of Axis forces in Africa. It made Goering a laughing stock; it also caused deep disgust and anger at his disloyalty to his men and his ignorance of their efforts. Resources were spread thinly. Sardinia was protected by a large number of Italian aircraft but only a token force from the Jagdwaffe (II. and III./JG51); Sicily would need all the aircraft it could get. Galland had at his disposal several Schlachtgruppen of Fw190s, and would keep the Bf109s for the air superiority role. The welcome new Bf109G-6 was now being delivered in quantity; and some would go to a new IV./JG27.

A general reorganisation in the Mediterranean theatre now saw Luftflotte 2, commanded by Wolfram von Richthofen, covering Italy and the central Mediterranean; the eastern region incorporating Greece, Crete and the Balkans as well as south-east Europe would be known as Luftwaffe Command South-East under Gen Hoffman von Waldau. Kesselring was in overall command of all land, sea and air units in the theatre. II.Fliegerkorps was commanded by Gen

Buelowius and tactical command of Sicily was placed in the hands of Genlt Mahnke, both of them from the Russian Front.

This was the first time Galland had been in full charge of a major Luftwaffe fighter operation since 'Thunderbolt' in February 1942. With few resources and meagre supplies he set up headquarters in Trapani; and organised a fighter attack on Allied bombers over the Straits of Messina. Galland gambled that a major strike at the B-17s would seriously impair the ability of the Allied air forces to bomb the island's defences and, perhaps, delay the invasion. For several weeks the USAAF had been pounding Sicily in a softening-up process before invasion, planned for 9-10 July as the biggest seaborne operation to date, involving 2,590 ships and 180,000 men.

Applying the tactics developed in north-west Europe, Galland threw his fighter Gruppen into the bombers; but the formations got caught between high flying B-17s and low flying B-26 Marauders and became disorientated, missing both. The attack was less than successful, and Galland gave the Jagdflieger a tongue-lashing on their return. Only Maj Johannes 'Macki' Steinhoff – Muencheberg's replacement at JG77, fresh from the Eastern Front – had engaged the B-17s and shot one down. Steinhoff did not take the general's dressing-down quietly, and argued with Galland about the proper way to attack bombers; Gen Steinhoff would recall in later years the piercingly threatening glare which Galland turned upon him. Goering rose to the occasion, as ever: he sent Galland a telex instructing him to select one officer from each Gruppe for trial by court martial on charges of cowardice. It is needless to add what Galland did with the telex.

The lesson had been learned: each theatre needed its own particular operational guidelines and its own tactics. For the rest of the war Galland would be shackled by the inability of fighter units to switch quickly from one theatre to another while retaining their fighting edge.

On Sicily the numerical imbalance made defeat inevitable; nevertheless the Luftwaffe poured men and aircraft into the area. The tally of single-engined fighters in the central Mediterranean grew from 180 on 14 May to 380 on 3 July, and the number in the eastern Mediterranean from 10 to 70. Fighter unit availability averages rose from 43 per cent to 49 per cent; and despite the relatively limited resources Galland's Jagdflieger gave a good account of themselves in the closing weeks before the invasion. (On 2 July pilots from II./JG77 managed to chase and shoot down one of the elusive RAF Mosquitos, a rare and coveted prize[8].) When the landings began on 10 July Galland had few usable airfields left for his fighters. II./JG51 was flown back to Sicily from Sardinia to join in the crowded air battles that broke out all across the island. The army called for the fighters to carry out ground-attack sorties, splitting the available forces between that requirement and the need to blunt the massive air offensive. In just three days the Luftwaffe was effectively wiped out of Sicilian skies.

Pulling back first to Comiso and then to Catania, Galland organised the general withdrawal. By 13 July all Jagdwaffe units but II./JG51 had moved to southern Italy, where they, like the rest of the Wehrmacht, were received as an occupation force; relations between Germany and Italy had been soured to the point of fracture, and the German forces were regarded with hostility by most Italians.

Without fuel, ammunition or supplies, Galland saved what he could from the island, but the Jagdflieger left behind wrecked aircraft and spent hopes. With few aircraft left in the toe of Italy to cover a withdrawal of German troops from Sicily, most of the fighter units were moved north-east and north-west – where they would be needed in earnest over the coming months.

* * *

This bitter experience would not be completely without value to the Jagdwaffe. Galland used lessons learned during the retreat from North Africa and Sicily to prepare recommendations that would contribute toward the defence of the Western Front. When he returned to Berlin he wrote a detailed report on operational problems; and paramount among these was a need for well-prepared, pre-supplied airfields that could be used in emergencies when their primary bases were not available to the fighter units. The lack of adequate ground facilities to fall back upon was, in Galland's view, a major cause of losses both in equipment and men. These airfields, he argued, should be camouflaged, supplied in advance with fuel, ammunition and spare parts, and equipped with servicing facilities. During 1943 he sought to set up these secondary airfields which could be used to recover fighters which could not make it back to their home fields after operations; this would save time, resources, and sometimes lives. Airfield construction had been much neglected during the past four years and the lack of such facilities hindered the smooth operation of defending fighters. Increasingly during 1943 Goering and the Fuehrungsstab were calling for fighters to fly more than one sortie each day against the USAAF raids. Working through the Luftwaffenbefehlshaber Mitte – Genobst Hubert Weise – and I.Jagdkorps, Galland organised in northern France, Holland, Belgium, and Germany a network of airfields where fighter pilots from any unit anywhere in Reich territory could land and find fuel, ammunition, spares, a situation room, weather room, refreshment and medical facilities, and a direct, secure telephone link with the appropriate Jagddivision headquarters. Galland ensured that not only could these airfields provide essential emergency support for diverted pilots; but also the facility for making a second sortie that day.

He did this by setting up procedures whereby fighters collected at such airfields would be commanded by the senior pilot present, who would make them available to the Jagddivision headquarters for a second sortie in force. Once airborne the pilots would tune in to the local frequency for the *Reichsjaegerwelle*, the national air raid commentary, for information about enemy activity that could be attacked by an *ad hoc* formation. This logical deployment was taken a stage further when Galland reasoned that, with increasing numbers of air raids, it was illogical to attempt to rise in force against each one. Much better, he said, to stagger the attacks so as not to cause bottlenecks in turnaround. There was opposition to this suggestion.

The policy of flying second missions on any day was sound so long as the raiders' formations had already been loosened and they had relatively weak escorts. When the boxes were still tight and escorts were numerous and aggressive the inevitably weak second sortie failed. Unaccustomed to flying with one another or to their temporary leader, the pilots were not as efficient and the formation as a whole was less effective, combat often taking on the dangerous profile of separate individual dogfights which left the Jagdflieger vulnerable to the highly organised escort pilots.

For Galland the situation got out of hand when Goering began to argue for three fighter sorties per pilot during the five hours the individual bombers were over Germany on a single raid. Galland worked hard to make this possible but in 1943 there were few times when it could be implemented. Under the pressure of intense operations too many aircraft were coming down at airfields where mechanics were unfamiliar with the type, and delays were caused when aircraft were backed up in the repair bays. By 1944 there were no opportunities to fly three sorties per pilot per day and, quietly, the separate Jagddivisionen worked out their own operational detail. The usual, unofficial guideline limited second sorties to *ad hoc* formations of not less than 25 aircraft, at which level they were of some use; below that figure the losses were simply too high.

Toward the end of 1943 Galland discussed with Goering the setting up of light and heavy Gruppen within each Jagdgeschwader. Galland had to recognise that some pilots were more confident than others in facing the increasingly large and formidably defended bomber formations; at the crucial moment some were gripped by what was termed 'Jaegerschreck' - what an RAF pilot might have called 'the twitch'. Unlike Goering with his demeaning rant about cowardice, Galland understood this; and he reasoned that one way round the problem might be to provide heavier armament so that their efforts, when seen to be more effective, would encourage a bolder approach. Heavy Gruppen would operate Bf109Gs fitted with 20mm MG151 underwing armament or Fw190As carrying four MG151s in the wings and wing roots. Light Gruppen would be equipped with DB605A-powered Bf109s optimised for high altitude. The idea was that the heavy Gruppen would carve into the bombers with their cannon, leaving the light Gruppen to go after the escort fighters. Galland nursed the hope that Geschwader commanders would assign pilots to these different roles according to their individual temperament.

Galland was given a free hand, and gradually set to work on restructuring the Jagdgeschwader to accommodate the new approach; he even wrote a new set of tactical instructions. When the assignments were made and the operations got under way, however, there was a tendency to use the light Gruppen to actually fly escort on the heavy Gruppen, which was not the idea at all. Nevertheless, this experiment formed the foundation for Galland's Sturmgruppe or 'assault group' concept, which was successfully introduced during 1944.

Goering and the Fuehrungsstab thought the separation of Geschwader and Gruppen between the Jagddivisionen left too many raids unmolested, so they ordered fighters from one to be transferred to the operational area of another to join in heavy engagements. This called for long cross-country flights, sometimes right across Germany, thus taxing the pilots and reducing the aircraft's combat endurance. It stretched pilots to the limit and kept them away from combat far longer than if they were retained in their assigned sector. Galland could get no change in this policy until 1944, when it became clear that it was also wasting fuel.

As early as spring 1943 the idea of moving fighters from sector to sector in order to vector larger formations on to the bombers gave rise to the employment of night fighters on day operations. With their greater range and longer duration they could maximise the greater navigational skills of their crews, and their heavier armament ensured greater success at the target. Galland was against this; to take a very specifically trained group of pilots away from their normal combat environment and commit them to battle in an unfamiliar scenario was a recipe for disaster. For several months Galland argued with the Fuehrungsstab that the heavy losses being incurred by these redeployed night fighters would deplete the defence put in place against the RAF night bombers. The relatively slow twin-engined night fighters were vulnerable to the bomber airgunners, suffering appreciably heavier losses than single-engined types; and if they encountered the P-47 escort fighters they were easy pickings. Their heavy multi-cannon armament was intended for use 'from ambush' after a stalk into a perfect firing position under the cover of night, and they were quite unable to bring it to bear in a daylight dogfight against much more manoeuvrable opponents.

The Fuehrungsstab listened to Galland's protests, and those of the Nachtjagdflieger themselves; but they only modified the policy as far as giving instructions that the twin-engined fighters were to limit their attacks to stragglers. By the end of 1943 the attrition of night fighters – with their carefully trained specialist crews, and their sophisticated on-board radar equipment – was so great that the impact on night victory figures against RAF Bomber Command was evident. Only after long and bitter lobbying did the Fuehrungsstab abandon the idea – too late for many good aircrew.

* * *

For most Germans the RAF's area bombing raids by night had much more impact than the USAAF daylight 'precision' raids on industrial and other targets. The 1,000-bomber raids of 1942 had struck a terrible blow at German cities and brought destruction on a scale unseen before; but the severity of the effects of a series of raids on Hamburg over a few nights at the end of July 1943 was as totally unexpected to the British as to the Germans. It introduced a new word to strategic bombing: firestorm.

Hamburg, Germany's second city and the largest port in Europe, had suffered scores of air raids before, but had not yet been subjected to one of 'Bomber' Harris's mass assaults. The first raid, by some 750 aircraft, hit Hamburg on the night of 24 July, protected for the first time by the massive use of 'Window' – bundles of 30cm aluminium foil strips which jammed the Wuerzburg flak control radar, the Giant Wuerzberg night fighter control radar, and the night fighters' Lichtenstein on-board target acquisition radar. Hamburg was rendered virtually defenceless; and a seven-mile carpet of incendiaries started massive and persistent fires. Only 12 aircraft were shot down, mostly by blind luck – a quarter of the usual 6 per cent loss rate.

The USAAF raided targets in still-burning Hamburg during the 25th and 26th; and on the night of the 27th the RAF returned, more than 700 aircraft dropping 2,300 tons of bombs[9]. So accurate was the aim that almost 80 per cent of the bombs were dropped into an area of only two miles by one mile. This extraordinary concentration combined with a month of particularly hot, dry weather to create a conflagration of such violence that a convection effect was created on a massive scale: a vertical funnel of fire rose into the sky, dragging colder air inwards below it at up to 240kph (150mph), which fanned and fuelled the continuing effect. Huge areas of the city were consumed; temperatures reached 1,000 degrees C, and some 40,000 people died in scenes of the utmost horror – almost as many as had died in the entire months-long Blitz of 1940-41 on Britain. Next day more than a million people fled the city in terror; the fires could be seen as a glow in the night sky 120 miles away and were still burning when, on the night of the 29th, the bombers returned.... .

The Hamburg raids completely paralysed the emergency services, and so deeply shocked the authorities that for a brief instant they almost collapsed. The fear of what was done to Hamburg spread throughout Germany to a population numbed to the long lists of dead and wounded on far-flung battlefields, but totally unprepared for such terrifying violence to be visited on Germany itself. Galland would say that he believed this single event to have been the moment when every German realised that the war could be, and probably would be lost.

Galland believed that the fatalism which set in after Hamburg was a reaction to the complacency of the preceding years of war. He had felt since 1940 that the German people had not fully absorbed the impact of what the war was leading to; but he also felt that although Germany had suffered military catastrophes in the year before Hamburg, she had ample resources, territories and potential to reinvigorate herself for the continuing struggle. As he would say, 'Hamburg only came as a surprise to those who had closed their eyes to the general development of the war in the air and had blindly followed their optimism ... [but] none of the components of the Allied success represented something which we were powerless to overcome.' Galland recalled that Goering refused to go to Hamburg, sending instead a letter of condolence to the Gauleiter. It was never published and would, in Galland's view, have caused a riot if it had been. Gen Bodenschatz was sent to evaluate the situation and report back.

At the Fuehrer's headquarters Goering organised a conference attended by, among others, Korten, Milch, the senior bomber officer Dietrich Peltz, and members of the general staff. Galland was there, in an unenviable position, to represent the fighter forces. But it seemed that Goering was, at last, shocked into a real commitment to the defence of German airspace against these crippling raids. For the first time since the war began all who attended the conference were agreed upon this single aim to the exclusion of all other objectives. There was no longer talk of territorial expansion, or the establishment of a Greater German Reich; simply the protection of the German people and the nation. Galland recalled that there was an unprecedented feeling of unity of purpose between the normally competitive factions of fighter and bomber staffs, the high command, industry – and between Goering and his subordinates.

The Reichsmarschall appeared elevated by this unanimous agreement and left to consult Hitler in his quarters, striding confidently out of the room as if on some Messianic mission to his leader. When he returned, accompanied by his aide, he strode between them with an unwavering stare and walked straight through into the next room, closing the door behind him. His adjutant was left to apologetically reveal the Fuehrer's response. Hitler had completely rejected the recommendation, and demanded instead a reinvigorated offensive against Britain. Peltz and Galland, hitherto opposing champions for their respective corners of the air force, were summoned to Goering alone. What Galland saw stunned him.

'We were met with a shattering picture. Goering had completely broken down. With his head buried in his arms on the table, he moaned some indistinguishable words. We stood there for some time in embarrassment until at last he pulled himself together, and said we were witnessing his deepest moments of despair. The Fuehrer had lost faith in him. The Fuehrer had announced that the Luftwaffe had disappointed him too often, and a changeover from offense to defence in the air war against the West was out of the question. He would give the Luftwaffe a last chance to rehabilitate itself by a resumption of air attacks against England, but this time on a bigger scale.'

Galland could hardly believe the verdict. He considered resigning there and then, but realised in time that nothing would reverse the decision, and that he would have wasted 18 months' work in trying to advance the interests of the Jagdwaffe. All he could do was return to his office, and do the best he could to resist the bombers. Much of Galland's time was now to be spent devising ways to optimise the equipment and the tactics for this, the overriding priority. An all-out effort to knock down the bombers at this stage could stop the escalation of daylight bombing.

The combined bomber offensive, logically, must be a prelude to invasion. Just as success against Britain in 1940 would have cleared the skies for invasion, so too would the remorseless grinding down of German resistance presage the onslaught against occupied Europe. Galland would never know, before the end of the war, how close his Jagdflieger would in fact come to forcing the USAAF to abandon the large scale daylight bombing offensive in the summer of 1943. Inevitably, with increasing numbers of P-47s, the situation would have swung back in favour of the Americans – but only to a limited degree before the very long range P-51 Mustang appeared in large numbers during 1944. Had they known it at the time, the Fuehrungsstab could have bought at least six to nine months of respite in the precision bombing campaign by day, which, arguably, was the one which hurt German industrial production the most.

An unattributed consequence of the night area bombing campaign was that, inadvertently, it deflected Hitler and the Luftwaffe high command from a logical and measured response that could have seriously hurt the Americans and tipped the odds their way. It was also the RAF night bombing which gave one distinguished Luftwaffe bomber pilot, Oblt Hajo Herrmann, the opportunity to try out a new tactic. A former Gruppenkommandeur who had served with KG4 and KG30 before moving to Berlin in a staff job in July 1942, Herrmann was a radical thinker, and he and Galland found some common ground.

Herrmann's first suggestion was too radical to be taken seriously in the middle of a war. Broadly, he reasoned that the conventional categories into which aircraft and trained aircrew were rigidly divided – medium and heavy bomber, dive-bomber, day and night fighter – had only limited usefulness in a modern war; and that these categories should be abandoned in favour of a multi-role approach, with cross-training to direct available talent to the most urgent needs of the day. He went further, and argued for development of a unique single-seat, multi-purpose aircraft capable of ground-attack with a high warload, or interception and dogfighting, as required. Seen with the hindsight of fifty years his concept seems visionary, but given Germany's circumstances in 1943 it would have required a complete transformation of training, tactics and doctrine, to say nothing of aircraft production and supply.

Herrmann's searching mind fastened on to another idea: that day fighters could achieve success against massed bomber streams at night by getting in close right over the target, where searchlights and fires below should allow visual contact. He tested the concept one night by intercepting a Mosquito over Berlin, using the searchlights to get general directions, and shooting down the fast-flying Pathfinder – to the amazement of the fighter staff.

Galland backed Herrmann to the extent of making some aircraft available to him for further experiments, using instructors from the training school at Brandenburg-Briest to conduct these operations in their spare time. He allowed Herrmann to use a full Gruppe based at Bonn-Hangelar and Fw190s from two day fighter Gruppen at Rheine and Oldenburg. Thus was born the 'Wilde Sau' – Wild Boar – tactic; in June 1943 he formed JG300, followed by JG301 and JG302 that October, a month before Jagddivision 30 was established to carry out these duties with Bf109s and Fw190s. JG301 and JG302 disbanded a year later, but JG300 survived to the end of the war. In all Herrmann personally knocked down nine four-engined bombers; he received his Oak Leaves on 2 August 1943 and was promoted to Major, followed by the Swords on 23 January 1944. Galland would encounter Maj Herrmann's inventive mind again before the war was over.

As if the burden of his responsibilities was not heavy enough, on 17 August 1943 – one of the Jagdwaffe's most victorious days for many months – Galland took a telephone call from 'Pips' Priller at JG26 to tell him that his second brother had been killed in action. A talented fighter pilot, the 28-year-old Hptmn Wilhelm-Ferdinand Galland had been awarded the Knight's Cross on 18 May when he had 41 victories; by the time of his death he had increased that score to 55, including 8 four-engined bombers, in 186 sorties.

On the day he died 'Wutz' had been part of the massed assault on the US 8th AAF's two-pronged raid against the Schweinfurt ball-bearing works and the Messerschmitt factory at Regensburg – the deepest daylight penetration into Germany yet, much of it beyond the range of the P-47 escorts. The 147 bombers assigned to Regensburg were attacked by relays of fighters for about an hour and a half, and lost 24 destroyed; but while the Jagdflieger landed to refuel and rearm before catching them on the way home the Fortresses left the target flying south, to land eventually in North Africa. The Schweinfurt force of 230 B-17s had been supposed to follow close enough behind the first element to catch the fighters on the ground, but the vagaries of the weather delayed them. It was three hours before they crossed the German border on a two-way mission; and the tired Jagdflieger came up again in their scores. In all 21 B-17s were shot down before reaching the target, one fell to flak at Schweinfurt, and 14 more to fighters on the way home. More than 300 Jagdflieger rose to fight that day; of the 363 Fortresses, 60 were destroyed – with 600 aircrew lost – and as many seriously damaged, for a loss of 25 fighters. The arithmetic was not so satisfactory if one of the 25 was your young brother.

On their return leg the B-17s from Schweinfurt faced the fresh pilots of II./ JG26, 'Wutz' Galland leading his Stabsschwarme and three Staffeln in from the south-east just on the German side of the Belgian border. In a head-on attack they shot down two Fortresses, made their escape over the top of the lead wing of the rear box formation, and turned back to repeat the process. Suddenly, Col 'Hub' Zemke's P-47s of the 56th Fighter Group stormed into the Fw190s from their rear, having overflown the formation on the outward leg of a rendezvous flight from England, wheeled around unobserved, and jumped the Jagdflieger from above. Cut down almost instantaneously, perhaps by Capt Walker Mahurin, 'Wutz' disappeared when his Fw190 simply exploded in mid-air, leaving a ball of smoke to mark the spot. He fell to earth entombed in the remains of his aircraft, striking the ground in a field near Maastricht. As so often, the weight of the engine took him deep; his remains were recovered from 12ft underground more than two months later. Adolf Galland was deeply upset by the loss of this second brother; although he had always known in his heart that the odds were against both surviving the war, he had never really accepted it as a fact – let alone that he would bury them both.

* * *

The daylight offensive grew more intense as 1943 progressed, and significant numbers of escorts were regularly being encountered. There was still a need to bring fighters long distances to mass them against bomber formations, and drop tanks were now standard. The landing gear on the Bf109 was too frail to support the addition of more than one tank, however, so the potential range extension of this type was limited compared to the Fw190, capable of carrying two 360 litre (79gal) tanks. With an increased flying time giving the fighters up to two hours in the air, Goering wanted the pilots to retain this advantage by not dropping the tank until the aircraft was actually hit by gunfire. Oblivious to the handicap drop tanks placed on performance, the Reichsmarschall wanted the pilots to preserve the option of being diverted to another raid, which they could not do if they released the tank. Only when several pilots were killed as their tanks exploded like bombs under gunfire was the demand dropped.

One technique for ravaging the bombers tried by Galland was the staff recommendation of attacks at full Geschwader strength; but this proved difficult. It had been the practice to attack at Gruppe strength, but after the first escorts began to appear the plan for co-ordinated attacks was often disturbed. Dispersed geographically, each Gruppe would be scrambled the instant the bombers crossed the coast, necessitating those closest to form up and wait for the others to arrive from a greater distance. Almost no wing could form up in the air at full strength; only Walter Oesau, Kommodore of JG1, could get it to work. The Fuehrungsstab refused to change this policy and toward the end of 1943 Gruppen were moved back from the coastal areas in the interests of better co-ordinated interception. Only then was it possible to get the 60-80 operational aircraft from a full Geschwader vectored to the bombers as a single attack force.

Effective control over the fighters from the interception command centre bunkers required some form of radio communication and two separate systems were in contest. One, dubbed 'Benito' by the Allies, had been around since 1941 when the Luftwaffe took a leaf from the RAF's fighter control book. It called for installation of a FuG16YZ set, essentially a radio-telephone with special attachment to receive the signal. This primitive system required a checkout flight every day to test the tuning frequency. Only one formation could be vectored at a time because there was only one frequency, 1.9MHz, on which the pilot could re-transmit for range information. The limitations of the system required 140 ground operators for one fighter at a time. Fighter control on the Eastern Front used both 'Benito' and 'Egon' systems with six Jaegerleitzuge, or fighter control units, installed in rail cars at strategic locations behind the front line and tied in to the Horchdienst, the reporting and radio interception service. (Problems emerged when the Soviet advance accelerated and overran the rail cars.)

The system was really only useful for night fighters, whose pilots had time to switch it off and on again, allowing other units from other geographic locations to receive direction-finding signals. Galland was opposed to the 'Benito' system because of its limitations and the confusion that could result in the air. He wanted a more advanced system capable of handling four or five formations at the same time. Working through a FuG.25a set, the 'Egon' system was able to operate with less servicing and without the daily checkout flights before operations could begin; but the night fighters had already committed to 'Benito', and there were insufficient resources for two systems. Galland bided his time, and was able to get 'Egon' fully integrated by late 1944, when it helped improve aircraft control and vectoring for the day fighters.

But fighter control was only one part of the equation. Day fighters needed more information than could be obtained from the ground. Weather up-dates could influence the tactical approach to the threat. Basic details of force size, altitude and escort fighters were also very useful pieces of information to have when going into battle against the day bombers. Galland reasoned that a special Staffel attached to each Geschwader for the specific purpose of maintaining contact with the intruders, albeit at some distance, could provide this information to the approaching interceptors. Selecting both ex-bomber and ex-fighter pilots he introduced so-called Fuehlungshalter, or battle observation aircraft, using Bf110s, Me410s and Ju88s unsuitable for interception and attack. These units did useful work, building a background to the attack and giving the fighters quality information for local tactical decisions. As the escorts became more numerous and accompanied the bombers deeper into Germany the Fuehlungshalter suffered heavier losses, and the system was dropped in mid-1944.

One of the most pressing problems for Galland during 1943 and early 1944 was the unrealistic insistence by Goering that pilots knock out the bombers and disregard the escort fighters. Increasingly, the P-47s were taking their toll of the Jagdflieger; if the interceptors were engaged by the Thunderbolts while trying to obey standing orders to mount an attack on the bombers, they would frequently cut to a split-S and dive away rather than get involved in a dogfight which would take them away from the bombers. Because the huge P-47s were faster in the dive the Jagdflieger were often cut to pieces before they could escape. Only the best Geschwader were able to retain consistently the head-on attack formulated by Galland during 1942. Once again the cheap accusations of 'Jaegerschreck' were flung about by Goering. Too many Jagdflieger were breaking off their attacks at the first sight of P-47s and, from early 1944, long range P-51s; but there was an understandable confusion among the younger pilots – what were they expected to do when orders circulated to the Geschwader from the Jagddivisionen, Jagdkorps and even the Fuehrungsstab cut across tactical notes from Galland? Galland was aware of this but could do very little, except in two distinct directions: training, and familiarisation. He wanted better and more scientific methods of preparing pilots for battle, and he wanted to make them see that the B-17s and B-24s were not invulnerable.

At first, addressing the fighter training issue, he tried to get his tactical ideas included in the school curricula, but without much success; they were strictly regulated and had to be adhered to at all costs. Galland's struggles with the flying training schools had begun in 1942 when he became concerned at the adverse effects of the selection criteria used for allocating pupils to bomber or fighter schools. Because the bomber crews had to have wider technical skills the more educationally mature candidates were sent for bomber training. Disturbed at the lower calibre of pilot coming through the training process, Galland began to put his own instructors in to tighten up the programmes, but the supply of such instructors was limited. Next he tried to get each Geschwader to contribute an instructor to the Ergaenzungsjagdgruppe from which it received its pilots, arguing that the graduates would arrive on the Staffel already tutored in the favoured combat techniques. It seemed to make good sense, and for a while the reciprocal arrangement worked: the Geschwaderkommodore sending good instructors, in the expectation of being fed with graduates who had been taught his philosophy and methods. It broke down after the Allied invasion of June 1944, however, due to the sheer pressure of replacement needs.

The generally lower educational level of the fighter pilots was reflected in the ratio of officers to men. At peak the Luftwaffe had more than two million men and 70,000 officers, only 800 of the latter serving in operational fighter units. These concerns drew Galland's attention to the entire recruitment process; the fact was that the Luftwaffe lacked a well orchestrated recruiting programme comparable to those run by the Waffen-SS and the Kriegsmarine, which made determined efforts to attract young volunteers. Although the NSFK – the Nazi Party's air organisation – had programmes for air-minded boys, the element of Party indoctrination was unhelpful, and all these teenagers had to serve their time afterwards in the Reich Labour Service (RAD); Galland felt that this broke the link with flying, and exposed them to the aggressive recruiting drives of other services. He backed an ingenious idea from an Obst Dickfeld for a range of Wehrertuchtigungs Lagern, camps where young men could get pre-flight training as well as the physical exercise which city boys needed – the Luftwaffe did better for recruits in urban than rural areas. However, the idea foundered because it was not recognised as a legitimate alternative to Hitler Jugend membership.

For the more immediate goal of improving training Galland put together a proposal which took root, and was to go some way towards raising the quality of graduates flowing from the academic and practical training system. He proposed that pilots should be chosen for fighter, bomber or other duties on the basis of psychological tests performed before they began to fly, and that flight training should be specialised from an early stage according to this selection process. To accomplish this, 12 A/B Schools would have to be converted to Jaegervorschulen, preliminary fighter schools, with three Jaeger Luftkriegschulen set up specially for officers – another attempt by Galland to bypass the standardised curriculum of the Luftwaffe staff academy. In this organisation too Galland wanted to use good fighter pilots as instructors to generally improve the quality and relevance of the instruction. Gen Karl Koller, chief of the operations staff, did not accept the proposal in the form presented; but some changes were subsequently made (without telling Galland that they had been implemented).

Even if the entire training system could not be transformed in the way he wanted, Galland did add some useful elements. He initiated special blind flying training in the A/B Schools, something they had not tried until prompted. Some attempt was made to establish a special night flying and bad weather school at Altenburg linked to an Ergaenzungsgruppe at Ludwigslust, but lack of fuel prevented much progress being made; Galland had intended that graduating pilots should be posted to the 'Wilde Sau' units.

Some attempt was also made by Galland to encourage conversion from one type of aircraft to another, and late in 1943 he set up the so-called 'Windhund' course; here pilots were physically examined for their suitability to fly under different conditions and their records checked to help determine which sort of aircraft would suit them best. Galland established a Flieger Sichtungstelle at Hottengrund, through which 12,000 men passed in the first year, with 8,000 successfully completing conversion courses. This course saved a considerable amount of fuel by screening out in advance competent pilots from other categories who turned out to be insuitable for the 'three dimensional chess game' of fighter combat. Those screened out of the fighter conversion programme were converted as Schlachtflieger or night fighters.

Galland became concerned at the apparent lack of proper training in how to lead and attack in formation. Recognising that his own success in the early days of the war had been a combination of trial and error and learning from experienced pilots, he set up in autumn 1943 at Konigsborg-Neumark a Verbandsfuehrer Lehrgang, formation leader's course, to train officers how to lead formations at every level from Staffel to Geschwader. Galland put together a small team from his own office to lecture at these courses; they would show off the latest equipment, describe new weapon systems, and demonstrate how best to organise and co-ordinate formation attacks on a wide range of targets. Different tactical methods were debated and officers were encouraged to develop innovations. The school was encouraged to fly operational sorties itself, and this continued into 1944 until the pressures became too high and the losses too great. From then on the students were attached to other operational units in the Berlin area.

Galland always felt that the root of a lot of the command and leadership problems stemmed from the fighter pilots' poor representation at the Luftkriegsakademie at Berlin-Gatow, the Luftwaffe's general staff college, whose faculty were mostly older men with a bomber background. The bias against the fighter arm was so marked that Galland reached the point where he stopped sending any more officers forward. He believed that problems which developed with the establishment of the Jagddivisionen stemmed from the shortage of good staff officers among the fighter pilot pool. The general absence of efficiency which Galland detected would be remedied to some extent, but only marginally and far too late.

Aside from training, one way Galland wanted to improve the tactics for attacking enemy bombers and eliminate the crippling 'Jagerschreck' was to set up a special demonstration unit using captured Allied aircraft. He recruited the services of one Hptmn Razarius, and formed a Sonderstaffel Wanderzirkus – 'special travelling circus squadron'. This travelled around the Gruppen giving pilots the chance to climb all over enemy aircraft, examine their weaknesses and strengths, devise optimum methods of attack, and generally de-mystify the fear they engendered – not only in the young pilots, but in experienced fighter leaders as well. Galland recalled that fighter pilots who had sat in the gun turret of an enemy bomber had a more realistic attitude about the limitations of the gunners they faced. Unfortunately most Allied aircraft used high octane fuel, which was increasingly in short supply.

* * *

Galland knew, of course, that there was another element – beyond better selection procedures, proper training and de-mystifying the enemy – which determined whether or not a fighter pilot would pull away and dive for the ground. That was the ingredient which only those who had tasted combat over weary months and years could truly understand: the smell of death – the increasing awareness that the probability of being killed was greater than the probability of survival. This could become a corrosive force that drained energy and stamina; but Galland had personal experience of fear, and knew that if harnessed it was a positive, even essential force – that pilots who cease to experience fear no longer understand what they are doing[10].

Many years after the war Galland recalled how one day early in 1941 he was experimenting with two 13mm machine guns on his Bf109F when the synchronisation gear failed off the coast of England; sparks flew from propeller blades and the engine coughed and spluttered. Throttling back, he fired again, but the guns jammed. Turning back toward the coast of France he was suddenly aware of a Spitfire immediately below his port wing, so close 'I could almost have touched it'. Paralysed with fear, he watched the pilot pull closer, give him a broad grin, wave and pull away. When he landed he was still so shocked that he had to be helped from his aircraft, his legs in uncontrollable spasm. This experience, and others like it, made him deeply interested in the balance between control and panic. Did this lie beyond any rational analysis, or was it something that could be defined and harnessed?

There were those who could see no further than cant about bad breeding or cowardice – the same people who had shot the wretched victims of shell-shock in his uncles' war. There were others still, in his own war, who thought this fear could be bred out of an elite guard of dedicated airmen. Towards the end of 1943 the Luftwaffe received numerous requests from the Reichs Jugend Fuehrung that a special Geschwader 'Hitler Jugend' be set up with volunteers from the national youth movement. The HJ had strong connections to the SS, and the attempt to set up an elite fighting unit of dedicated young Nazi airmen went forward with some enthusiasm. Goering was wary of this and did little to encourage it; but he had to walk a thin line between openly seeming to discourage a focus of Party fervour in the Luftwaffe, and blocking the attempts of the SS to infiltrate the service – a prospect which Goering always feared. Galland was disgusted at the suggestion; but on the other hand, the chance of high quality recruitment was too good to ignore entirely. In 1944 plans went ahead to train these volunteers and put them into JG1; when sufficient numbers had been inducted it was to be named Jagdgeschwader 1 'Oesau' – after its former commander Obst Walter Oesau, who had been killed on 11 May 1944, with 123 victories to his credit in 300 missions. As the military situation worsened the idea unravelled, and only a few of the HJ volunteers from the programme ever got to join the Geschwader.

Outside the realm of recruitment and training, there was the pressing need to improve the ability of existing pilots to exploit an ever growing range of advanced weapons. Skill in basic marksmanship was always emphasised by Galland, who set up six Schiesslehrstabe – gunnery instructional teams, equipped with the latest gunsights, weapons and training aids – to travel around the Gruppen. Too late, as he later admitted, Galland tried to improve the poor standards among new pilots, but was sometimes resisted by their superiors who preferred to keep ammunition and increasingly precious fuel for combat rather than improving the skills of their Jagdflieger. He had wanted to set up special air combat training zones where pilots could check their results with gun cameras, but it was not to be.

Where Galland he did achieve success, however, was in co-ordinating a wide range of weapons experiments conducted at Gruppe and Geschwader level into a well organised programme applicable to all fighting units everywhere. Throughout 1942 and 1943 the changing pattern of air combat over Europe introduced novel innovations for dealing with the enemy. Feeling that they were falling behind technical developments and equipment possessed by the Allies, pilots were keen to try new devices. To feed this need at an appropriate technical and scientific level, Galland set up an experimental weapons testing unit, Erprobungskommando 25, with his own staff based at Achmer under the command of Hptmn Eduard Tatt. Through its two Staffeln a large and exotic variety of weapons concepts were tested in the air and on the ground. Among the various weapons tested were 500lb rocket bombs, cable-bombs reeled out and trailed through bomber formations, and various large calibre cannon.

Purportedly at the insistence of Hitler, Goering ordered Galland to fit a 50mm BK5 cannon from an armoured car – weighing 900kg (2,000lbs) – into the nose of a Me410 twin-engined Zerstoerer, complete with its 21-round magazine. The gun was fitted to the Me410 at Staaken during August 1943 and delivered to Tarnewitz for firing trials. Galland's Test Unit 25 took the project over, and determined that the enormous size and slow rate of fire – just one round per second – would obviate any advantages. With an enormous recoil, the gun frequently jammed after a few shots, which were anyway not effective unless the pilot got to within 300m (1,000ft) of the target. Other more successful developments included the devastating 30mm MK103 underwing cannon for the Fw190A, the 21cm WGr.21 rocket mortar fired from underwing tubes on the Bf109G and Fw190A, and the 55mm R4M battery rockets principally used by the Me262 jet fighter. Not all were suitable for widespread application even if they worked. There was 'Krebs', a 50cm rearward and backward firing rocket discharged by an Fw190 after it had passed across the top of a bomber formation lead aircraft at 150ft, sending the projectiles back into the middle of the formation where they did the most damage.

Ignorant and wrong-headed interference from Goering, in many matters apart from armament and equipment, added to a hostility which grew steadily worse throughout 1943, and two incidents highlight the growing rift. Early in 1943, at a special conference at Schleissheim involving a large group of Jagddvision and Luftgau representatives, Goering insulted the Jagdflieger by claiming that they lied about their victory scores in order to qualify for the Knight's Cross. Enraged, Galland wrenched the decoration from his throat and slammed it down on the table; other officers made to follow suit but Galland refused to let them implicate themselves, feeling that his gesture, as General der Jagdflieger, was sufficient. Although Goering apologised some time later, not for almost a year would Galland resume wearing the decoration.

During autumn 1943 Goering invited Galland to Schloss Veltenstein, where he attempted to persuade him to be take a more conciliatory line, and not to resist changes demanded by the Fuehrer. The issue of the 50cm BK5 cannon came up and, stubborn to a fault, Galland refused to give ground, telling Goering that he was wrong and Hitler was wrong, it was simply not the right weapon for the job. Both men lost their tempers, and Goering's voice rose in abuse so furious that he could be heard by local villagers passing outside the castle. He did not want to know what Galland thought, he was ordering him to get the weapon installed, and that was an end to it. Galland told Goering that he felt he could no longer carry out the duties of General der Jagdflieger, and resigned. Goering had one word: 'Granted!' Turning on his heel, Galland strode out of Veltenstein and drove to nearby Nuremberg airfield. When he arrived there was a telephone call from Goering's adjutant to say that he was to remain in office until a successor had been selected. Two weeks later Goering telephoned, apologised and reinstated him.

Notes to Chapter 17

1   Galland was the first product of the fighter arm of the new Luftwaffe to reach general officer rank; and it was good for the morale of all Jagdflieger to have their own 'General of Fighter Pilots' by rank as well as by courtesy. His duties as 'Inspector' did not change with the promotion in any practical sense, but general rank brought added authority and prestige to the appointment, and eased Galland's efforts to introduce some positive changes.

2   Egon Mayer had been with JG2 since December 1939; he was awarded the Knight's Cross for his 20th victory on 1 August 1941, reached his 50th on 19 August 1942, and in one three-week period during that summer shot down 16 aircraft. In November 1942 Galland approved his appointment as Gruppenkommandeur III./ JG2; Mayer was awarded the Oak Leaves on 16 April 1943 for achieving 63 kills, and promoted Hauptmann. The most artful exponent of attacks on four-engined bombers, he was appointed Geschwaderkommodore of JG2 on 1 July 1943. With 102 kills (25 of them four-engined bombers) in 353 sorties, he was killed on 2 March 1944 in a fight with P-47s, and was posthumously awarded the Swords.

3   The firing time from 800m would be 3 to 4 seconds only; the four cannon and two MG of an Fw190A would fire a total of 130-150 rounds in that time. Unless a lucky hit was scored it usually took an average of 20 hits from a 20mm cannon to knock down a heavy bomber.

4   JG11 would form in April 1943, but at the time of the conference no Geschwaderkommodore had been appointed.

5   Lit: 'Break your neck and leg!' German 'good luck' slang, like an actor's 'Break a leg!'

6   The Republic P-47 Thunderbolt had been introduced to the European theatre with the arrival of the first at RAF Debden in January 1943, and saw action for the first time on 8 April 1943 flown by Maj Hubert Zemke's 56th Fighter Group. A massive fighter compared to the Fw190 and the Bf109, the 'Jug' carried a formidable armament of six or even eight .50 machine guns in the wings; the 2,300hp Pratt & Whitney radial engine delivered top speeds of 570kph (353mph) at 1,525m (5,000ft), and 650kph (406mph) at 6,100m (20,000ft).

7   Between the beginning of August and the end of October 1942 some 21,500 transport sorties had been flown, carrying 43,000 tons of fuel and supplies into Stalingrad. When the Soviet counter-offensive opened in November He111 bombers from the Mediterranean were moved to the Ukraine to serve as transport aircraft; training units were required to give up Ju52s, He111s and even ancient Ju86s; and finally the bomber fleet in Southern Russia was turned to the task, including the scarce He177 heavy bombers from I./KG 50.

8   The intrusion by RAF Mosquitos on reconnaissance flights, traversing the skies of occupied Europe with apparent impunity, was a constant provocation to Goering. Developed as a fast twin-engined medium bomber, the De Havilland Mosquito was built largely from wood to conserve strategic materials. Almost from the outset the Mosquito was developed into bomber, fighter and photo-reconnaissance versions. The latter, introduced early in 1943, had a top speed of 700kph (436mph), a ceiling of 11,700m (38,000ft), and a range of 4,100km (2,550 miles); they were a formidable asset to the Allies.

9   By July 1943 Bomber Command had some 20 operational squadrons of Avro Lancasters; this would rise to about fifty. With a range of 2,785km (1,730 miles) with a bomb load of 5,440kg (12,000lbs), and a maximum capacity of up to 8,165kg (18,000lbs), it was a vast improvement over other four-engined bombers. Although

Bomber Command casualties, at an average of 5 per cent of aircraft committed per sortie, were cumulatively very high, the Lancaster's 'survivability' compared well with older types at 132 tons of bombs dropped for every aircraft lost; the figures for the Halifax and Stirling were 56 tons and 41 tons per loss respectively.

10 The author had considerable experience of this during the 1960s when researching criteria for the selection of test pilots and astronauts. It was found that those pilots who routinely admitted being afraid were preferable in emergency situations to those who denied the emotion. Galland agreed that when he was Geschwaderkommodore he would never allow a pilot to fly on operations unless he could control, rather than deny, his fears. It is always said that a pilot who cannot define his limits has no stability, because he has no co-ordinate system in which to balance his emotions.

CHAPTER 18

October 1943 – July 1944

The losses incurred during its daylight bombing offensive of 1943 failed to deter the US 8th Army Air Force until 14 October 1943, and the second raid on the ball-bearing works at Schweinfurt. Escorted by 196 P-47s to the extent of their inadequate range, a force of 229 bombers lost a staggering 77 aircraft either destroyed or written off – one third of the force – with more than 600 crew members either killed or taken prisoner and 43 wounded. The price being paid for unescorted deep penetration bombing was too high, and the deep raids into Germany were suspended until the long range P-51B Mustang escort fighter became available for escort duty at the end of the year. The future of daylight bombing of Germany itself depended on neutralising the Jagdflieger.

The number of serviceable bombers available to the 8th AAF had increased from around 155 in January 1943 to more than 1,000 in December; but loss rates (defined as total write-offs from whatever cause) increased from 13 per cent in January to a peak of 26 per cent in October, when 198 bombers were lost out of a total availability of 763 – an unsustainable attrition rate. Crew loss rates increased from 21 per cent in January 1943 to around 37 per cent for most of the summer and autumn months.

It was the build-up of American strength during 1943 which stimulated German aircraft production, as the Allied raids galvanised the Luftwaffe high command into an expansion in fighter production which revealed the extraordinary recuperative powers of severely bomb-damaged factories. Urged on by Galland and implemented by Milch, fighter production had increased from around 500 a month at the start of the year to the planned goal of 1,000 by May 1943. Thereafter it averaged 1,100-1,200 a month until the big raids of October reduced production temporarily: 985 fighters were built in November and 687 in December, climbing again to 1,555 in January 1944. Before the end of 1944 production would average close on 3,000 a month. At long last the single-engined fighter was getting manufacturing priority, and annual production figures reflected this. From 24 per cent of total aircraft production in 1941, the fighters' share rose to 29 per cent in 1942, and 38 per cent – 9,626 fighters – in 1943. The credit for this must go to Milch; but it was the spur of Galland's relentless arguments which convinced Milch to make a personal commitment to these goals.

Throughout the year most of the Nazi hierarchy refused to accept the reality behind the incessant bombing and the remorseless destruction of German cities by night and industry by day. But with fighter production uppermost in his mind, Galland had frequent call upon the assistance of Albert Speer, who had been appointed minister of armaments and munitions on 8 February 1942, and who more or less controlled Germany's war economy from July 1943. Speer was by far the most intelligent and pragmatic of the senior decision-makers whom Galland came in contact with; he shared with the General of Fighters a grasp on reality – a rare quality around the Fuehrerhauptquartier.

Increasingly concerned at the lack of direction from the political leadership, Speer and Milch organised a conference in September 1943 at the Rechlin experimental station to discuss the situation with senior Luftwaffe staff. With a mass of supporting evidence, figures were presented comparing American aircraft production with projected German output: enemy production of four-engined bombers was proceeding at an alarming rate, and there would be insufficient fighters to counter this threat. Speer supported Galland's campaign for less emphasis on the construction of bombers and 'terror weapons' and greater priority for weapon systems capable of defending Germany; but at the Rechlin conference he was preaching to the converted. Since the spring Milch had been trying to get Goering to accept the figures; but the Reichsmarschall refused to oppose Hitler's conviction that they were propaganda lies, worked up by defeatists in the RLM.

In one telling incident during autumn 1943, Galland briefed Hitler on the increasing numbers of USAAF escort fighters, and told him that some had been shot down over Aachen, close to the Belgian/German border. Goering had always denied to Hitler that escort fighters had that kind of range; now, in the presence of Speer, Galland confirmed to Hitler that they were, in fact, reaching into German airspace, and warned of the consequences should the Americans field longer range escorts capable of accompanying the bombers deep into the Reich. Goering later berated Galland for telling the Fuehrer such 'lies'; but Galland stood his ground, saying that if the Reichsmarschall did not believe him the evidence was there for him to see – in Aachen. According to Speer, Goering spoke even more vehemently: 'That's nonsense, Galland. What gives you such fantasies? That's pure bluff!... I'm an experienced fighter pilot myself. I know what is possible. But I know what isn't, too. Admit you made a mistake.' Galland could only shake his head. 'What must have happened', said Goering, 'is that they were shot down farther west. I mean, if they were very high when they were shot down they could have glided quite a distance before they crashed.' Puffing himself up, he issued a final pronouncement: 'I hereby give you an official order that they weren't there! Do you understand? The American fighters were not there! Get that! I intend to report that to the Fuehrer!' So saying, he turned and walked away.

When the unchallengeable leadership of a great power in the crucial stage of a world war was exercised on such a basis, it is hardly surprising that on 18 August 1943 the Luftwaffe chief of staff, Genobst Hans Jeschonnek, had put a gun to his head and blown his brains out.

Monthly German fighter losses had increased from around 300-400 in January 1943 to a peak of 782 in July – the month of the battles for Sicily and Kursk – falling off to 380 in November. The dramatic reduction in losses on the

Mediterranean and Eastern Fronts was more than balanced by sustained loss rates on the Western Front, where every month the Jagdwaffe was losing on average 250-330 aircraft; in November 1943 only 99 aircraft were lost in the other two theatres combined. While Allied claims, particularly by bomber airgunners, were far in excess of the true figures, such attrition remained serious.

During the spring and summer of 1943 the OKL had pulled back to Germany all but the six Gruppen of JG2 and JG26 left in France. There were now 19 Jagdgruppen in central Germany, with JG1 , JG3 , JG11 and JG300 at full strength and various Gruppen from JG5, JG27 , JG51 and JG54. When Galland failed to get approval for his Jagdflieger to attack the American escort fighters rather than the bombers he had proposed that JG2 and JG26 alone should go for the P-47s, causing them to drop their belly tanks which, even if they were not shot down, would prevent them escorting the bombers. This was tried on one occasion and proved highly successful; but OKL refused to approve the scheme for general application.

A significant engagement took place near Cologne on 4 October during a daylight raid on Frankfurt: at the very limit of their range, P-47s of the 56th Fighter Group caught a Gruppe of Bf110s preparing to attack the bomber formation with heavy weapons. The Zerstoerer squadrons had sometimes proved very effective, standing off and breaking up the Fortress boxes with the various rocket weapons and multiple cannon which their size allowed them to carry – once a bomber was forced out of formation it was relatively easy meat for the Jagdflieger. On 4 October the Zerstoerer group, more or less helpless against true fighters, suffered about ten losses. Soon they would be unable to operate west of the line Bremen-Kassel-Frankfurt.

The General der Jagdflieger had additional responsibilities forced upon him in November 1943 when he was given authority over the night fighter force. Raised largely through the personal energy and commitment of Gen Josef Kammhuber in 1940, the Nachtjagdflieger had been moulded by 1942 into a formidable defence in depth, efficiently directed by a tight system of ground control served by an extensive radar network. It waged a see-saw war of technical and tactical innovation against RAF Bomber Command, who took it very seriously indeed. It had fewer aircraft than Kammhuber wanted, but when in July 1943 he requested a major expansion Hitler assured him it would not be necessary. Operating through XII.Fliegerkorps, Kammhuber controlled almost all Nachtjagdflieger, and had resisted any call for a major reorganisation of the air defence of the Reich. What he objected to was full integration of the Nachtjagdflieger with the air raid reporting service, a motley collection of organisations which he felt would confuse rather than simplify the task of bringing the bombers down. His detractors argued that only when this integration of the radar and the reporting service took place could the system operate effectively. The failure to effectively intercept a raid on Kassel on 3 October was used against him, and the following month the functions of Inspekteur der Nachtjaeger were absorbed into those of the inspectorate of day fighters. Galland protested against this, arguing his ignorance of this specialised form of air fighting, but to no avail.

There had, however, been some respite from other pressures: only the previous month the ground support elements had been taken from him when a General der Schlachtflieger had been appointed. He had never wanted the Schlachtflieger under his command, claiming that it was only the common use of the Fw190 series which provided any link with the Jagdwaffe. Later in the year there was also a rationalisation of the air raid reporting service, which was given to the Jagddivisionen with observer and radar reports integrated and passed to the fighter units. Galland leaned heavily on Maj Herrmann, and later Obst Streib, in his dealings with the night fighter arm.

* * *

Throughout 1943 and early 1944 the struggle to increase fighter output and to select the best types for production was complicated by the appearance of prototype aircraft whose potential appeared to far outweigh that of normal piston-engined fighters the – Me163 and Me262. The rocket-powered Me163 was, in reality, a pilot-killing dead end, but the raw figures were deceptively impressive to those of a Wagnerian rather than a technical bent. Its rocket motor was powered by an exotic and highly unstable mixture of two propellants; with 1,500kg (3,300lb) thrust, it had a top speed of more than 885kph (550mph) and a phenomenal climb rate, reaching almost 10,000m (33,000ft) in little more than three minutes from a standing start. Equipped with a pair of 20mm or 30mm cannon, it looked formidable on paper; but its limitations – specifically, an endurance of less than five minutes, and the volatility of its dangerous fuel – greatly restricted its operational value.

The Me262 was altogether far more promising, and had caught Galland's interest when he first heard about it during a conference with Milch in early 1942; its first jet-powered flight had taken place on 18 July that year. It would become the world's first operational jet fighter; but its introduction in this role would be complicated by the view held since 1942 by the influential 'bomber lobby' within the RLM that it should be developed as a 'Blitz-bomber', a ground-attack and strike aircraft. As soon as he learned about the project Galland was pitched headlong into the debate, demanding that it should be designed and built as a high-speed interceptor[1].

A year after he had first heard about the Me262, Galland had visited the Messerschmitt works to fly a prototype for himself; he had been pressed by Willi Messerschmitt to back its development as a fighter. In taking over production responsibilities from Udet, Erhard Milch had inherited Udet's prejudice against jet-powered aircraft, but had eventually been convinced of their usefulness as part of the overall production plan. Milch and Galland had been taken to Lechfeld on 22 May 1943 with the test pilot Maj Wolfgang Spaete, who was aglow with enthusiasm from his first few flights in the V4, powered like its predecessor by two 840kg (1,850lb) thrust Junkers Jumo 004 turbojet engines. With a wingspan and length almost as great as that of the Ju87 Stuka and a loaded weight 50 per cent greater than a Fw190, the Me262 was a big aeroplane. What Galland had been told about the aircraft could not have prepared him for what he had seen that day: as he arrived at Lechfeld he had glimpsed two gleaming silver shapes, precursors of a whole new age of jet-powered fighters with performance characteristics of which pilots had only dreamed.

Technicians had prepared the Me262-V3 for Galland's initial flight; it had already flown 18 times since the previous July, including a brief check flight that day. Galland had wanted to know the equivalent horsepower; with slide-rule, pencil and envelope a rough calculation produced an astonishing figure of around 74,000. Its maximum speed was around 885kph (550mph), about 225km (140mph) faster than the Bf109G-6. Test pilot Fritz Wendel had first put the V3 through its paces in an 18-minute flight which seriously impressed Galland, now eager to take it into the air himself. The aircraft had rolled to a halt with smoke and steam pouring out of the two underslung engine nacelles; resting back on its tail wheel, nose high in the air, it had looked like a mechanical bird from a different world. Now it was his turn. It had taken about ten minutes to brief Galland, advising him of a trick learned by the test pilots to get the Me262 airborne: at 180kph (112mph) a gentle stroke on the brakes would tip the nose forward, bringing up the tail and putting the elevators into free air; at 190kph (120mph) the Me262 would fly itself off the runway. He should watch the critical throttle setting to avoid stalling or overheating the engines and, once in the air, must handle the throttle gently – roughness could induce a flame-out. Few things could be worse than a flame-out on take-off: it would wrench the aircraft to one side and probably destroy prototype and pilot.

As the first engine started everything had seemed fine; it crackled and roared to life as technicians began to start the second engine. Suddenly, a flash of flame had licked the nacelle and it caught fire. Frantically signalling for Galland to get out of the cockpit, the groundcrew had dowsed the flames. So it was to be in the Me262-V4, only seven days after its first flight, that Galland got to fly the 'silver bird'.

Bearing the markings PC+UD, the fourth prototype had begun to roll down the runway as Galland strained left and right to see around the high nose. He had kept a close eye on the temperature gauges to monitor the temperamental engines as, carefully inching the throttle forward, he accelerated rapidly. Maintaining a straight line by looking to either side of the runway, he had got the nose down at around 130kph (80mph), touching the brakes when he crossed a specially painted white line, and was airborne at the predicted speed. It felt, he would recall later, 'as though an angel was pushing me'. Nothing had prepared him for this sensation. Gone was the vibration inseparable from piston engines; gone was the noise of the beating propeller; gone was the torque that persistently tried to pull the aeroplane around: instead there was a constant rushing sound, extraordinary speed, and flight as smooth as silk.

After getting the feel of the aircraft and noting its excellent aerodynamic characteristics, Galland had seen in the distance a four-engined Me264, the highly secret 'Amerika bomber' prototype, engaged on its own flying trials. Deciding there and then that this would be a good opportunity to test the Me262's interception abilities, he had roared after it and performed a mock attack, albeit with due caution – it would not have helped the programme to have destroyed one of only two prototypes then flying. Returning to Lechfeld, Galland had felt convinced that the Luftwaffe had a winner, an interceptor of such capability that he was certain it would play a crucial role in the defence of the Reich. He always remembered that as simply the most exciting day of his life.

Three days later, on Tuesday 25 May 1943, he had written a brief report to Milch thoroughly endorsing the new jet and recommending a major production commitment. Galland wanted the Me262 and the Fw190 to form the core of a fighter production programme, abandoning the Bf109 for Butcher Birds powered by the BMW801 series for conventional variants, the DB603 for high-altitude variants, and the 1,776hp Junkers Jumo 213 in-line engine for developed versions – in late 1944 the Jumo 213 would give the Fw190D series a top speed of 685kph (426mph) and a climb time of only two minutes to 4,000m (13,000ft). The Me262, thought Galland, should form 25 per cent of the total fighter output; and the day after he had submitted his report to Milch he had gone to see Goering and stressed the importance of getting the jet into service as a fighter.

Goering had played down the need for such a radical shift in fighter production; nevertheless, responding in part to urging from Galland, Milch had ordered series production of the Me262 on 25 May 1943. Three days later the RLM had decided the production standard for the first 100 aircraft, and on 2 June series production had been authorised for the manufacture of 60 a month beginning in May 1944. Galland was delighted with plans to put the fighter into production but incensed over the cautious attitude. He had been to see Milch, who explained that Hitler had reservations about the viability of the new jet and had urged restraint. As in so many instances, Hitler had little feel for the operational value of scientific and technical advances, preferring to listen to those who played up to his prejudices.

The gradual shift of emphasis toward the Me262 as a bomber began in earnest on 11 September when two engineers from the Messerschmitt design bureau, Degel and Althoff, prepared a document detailing eight potential variants of the Me262 , including two types for reconnaissance, two for high-speed bombing, three for fighter interception and one for training. The bomber version was envisaged as carrying a 1,000kg (2,200lb) load, while one of the proposed interceptors was described as having six MK108 30mm cannon. In the event the aircraft would mount four MK108s in the nose, with 100 rounds per gun for the top pair and 80 rounds each for the others. Galland was delighted with this armament: the close grouping gave the 'Experten' a concentration of fire which maximised the effect. Early versions of the MK108 fired 10 rounds/second, later models increasing this to 14.3 rounds/second.

The question of role was still being argued, however: those who saw the Me262 as a bomber argued their case at the RLM, and from there to Goering personally. The Reichsmarschall was also approached by the fighter lobby, concern at the planned production rate leading to a direct appeal by Willi Messerschmitt and Galland. On 2 November 1943, after talking to Hitler, Goering set up a special commission under Obst Petersen at the Technisches Amt to oversee development. By going straight to Goering over Milch's head the intention had been to get approval for increased production, but in fact the fighter lobby simply drew the attention of men who knew little about modern air warfare. The day Goering set up the commission he visited Augsburg. He had been asked by Hitler to make a personal tour of the Messerschmitt works and was accompanied by Milch, Galland and Genmaj Vorwald of the Technisches Amt.

Progress was satisfactory; to give the aircraft a more sympathetic take-off and landing attitude the Me262-V6 had a nosewheel undercarriage, and had flown successfully on 17 October. Knowing Hitler's prejudices, Goering asked Messerschmitt whether the aircraft could carry bombs. Thinking of the Degel/ Althoff schemes, the designer assured him that it could easily carry a useful warload and that it would only take a couple of weeks to design the appropriate shackles. Galland was dumbstruck: the tone of the conversation was changing, and he knew Goering was up to something. Shortly afterwards, Goering told Hitler that he had personally arranged for the latest jet aircraft to be used as a Blitz-bomber – the role closest to the sickly dictator's heart, given his obsession with revenge.

On 12 November Milch questioned the wide use of resources on the Me262 programme and drew attention to the manpower levels requested. Genmaj Vorwald was asked whether the programme was ready to move to production during 1944 and, after consultation with Galland, gave a strong affirmative. He was being optimistic; Augsburg was in chaos, due in part to air raids during August and October, and full production would be delayed. When the RAF hit Augsburg on the night of 25 February 1944 with a force of almost 600 bombers they would accelerate plans already under way to disperse manufacture and assembly of the all-important jet.

Hitler still remained to be convinced that the aircraft was, in any event, worth pursuing. Goering, desperate to regain Hitler's favour, courted the pro-bomber lobby at the RLM, and arranged for the Fuehrer to see a demonstration at Insterburg, East Prussia, on 26 November. Hitler was stunned; and Galland heard him ask Willi Messerschmitt if the aircraft could carry bombs. Unable to resist giving the answer which Germany's most powerful man clearly wanted, Messerschmitt confirmed it – an act for which he would curse himself within moments. Unable to move his arm, and with a sickly pallor, Hitler turned upon the group and – much as he had done when replacing Galland's diamonds – went into an act of superior insight. Primed by Goering, he railed against their lack of imagination: 'Not one of you has come to the idea that this is the Blitz-bomber which I have been demanding for the last ten years ... This is the aircraft with which I will fight and repel the imminent Allied invasion.'

On 5 December a telegram to Goering confirmed that 'The Fuehrer has again called attention to the importance of producing all jet aircraft as fighter-bombers. It is vital that the Luftwaffe has a number of these aircraft available by spring 1944 and any deficiency in materials at the manufacturer is to be made up through Luftwaffe resources. The Fuehrer is adamant that any delay in this programme would constitute irresponsible negligence.' Moreover, Hitler wanted bi-monthly reports on the Me262 and Arado Ar234 – the latter a four-engined jet bomber capable of carrying a 1,500kg (3,500lb) warload.

Galland was silently determined not to let this vital weapon in his fight against the Allied bombers be taken from him; and the whole group responsible for bringing the Me262 to operational status shared the belief that this was one

Fuehrer order that was simply too damaging to obey. In the meantime the aircraft had to be built, bomb shackles or no bomb shackles. Encouraged by Galland, Speer put his weight behind the Me262 programme and, although considerable development work lay ahead, gave priority to its production.

* * *

Galland and Speer discussed production of the Me262 in detail; there were problems inherent in the main Augsburg works, which was clearly a prime target for the Allies. As things stood, fuselage sections were being produced at the Regensburg works and then moved to Augsburg, where wings and nose sections were built; final assembly took place at Leipheim airfield – already overcrowded with work on the giant Me323 transport. Speer was looking for a major change in the way munitions were produced, and the Me262 was representative of an increasingly difficult situation. In a sweeping decentralisation programme, assembly lines would be dispersed into the surrounding countryside; and following the RAF raid of 25 February 1944 a determined effort was made to consolidate Me262 production in forest factories around the Augsburg region. (In fact, the Me262 was absorbed into a plan that had already been worked out in mid-1943 by Wehrmacht engineers on the express orders of Hitler, for the protection of aircraft production lines in three phases: by dispersal, by the use of existing mines and tunnels, and by construction of large bomb-proof shelters.)

Galland had many meetings with Speer during the first half of 1944 as these activities got under way and additional factory sites were planned. These manufacturing, component and assembly works would quickly spread right across south-eastern Germany, primarily in the area between Stuttgart and Passau. The forest factories were placed near sections of autobahn from which the aircraft could make test flights and be delivered to their distribution points. The first such factory, Kuno I near Leipheim, was completed by March 1944 in woodland close to a 2km (1.25 miles) straight section of the Munich-Stuttgart road, which provided an excellent runway. Elaborate camouflage hid the factories from air observation. Set within pine forest in remote areas, the machining and assembly shops were built on large concrete bases and covered with wooden canopies and camouflage nets. Alongside were gun-pits for test firing, test stands for engines, and a heavily camouflaged checkout facility.

Kuno I was the focal point for production dispersed over a wide area. Hundreds of components were fabricated in isolated workings set in dense forest or camouflaged clearings, linked by tracks and small roads along which regular traffic on a one-way loop would serve as a non-stop delivery belt. The wings were assembled and finished in a specially converted tunnel covering a section of autobahn near Leonburg just outside Stuttgart; fuselages were delivered from forest works near Passau and Hagelstadt; nose sections came from similar shops at Gunzburg, and flaps, engine cowlings and undercarriage doors from Wasserburg. However, even this ingenuity could not keep the Me262 entirely safe from the bombing: on 24 April 1944, 98 B-24s dropped 236,000kg (232 tons) of bombs on Leipheim, destroying 53 Me262s from the Kuno I works. For much of the year the forest factory itself went undetected, until attacked by air on 18 November 1944; but long before this a second factory, Kuno II, had been opened to the east, and final assembly works at Schwabisch Hall had been operating since May. A third factory near Regensburg began to produce aircraft in December 1944, and a plant at Neuberg/Donau started operations in January 1945.

The second phase of the protection plan started in early 1944 when construction of the 'Reichsmarschall Hermann Goering Factory' got under way in redundant china clay galleries at Walpersburg near Kahla. Linked by interconnecting tunnels, the galleries formed assembly points for components and parts put together at the extremities of the complex. They converged on a central underground assembly hall where taxyways gave access to similarly enclosed test ranges for engines and guns. At the end of one taxyway aircraft were placed on a specially inclined lift which pulled them up to a mountain ridge, on top of which a 1,220m (4,000ft) runway supported fuelling facilities and test stands for final flight preparation. Launched with additional thrust from rocket packs, the Me262s were hurled into the air from the ridge to fly to nearby airfields. Because landings were impossible on the precarious ridge, pilots had first to be trained at Zerbst before travelling to Kahla and taking away the completed jets. Not before 1945 was the facility finished, although 27 fighters were completed and despatched from the ridge.

The third phase was a bomb-proof assembly facility with the code-name 'Weingut II'. During the first two months of 1944 final drawings were completed for a production facility to be built near Kaufering alongside a railway line about six miles north of Landsberg. Additional railway lines were to have linked the facility with Augsburg and Munich, and large communal housing estates were to have provided accommodation for the estimated 90,000 workers necessary to complete the project. Construction work began in March 1944 – five floors enclosed by a massive concrete arch structure 1,145m (3,750ft) long and 400m (1,300ft) wide. The outside was covered by turf and grasses to blend it in with the surrounding countryside. About 50m (150ft) high at the centre, the semicircular arch was blanked off at one end by giant doors. Four of the five interior floors were to be given over to manufacturing and assembly; the top floor was an enclosed runway along which completed aircraft would be hurled into the air by rocket-assisted take-off. For the construction of this immense structure, 10,000 Hungarian labourers were brought in by labour minister Fritz Sauckel to a newly established work camp near Kaufering[2]. 'Weingut II' was never completed in time to produce finished aircraft; but ground clearance began at Wasserburg for the second of six such sites, planned to produce around 4,000 aircraft a month.

Organisation on this scale was only possible because a clear and decisive chain of command led from the tiny lathe in a forest to the offices of Albert Speer in Berlin. Galland found in Speer a means by which he could bypass the increasingly distracted leadership, and work to organise the massive expansion of the fighter forces, which required the construction of facilities on this colossal scale.

* * *

The threats that would determine Galland's recommendations on fighter strengths and type-by-type priorities emerged in the first half of 1944 as an intensification and expansion of US daylight raids, and the appearance of the P-51B Mustang[3] long-range fighter over German territory from 13 December 1943. From March 1944 the Mustangs were flying all the way to Berlin and back; single-handed, the P-51 would save the US daylight bombing offensive from unacceptable attrition, chopping B-17 and B-24 losses from 19-25 per cent in the first four months of 1944 to an acceptable 11-13 per cent by June 1944.

For the Jagdwaffe the situation was fast deteriorating. During the first half of 1944 fighter loss rates went up from 30 per cent in January to around 50 per cent in May and June, actually peaking at 56 per cent during March. Perhaps predictably, when escort fighters were reported over Hannover in central Germany Goering refused to believe it. Galland was determined to see for himself and arranged to go up and investigate, taking along Obst Trautloft, now his chief inspector of day fighters; his disregard of the order grounding him from combat operations was becoming commonplace. The two pilots duly encountered the reported Mustangs, and got chased all the way back to Berlin. There was no doubt about the P-51's ability to stay with the bombers.

In a single stroke, restrictions on 8th AAF daylight operations disappeared. The Americans were to suffer heavy losses to Galland's fighters during the first four months largely because the Jagdwaffe concentrated its defensive structure and because the 8th AAF were not yet able to put up enough P-51s, but this would not last. The sheer pressure of numbers and the increased frequency of the raids worried Galland intensely. The 8th AAF had increased its operational strength from fewer than 500 bombers in September 1943 to just over 750 by the end of the year, to almost 1,050 in February 1944, and more than 1,300 in April 1944.

Pilot losses among the Jagdflieger constantly reduced the number of experienced officers, and compressed training programmes increased the ratio of new pilots to veterans. Simultaneously a major training programme for 'Mighty Eighth' escort pilots increased the available number of P-51s and P-47s. The number of operational escort fighters increased from fewer than 300 in September 1943 to around 1,000 by mid-1944. This armada was wielded by mature and sophisticated commanders. LtGen Doolittle[4] made a wise decision when he released his escort pilots from the apron-strings of the bombers and gave them a far greater operational freedom than Galland had been able to extract from Goering. From the end of February, when bad weather gave way to clearer skies, the American fighters went on the offensive; and Galland would never forget the impression they made.

The fresh, aggressive USAAF fighter pilots not only had excellent aircraft; their tactics, and their flying skills, were simply superior to those of the Jagdflieger of 1944. The sheer intensity of the American onslaught was breathtaking. Sweeping widely ahead of and to the flanks of the massed bomber formations, the fighters quickly hunted down any gathering group of German interceptors, denying them the chance to assemble in the large numbers which alone would make their attacks effective. This was air warfare on a grand scale.

From 20 to 25 February 1944 – 'Big Week' – the USAAF mounted a massive assault on the German aircraft industry, striking directly at Germany's ability to control her own airspace. Allied and German propaganda made of it what served their respective purposes; and while the figures looked impressive, the outcome was unexpected. While as many bombs were dropped in this one week – 10 million kg (10,000 tons) – as the 8th AAF had dropped in the whole of 1943, the most enduring result was to accelerate the German production dispersal plan set out several months earlier. Of the 2,351 bombing sorties flown, 157 US aircraft were lost – around 6.6 per cent of the total. A total of 4 million kg (4,000 tons) of bombs actually hit the aircraft production plants; 75 per cent of the buildings and facilities accounting for 90 per cent of German aircraft production were either damaged or destroyed.

For Galland the real issue of 'Big Week' was that it represented the beginning of a sustained campaign leading up to the inevitable invasion of occupied Europe. The Luftwaffe was in the front line; control of the skies was vital for the Allied effort. The Luftwaffe's losses went from just under 15 per cent of front line strength in January 1944 to around 28 per cent in April and May, with Luftwaffe bomber losses reaching 34 per cent of strength by April. Galland knew the onslaught he had prophesied for so long had arrived, and the casualties wrote that reality in blood.

The German leadership was stung into a maelstrom of activity, some of it productive but a lot of it wasted on fruitless discussions at hastily convened conferences. The plans to disperse production were accelerated; and Goering wanted, again, to know why the bombers were getting through. Galland wanted to remind him that it was precisely because too little attention had been paid to defensive fighters for the Reich, and because the tactics being employed were, quite simply, losing the war. That he did not was more out of a need to keep at least the semblance of a dialogue alive than from any natural reticence. At all costs he had to keep pushing for more fighters and a better use of the existing resources. As it was, the remarkable recuperative powers of German industry made 'Big Week' a mere blip on the chart.

Overall, production slipped back from 2,445 aircraft in January to 2,015 in February, before resuming its climb to 2,672 in March and 3,034 in April. Galland watched the fighter component of that total with eager eyes: dropping from 1,555 in January to 1,104 in February, rising to 1,638 in March and 2,021 in April. So it would go on, rising inexorably until a total of 3,375 fighters were produced in September, 82 per cent of all aircraft production that month. These figures were seriously underestimated by Allied intelligence, their reports citing an average monthly total production of 645 for the first half of 1943 (851 in reality), and 655 a month in the first half of 1944 (1,581 in fact). The spurt in fighter production during 1944 came as a direct result of plans laid down in March and April, when new goals and production levels were agreed.

Under Karl-Otto Sauer's leadership the production programme had expanded enormously, and during March and April fundamental decisions about future output were put in place. At the urging of Galland the RLM had set up on 1 March 1944 the 'Jaegerstab' or Fighter Staff, which Sauer would head with Milch and Speer as joint chairmen. Functioning under Speer's ministry, it took direct control of fighter production, co-ordinating not only the dispersal of production facilities but also the allocation and distribution of essential materials. From approximately 200 different types and variants it pruned the number of production types to less than 20, restricting production to aircraft demanding the least materials and manpower and rejecting exotic types and advanced, high-performance designs. Of these only the Me163 and the Me262 were rushed through; an aircraft such as the successor to the Fw190D, the Focke-Wolf Ta152, while showing great promise and outstanding performance, was simply too complex to get into volume production. This, as much as the Allied bombing effort, was responsible for the low output of that type; numbers were what mattered, and it was better to have ten Bf109Gs than three Ta152s.

The Jaegerstab closed the circle that contained Galland, Sauer, Milch and Speer, and production decisions were made on the basis of expediency and not the exotic attractions of the 'super-weapons' which so excited Hitler and Goering. Severe decisions had to be made; among the types which fell foul of this rationalisation process were the Dornier Do335, the Focke-Wolf Ta154, and the equally promising Heinkel He219. Galland was kept constantly in touch with the various groups providing details for the RLM. The proposed programme envisaged production of 5,000 aircraft a month, and Galland was able to secure a fighter target of 3,000 of those.

Goering, predictably, wanted bombers, to carry out the promise made by Gen Karl Koller and Gen Guenther Korten to turn back the invading Allies on the beaches with massive raids[5]. Galland, equally predictably, believed that Koller's plan, drawn up while he was head of the Fuehrungsstab, was unrealistic, but Goering refused to abandon it; in his eyes the priority was probably to bomb himself back into Hitler's favour. Galland did not object to the production of bombers so much because they took resources from the fighter production lines, but rather because bombers devoured aircrews, fuel and manpower in pursuit of what he considered a fruitless exercise, while fighters capable of smashing up the bomber formations were kept inactive for lack of them.

At Berchtesgaden, Goering reviewed the new production proposals put together by those responsible for different elements in the air force, including Galland, and after several changes the document was submitted for Hitler's approval at a conference on 23 May 1944 attended by Goering, Milch, Speer, Sauer and senior representatives of industry. Hitler noticed that the Me262 was down in the production figures as a fighter. In uncontrollable rage he accused everyone of disobeying orders, of betraying his will and of sabotaging the war effort; henceforth, he ordered, the Me262 would be known as a 'Blitz-bomber'. Milch tried to explain it away as an administrative categorisation that hid the reality; that only a few pre-production aircraft were in those figures, and that the bomb shackles were indeed being designed and would be fitted as directed. It was not enough, and Hitler raged on.

Four days later Galland was at another conference on the Obersalzburg, this time without the Fuehrer; attended by Bodenschatz, Willi Messerschmitt, Petersen and others, it was convened specifically to discuss the Me262. Goering requested that in future the aircraft be categorised as a 'super-speed bomber' and that it should never again be referred to as a fighter; Messerschmitt was admonished for so doing, and Goering pleaded that no one do anything to upset the Fuehrer on this matter – to placate the Fuehrer, Goering was going to give direction of the Me262 programme to the General der Kampfflieger. But already, by the end of May 1944, Galland was beginning to see through the charade. Little more than a week later Karl-Otto Sauer came to reassure Galland that it was not the Fuehrer who wanted the aircraft built exclusively as a bomber, despite the impression he gave at meetings. It was Goering who insisted that the Me262 be disregarded as a fighter; and Sauer brought clear and unequivocal evidence.

This came in the form of a Fuehrerbefehl which historians would later claim dealt the Me262 a debilitating blow. The opening passages do indeed read like a defining commitment, demanding that '... under no circumstances is bomber production to be delayed'. But Galland read further, to learn that Hitler would indeed permit fighter production to proceed, and that when bomb-carrying tests had been completed 'there is no reason why production cannot be divided between the two models'. Galland took the order, and a memorandum of an earlier meeting on 7 June between Hitler and Sauer, to Speer, and together the three men worked out how Goering could be kept in the dark and Hitler reassured that his orders were being carried out.

Trouble with the Me262 programme would linger on throughout the summer and autumn. Long after the war the selective reading of the Hitler edict would muddy the waters. Everyone close to the Me262's protracted development felt that too many expectations had been raised, not least Sauer who, in late June 1944, turned on his fellow members of the Jaegerstab and accused them all of making rash promises. Under Sauer's more sober plan 60 Me262s were to be produced in July, 100 in August, 150 in September, 225 in October, 325 in November and 500 in December. Of that revised production target of 1,360 for the second half of 1944, only 513 would be built. The engines were late, the general production of the aircraft fell far behind schedules set months earlier, and technical problems with the airframe and equipment kept it out of operational service more than a year beyond expectations. Equipping it for fighter-bomber duties in fact had little or no impact on its availability; but the myth prevails.

* * *

Between January and May 1944 the Jagdwaffe lost 99 per cent of its average personnel strength: 2,262 killed or seriously injured, against an average paper strength of 2,283. In March the US 8th Army Air Force extended its raids all the way to Berlin; and while the Goebbels propaganda machine told the public through the *Voelkischer Beobachter* that such attacks should not be 'interpreted as a sign of strength', Galland was warned in a coded message to his headquarters on 8 March that the Allied air forces were getting wise as well as strong: 'The enemy has recognised our tactics of taking off and getting away from the airfield with all serviceable aircraft before attacks on our ground organisation. In the West, he has recently put aside a part of the escorting force to attack these aircraft, and has achieved successes in this connection.' Little more than two weeks later, Luftflotte Reich sent Galland a coded signal:

'During flights into the home war zone, enemy fighters have repeatedly carried out attacks on aircraft which were landing or on the airfields themselves. In doing so, they imitate the landing procedure of German fighters or gain surprise by approaching the airfield in fast and level flight. The difficulty in distinguishing friend from foe often makes it impossible for the flak artillery to fire on them.'

Released from the rigid escort role, the enemy pilots were free to fly and fight as they thought fit. Galland watched this development keenly; he knew that attrition of the pilot pool could threaten the ability of his fighter units to put aircraft in the air. Accordingly, he sent out a request for volunteers:

'The strained manpower situation in units operating in defence of the Reich urgently demands a further influx of experienced flying personnel from other arms of the service. In particular, for the maintenance of the fighting power of the air arm, experienced pilots of ground-attack and bomber units, especially officers suitable as formation leaders, must now be drawn upon.'

In the interests of making the most of existing resources Galland had the RLM circulate the following, drafted by his own hand:

'The extraordinarily difficult situation in the air defence of the homeland requires, with all emphasis:

(1) The speedy salvage of all fighter and heavy fighter aircraft and their immediate return for repair.

(2) The unrestricted employment of salvage personnel for salvage tasks. Subordinate units are expressly forbidden to employ them for any other purpose.

(3) That spare parts be acquired by repair and salvage units by removal from [damaged aircraft which are judged] worth salvaging only in case of absolute necessity.

(4) That repair of aircraft in your area be energetically speeded up in order to increase serviceability and to relieve supply.'

In the final days before the invasion of France, Galland put together an expansion plan for the Jagdgeschwader to increase their strength in much the way he had proposed in 1943. This envisaged the addition of a fourth Staffel to each Gruppe, or a fourth Gruppe to each Geschwader, with Staffel establishment rising from 12 to 16 aircraft. This expansion policy, begun in JG2 and JG26, would continue throughout the Jagdwaffe. Moreover, Galland proposed to Goering that the new reserves be held in Germany until fully trained for operational duty. From previous experience he knew that the Jagdgeschwader would quickly absorb the new sub-units if they were sent across all at once; whereas if they were filtered into the front line at intervals, the new forces would be more effective.

It was over the policy for Reich defence that Galland was at odds with Goering. On 1 April 1944 Luftflotte Reich had been theoretically allocated 50 per cent of the Luftwaffe fighter force, a total amounting to about 850 fighters; and on 19 May Galland proposed that the entire fighter complement in Luftflotte 3 be given over to Luftflotte Reich. This was turned down; Goering wanted to retain the means to comply with Hitler's insistence that the invasion, when it came, must be stopped on the beaches. Once again Milch, Speer and Galland pressed for a stronger reserve in Germany to stem the bombers. Goering agreed that this was desirable, and ordered that 2,000 fighters be assembled for that purpose. Galland knew that such a figure was impossible, but got approval to build up to a force of 1,800 – even that would take several weeks to achieve.

To start the process he took the third Staffel from each Gruppe on the Eastern Front and recalled them to Germany for intensive training; as experience had shown, it was unwise to take a pilot from one front and expect him to fight effectively as soon as he arrived on another. Replacements for the Eastern Front would come from the flying schools, as Russia was relatively the least dangerous place for the inexperienced to practise newly acquired skills. In addition, each Jagdschule and Ergaenzungsjagdgruppe would contribute one Staffel for Reich defence. Thus he hoped to build the numbers up to 1,800 by the end of June. But by 1 June Gen Stumpff, commanding Luftflotte Reich, had only 700 single-seat fighters, of which only 444 were fully serviceable; and the invasion would end all hope of maintaining the commitment to build up the home defence reserve, throwing the fighter forces into chaos by the sheer weight of Allied air power.

Under detailed plans drawn up for the invasion, Jagdgeschwader were to move en masse to the Western Front to deliver the deadly punch that would repulse the invaders; only JG300, JG301, ZG26 and ZG76 would remain in Germany. A special staff study determined that all Jagdgeschwader would be transferred to II.Jagdkorps in the West when invasion began. In reality, preparations to repulse the invasion may be said to have begun with the transfer in August 1943 of Genmaj Dietrich Peltz from Italy to command all bomber forces in the West, where he was given command of IX.Fliegerkorps. In February 1944, II.Flieger-korps under the command of Gen Alfred Buelowius was taken from the Italian theatre to build up additional airfields, supply routes, communication systems and ground organisation in France; the mass movement of the fighter forces to the West would need a large number of airfields and operating bases. In mid-March 1944 Fliegerfuehrer Atlantik was expanded to the status of a Fliegerkorps; its long range aircraft would operate from bases in south-western France against ships of the invasion force. Genlt Holle and X.Fliegerkorps were brought up from the Mediterranean to form the basis for the new corps. Subordinated to X.Fliegerkorps, II.Fliegerdivision deployed torpedo-bombers to southern France in case an invasion came from that direction, and Galland was responsible for setting up a Jafu Southern France to direct fighter operations in that eventuality.

The question of fuel demand had been anticipated; strict economy measures and increased production during the winter of 1943-44 and the following spring had built up an unprecedented reserve. Galland knew that this could vanish within weeks if the Allies conducted a serious bombing campaign against the refineries, but there was nothing that could be done about that other than push for as many fighters as possible to hold back for Reich defence. Reserves had increased from 280,000 tons in September 1943 to 390,000 tons in December; by April 1944 Germany had 420,000 tons of fuel oil with a further 120,000 tons in a strategic reserve. In May Luftflotte 3 had a reserve stockpile of 20,000 tons, more than enough for a month of intensive operational flying. Reserves were stronger than they had been at any time since 1940. The main bulk reserve was the primary source of fuel for air operations, but at Gruppe level local commanders had their own emergency reserves. The strategic reserve, hitherto released at the authority of a senior commander, was now labelled the 'Fuehrer Reserve', to be released only on the express order of Hitler.

In reviewing the situation regarding pilots, Galland was moderately satisfied with the numbers now coming through. Generally speaking the flying schools had done a remarkable job of expanding their output, increasing the graduate pilot total from 1,962 in 1942 to 3,231 in 1943. The numbers of single-seat fighter pilots had increased the most, with 1,662 in 1942 and 3,276 the following year. To Galland's mind, however, the quality of the modern fighter pilot left a lot to be desired. Day fighter pilots were coming out with less than 100 hours' flying time, while night fighter pilots had 110-155 hours; and the time would soon come when the new Jagdflieger would arrive on his Staffel with only 30 hours in his logbook. (By comparison, British pilots now had 200-220 flying hours when they joined their units.)

Galland knew that the invasion was near. His intelligence information told him that the Allies were putting in a superhuman effort. Most significantly, even RAF Bomber Command (over the protests of 'Bomber' Harris) had gradually been switched from area bombing in Germany to the destruction of the rail and communications systems prior to an invasion of enemy-occupied France. In March 1944 only 30 per cent of Bomber Command's targets lay outside Germany, in April 66 per cent, and in May more than 75 per cent. By 6 June the volume of traffic on the French rail system had fallen to 30 per cent of its January level, and within weeks it would fall to 10 per cent. In the two weeks prior to D-Day the Allies flew 195,000 sorties from Britain – two-thirds by the Americans – dropping 215,000 tons of bombs. This had been achieved at high cost: in that period the Allies lost 2,000 aircraft and 12,000 airmen. On 21 May Galland received worrying news that massive sweeps by Allied aircraft were disrupting rail and road traffic. In a little over a week unrestrained attacks by almost 800 Spitfires, P-47s and Typhoons damaged or destroyed 500 locomotives.

Despite the cost in Allied airmen, comparative figures gave no cause for confidence. In May alone the Luftwaffe lost 50.4 per cent of its fighter force and 25 per cent of its Bf109 and Fw190 pilots. The extraordinary production effort compensated to some degree for these losses, but units were badly depleted and had no reserve. At the end of May the Luftwaffe had approximately 4,500 serviceable aircraft of all types. Resident on the Western Front with Luftflotte 3 were JG2, with only 44 serviceable aircraft out of 64 on hand; and JG26, with a mere 71 aircraft operational out of a strength of 104. In the event of invasion, the Luftwaffe had 115 day fighters to repulse the aerial armada.

It was a pattern repeated elsewhere, but not universally. Luftflotte Reich had 19 Gruppen with a total strength of 641 aircraft, of which only 319 less than 50 per cent were serviceable. In early June 1944 Luftflotten 1, 4, 5 and 6 in the East were faring much better, however: of the 443 aircraft on charge to their ten day fighter Gruppen, 373 (84 per cent) were operational. In the Mediterranean theatre, Luftflotte 2 had four Gruppen with 105 aircraft on charge and 71 serviceable, while Luftflotte 'Kommando Sudost' in the Balkans had two day fighter Gruppen and 64 aircraft with 54 serviceable.

Galland knew that when the invasion came differences of command opinion would pull the available fighter forces in opposite directions and fragment the defences. Feldmarschall von Rundstedt, as Commander-in-Chief West, bore overall responsibility for the defence of mainland Europe from attack by the Western Allies. During 1943 Feldmarschall Rommel had been given Army Group B under von Rundstedt, established to repel an invasion. From the outset the two differed over the best way to prepare the defence. Von Rundstedt did not believe the invaders could be repulsed on the Atlantic Wall, and wanted a large mobile reserve ready to attack the invaders wherever they were vulnerable. Rommel believed that Allied air supremacy would all but halt rapid movement of large-scale reserves, and opted for a strategy of defence in depth along the entire coastline, with reserves brought close up to consolidate in the landing area.

The seemingly irreconcilable views of von Rundstedt and Rommel were made even more divisive by the organisational structure. Rommel's Army Group B reported to von Rundstedt, who in turn reported to Keitel at the OKW. However, Rommel had personal access to Hitler – as did all field marshals – and in theory this might allow him to persuade the Fuehrer to accept his defence concept. With the 15th Army in the Pas de Calais and the 7th Army in Normandy, however, Rommel had little freedom to make the strategic decisions crucial to rapid response. Moreover, worried Galland, Luftflotte 3 reported to the OKL – ultimately, Goering, who in turn had to respond to Hitler's edicts. In no circumstance could the Heer and the Luftwaffe be co-ordinated under a common command structure – neither for that matter could the Kriegsmarine. And ultimately, both Keitel and Goering were under the authority of their Fuehrer, who had never risen beyond the rank of corporal.

By choosing to attack in the Mediterranean first, the Allies had succeeded in drawing large numbers of German troops to the south and the Balkans which, together with the Eastern Front, limited the forces available to von Rundstedt. On 6 June the Wehrmacht had 165 divisions in the East, 28 in south-eastern Europe, 28 in Italy, 18 in Norway and Denmark, and 59 in France and the Low Countries – only 20 per cent of the German army was available for defence of the Atlantic Wall, and less than 14 per cent (41 divisions) were north of the Loire. However, the threat of invasion had already drawn high quality assets from the East: in January 1944 there had been 24 Panzer divisions in the East and eight in Europe; by 6 June there were 18 Panzer divisions in the East and 15 in the West.

Galland knew that when the invasion came there would be an irrepressible urge to throw the weight of the Luftwaffe at the enemy landings, and that the fighter forces would be called upon to do their fair share. He also knew that this would play into the enemy's hands, leaving much of Germany undefended against massed air raids on the oil reserves and the factories. He proposed keeping either two full Geschwader or one Gruppe from each Geschwader back in Germany for Reich defence. If they were not needed for this task they would serve as reserves for the Western Front. After consultation with Goering, the RLM denied this request, believing that only by the ultimate concentration of forces against the bridgehead could the Allies be defeated before they gained a foothold.

There was, at least, no likelihood of the Jagdflieger being shackled to close escort of bombers; the fighters would be free to fight unimpeded – although a number would inevitably be drained away to operate as Jabos. There were few enough bombers left to escort anywhere: the remaining squadrons had been overcommitted by Peltz to the 'renewed assault on Britain' which had begun in January 1944. This Operation 'Steinbock' had seen bomber losses increasing from 15 per cent at the beginning of the year to 34 per cent by the end of May when the offensive dwindled and died.

* * *

When the Allied invasion came on the morning of 6 June 1944 it proved, in a sense, anticlimatic for Galland, who could do little of immediate value. The Allies had at their disposal approximately 12,000 combat aircraft of which more than 5,000 were fighters. On that first day alone the combined air forces flew more than 14,000 sorties. Only JG2 and JG26, with their 115 Fw190s and Bf109s, stood in their path. In fact only 70 day fighter sorties were flown against the invasion forces on 6 June; the Allies had complete control of the skies over the Normandy landing beaches, and a *cordon sanitaire* extending far into France had been established by the Spitfires, Typhoons, P-47s and P-51s. During the entire day only two aircraft managed to slip through and attack the troops on the beaches: the Fw190s flown by 'Pips' Priller, Geschwaderkommodore of JG26, and his wingman, who made one reckless strafing pass before flying for their lives. As it turned out, there were no wonder-weapons here, no 'magic wand on winged flight' to save the day. The Me262 was still a long way from operational readiness; everything was too late.

The landings caught everyone by surprise; the Luftwaffe weather service had misread the forecast, believing that the invasion could not possibly take place for several days at least. Poor weather over the Channel inhibited Luftflotte 3 from making any reconnaissance flights, and the greatest armada in history crossed the Channel unobserved. Communications were a shambles from the outset. At Compiègne, the headquarters of II.Jagdkorps only received word of the invasion at 08.00, by which time troops were pouring ashore. Not before 09.35 did Schlachtgeschwader 4 receive word to move forward to operating bases at Laval and Tours from where they would conduct ground attacks. Confusion reigned amid the high command where everyone, from Hitler down, had his own ideas about the invasion; most, Hitler included, believed that the main assault would come in the Pas de Calais, and the vital reserves were not released. Goering ordered caution; he was terrified of upsetting the Fuehrer, especially since the mid-May debacle over the use of the Me262 as a bomber. By the end of the first day Luftflotte 3 had lost 36 aircraft with 18 damaged; and the Allies had landed more than 100,000 men on the Normandy beaches.

On 6 June few units had moved forward from Germany to the West, and it was not until the morning of the 7th that the order was finally given to activate the invasion contingency plan. Fighters from Luftflotte Reich, it was said, would fly top cover for the Schlachtflieger and the hastily converted fighter-bombers as they attacked the beaches. The order did not come from von Rundstedt, who remained suspicious that the Normandy landing was a feint; it was at the initiative of the Luftwaffe itself. The difficulties of redeployment began when the Luftflotte Reich Gruppen flew to airfields presupplied with fuel and resources. During the intensive bombing of the previous months many of these had been obliterated, and other makeshift airfields had to be pressed into service. To make matters worse, the ravaged rail and communications systems were close to saturation, and while advance parties would fly in aboard Ju52s, the rest of the Gruppen would take days or even weeks to arrive by rail.

Galland saw irony in many of the events of that day, with little or no cohesion visible despite all the extensive planning that he and others had done to smooth the movement of aircraft west. It was an irony made the sourer by a message from Sperrle which landed on Galland's desk that afternoon, a copy of the telegram which had been distributed to Luftflotte 3:

'The enemy has launched the long-announced invasion. Long have we waited for this moment, long have we prepared ourselves, both inwardly and on the field of battle, by untiring, unending toil. Our task is now to defeat the enemy. I know that each one of you, true to his oath to the colours, will carry out his duties ... Great things will be asked of you and you will show the bravest fighting valour. Heil Hitler!'

Galland muttered his own comment, which may be imagined but not repeated.

Military actions on the ground were going to decide the fate of the air elements of Luftflotte 3; it was inevitable that sooner or later a major German counter-attack would see the strategic reserves committed, and that was the moment Galland feared. He knew that it was then that his Jagdflieger would be thrown into battle – and he strongly suspected that they would be entirely subordinated to the army's planning, and denied the opportunity to fight an air war against an air threat. What would become then of his careful plans for building a Reich defence reserve of 1,800 interceptors?

As units began moving forward on 7 June the pilots ran into immediate problems. Accustomed to operating under the relatively sophisticated fighter control network that had evolved during 1942 and 1943, the pilots of Luftflotte Reich were not used to 'seat-of-the-pants' navigation; many, even formation leaders, were unable to locate their designated airfields. When they did arrive they found that many of the promised supply stockpiles had been pillaged by Luftflotte 3 during the preceding weeks as the Allies hammered hard at JG2 and JG26. Moreover, many pilots on delivery flights were bounced by Allied fighters, and in the ensuing fights they either lost their way or fell to the guns of a more experienced adversary.

It took Galland two days to gather detailed information from right across the sector, seeking status reports from all the Gruppen operating under II.Jagdkorps in the West and I.Jagdkorps in Holland and north-west Germany. As part of II.Jagdkorps, II.Fliegerkorps was hard pressed and had few airfields close to the Normandy front where the aircraft were needed most. A large percentage of the preassigned forward bases were in the vicinity of Paris; and the confidence of the Allied fighter pilots took them far to the south and east of the invasion front to harry the migrating cross-country Jagdflieger. Meanwhile, operational orders outside Galland's remit put more emphasis on the fighter-bomber role; as he had feared, increasing numbers of fighters were converted to bomb-trucks under the immediate pressure of events, and within four days of the Allied landings more than 25 per cent of the fighter force had been converted for this task – a wasted effort which had minimal positive results.

With the results in from his survey of operations across the breadth of II.Jagdkorps, Galland found that the ferry pilots from the Ueberfuehrungsgesch-wader were incompetent in navigation and fighting alike, and that they were retarding the flow of aircraft out to the units in France. He set to work on a new distribution plan which involved centralised dispersal points for the flow of fighters. Fed from a main transit base at Wiesbaden, these were set up at Cologne and Mannheim, where pilots and their new aircraft would assemble for the flight to France. Galland put II.Jagdkorps in overall control of unit allocations and issued orders as to when the flights were to take place, usually in the evenings when they were less likely to be jumped by Allied fighters. He was amazed at how long these transit bases survived, and often thought that had the Allies known about them they would have made vulnerable targets. They actually survived until they were overrun by ground forces.

One operational disadvantage sprang from the forced location of the new makeshift airfields, which had to be located north and north-west of Paris due to the badly damaged communications and ground transport network to the south and south-west. Attacks on the Allied positions, consolidating west of Caen, could only take place from the flank, preventing the Jagdflieger from attacking across the enemy positions. Cut off from the ground war, they were hacked about by swarms of British and American fighters which greatly outnumbered them. Only slowly did the fighter forces build up their strength, and four days after the landings only 300 additional fighters had been moved to France. Nevertheless, on 8 June some 500 ground-support sorties were flown.

Galland began to receive reports on the performance of the converted Jabos, now accounting for no less than one-third of all German day fighters in the West. Inadequate training for ground-attack work and the loss of performance resulting from the extra load and reduced aerodynamic efficiency made them easy targets, and losses began to rise unacceptably. Finally, by 12 June, Galland was able to hammer home the message, and it was decided to abandon fighter-bomber operations. Now the fighters were given new orders, to concentrate on attacking the Allied aircraft over the battlefield in the vain hope of clearing the skies of enemy fighters. II.Fliegerkorps was removed from the front and Gen Buelowius was relieved of his command for having failed to get the new airfields ready as ordered.

II.Jagdkorps took over control of all fighter forces in the sector and was given a free hand to run operations. During the rest of June the situation deteriorated markedly. By the middle of the month more than 425,000 men and 62,000 vehicles had come ashore in Normandy. Units of the Wehrmacht were taking days rather than hours to reach their destinations; transport became a crucial factor even in the movement of small units, and the supply situation began to break down. With a conflicting mandate to provide general air cover over the Cherbourg peninsula and to contain the Normandy bridgehead, Jagdwaffe resources were spread too thin and the fighters were unable to prevent the fall of Cherbourg, giving the Allies a deep water port by late June. By this time the Allied air bombardment had driven the fighter bases back to the Paris region, from where they had as far to fly to the battlefront as did Allied aircraft from England.

Long before the end of June Galland was bombarded with requests for directions on tactical deployment. Throughout the daylight hours the Normandy front was a happy hunting ground for Allied fighters, flying very low and keen for the fight. Existing airfields were becoming unusable, and individual aircraft had to be pulled under cover of woodland and carefully camouflaged. Serviceability rates began to sink dramatically because the transport bottlenecks prevented spares and munitions getting through. Galland had already sent Hannes Trautloft, his inspector of day fighters in the West, to see the situation for himself; when he returned the message was gloomy. He recognised a serious mismatch between the expectations of Jagdkorps headquarters and activities in the field. The Gruppen were becoming disconnected from their Geschwader staffs, and communication was breaking down.

While Trautloft was in France he established a telephone link with Galland, and together they bypassed Jagdkorps and sorted out the situation direct with the unit commanders. Next Trautloft, under Galland's guidance, wrote new regulations for the fighter sweeps including free hunts, low altitude strafing and bombing, and protection of vital supply lines. When Trautloft ran into problems or administrative obstacles that needed a clear order from a senior officer, he telephoned Galland who gave the necessary authorisation.

As the Allied land forces were advancing on Avranches there was a brief lull during which Galland visited the front to get a first hand impression of the situation. Visiting all the Gruppen in turn, he put together a grim list of problems: lack of ground preparation, poor signals preparations, numerical inferiority in force levels, poor intelligence of the general air picture, poor airfield facilities at makeshift bases, bad unit training and pilot replacement, poor quality of formation leaders, general lack of pilot combat experience, poor planning for unit transfer corridors with exposed flanks, too many missions with too many diverse objectives, poor concentration of forces, orders too detailed compromising initiative, and technical inferiority of German aircraft....

On through July the situation continued to deteriorate, and when the Allies began the big push through Avranches the Luftwaffe units west of Paris were forced to retreat. Gradually the Reich defence force gave up its fighters to replace those lost in the West. At the end of June there were only 425 fighters on the Western Front and 370 in Luftflotte Reich; the overall fighter force on all fronts totalled only 1,375. During the month the situation on other fronts became disastrous, with almost no fighters left in Romania to defend the oilfields. It was now that the Allied bombing offensive turned to the oil reserves. Where there had been strong reserves there was now a worsening shortage. The use had been so high, and production had fallen so sharply, that stocks were falling to dangerous levels. The daylight offensive turned its attention to the synthetic oil production plants, and then to the crude refineries in Romania, Hungary, Poland and Germany.

In a secret memorandum dated 31 July 1944, noting the minutes of a discussion with the chief of the OKW operations staff, Genobst Jodl, Hitler began to rearrange the priorities placed upon the Reich fighter reserve by Galland:

'I am of the opinion that we ought to do everything possible however hard it may be at the moment to hold the Luftwaffe units now being formed in the Reich in readiness as a last reserve for an extreme emergency, so that they may be sent to a spot where it might be possible to bring about a change of events. Today I cannot say where the last die may be cast.'

During the second week of August Galland received a directive from Hitler to say that the Reich reserve of about 800 aircraft was to be thrown in on the Western Front to help stem a major breakout that would, if left unchecked, carry the Americans straight to Paris. Galland was beside himself: the reserve had been built for a major attack on the Allied bombers which threatened to cut Germany's lifelines of oil and strategic supplies. If committed to the West they would be decimated, and Germany would be roofless.

Speer was required to be at a situation conference with Hitler at Rastenburg and, accompanied by Galland, Sauer and Gen Kreipe, he tried to put the logical case. Hitler deftly skirted round the matter and agreed to see the four men later in private, which he did. He explained that he was dissatisfied with the fighter arm and was going to reduce the fighter forces down to just a few Gruppen equipped with one type of aircraft, possibly the Me262. He emphatically restated his intention to use the fighter reserve to prevent the Allied breakout towards Paris, and Kreipe sided with him, claiming that the 800 fighters could easily make 1,000 sorties a day. Galland could hardly control himself, knowing that there was no chance for the fighters if they were suddenly transferred to the West without careful training for the very different fighting conditions.

Hitler listened as Speer began to explain the consequences of ignoring the Allied bombers, reiterating an earlier claim that he had worked out with Galland showing that one bomber could be shot down for the loss of each fighter, and that if more than 1,000 fighters could be sent up at once the Americans would suffer such a blow that they would reel under the losses and give Germany respite. Furthermore, because of the relative material needs, six times the resources would be lost with each American bomber shot down than with one German fighter that failed to return; and that two American pilots would be lost for every German pilot – more than this, because one in every two German pilots shot down would parachute into friendly territory, so the pilot loss ratio would be 1:4 in favour of the Luftwaffe. In addition, Galland had calculated that the massive bomber boxes now being flown stretched back 600 miles, exposing a vulnerable flank that would be relatively easy to attack.

Before Speer could finish, Hitler began to react. In Speer's own words: 'Although he listened in silence, I could see by his expression, by the lively fluttering of his hands, the way he chewed his fingernails, that he was growing increasingly tense. When I finished … Hitler was no longer in control of himself. His face had flushed deep red; his eyes had turned lifeless and fixed. Then he roared out at the top of his lungs: "Operative measures are my concern! … this is none of your business! I have no more time for you." Deeply perplexed, I returned to my barracks with Galland.'

That evening the two men discussed options, and resolved to work closer together to do what was right for Germany rather than serving any longer the warped and distorted mind of a dreadfully sick man. The following day the two men were on the point of returning to Berlin when SS-Gruppenfuehrer Julius Schaub, Hitler's adjutant, rang to say that the Fuehrer wanted to see them again. This time Hitler was in an even greater rage, stumbling over his words and shouting at the top of his voice:

'I want no more fighter aircraft produced at all. The fighter arm is to be dissolved. Stop production! Stop it at once, understand? You're always complaining about the shortage of skilled workers, aren't you? Put them into flak production at once. Let all the workers produce anti-aircraft guns. Use all the material for that too! That's an order. Send Sauer to headquarters immediately. A programme for flak production must be set up. Tell Sauer that too. A programme five times what we have now … We'll shift hundreds of workers into flak production … .'

He continued by referring to American and British press reports of how much the bomber crews feared the German anti-aircraft guns. Galland began to explain how many bombers the fighters would shoot down if they were allowed to attack in large numbers, but he was cut off in mid-sentence and both men were thrown out.

Stopping off at his quarters, Speer poured a drink for them both. Galland could not come to terms with what he had just experienced, but Speer was getting used to it, and reassured him that there was no conceivable way the aircraft programme could suddenly be converted to production of anti-aircraft guns. Moreover, the problem was not one of shortages in guns but of shortages in explosives – soon, most German explosives would contain 20 per cent rock salt; and there were insufficient raw materials to manufacture high-grade weapons. Galland told Speer of his frustration at not being able to push through his Reich reserve programme, and the munitions minister assured him that he would do whatever he could to get the decision reversed.

Galland explained at length how important it was that the Reich fighter reserve was held back for the work it had been trained to do. Speer said he feared he could do nothing to change the Fuehrer's mind on that matter, but that he would approach Hitler with a modified plan for limited fighter production. When Speer returned to Rastenburg to examine the fine detail of the new orders he again tried to get the fighter programme reinstated, but to no avail. Nevertheless, Speer was able to get the order for a five-fold increase in flak guns halved.

He later rang Galland and invited him to a meeting with representatives of the aircraft industry on 24 August.

On that occasion, in unequivocal terms, in Galland's presence, Speer encouraged the industrial representatives to prepare for a further increase in fighter production orders, assuring them that 'By sending the production of fighter aircraft soaring we can meet the greatest danger we face: the crushing of our armaments manufacture on the home front.' Galland felt the abyss into which he had been falling recede; cool logic was replacing insanity.

Before the meeting broke up a message was delivered to Speer, bearing the Fuehrer's crest. Hitler had approved the programme of limited fighter production. The Fuehrer still harboured an attachment to Galland; and Speer, at least, believed that this was one of the greatest victories the General der Jagdflieger had ever achieved. He assured Galland that the 'limited' fighter programme would in fact be constrained only by the ability of German industry to produce the aircraft. As Speer would later recall, it was the first order from Hitler that he openly disobeyed. It would not be the last.

Notes to Chapter 18

1 Projekt 1065, which became the Me262, was designed as a high performance fighter in response to a specification issued by the Technisches Amt of the RLM dated 4 January 1939 calling for a jet-powered fighter with a top speed of 900kph (560mph). Information about the growing number of jet projects leaked to Galland in 1942; what he probably did not know was that the British and American jet projects were also nearing completion – the Gloster E.28/39, powered by a Whittle engine, first flew on 15 May 1941, and the Bell Airacomet on 2 October 1942.

2 Fritz Sauckel, Gauleiter of Thuringia, was Reich defence commissioner with responsibility for allocation of German and foreign labour; in all he would mobilise some 5 million men and women, many by what can only be described as slave raids, to work on sites and in factories of all kinds, including those devoted to aircraft production. Their conditions varied from the barely tolerable to the atrocious, and the death rate was high. Sauckel was hanged after the Nuremberg trials.

3 With a range of 2,000km (1,300 miles) on internal fuel and almost 3,400km (2,100 miles) with two 416 litre (110 US gal) drop tanks, the North American P-51B Mustang mounted four .50 machine guns; top speed was 710kph (440mph) at 9,100m (30,000ft), climb time 12min 30sec to that height, and ceiling 12,800m (42,000ft). The P-51D variant arrived in May 1944; slightly slower, it had six machine guns, a superior 'bubble' cockpit canopy, and could carry much more fuel.

4 LtGen James Doolittle, leader of the famous April 1942 raid on Tokyo by B-25s taking off from the carrier USS *Hornet*, took command of the 8th Army Air Force after leading the 15th AAF in the Mediterranean.

5 Genobst Guenther Korten was chief of staff at Luftflotte 4 during the Polish campaign; following the suicide of Jeschonnek in August 1943 he became chief of the general staff of the Luftwaffe, dying from injuries received in the 20 July 1944 bomb attempt on Hitler, and being succeeded until November by Gen Werner Kreipe. Gen Karl Koller was chief of staff at Luftflotte 3 from January 1941; in September 1943 he was appointed head of the Luftwaffe operations staff, and in November 1944 succeeded Kreipe as chief of the general staff of the Luftwaffe.

CHAPTER 19

August – 7 November 1944

Galland's carefully hoarded reserve of 800 fighters, all that could be assembled in reality against the grand plan for a knock-out force of 1,800, bled to death in the course of the overall German retreat. Piecemeal, they were fed into the dwindling units in France, and swallowed up by the battle; Galland had always known that Hitler's boast of turning back Patton's break-out by concentrated fighter attacks was a fantasy. The co-ordination to use the fighters effectively was lacking. Airfields, their operations hampered by the need for dispersal and concealment, were nevertheless constantly strafed by Allied fighters; and the pilots were totally unprepared for the hedge-hopping gunfights which developed – they were trained for high altitude assaults against boxed bomber formations. Many aircraft were lost in accidents; the Bf109 was notoriously hard to handle on rough ground, and take-off and landing were especially difficult in the conditions faced by these unsuspecting pilots, used to the concrete runways of the Reich.

Galland kept a cynical note of the fate of these aircraft from his cherished reserve. Of the 800 fighters, some 200 were lost on their open airstrips to roaming Allied fighters or advancing ground forces. Another 200 were shot down as they simply attempted to reach their respective destinations. Of the rest, eventually lost through general attrition, Galland's reports indicated that they accounted for no more than 25 Allied aircraft.

As the British and American troops advanced Wehrmacht and SS units would commandeer Luftwaffe ground transport at gunpoint, leaving the ground crews to fight a rearguard action as infantry if they chose. Mechanics and administrative officers were abandoned to destroy their equipment rather than let it fall into enemy hands. Frequently, pilots would fly their aircraft to another field only to wait in vain for the rest of the Staffel to arrive. There was nothing Galland could do to help his dying squadrons.

Although August 1944 was a bleak month for the whole German war machine, Galland found in Speer an unassailable optimism that he admired; it chimed with his own dogged resistance to defeatism. Speer convinced Galland that there were many areas for improvement, vast reserves in the German nation that could be mobilised for the war effort. Did Galland know, asked Speer, that in addition to the 1.8 million people employed in the basic power, fuel and energy industries and the 5.2 million working on armaments, there were still 6 million labouring over the production of cookers, electric fires, furniture, kitchenware and other consumer products? Did he know that just before the Allied invasion Germany was still producing an annual average of 364,000 spurs for horsemen, 800 tons of piano wire, and 150,000 electric cushions? The energy and manpower required for producing these unnecessary civilian goods could be applied to essential war materials. Speer's obvious organisational flair and practical determination were very heartening in this summer of defeats, especially after Galland had been exposed to Hitler's fantasies and Goering's ranting.

Unbeknown to him, his own stock was rising too. His furious efforts to sort out the situation in France; the good work done by Trautloft; the general improvement in organisation and control that resulted from Galland's direct intervention below Jagdkorps level; these had been responsible for getting many units into battle which otherwise would have been trapped by logistic failures – and it had been noticed.

During August the Luftwaffe on the Western Front reached its lowest level of operational effectiveness since the war began. On 14 August, one day before the Allied landings in southern France and immediately prior to the use of Luftflotte Reich as reinforcements, Luftflotte 3 had just 75 operational fighters. By the end of the month it had lost 482 fighters, while Luftflotte Reich had lost 375. In total, during that one month, the Luftwaffe lost 44% of its available fighter force, and of the remainder less than 50% were serviceable and fit for combat. Nevertheless, fighter production expanded to new heights: from 2,449 in June, to 2,954 in July, 3,020 in August, and a peak of 3,375 in September, representing 82% of all German aircraft production. Behind these figures lay a dramatic change in policy. During late August Goering finally became convinced that only fighters could save the day; and it transpired that despite Hitler's deranged outburst in mid-August, he too had in fact already accepted that bomber production should be curtailed in favour of interceptors.

This dramatic reversal was presumably the work of the US 8th AAF, who on 20 June had sent 1,600 US bombers with 1,100 escorts to hit oil refineries in central Germany and Poland, dropping almost 4 million kg (4,000 tons) of bombs, for the loss of 63 aircraft. The following day 1,200 bombers and 1,300 fighters flew to Berlin and the Ruhr. On 3 July the Emergency Fighter Programme was announced; bomber production fell from 767 in June to 326 in October, and production of all transport aircraft virtually stopped.

Just when the fighter forces had been rendered virtually impotent, expanded fighter production spurred by renewed political will and effective production methods coincided with a slowing of the ground war. As the Allies, at the end of overstretched supply lines and still without ports in the eastern Channel, were forced to pause before deciding the next move, the German military machine had a respite for renewed effort.

Galland was unable, however, to win his argument that production should be concentrated on just three types. In addition to the conventional Fw190, Bf109 and the jet-powered Me262, three other aircraft were also selected for future production: the Arado Ar234, the Dornier Do335, and the Heinkel He162. The first was a jet-powered 'Blitz-bomber' which did see action before the end of the war, but because of its small numbers and limited warload it remained more a technical curiosity than a serious contribution to the war effort. The Dornier, a weird device with both pusher and puller propellers, was even less militarily significant, and as already mentioned would fall victim to the 'triage' of resources. The He162, however, was seriously considered – by some – for mass production.

The He162 originated with Karl-Otto Sauer, who envisaged a *Volksjaeger*, or People's Fighter, produced in large numbers by semi-skilled labour from inexpensive materials and powered by a single jet engine. Galland was opposed to the concept from the outset and when, on 14 September 1944, draft proposals were submitted by several manufacturers, he recruited the help of Willi Messerschmitt to argue instead for increased production quotas for the Me262. Galland worked feverishly to kill the He162 programme, preparing detailed reports to show that it would divert resources and reduce overall production. Nevertheless, Goering gave the Heinkel submission his approval on 30 September.

The *Volksjaeger* was more than an exotic aircraft project; it was a weapon in Goering's struggle against Himmler to retain his powerbase among the leaders of the Reich. Less than a week earlier the Reichsfuehrer-SS had instituted the Volksturm programme, mobilising tens of thousands of the young and the old in a makeshift Home Guard. Goering hastily convened a meeting with Genobst Keller, chief of the NSFK, and Reichsjugendfuehrer Artur Axmann, head of the Hitler Youth, to arrange for a year's HJ intake of German youths to be trained on gliders and then to convert onto the new *Volksjaeger*, for which fantastic production plans of 2,000 a month were bandied about. For security this unhinged programme was codenamed 'Salamander'.

Galland was deeply concerned that this toy of Goering's failing grip on reality could undo everything that he and Speer had worked for. Speer confirmed that Goering was motivated by his fear that Himmler would attempt to seize control of the armed forces and the country; he advised Galland to tread softly, while Speer quietly ensured that the 'Salamander' programme did not disrupt the production of serious aircraft. In the event the He162's technical immaturity would prevent the project getting far[1].

* * *

Galland placed supreme importance on the Me262 programme; but getting it into service depended upon it being ostensibly produced as a fighter-bomber rather than – or with priority over – the interceptor for which Galland yearned and which Speer and Milch supported. Hitler still needed convincing, and this issue would cost the chief of the Luftwaffe general staff his job. After extracting a concession from Hitler on 30 August that every 20th aircraft off the production line could be completed as a fighter, Werner Kreipe returned a month later to argue for a stronger commitment to the defensive rather than the offensive potential of this extraordinary aircraft.

Appointed successor to Gen Guenther Korten, killed in the 20 July bomb plot on Hitler's life, Kreipe was a staunch advocate of Reich defence. But Hitler had now tightened his grip on the Luftwaffe to such an extent that even minor movements had to be approved by the Fuehrer; and after a furious argument on

18 September Kreipe resigned his post, to be replaced by Gen Karl Koller. Galland lost another ardent supporter of the Me262 fighter when, on 1 October, Milch was injured in a car crash and remained immobilised for three months. Hitler's final position on the Me262 was delivered on 4 November: he approved its production as a fighter, provided that every aircraft be equipped with the necessary shackles and release gear for 250kg (550lb) bombs.

Factories in the Augsburg region had been steadily building up deliveries of the Me262. Between May and August 1944 they had rolled out 124 aircraft, with 92 in September and 108 during October. In these last two months the first deliveries emerged from the Regensburg works, 12 being delivered before the end of October. From these two facilities 101 were produced in November and 131 in December.

Galland had for many months been paying particular attention to the experimental test and conversion unit, Erprobungskommando 262 (Ekdo262), which comprised two Staffeln from III./ZG26 and a Stab flight. Formed at Lager-Lechfeld on 19 December 1943, with 8.Staffel based at Swabisch Hall and 9.Staffel at Leipheim, it did not get its first aircraft until April 1944. Commanded by Hptmn Werner Thierfelder, a veteran of the battles for France, Britain, the Balkans and Crete, Ekdo262 began training pilots in May 1944. However, the conversion course worked out was merely the minimum deemed necessary to give pilots the essentials. Galland was concerned that the course was not adequate to prepare the pilots for this new age of jet combat, and he worked with the instructors to develop a programme that would.

Training required 20 hours on a Bf110 or Me410 with fixed throttles to give the pilots experience of handling aircraft in this manner; the Me262 had a temperamental engine which worked better if left at constant thrust as long as possible. After the requisite hours, pilots made the transition to the jet and began a series of nine familiarisation stages. Two 30-minute sessions of circuits were followed by two separate one-hour sessions of aerobatics; one hour of high altitude flying at 9,100m (30,000ft); one hour of cross-country flying at 3,700-4,500m (12-15,000ft); two separate one-hour sessions flying in a Rotte; and finally, gunnery practice.

By June 1944 the Me262 was ready for operational use, and Ekdo262 had managed to develop tactics for the new aircraft. Galland had not been closely involved with selecting the unit from which the core combat element would be formed; its introduction to service was the prerogative of the bomber men. On 3 June 1944, Obst Wolf Dietrich Meister was ordered to send III.Gruppe of his bomber wing KG51 'Edelweiss' to Lechfeld, where they would exchange their Ju88s for Me262s. The following month he sent I. and IV.Gruppen to begin combat operations training at Munich-Reim, followed by II.Gruppe in October to Rheine-Hopsten.

The Me262 was heavily compromised in performance by the two 250kg (550lb) bombs carried on pylons under the forward fuselage. To compensate for the change in centre of gravity, additional fuel was carried in supplementary tanks behind the pilot's seat and behind the rear main tank, while two of the four cannon were removed from the nose. Fuel had to be consumed from the rearmost tank first, and if the aircraft was attacked shortly after take-off the bombs could not be jettisoned for fear that it would rear up and stall.

For take-off, the throttle had to be set precisely. The Jumo 004B engine was sensitive to throttle settings and, if not handled with delicacy, could cause serious problems especially during preparation for flight. B4 fuel was fed in until a throttle setting of 6,000rpm was reached, at which point the J2 diesel fuel cut in. Steadily advanced to 8,000rpm for stable combustion, the engine was slowly throttled back to 5,000rpm, at which level the wheel chocks were removed. Advanced to 7,000rpm, the aircraft would begin to move and at 8,000rpm it would fly – this was the minimum setting for sustained flight.

Sudden throttle movement would cause the turbines to burn out; but a regulator was designed to control fuel flow above 6,000rpm irrespective of the rate at which the throttle was advanced, and this left the pilot freer to concentrate on flying and fighting. Pilots found the aircraft easier to fly than a Bf109G, although turns were not as tight and acceleration and deceleration were slower. Although the aircraft could dive very fast it was important not to pass the critical Mach number; in June 1944 one Me262 performed a power dive at 1,054kph (624mph).

The attention to detail paid off, and the aircraft began to show its mettle, albeit in a stunted role. KG51 used the Me262 as a dive-bomber, but since it was prohibited from dropping its bombs below 4,000m (13,000ft) this was a useless exercise. Despite these handicaps, on 26 June 1944 a Mosquito flown by Flt Lt A.E.Wall and his navigator Plt Off A.S.Lobban of No.544 Sqn RAF became the first of 357 aircraft which would be claimed shot down by Me262 pilots over the next ten months. When Galland heard the news it whetted his frustration at the manacles which still kept this wonderful aircraft from its obvious destiny as a pure fighter. He was not to know that they were soon to be removed as a result of pressure from a most unexpected and sinister quarter.

Although it was Goering who first suggested to Galland that he should set up a jet fighter training unit in preparation for the deployment of the Me262 in that role, it was Heinrich Himmler who had gently leaned on the Reichsmarschall to give the order. For much of the summer in that last year of war Galland had been unhappily aware of the increasing and undisguised interest being taken by Himmler's SS in the armed services, and in particular in the many technical developments which held promise for the war effort. In the aftermath of the 20 July bomb attempt Hitler's long-simmering distrust of the traditional officer corps of the armed services had become inflamed; and the SS seized many opportunities to extend their influence, which already spread far beyond their explicit security role. Now even Hermann Goering, who deeply distrusted Himmler's new interest in the armed forces, did not choose to dispute the Reichsfuehrer's suggestion about jet fighter training.

Galland had not been above some mild subterfuge in pressing his case for the Me262 fighter, and he had not lacked supporters. In his position as General der Jagdflieger he kept in close contact with the 'Experten' – the unofficial brotherhood of high-scoring fighter aces, many of whose scores now ran into three figures. One such was Maj Walter Nowotny, who had been at the Wiener-

Neustadt training school with Paul Galland during 1940 and who, by September 1944, had scored 256 confirmed kills in three years of combat flying. Maj Nowotny had frequently added his voice to Galland's campaign; and had circulated among his fellow 'experts' an intelligence report to the effect that an American pilot held at Auswertestelle West (Dulag Luft) prisoner-of-war camp had commented on the foolishness of using the jet as a bomber, saying that Allied pilots dreaded the day it would appear as an interceptor. This report, widely circulated inside and outside the Luftwaffe, came to the notice of Himmler, who saw in it another welcome chance to embarrass Goering.

Being one of the illustrious nine bearing the Knight's Cross with Oak Leaves, Swords and Diamonds, Walter Nowotny was Galland's natural choice to head the first jet fighter trials unit Kommando Nowotny at Achmer near Osnabrueck. Pilots from Ekdo262 came to help form the unit, which was to have grown into a full Geschwader. Declared operational on 3 October, only ten days after Nowotny's appointment, the unit was deployed to the West rather than in defence of Germany. Galland objected to this, believing the tactical environment over the front lines was too demanding for this new aircraft. The Me262 was extremely vulnerable on take-off and landing; so III./JG54, commanded by Hptmn Robert Weiss, was ordered up to Achmer and a nearby airfield at Hesepe to fly protective patrols with its Fw190D-9 fighters. In addition, a flak corridor several miles long was set up in a straight line out from the main runway, to protect the jets from unwelcome visitors during their approach. Galland knew it could only be a matter of time before the Allies discovered the unit's location; the scorch marks on the concrete runways were a certain giveaway.

Kommando Nowotny scored its first kills on 7 October 1944 when Lt Schall and Ofw Lennartz each downed a B-24 Liberator. Other kills followed on 10 and 12 October when Oblt Bley and Ofw Lennartz each bagged a P-51 Mustang. Three days later the Fw190D-9s arrived to fly cover for what was to have been a jet sortie, the take-off protected by two aircraft at low level and four at 1,800m (6,000ft). With the Allies virtually controlling the skies, it was no place to be at a disadvantage; and when radar alerted the fighters to an approaching force of 40 P-51s it was decided to land again and disperse. Before they could get back on the ground the P-51s of the 78th Fighter Group appeared at treetop height and tore into the Fw190s. Turning to defend themselves, the Jagdflieger were cut to pieces, only one aircraft escaping to the nearby airfield at Muenster-Handorf. Before the end of the day a further four Fw190s had been shot down. Despite the ever-present danger from Allied fighters, however, over several weeks Kommando Nowotny built up its score as pilots learned how best to operate the new fighter. Limited availability meant flying in groups of one, two or three Rotten, low numbers which severely hampered their operational flexibility.

On 1 November 1944 Galland was promoted Generalleutnant, at 32 still the youngest general in the German armed forces. On the morning of the 8th he arrived at Achmer to get a first-hand report on operations and tactics, information he would use to prepare guidelines for the first fully operational Me262 Geschwader, JG7, which was about to form. No sooner had he arrived than the air raid sirens wailed mournfully across the airfield. Maj Nowotny and Oblt

Wegmann leapt to their aircraft, and at nearby Hesepe Lt Schall and Ofw Buttner prepared to take off. The aircraft flown by Nowotny suffered technical failure and the one flown by Buttner was damaged while taxying, leaving only Wegmann and Schall to take to the skies; each pilot shot down a P-51 before returning to base. Almost at once there was another air raid warning; this time Nowotny, Schall and Ofw Baudach took off to attack bombers heading for Merseburg and Rheine. Galland watched the action through reports coming in to the fighter control headquarters, as the Fw190Ds tried to keep the USAAF fighters at bay while the Me262s gained speed and height.

Lt Schall quickly engaged P-47s from the 359th Fighter Group, downing one and damaging a second, which was finished off by an Fw190D-9 from III./JG54 looking for strays. A Mustang from the 357th Fighter Group attacked an Me262, but was deflected by a swarm of other P-51s flashing past; unsettled and probably damaged, the Me262 – flown by Baudach – rolled over and spun into the ground. Schall went on to claim two P-51s escorting B-17s in the vicinity of Lake Dummer, and Nowotny downed a B-24 and a Mustang, bringing his personal score to 258 kills. Within minutes he radioed to base that he had a turbine failure; seconds later there came a frantic cry that his aircraft was on fire. Galland leapt from the control room and ran outside to the airfield. He was listening to the sound of the ailing jet approaching unseen when the rattle of gunfire was heard; through low cloud a lone Me262 plunged straight into the ground, exploding less than a mile from where Galland stood with Hptmn Georg-Peter Eder.

It was shortly before 13.00 when Maj Nowotny fell victim to the guns of a P-51 flown by Lt R.W. Stevens of the 364th Fighter Group. On the spot, Galland appointed Hptmn Eder to command of Kommando Nowotny. Lt Schall had baled out of his Me262 minutes before, shot down by Lt James Kenney of the 357th Fighter Group. That was another thing that worried Galland: the promised ejection seats had not appeared. Without their aid the Me262 pilot had to slow right down before the air pressure allowed him to get rid of the canopy and clamber free, and in those moments – even if the jet did not explode or spin – it was all too easy for an enemy fighter to administer a lethal *coup de grace*.

Three days later Kommando Nowotny was administratively disbanded, and reformed as III.(Ergaenzungs)/JG2 at Lechfeld on 14 November; several pilots from this training unit would graduate to JG7. The events of Galland's visit to Achmer lent emphasis to his feeling that the jets were facing unnecessary risks by operating under the noses of patrolling Tempests and Mustangs; he ordered their immediate withdrawal to Brandenburg, where they would not be exposed to daily attacks on the runways. There the aircraft were turned over to III./JG7 which, on 19 November, became the first operational jet fighter Gruppe to form.

In the weeks ahead Galland prepared his report and wrote tactical guidelines, suggesting that the jets should be flown in paired flights of three, one watching the other into combat. The optimum size for an Me262 Gruppe would be about 40 aircraft which, given the serviceability rates, would produce perhaps 25 available for flight at any one time. That was about the maximum any field unit could handle and any airfield could support for take-off and landing clearance under prevailing conditions. Galland was adamant that the jets had to be based well back where they were less susceptible to surprise attack during take-off and landing.

The training programme obviously still left much to be desired; accordingly, a two-seat trainer designated Me262B-1A was developed by Messerschmitt and introduced to III.(Erg)/JG2 at the end of 1944. The second seat occupied the place taken up by the rear main fuel tank, replaced by two 300 litre (66gal) teardrop tanks suspended from the forward fuselage. (From this version would grow the Me262B-1A/U1 night fighter promoted by Maj Hajo Herrmann and operated by a test unit commanded by Maj Gerhard Stamp on Wilde Sau patrols.)

* * *

Goering had already appointed ex-night fighter chief Gen Josef Kammhuber as his special commissioner for jet aircraft; he had wide powers, and was prone to interfere in a programme about which he had little knowledge. Simultaneously the SS had also extended its tentacles into the realm of exotic Luftwaffe weapon systems by the appointment of an inspector of jet aircraft, SS-Obergruppenfuehrer Hans Kammler, who on 8 August 1944 had been given total control over the V-2 rocket programme. This more than usually unpleasant representative of Himmler's conspiracies was yet another irritant that Galland could do without[2].

While the temperamental jets were being nursed into service, Galland was also wrestling with the daily problems of the conventional fighter force. During autumn 1944 he finally convinced the Fuehrungsstab to pull units out of the line and back to Germany for rest and recuperation after their many months of continual fighting against overwhelming odds. Undismayed by the loss of his 800 Reich defence reserves in France, he once again proposed that a major fighter force should be built up to strike a knock-out blow at the daylight bombers; he was determined to exploit the excellent new production levels to mount a decisive series of attacks rather than rest content with the daily trickle of interceptions. He argued that such an operation – 'Der Grosse Schlag', or 'Big Punch' – could achieve at least a temporary halt to raids on the oil and steel works upon which Germany relied for the sinews of resistance to her most feared enemy, the Red Army. He predicted that sudden, unacceptable rates of bomber losses to attacks by massed interceptors would force the USAAF to switch targets to the aircraft factories, whose output they were now less likely to damage seriously.

Galland also believed that if the Jagdwaffe could inflict shocking casualties on the strategic bombers Germany's chances of concluding a separate peace with the Western Allies would be improved. In this, if nothing else, he was like Hitler: he was unable to comprehend the wartime alliance between such fundamentally antagonistic systems as Western capitalist democracy and Soviet Marxism. There were many senior German officers who nurtured almost to the end an illusion that the anti-German alliance could be split by inflicting a severe reverse on the Western Allies, and then immediately offering them attractive terms for, if not an anti-Russian alliance, then at least a compromise peace which would leave Germany free to turn all her remaining forces eastwards. From his recorded conversations it is easy to believe that the same hopes lay behind Hitler's plan for the Ardennes counter-offensive; but while Galland was arguing for his 'Big Punch' at the USAAF he had no inkling of that plan.

If Galland's dream of assembling a decisive force of interceptors were ever to come true he would need to pursue innovative schemes for improving the numerical build-up. Reorganisation of force disposition was one way he found of maximising the potential of fighter units spread right across Europe. First, fighters were to be withdrawn from the Southern Front and from Austria. Two Gruppen of Bf109s under Obst Eduard Neumann, a friend of Galland's from the Spanish Civil War, recruited volunteer Italian pilots; and plans were also laid for a special unit operating Me163 rocket fighters. Galland organised training for 20 Italians, but that project fizzled out when fuel reserves fell to prohibitive levels. Galland liked the idea of the rocket-propelled Me163 for point defence over airfields and similar vulnerable targets where its brief mission endurance could be accomodated by hit-and-run tactics; however, fuel shortages would always frustrate the attempt to put significant numbers of Me163s into the air.

Further expansion of Gruppe establishment went ahead, with an increase to 68 aircraft for the four Staffeln nominally forming each Gruppe. Galland also instituted a special training session involving 15 hours on Reich defence tactics. From September 1944 control of Luftflotte 3 fighters was subordinated to Luftflotte Reich, which consolidated the command structure and allowed greater flexibility of deployment. For the time being the disposition of fighter elements remained unchanged. In the West were JG2, JG26, JG27 and JG53; in defence of the Reich itself were JG3, JG300 and JG301; in the East were JG5, JG51, JG52 and JG54. Resting in Germany were JG1, JG6, JG11 and JG77; while new Geschwader – including JG4, JG7 (soon to be called 'Nowotny') and JG76 – were working up.

By 15 September the Allied advance on the ground had extended as far as the German border, taking a line from Ostend to Antwerp, Maastricht, Luxembourg, Metz and Nancy. The momentum of the great Allied advance from the Cherbourg peninsula was faltering; there was disagreement over the respective merits of a fast, narrow thrust into northern Germany, and a more deliberate advance across the Rhine and into Germany on a broad front.

German munitions production was markedly improved, and despite being dispersed from fewer than 30 factories to more than 700 manufacturing and assembly sites the aircraft industry was pouring out equipment at a faster rate than ever. As enlargement of Geschwader went ahead and squadrons were rested, JG27 was moved to central Germany to help with the consolidation of other fighter units. Fuel was always going to be a problem now; to avoid unnecessary movements to bring Staffeln, Gruppen and Geschwader together, Galland organised a complete renumbering system to avoid major relocation.

On 19 August Hitler had called a meeting of senior Nazi officials and SS leaders to inform them about a major offensive which he planned to launch at the beginning of November. Then, when heavy rains, fog and poor visibility would make a German counter-offensive seem unlikely, he would strike a heavy blow at the Allied armies while poor flying conditions kept Allied aircraft on the ground. The plan depended upon the utmost secrecy, and Hitler determined to lay a smokescreen to protect his preparations not only from Allied intelligence but also from a large part of the Wehrmacht high command. Central to the plan would be Generalfeldmarschall Gerd von Rundstedt, recently dismissed from his post as commander-in-chief of defences in the West. On 1 September he was called to the Wolfsschanze, and asked if he would return to command the defence of Germany in the West. Hitler delivered a long lecture to the effect that it was impossible to mount a major offensive, given Germany's depleted resources, and that he wanted a strong and capable hand on the tiller.

In fact Hitler nursed an intense personal dislike for von Rundstedt, who represented the old Hohenzollern guard of another age. Although impeccably disciplined, this living embodiment of all that was dignified, honourable and professional in the two hundred year old Junker tradition regarded the Fuehrer's delusions of military competence with ill-disguised contempt. It was von Rundstedt's conventional military philosophy and professional caution which made him a vital part of the deception. In noting the shift of command the Allies would interpret his reinstatement as a sign that Hitler intended to adopt classic lines of defence and consolidation. Hitler even chose a studiedly unexciting code name for von Rundstedt's orders: *Wacht am Rhein* (Watch on the Rhine), hinting broadly at a commitment to standing firm on the banks of the river.

Meanwhile, completely unknown to von Rundstedt, Hitler set in motion preparations for the secret counter-offensive. As it was finally to be planned by Jodl and approved by Hitler in early October, the spearhead of the offensive thrust from the Ardennes towards the vital port of Antwerp would be the 6th SS Panzer Army, formed from four SS Panzer and five infantry divisions and commanded by SS-Obergruppenfuehrer Josef Dietrich. This would be supported to the south by Gen Hasso von Manteuffel's 5th Panzer Army (three Panzer and four infantry divisions), with the infantry of Genlt Erich Brandenberger's weak 7th Army on the far left flank; altogether some 30 divisions were earmarked for the operation, including most of Germany's remaining high quality tank battalions of Panthers and King Tigers. When the plan was finally revealed, on 22 October, to the sophisticated military scrutiny of von Rundstedt and Generalfeldmarschall Model – his deputy as commander of Army Group B – their reaction was pessimistic; and it was shared by the commander of the 6th SS Panzer Army. 'Sepp' Dietrich, as a ruthless henchman from Hitler's earliest days, owed his rapid promotion in the Waffen-SS to favouritism rather than any great military skills, but he was by no means a fool; in an earlier century he might have risen to general rank by his own merits, and he could clearly see the flaws in this operation. Hitler would brook no argment, although he did allow the date to be postponed until mid-December.

As these preparations took shape in the late summer and early autumn of 1944 Galland remained completely unaware of them, and specifically of their planned impact upon the massed fighter force which he was patiently building up for his 'Big Punch' at the daylight bomber offensive. Considerable resources were expended preparing for massed formation intercepts of Allied bombers even while senior Luftwaffe staff officers knew that they would never take place. As Galland toiled over the tactics and training of specially reserved units, an alternative use for his fighters was already being schemed. Paradoxically, Galland could have supported a major offensive in the West and understood the reasoning behind it: the real enemy lay to the East, but the Russians were still on the Vistula more than 480km (300 miles) from Berlin. Galland would have needed little persuading of the wisdom of temporarily trading some soil in the East for the chance to concentrate resources in the West, if that achieved decisive success and a compromise peace, and left the entire Wehrmacht free to face the natural enemy. (In nursing this hope Hitler based his reasoning on the success of Frederick the Great in the Seven Years' War, when the enemies of a small and surrounded Prussia had been separated and picked off one by one. Given Hitler's world view, it is hardly surprising that he failed to grasp the essential differences between the military chess-playing of unchallengeable 18th century monarchs with small professional armies, and the choices open to elected governments commanding the citizenry-in-arms of the mid-20th century.)

As it was, Galland's argument for a major strike at the bomber offensive seemed to be supported by Albert Speer, one of the few talented advisors whom Hitler still tolerated. On 30 August 1944 Speer's routine monthly report to Hitler opined that in view of the crippling effects of the Allied bombing on these industries, 'We will do the troops a bad service by sending fighter aircraft from home defence to the front [if we thereby allow] the vital materials needed at the front (munitions, explosives and fuel) to be battered.' Speer reminded Hitler that 'The Luftwaffe must be ready for this last great stake by the middle of September at the latest. It must throw into this undertaking all its best personnel, its flying instructors and its most successful fighter pilots. At least 1,200 of the most modern fighters must be made available for this operation.'

Galland was resolute in his determination to do all in his power to halt the advancing Russians by first stopping the destructive assault on Germany's war production by the combined efforts of the Reich air defence fighters. Hitler read the reports from Speer, who was probably giving the clearest picture of the real situation, and concluded differently. Although he knew the British and the Americans had to be stopped before they crossed the Rhine – Speer was sending almost continuous reports on the fragility of the ministry's preservation of the Ruhr as a source of munitions supply – he had no concept of air power defeating the bombers. For him, it had to be action on a vast canvas: huge armies sweeping across the maps, scything through the enemy's armies one by one: in this case, a massive assault through the Ardennes to capture Antwerp. For Hitler the Ardennes held a special significance; those 5,000sq/km (2,000 sq/miles) of forested hills straddling the valleys of the Meuse and the Aisne were the scene of German victories from the French Revolutionary Wars of the 1790s to the successful breakthrough near Sedan in 1940, and it had been in the Ardennes that the Americans had made their first major commitment during World War I.

* * *

Galland was not the only officer whose mind constantly turned to ways of defeating the 'heavy babies' of the 8th AAF; and one who thought he had come up with an answer was the ex-bomber pilot Hajo Herrmann. Back in September 1943, newly promoted Major and awarded the Oak Leaves for his good work with the 'Wild Boar' night fighters, Herrmann had submitted to a conference at Treuenbriertzen a memorandum suggesting the setting up of a special unit of volunteers for the deliberate ramming of enemy bombers. Galland had dismissed the idea, which ran counter to all his instincts: he believed that fighter pilots should be given the freedom to fly and fight, not be sent on one-man suicide missions – and anyway, he was not convinced that ramming would necessarily bring a bomber down. Shortly after that conference Herrmann was posted, under something of a cloud, to the Fuehrerreserve at Koenigsberg/Neumark; but this was only a pause in his career advancement, and he was not to be put off so easily. He had useful contacts among the 'bomber lobby' – among them Obst Dietrich Peltz, who would be appointed General der Kampfflieger – with whom he would keep in touch.

Herrmann's radical suggestion may have been sparked by the fact that at around the time of the Treuenbriertzen conference Galland had been working on bringing into practice the Sturmgruppe ('assault group') concept. This envisaged concentrations of heavily armed and armoured Fw190s committed to pressing home attacks on the rear of bomber formations while the lighter Bf109Gs kept the escorts away from them. (In practice, much of the heavy armour and strengthened glass added for protection was removed when pilots saw how much it slowed their aircraft.) The idea was to concentrate several Gruppen of assault and conventional fighters, up to 300 aircraft in all, in a so-called *Gefechtsverbande* strong enough to break through the defensive perimeter of the escorted bomber formations. The close attack from the rear, performed by determined pilots willing to risk the additional danger from tail gunners, gave a longer firing time and thus a better chance of kills than a head-on attack. With encouragement from Galland, JG1 had employed this tactic with older pilots returning to combat who had developed a fear of close-in attacks on the heavily defended bombers. By accompanying them close up to their targets the escorting Bf109G pilots would demonstrate that there was little extra danger in pushing the attack right home.

Concurrent with the introduction of the Sturmgruppe tactics, Galland received numerous letters from pilots throughout the Jagdwaffe – and other branches of the Luftwaffe – volunteering to try ramming bombers and taking their chances of baling out after the impact. Opposed to the principle of the idea, Galland decided to try to harness this surge of enthusiasm while controlling its wilder excesses. In early 1944 he discussed trial operations with JG3, and Maj Heinz Bar of IV.Gruppe agreed to command a Sturmgruppe inducting pilots who swore an oath either to shoot down a bomber or ram it every time they engaged the enemy. Maj Bar was a remarkable pilot and an experienced leader whom Galland knew well, and admired; his style was more flamboyant and impulsive than Galland's, but successful nonetheless.

Galland put together a training programme which gave pilots experience in flying heavily armed versions of the Fw190 and attacking the bombers using these assault tactics. The Focke-Wulfs were armed with four 15mm MG151s, or two each 13mm MG131s and MG151s, plus two 30mm MK108 cannon in underwing pods; tests showed that four cannon shells from an MK108 were sufficient to bring down a four-engined bomber. (Some aircraft had six MG151s instead.) Galland had always maintained strong links with the armament experimental stations, and supported work to strengthen the fuselage and wings of the Fw190 to allow it to carry heavier weapons. From this work emerged the Fw190A-6 capable of carrying 30mm cannon and the larger ammunition boxes they required. One variant carried two 7.9mm MG17s, two MG151s, two MK108s and two WGr21 rocket tubes.

When tests at the Rechlin weapons research establishment showed how effective the 21cm rocket could be when fired from an aircraft, Galland personally authorised trials and flew a suitably modified Fw190 himself. A development from the army's Nebelwerfer rocket mortar bomb, the weapon had a circular probability grouping (50 per cent falling within the prescribed diameter) of 30m (97ft) at a range of 2,000m (6,560ft). Galland tested the Revi C12d gunsight and found it useful, but this was later changed to the type 16F optimised for improved accuracy at greater range. Combinations of the 21cm rocket projectile and the 16F sight enabled Sturmgruppe pilots to attack bombers from outside the accurate range of their defensive guns. The WGr21 'Dodel' was never accurate enough for true aimed fire at individual targets, but when pilots did achieve a hit by firing into the overlapping mass of B-17s the results were spectacular. More importantly, they had some value in breaking up formations to provide isolated, vulnerable targets for the subsequent attack runs with multiple cannon.

By spring 1944 these plans had matured to the point where Sturmgruppen were being set up in several Jagdgeschwader, although the change in priorities that came with the D-Day landings upset the assignments. However, Galland challenged the logic of the original tactic of flying equal numbers of assault fighters and light fighters, which tended to stick too closely together. His own rule of first principle was that a fighter should never fly defensively; in operations where the 'escorts' stayed close to the heavy assault fighters they fell prey to the P-51s, simply leaving the heavy Fw190s – singlemindedly committed to their runs at the bombers – as vulnerable as if they had not been accompanied. When Goering ordered that Sturmgruppen should be attached to the reserve Reich defence force, Galland pushed for a change in tactics whereby the Sturmgruppen incorporated one-third heavy Fw190s, one-third 'close escort' fighters, and one-third 'stand-off' fighters aggressively hunting down and attacking American fighters. When the fighter wings protecting Germany incorporated these Sturmgruppe tactics, they succeeded in shooting down large numbers of enemy aircraft.

It was this success that now encouraged Hajo Herrmann to dust off his earlier idea about ramming and submit his proposals to Galland. Appointed to command 1.Jagddivision on 23 March 1944, Herrmann wanted to show his initiative. To him, Galland represented a group of elitist early war fighter aces who were out of touch with the violence and scale of war in the mid-1940s. He looked upon them much as Galland had himself regarded the old men of the Luftwaffe ten years before. To some extent Herrmann was right, but in the way he sought to apply his insights he was wrong. Herrmann telephoned Galland and suggested he should set up a special group of pilots volunteering to ram enemy aircraft. Somewhere along the line Herrmann had read Galland's report showing that if sufficient fighters were employed one fighter lost in combat could account for one bomber destroyed. Why risk merely damaging a bomber that would return to attack Germany again, when it could be destroyed through ramming?

Galland responded by asking Herrmann where he would be while his brave young pilots were giving away their lives in this dubious entrprise. On the ground controlling operations, replied Herrmann. Galland told him to go away and come back when he was prepared to fly the first Rammjaeger operation himself. Then, if it worked, he, Galland, would immediately institute such a policy. Rebuffed and insulted, Herrmann – whose record proved his personal courage – sought support elsewhere, deepening his involvement with political elements in the Luftwaffe who sought the means to wrest control from the current leadership. Galland had given due credit in the past to Herrmann's energy and imagination; now he began to see him as a disruptive element who could damage all the hard work he had done to prevent panic schemes and misuse of resources. He failed to see, however, that he was laying up trouble by dismissing Herrmann with such flippancy.

* * *

By October 1944 Galland's fighter reserves were almost ready for 'Big Punch'. He had put Oberst Handrick in charge of training and had approximately 2,700 fighters assembled for the task. With the slowdown in the Allied advance and a massive increase in aircraft production, the Luftwaffe now had greater numerical forces than at any other time in its history. Galland had worked with unit commanders to rationalise the several different types of formation employed by the American bombers, and broke them down into six types, evolving a separate set of tactical notes for attacking each type. Unit officers had been involved in the planning from the outset and knew what to expect. The entire operation would be under the command of I.Jagdkorps, with no fewer than 11 Gefechtsverbaende flying against the bombers as they penetrated Germany itself. The vulnerability of Gefechtsverbaende in Sturmgruppe attacks would be offset by the sheer weight of numbers comprising the new attack formations. To handle this number of aircraft, Handrick organised a special operational staff known as Jagddivision zbV to control four Jagdgeschwader operating throughout Germany. To the west of the main battle, Galland organised JG2, JG26 and JG53 under II.Jagdkorps to hit the bombers and their escorts as they came in from England and to harry them as they left.

Galland envisioned at least 2,500 sorties launched in the first wave, with fighting carrying some Jagdflieger toward the west as the American aircraft left Germany. To facilitate further sorties before these raiders escaped, Galland instituted a plan that had worked well during Operation 'Thunderbolt' in 1942, when fighters had leapfrogged to forward airfields; he arranged for some Geschwader from I.Jagdkorps to use airfields assigned to II.Jagdkorps for rapid refuelling and rearming. In this way he calculated that 500 fighters would return to the fray in a second wave, bringing to more than 3,000 the total number of sorties launched against an attacking force of 1,500-2,000 aircraft spread right across western Europe. Finally, he alerted almost 100 night fighters located in Denmark and south-west Germany to hunt down stragglers. Galland knew that the right conditions were essential to success; but he believed that with careful planning and preparation he could bring down approximately 400-500 bombers for an equal loss of fighters, and a cost of around 150 Jagdflieger.

Galland took the plan to Speer, who had the latest production figures, to discuss the consequences of his 'Big Punch' and consolidate his argument. Speer agreed with his conclusions. German intelligence knew that throughout 1944 the Americans had been building four-engined bombers at the rate of approximately 1,250 each month. German fighter production was now running at approximately 3,000 a month, more than had been produced for the whole of 1940. With three times the resources and manpower needed to build a bomber compared to a fighter the argument spoke for itself, said Galland. The Americans could not afford to lose bombers – and as important, their ten-man crews – at the level of attrition exacted by 'Big Punch'. The flaws in Galland's argument lay in the fragile serviceability rates, pushed to 71 per cent in September as the peak for 1944 but not sustainable at that level; and in the depleted fuel supplies which, although better in late 1944 than they had been earlier in the year, would not support any sustained series of operations on the scale envisaged by Galland.

Nevertheless, it was impossible to hold back such a potentially valuable force for long while waiting for the perfect conditions. The resurgence of Luftwaffe strength had surprised British and American leaders. The bombing campaign to destroy German industries, fuel stocks, refineries and tool factories went on relentlessly. US intelligence reported activity increasing by the day, and the growing numbers of fighters encountered were having a telling effect. In a totally unsuspected way, Germany had turned its back on mass production and had returned to the age of the artisan; hundreds of thousands of workers laboured in forest clearings, caves and tunnels to manufacture all the myriad parts for Galland's fighters.

On 2 November, after three weeks of hoarding fuel and getting every fighter possible ready for flight, the Jagdflieger were unleashed in what was, to Galland's mind, a dress rehearsal for the 'Big Punch' which he planned for later that month. The prime target for the 8th Army Air Force that Thursday was Merseburg oil refinery, together with rail targets such as the Bielefeld marshalling yards and installations in the vicinity. The raid had all the characteristics required for a 'Big Punch' response, although the numbers of German fighters sent against it on 2 November would be small by comparison. The 1,100 American bombers and 873 escort fighters attracted 490 German fighters from ten Gruppen. 'Sturmbock' Fw190s from IV. (Sturm)/JG3 blasted 13 Fortresses from the 91st Bomb Group's formations; but escorting P-51s hit fast and hard, tearing into the Bf109s with furious determination. An attempt to launch rocket-propelled Me163s from Brandis resulted in one crashing on take-off and three shot down by escorts without a single claim. The Me262s fared little better, loosing off underwing batteries of 55mm unguided R4M rockets against B-24s without result. At the end of the day the Jagdwaffe had lost 120 aircraft and 98 pilots, 70 of them dead; a total of 40 bombers and 16 Allied fighters were destroyed – but of those 56, 30 were claimed by the Flakartillerie.

Just four days later at a Fuehrer conference Hitler examined the figures in detail, and concluded that throwing fighters at the massed Allied bomber formations was a futile exercise. Despite the undeniable failure of 2 November, Galland continued to argue that there was a critical number above which success would be assured, a critical mass of fighters that would saturate the escorts and allow much greater success in shooting down the bombers. Hitler would have none of it; his eyes were fixed on the offensive through the Ardennes, and he wanted those fighters for another purpose. Galland was not to know this for a further two weeks, but Hitler's mind had been crystal clear at the conference on 6 November – one of the now rare moments when he was able to absorb facts and define rational options. Goering was also present, and railed against the Luftwaffe for betraying the Fuehrer. Long since fallen from favour, he was included in such meetings as little more than a courtesy, and his interventions were frequently embarrassing.

On 7 November, the day after the Fuehrer conference, Goering gathered all the senior day and night fighter officers at the Luftflotte Reich headquarters building at Berlin-Wansee. The meeting was attended by the greatest fighting pilots who still drew breath after five years of continual combat. It was the last time that Goering would address the leadership of his Jagdflieger down to squadron level. They had become accustomed to his abuse, but this time he excelled himself. In a monologue which droned on for a full three-and-a-half hours Goering raged against the fighter pilots, questioning their courage, insulting their honour, assaulting their pride. Men with more than 1,000 combat sorties in their logbooks; men with more than 200 air-to-air victories; men with tortured limbs and ugly burn scars on their faces; hollow-eyed, chain-smoking men wearing the highest decorations for valour their country could bestow; men who were now the only survivors of their training school classes – these men were forced to listen while the porcine Reichsmarschall hurled reproaches and irrational accusations in their faces.

At the end Goering had the recording of his speech distributed to every fighter unit with orders that each pilot was to be made to sit and listen to it in full. It did great harm to morale and depressed the men greatly. Galland could do little except bind himself firmly to the fate of his combat pilots, and vow to continue to defend their interests by whatever means remained to him. As he would soon learn, those means were meagre, and would evaporate completely in the weeks ahead.

Notes to Chapter 19

1 Built largely of wood, and powered by a single 'piggyback' turbojet, the He162 actually progressed from drawingboard to flight in ten weeks; but it was inherently unstable, and the prototype broke up in mid-air during the demonstration flight. How teenagers

with a few hours on gliders would have fared does not bear thinking about. In the end only two Gruppen took delivery in the last weeks of the war; I./JG1 was officially operational in April, but it is most unlikely that the He162 ever saw combat.

2 It is reported that on one occasion Kammler had 250 prisoners of war shot merely to impress subordinates with his ruthlessness. Just before the end of the war Hitler put him in charge of halting the Russian advance in Czechoslovakia. Supposedly, rather than suffer at the hands of the Russians he had his adjutant shoot him.

CHAPTER 20

8 November 1944 – April 1945

Goering's speech on 7 November was a final summary of life under the old order. Now he wanted a different way of working, and he called a further meeting during the second week of November at the Luftkriegsakademie at Gatow – the staff college where Galland had so frequently run into opposition to his reforming plans. Goering was about to bring in a new guard to replace the old; and in the process he would give opportunities of advancement to some men whose motives, and behaviour towards their comrades, did not bear much examination.

Goering put great faith in Dietrich Peltz, and wanted to promote him to a senior position. Peltz sent a telegram to Hajo Herrmann calling him from Koenigsberg/Neumark to join the 'Luftwaffe parliament', as Goering called it; and briefed Herrmann on the importance of the meeting. Goering had intimated that major changes were afoot and that he would have a senior job for Herrmann. Other bomber men called to the Luftkriegsakademie included Kraft von Delmensingen, von Brauchitsch, Schubert, Diesing, Kneemeyer, Obstlt Werner Baumbach, and Muller. Representing the fighter pilots were Schmid, Harlinghausen, Trautloft, Luetzow, Streib, von Maltzahn, Roedel, Weiss and Galland. But there were others present too: von Klosinski, Staub and Gordon Gollob, who represented the National Sozialistischen Fuehrungs Offiziere (NSFO) – a group committed to the Party cause. Not one member of the Fuehrungsstab was present.

As the meeting got under way Galland could see no useful purpose whatsoever in its alleged mandate: to define a means by which the Allied air effort could be stopped and the German army supported in the field. Goering began by claiming that he had been asked by Hitler to rebuild the Luftwaffe, and that the 30 men present were tasked with defining how that could be made to work. There was to be a free and uninhibited exchange of opinions, and those present were free to criticise anyone apart from the Fuehrer and himself. Turning to Peltz, Goering appointed him chairman and left. Soon the varied opinions about air war strategy began to fly freely. The bomber advocates wanted a return to strategic bombing, cutting off the enemy's production and raw materials – although it was far too late for that to mean anything, even if there were the bombers to carry it out, and it ignored the central fact that the Allies' great arsenal lay on the other side of the Atlantic. The fighter men wanted to keep all production devoted to fighters, and a concerted effort made to organise massive attacks on the bombers and their escorts.

Galland sat through most of this without speaking. As the meeting went on the subject turned from operations to morale and the general attitude of junior officers and unit leaders. When it was suggested that classical music be played to fighter pilots to soothe their stress and inspire them morally, Galland burst out laughing and dug Herrmann in the ribs. Nobody else laughed. Neither was there reason to laugh when Gollob[1] proposed a renewed dedication to the National Socialist spirit, and suggested that every fighter pilot should go on a four-week course of political indoctrination. Then pieces of paper were distributed on which everyone had to write the names of people they wanted removed from office, and the feuding began in earnest: bitter recriminations, old resentments aired and old wounds aggravated.

Galland left the room to relieve himself; he considered walking straight out of the building there and then, but could not quite bring himself to do it. When the 'parliament' ended nothing had changed. (When the members of the Fuehrungsstab heard about the meeting they were furious that they had not been consulted, and shorthand notes were translated into a briefing for Goering.) As he left the academy with Trautloft and Luetzow, Galland knew that at least he had his 'Big Punch' to finalise.

Preparations for the Ardennes offensive were being completed, but the precise date depended to a large extent upon the weather. Through signals intelligence the Allies knew about an impending attack, but their information was sufficiently imprecise to keep them guessing where and when the blow would fall. On 10 November Hitler signed the final operational order for the attack through the Ardennes. Two days later Galland reported to the Luftwaffe Fuehrungsstab that his fighter forces were ready for the 'Big Punch' against the bombers. Preparations were complete but poor weather would hold off the attack for several days. The following week Galland was summoned to a meeting at which it was explained that his fighters would be needed elsewhere. On 20 November he organised their transfer west, in the belief that they were being temporarily redeployed for tactical purposes against Allied air threats. He continued to work on the organisation of his planned operation, remaining available to the demands made on his time by unit commanders down to Staffel level.

Nevertheless, Galland could feel the ground shifting under his feet; he was already beginning to be overwhelmed by a fear that he was no longer in a position to influence the fate of the Jagdflieger to whom he had given his total loyalty. He had always been a champion for the individual fighter pilots, irrespective of rank. He had often intervened in operational, procurement or administrative matters; many had looked to him for help with their problems, and to put in a good word here or there, representing their interests among the higher echelons of command. How much longer would he be able to ensure that at least one stubborn voice spoke up for the exhausted, outnumbered young men in the cockpits?

* * *

As the war ground inexorably toward the final and crushing defeat of Germany, proclamations from the Allies that they would accept nothing but unconditional surrender spread a panic fear of the Russian vengeance to come. With the Red Army now in Poland and pushing toward Germany the trickle of refugees from the east would turn into a tidal wave. As the structure of totalitarian rule began to crumble round the edges, unscrupulous opportunists in authority were looking for scapegoats among the lower levels of command. Even the pretence of civilised forms of behaviour among the leadership was wearing thin; in the increasingly feverish atmosphere which had gripped Berlin since the July plot, military rank and decorations won in battle were no longer a guarantee of immunity. Galland began to feel that he had joined the ranks of marked men.

In his increasing frustration over his declining influence in the affairs of the fighter pilots, Galland continued to seek company outside his military world in his brief hours of relaxation. He had always kept a sharp line of demarcation between work and play; but some of the friends he held on to were far from instinctive supporters of the Party – and the creatures of the regime, in turn, were suspicious of his social links with liberals whom they considered potentially disloyal. Galland had been drawn into a circle increasingly ostracised and suspected by powerful figures in the Party. Always opinionated and forthcoming, Galland had defended in such company the need for a determined stand in defence of the country and the principles of loyalty. Yet, while trying to avoid politics, he had been less than willing to defend the regime itself. There were unsuspected eyes and ears in the most intimate of circles; and a dossier had long ago been raised on Galland by the RSHA's security police.

It was in the second week of December 1944 that his separation from power and influence were finally brought out into the open. At a meeting with the chief of the Luftwaffe general staff, Gen Karl Koller, Galland was told bluntly that Goering and Hitler wanted him removed, but that they were undecided on a successor. He also discovered that Gordon Gollob, a man who had once been on his own staff and whose career he had personally advanced, was implicated in a campaign to replace him. Galland disliked Gollob intensely; he believed him to be underhand in his dealings, and he had no sympathy for Gollob's political enthusiasm. Sidelined when Galland had relegated him to looking after Me163 and Me262 technical evaluation teams, the ambitious Gollob seems to have discussed with his political contacts the desirability – for the Luftwaffe and for the war effort – of replacing Galland. One way or another the grisly SS-Obergruppenfuehrer Ernst Kaltenbrunner[2] became involved in a plan to remove Galland by having him discredited and charged with treason.

Himmler, furthering his scheme for the SS to usurp power over the armed forces, instructed Kaltenbrunner to remove from office all those who were capable of adversely influencing large groups of military personnel; and Galland's name was raised as one who had a strong and loyal following in the Jagdwaffe and who was in a position to cause trouble. In the pursuit of his own murky personal and departmental agenda, Heinrich Mueller – as head of the Gestapo Himmler's subordinate, but a far from loyal lieutenant – convinced Kaltenbrunner to let him take care of Galland. During December Galland's telephone was tapped and transcripts of his conversations were prepared daily for Mueller's attention. Simultaneously, two or three clerical staff in Galland's office were removed and replaced by SS informers: Kaltenbrunner insisted that the Sicherheitsdienst should be directly involved as well as the Gestapo.

Meanwhile a thorough search began for evidence with which to incriminate Galland of treason. It is not certain exactly what the SS and the Gestapo were looking for, as the detailed reports have never been found. They could find nothing to incriminate him on grounds of military discipline, although it appears this was the main thrust of their efforts. (It must have been a minor irritation to them that earlier in the year Galland, among other notable pilots, had heard to his surprise that he had been declared an honorary Gruppenfuehrer in the NSFK, the Party aviation organisation; the Nazis were much given to the meaningless distribution of such interdepartmental baubles.) While Mueller had his staff examine every press report written about Galland, every radio broadcast he had recorded, and files on his every known friend and acquaintance, Galland – uneasy and depressed, but still not realising how close he was to disaster – continued to work feverishly to prepare his fighter forces for the 'Big Punch'. He might be under notice, but he was going to do everything he could for the Jagdflieger until the hour when he had to clear his desk.

During the second week of December Galland was finally told the truth. There would be no 'Big Punch'; the elite fighter forces prepared meticulously over many months to fly and fight in the skies above the Reich would instead be hurled into the foggy skies of the Ardennes, flying low from makeshift fields against an enemy they had not been trained to face. Galland understood at once that it would be a massacre, and that it would bring about the final defeat of the Luftwaffe. Few things troubled his conscience as much as the secret he carried in those final days before the battle. Bitter and disappointed, he was appalled by the treachery of former colleagues and men he had lifted to power and success.

His final act of influence on the activities of the Jagdwaffe was to plead, successfully, for a change in the way the fighter forces were disposed. Instead of spreading the squadrons thinly close behind the whole width of the front, he had them stepped back in depth, allowing one to cover the other during flights to and from the battle zone. The Luftwaffe operation, codenamed *Bodenplatte* ('Base-plate'), would involve almost 2,500 combat aircraft including more than 1,900 fighters. Its mission was to hit Allied airfields and destroy a large percentage of the available British and American aircraft on the ground, clearing the skies above the German armies. On 14 December Dietrich Peltz, commanding II.Jagdkorps and all the air operations, summoned unit commanders to his headquarters outside Altenkirchen to brief them on the 16 crucial airfields that were to be destroyed on the first day. Under conditions of utmost secrecy, the units had been moved forward under radio silence and at night with their aircraft hedge-hopping to evade detection.

Early on the morning of 16 December 1944 a short, intense artillery bombardment signalled the start of the offensive; but fog and drizzle kept the Luftwaffe and Allied aircraft alike grounded as the Panzers drove deeply into the American lines. That evening a planned paratroop drop on the strategic crossroads of Malmédy got under way 17 hours late when 68 Ju52s carried almost 900 men and their equipment into the mist. One crashed on take-off, ten failed to find their drop zones, and as the Fallschirmjaeger were dropped into high winds they were scattered all over the countryside. The following day ground-attack and strafing units flew 600 sorties, and that night Luftwaffe bombers hit troop concentrations in the Allied rear. Over the next few days the Luftwaffe did what it could to support the ground forces, and from the 22nd Allied aircraft were also active; but the weather failed to improve significantly before Christmas Eve. On that day, the first Arado Ar234 jet bombers to see action flew to drop their bombs on a factory at Liège as Me262 bombers from KG51 hit tactical targets. Patton's counter-attack against the German salient from the south was well under way by this point; and on the 26th the US paratroopers holding Bastogne were relieved. Day by day the Luftwaffe was being whittled away, and still the order for 'Baseplate' had not been given. Gen von Manteuffel's divisions fought in vain to push Patton back from around Bastogne, but the Allies only got stronger while the German troops – committed to an over-ambitious offensive without the strength in depth which it demanded – grew weaker by the day. By the end of December the Allies had recaptured all the ground they had lost; at a cost of some 80,000 men, the Wehrmacht had delayed the crossing of the Rhine by perhaps six weeks. For Galland, in a state of limbo, the final week of 1944 brought only frustration and bitterness. Not only had his hopes of striking a major blow at the Allied bomber offensive been dashed forever; but the fighter forces he had spent months building up were being wasted in a war of attrition against overwhelming odds.

It was during that final week of December that Goering summoned him to Karinhall. For almost three hours, amid the flamboyant vulgarity of a setting which now seemed utterly futile, Galland was lectured on his failures. He had to be replaced. He had, it seemed, betrayed his office by disobeying orders, devising unworkable tactics that wasted men and equipment, creating a private empire, and using his powers to pursue personal enmities. Right at the very end of the interview Goering told Galland that, personally speaking, he liked him very much; but that the responsibilities of office prevented him from acting in any other way. Patronisingly, he told Galland that he would be a difficult man to replace; but that Himmler had recommended Gordon Gollob for the post of General der Jagdflieger. (Given Himmler's long term programme, it does not require much imagination to see the appeal of having a protégé in a position to deliver the services of the world's only operational jet fighters.) Galland said nothing in his own defence; he merely asked to be sent to the front to fly again, this time with Me262s. Goering insisted that he should take some leave. Deeply depressed, bitter over all the wasted effort and incensed at the folly of it all, Galland left.

The carefully planned attack on Allied airfields had not happened, and most of the pilots and ground crews assumed that it probably never would. Torn between demands for ground support sorties and searching for enemy fighters in the misty skies, the Jagdflieger had lost all sense of strategic purpose. So it was with surprise that they received orders on the afternoon of 31 December to attend special briefings that night; and with surprise that they learned that 'Baseplate' had not been abandoned, but would take place the following morning at dawn. Moreover, because the bomber general Dietrich Peltz was in charge of the operational detail, the entire assault was planned and co-ordinated like a bombing raid. Aircraft were ordered to assembly points, their precise flight plans were conveyed to the pilots, and detailed briefings were given on targets and way points. The weather, it seemed, was favourable for an attack next day.

When 'Baseplate' was finally launched on New Year's Day 1945, there were only 900 fighters remaining for the attack on Allied airfields. The over-complex operational planning could not be followed in practice; and the attack lacked both flexibility and consistency. On that one day the Jagdwaffe lost 300 aircraft and 237 pilots killed or missing, which according to Galland's personnel records included three Geschwaderkommodore, 17 Gruppenkommandeure and 39 Staffelkapitaene – the irreplaceable core of the fighting squadrons. Ironically, about half the losses were to German flak units protecting V-2 launching sites over which large numbers of Jagdflieger had flown on the way to their targets. Peltz had not foreseen the consequences of putting so many aircraft into the sky at once; now long unused to seeing large numbers of friendly aircraft, the flak gunners naturally assumed that they were the enemy. Spectacular results were achieved against a few Allied airfields, but with insufficient effect to make any difference to the Allies fighting their way back through the Ardennes, who had already broken German resistance. In all, the Allies lost 144 aircraft destroyed and 62 damaged.

Yet even as the lifeblood of the Jagdwaffe was being shed in a hopeless cause, among the bones that remained there were careers to be considered. On 31 December Goering had invited Dietrich Peltz and Hajo Herrmann to Kronberg in the Taunus; it was a bitterly cold Saturday morning when the two men arrived to celebrate the New Year with the Reichsmarschall. Taking Herrmann apart for a walk in the grounds, Goering gave him a long lecture on the origins of the Luftwaffe, his hopes and aspirations for its success, and his criticism of key leaders, including Galland. Goering praised the bomber crews, pointing out that their extensive training in navigation and cross-country skills would make them better pilots for fighter-bombers. He wanted to restock the Jagdwaffe with such men, he said; and told him that Peltz would command Luftflotte Reich but that Herrmann was to replace Galland as General der Jagdflieger.

Herrmann was astounded and delighted. Now, at last, he could implement all those schemes and tactics that Galland had suppressed. When he returned to Kronberg, Goering ordered telexes sent to all senior Luftwaffe officers informing them of his decision. Herrmann telephoned Galland to ask for a meeting, which he refused on the pretext of a fever. Later, Herrmann again called Galland and asked for a copy of the telex from Goering announcing his promotion. Galland took some pleasure in telling him that no such telex had arrived. In fact, there was a mutiny afoot.

News of Galland's dismissal had spread like wildfire and triggered a reaction unforeseen by Goering. Luetzow and Trautloft gathered support for a petition to Hitler and refused to accept that the dismissal was irrevocable. First, they sought advice from Genobst Ritter von Greim, now in command of Luftflotten 5 and 6 in the East, and an officer whose loyalty to the Fuehrer could not be questioned.

They met with von Greim on 13 January; and on the 14th he telephoned chief of staff Gen Karl Koller – who had already been approached by Maj Gerd Mueller-Trimbusch, Galland's operations officer. Koller knew from these two contacts that the 'Experten' were trying to bypass Goering and get to Hitler. On 17 January Koller received Johannes Steinhoff and Obst Eduard Neumann, who left him in no doubt that if something was not done the majority of senior Jagdflieger would take matters into their own hands. Koller telephoned Goering and warned him that he practically had a revolt on his hands, and that he had better get matters back under control. Coming from an officer of unquestionable loyalty to the Fuehrer, Goering knew what that meant.

Without delay Goering contacted Steinhoff and Neumann who, together with Luetzow, went to see the Reichsmarschall at Karinhall. Goering listened, and agreed to call a meeting of all available Geschwaderkommodore at the Haus der Flieger in Berlin. Galland was not allowed to be present, but fellow officers kept him informed by telephone as the meeting progressed. Luetzow acted as spokesman for the group supporting Galland's reinstatement, and presented a list of demands calling for better tactics and a more efficient command and control system. Goering was incensed by their mutinous demands, and flew into a rage over their uncompromising attitude. No one, it seemed, was prepared to oppose the motion, although some kept quiet and watched the arguments unfold. As tempers rose and recriminations replaced logic, Goering threatened to have all the Geschwaderkommodore arrested and shot on the spot – a threat which did nothing to quell the disturbance. The meeting broke up in disarray, having agreed nothing. What it did accomplish, however, was effectively to block Hajo Herrmann as Galland's replacement; and to unleash opposition to Goering, some of it unexpectedly expressed. A staunch Nazi, von Klosinski from the NSFO talked with Luetzow and tried to promote a plan to get Goering removed from the office of chief of the Luftwaffe. Von Klosinski was promptly posted to Norway, where he stayed.

The revelation of the strength of feeling among Galland's comrades was taken more seriously; and on 19 January 1945, soon after the meeting at the Haus der Flieger, Goering ordered the arrest of Luetzow and Galland. Koller persuaded Goering that this would only exacerbate the situation; instead he sent Luetzow to Italy with the post of Jafu Italien, in charge of one Gruppe of Italian aircraft. As for Galland, he was ordered to report to the chief of the RLM personnel office, a tenacious little man called Meister, who ordered him to leave Berlin within 12 hours; he was told keep Meister informed of his whereabouts, and to consider himself under house arrest until further notice. Galland chose to go to Oberwiesenthal in the Harz mountains, and Goering sent telegraph messages to all Jagdwaffe units to say that he had retired because of ill health.

Goering did not tell Herrmann directly that he would not after all be made General der Jagdflieger as promised. Instead he heard the news as it was distributed on general notices, and learned that he was to command IX.Fliegerdivision. On 23 January Goering issued the order for Galland's replacement by Gordon Gollob. When his appointment was made official on 31 January 1945 Gollob held a huge Siegefest, a massive banquet, to celebrate his success and to emphasise the new style of the leader who would take over Galland's former office. But it was a far from happy transition. Almost all Galland's staff opposed Gollob, whose first two weeks in office were spent investigating his predecessor; he virtually ignored the responsibilities of his appointment, the fighter pilots under his command and the worsening situation across Germany. Galland's former staff wanted to resign en masse but Galland appealed to them to remain and do their duty. Gollob, meanwhile, was now working for two masters; and Himmler wanted the old guard buried.

When Galland returned to Berlin during the last week in January, after a week's leave, his car was confiscated. He was shocked to learn from friends that a major investigation had opened up around his activities since becoming General der Jagdflieger. The SS arrested his adjutant, Maj Rolf Meinardus, and put him in jail pending trial. Galland's faithful old batman, Uffz Benno Reiske, was forcefully interrogated at Gestapo headquarters, and released only on the promise that he would spy on Galland and report his every word. Somebody wanted a watertight case against Galland; and his successor ransacked all office paperwork and administrative files which had any bearing on expenditure, visits, meetings and personnel assignments which might provide ammunition. Trumped-up accusations of misuse of funds, excessive gambling, disloyalty, defeatism and incompetence were levied against him in preparation for formal charges. All members of Galland's staff over the previous three years were hunted down and interrogated. The SD men found people who had heard Galland say that the war was hopeless, that Germany had already lost. Then there were Monica and her friends, hardly sound referees for his political views (such as they were); they too were investigated by the SD for complicity. Goering brought in the Luftwaffe chief judge, von Hammerstein, and two other judges to investigate and prepare a trial.

Throughout the last days of January and the first half of February 1945 Galland remained at his home in Berlin under house arrest, only occasionally able to get word about the progress of the investigation from friends and former colleagues; far from spying on him, they kept open a secret channel of information to him. On occasion he was able to see Monica, who crept into his house while friends distracted shadowy figures watching doors and windows in the fashionable street where he lived. Deeply hurt and depressed, Galland brooded over the recollection of carefree days flying airliners to Spain; of the rough and tumble of J88 in the Civil War; and of his excitement in those first days of flying Bf109s in combat over Belgium and France. It was all a very distant memory; how he wished the last three years had been a dream. Friends began to notice his deterioration and worried over his state of mind. He had become morose, withdrawn, distant.

One night he gathered a company of close friends, including Monica, and poured out his heart. Some urged him to leave and give himself up to the Allies, but he could not. He remembered the attentions of the secret police when Anna Galland had petitioned to keep open a small Catholic school; how could he condemn his parents and his surviving brother to the consequences of his fleeing his country and giving himself up to the enemy in time of war? Reaching down into the depths of his soul he searched for a solution; he could find only one. To protect his family, there was nothing for it but to take his own life. He would not face a court that had already determined to find him guilty, and he swore that night never to be taken alive before the German people on a charge of treason.

Monica was beside herself and his friends were distraught. He was not the kind of man whose word was to be lightly dismissed, and neither could he be directly controlled. In their own ways each of them sympathised with him and undertood his dilemma; but they could not let him go, let him take his own life as so many others had been forced to do. Later that night Monica slipped out, and from the home of a friend tried to reach Speer by telephone – she knew it would be useless to try using Galland's line. She was lucky; she found Speer in, and the minister agreed to speak to her. He was appalled to learn her news, and he immediately called Hitler himself to tell him what was going on. Reportedly, Hitler was furious that so much had been undertaken in his name but without his authority. Within minutes Hitler got through to Kaltenbrunner of the SD and Mueller of the Gestapo, ordering them to drop all charges and call off the witch-hunt.

Monica returned to be with Galland. Shortly thereafter his telephone rang. It was SS-Obergruppenfuehrer Kaltenbrunner, to assure him that there had been a dreadful mistake and that the investigation was being dropped from that moment. Galland put down the telephone in bewilderment. Almost immediately it rang a second time. It was Mueller of the Gestapo: everything would be all right, and would he please not kill himself? What passed between Galland and Monica remains a confidence that time will not betray; but an hour or so later there came a knock at the door. It was a young Luftwaffe officer, who had been sent to stay with Galland for the night with instructions to discreetly remove the general's pistol and any other weapons which might be lying around. Galland didn't need this earnest, embarrassed young officer to keep him from his Maker; if he had ever doubted his friends, he had no reason now to question their loyalty and their love.

Next morning there was another call, this time from Obst Nicolaus von Below ordering Galland to the Reichskanzlei. There he received an explanation, and a personal apology conveyed from Hitler. The Fuehrer still had regard for him, said von Below; Goering had lied when he said the Fuehrer wanted him removed. It had all been a plot by the Reichsmarschall. Two days later Goering called Galland and asked him to visit Karinhall once more. When he entered the room he saw that Goering had two enormous piles of files and reports on him arranged on a table. He had to endure another long lecture on how he had deceived the Luftwaffe hierarchy and how he had betrayed a trust placed in him when he had been appointed fighter chief. However, said Goering, considering his combat record, he had personally intervened to save Galland from trial. Galland stood listening in silence. Goering completed his lecture by saying that it was Hitler's wish that he should organise an elite Me262 fighter unit composed of 'Experten', including Luetzow and Steinhoff. This had not, of course, been Hitler's suggestion at all; in February 1945 the Fuehrer had other things on his mind than the operational assignment of Adolf Galland. The idea had doubtless come from among the new men at the head of the dying Luftwaffe, and it had a certain elegance: the rebellious fighter aces would soon be dead, where they wanted to die, in the field of combat. Galland made one stipulation when he accepted the offer – that he would not be under the command of Gordon Gollob.

* * *

Johannes Steinhoff paid for his loyalty during the 'aces' mutiny' by losing command of JG7; but along with the faithful Guenther Luetzow he was immediately swept up in preparations for the formation of 'Jagdverband Galland', as the elite fighter unit was initially to be known. The new unit would be located on the airfield at Brandenburg-Briest near Berlin, where Steinhoff's previous unit was based. JG7 seemed to be under strict orders not to co-operate, although the fact was frequently forgotten in the face of their obvious common interests. However, when Galland put together a list of 24 'Experten' requested from other units, Gollob refused to release a single man. Galland had to resort to subterfuge with the help of Hannes Trautloft, recently appointed to command 4.Flieger-Schule-Division, from where he could assign leading instructors and the very best pupils to Galland's new unit.

When the unit formed on 22 February it was given the designation JV44 (Jagdverband 44); initially it had only a few Fw190Ds from IV./JG4 in one Staffel commanded by Lt Heinz Sachsenberg, retained for air defence. Steinhoff began to scour training schools and hospitals for gifted pilots and veterans; but word soon spread that 'Dolfo' Galland was forming an elite unit and wanted committed fighter pilots. Soon, in addition to Luetzow and Steinhoff his unit would include such names as Gerhard Barkhorn, Walter Krupinsky and Erich Hohagen. Others would soon achieve fame, and would carry with them for life the honour of having served in a Staffel-sized jet fighter unit commanded by a general. Galland had wanted Erich Hartmann, the highest scoring Luftwaffe ace, who would end the war with 352 confirmed kills; but he would not give up his Bf109G and the Eastern Front[4].

It took time to get the fighters, even though production of the Me262 was increasing, with 228 built in January and 296 in February. On formation JV44 had a nominal strength of 16 operational Me262s and 15 pilots, obtaining its ground personnel from 16./JG54 and III.(Erg)/JG2. Throughout March 1945 JV44 was working up, developing training procedures and devising tactics, despite enormous difficulties made worse by the intransigence of Gollob. Goering showed some sympathy for Galland's Herculean efforts to get his unit ready for combat; and Gen Kammhuber, the Reichsmarschall's overseer of jet fighters, asked him his opinion about the best way to use the aircraft.

His first recommendation was to convert KG51 into a fighter unit by changing its existing personnel for experienced Jagdflieger; by this late date there was a surfeit of good pilots – high-grade fuel shortages grounded large numbers of conventional fighters, while the jets used diesel. Galland's second recommendation was to remove Me262s from KG6 and KG27, which were behind in their conversion programmes, and give them to JG7 and KG54, which could then receive additional fighter pilots to maximise flying time. Thirdly, Galland suggested removing every good fighter pilot from existing Fw190 and Bf109 units and training them for jet flight. Fourth, he proposed that excess tanker lorries, servicing units and towing lorries be transferred to the Me262 units; and fifth, he wanted to stop the transfer of ground personnel away from the jet squadrons.

Galland reasoned that by equipping JG7, KG51 and KG54 fully the Jagdwaffe could put up 150 aircraft in a major attack against each American air raid. In reality, of course, the situation had deteriorated far beyond the point at which even these numbers could have had any appreciable effect on the air war, let alone the steamroller of British, American and Russian land forces. Nevertheless, he refused to give in; it was not in his nature to accept defeat. He had resolved to fight to the end, and had told his pilots firmly that if they were not prepared to do the same they should leave. As for his recommendations to Kammhuber, they got lost in the general collapse of serious strategic or tactical planning; by the end of March 1945 the military direction of the tiny and ever-shrinking Reich no longer displayed any clear purpose or logic. Conditions around Berlin were so bad that it was becoming impossible to fly; aircraft were hardly able to get out on the runways before they were caught in a hail of fire by strafing Allied fighters. It was time to move out and seek a more appropriate home from where the jets had some chance of operating effectively.

On 31 March, JV44 began the long move to Munich-Reim where it was to join KG(J)51. The 12 serviceable aircraft took off one by one and headed south toward the Harz mountains, flying through the Valley of the Golden Lea and on to Nuremberg, Ingolstadt and their destination. It took less than an hour to fly the 300 miles from Berlin to Munich, and all 12 jets made it safely. Within a few days they were operational – a remarkable feat in itself considering the equipment they needed, and the conditions of general collapse all around them.

Galland orchestrated a scramble against an American raid over south-eastern Germany on 5 April. Five jets pursued the bombers over Karlsruhe, shooting down one B-17 and so damaging two more that they were written off on landing. But the opportunity to engage in combat was elusive, for the unit was still building up its pilot pool and Galland insisted on an intensive training programme before throwing his men into action. Nevertheless, on 8 April Steinhoff scored against a B-24, but an escort fighter shot down his wingman Lt Fahrmann, and he had to bail out when another P-51 got him as he slowed down.

On 10 April Galland flew from Munich to Berchtesgaden, where he was rushed by car to Goering's villa at nearby Obersalzburg. He could not imagine why he had been summoned by the Reichsmarschall. It was a strained meeting on both sides; expecting the worst, Galland was braced for recriminations and insults. Instead he found Goering with the patriarchal side of his character on show, treating him with forced courtesy and thoughtfulness. Since their last meeting the Allies had pushed far into Germany and the end was clearly in sight. Galland recalled later of this meeting that the Reichsmarschall seemed almost in a trance, reminiscing with a dreamy detachment, agreeing with him that the Me262 was the perfect fighter and that he had been right to advocate its use in large numbers against the American daylight bombers. Goering wanted to know about JV44, its victories so far, and how things were in Munich. He seemed so different. Only later did it occur to Galland that, seeing the end in sight, the Reichsmarschall was trying to ingratiate himself with all those he had abused over so many years.

Elsewhere, the war was staggering to its final climax and desperate men were throwing anything they could at the enemy. Free now to exploit his unusual ideas, Hajo Herrmann had finally got approval to organise his Rammjaeger; but Goering would only let him take junior pupils from the training schools in an effort to save experienced pilots. Code-named 'Werewolf', the training scheme taught pilots how to fly lightweight Bf109G-10 or K-1 fighters stripped of armament except for one 13mm MG131 machine gun. After climbing to around 11,000m (36,000ft), the pilots were to dive at maximum speed and strike the weakest part of their target, usually the fuselage just forward of the tail, bringing down the bomber and leaving any surviving Rammflieger to take to their parachutes if they could. Herrmann envisaged a force of 800 aircraft each bringing down a single bomber. By the end of March he had assembled 250 pilots, but only 150 fighters were modified for this operation. On 7 April the only 'Werewolf' operation of the war took place when 120 Rammjaeger of Sonderkommando Elbe took off to hit a force of more than 1,200 B-17s and B-24s penetrating central Germany. Half the German force was destroyed, but only eight bombers were brought down by ramming. Galland smiled sourly to himself when he heard that Herrmann had been controlling operations from the ground.

Back at Munich-Reim, Galland gradually developed tactics based on Nowotny's experience of the previous year. Flying in Ketten of three aircraft and using the sheer speed of the Me262 to achieve surprise, Galland trained his pilots to exit flat and low across the top of the bombers. It worked as well as it had during 1943 – better, given the greater speed of the jets. Although he never had as many aircraft as he wanted, Galland believed his optimum formation was about 21 jets in loose Ketten; JV44 practised this, achieving good results.

Increasingly toward the middle of April his airfield came under attack from strafing fighters, and several aircraft were written off as a result. The shortages of equipment and spares became worse; and production of new Me262s had slowed, with 240 completed in March and 101 during April, when all deliveries ceased. In all, 1,433 of the revolutionary jets had been produced, but more than one-third suffered problems caused either by technical failure or by deliberate sabotage – even a slave-worker can strike his blow. Aircraft would be delivered incomplete, or tampered with so that when they took to the air a vital part would fail. Many Luftwaffe aircraft crashed and killed their pilots because a fuel-soaked rag was packed tight inside the engine casing, or a pin-hole in a hydraulic line bled off the fluid at a critical moment.

On 16 April Galland led JV44 into the air against a formation of B-26 Marauders, and within minutes he had shot two down using the R4M rockets, 12 of which were carried beneath each wing outboard of the two engines. These 55mm, 4kg (8.8lb) rockets each carried 0.5kg (17oz) of Hexagen, which had a lethal effect when used against bombers. The projectiles had the same trajectory as the MK108 cannon and were effective when aimed with a Revi 16B gunsight. Mounted on wooden racks flush with the wing, they could be fired together if necessary and would produce a spread equal to the span of a four-engined bomber at 550m (1,800ft). All too frequently the firing mechanism failed, however, as it did the next day when Galland led nine Me262s in an attack on bombers over Munich and Steinhoff was unable to get off his rockets at a B-17. Another Me262 was hit by gunfire and sliced the tail off a B-17, which carried them both to the ground. Galland failed to score before they had to return to Munich-Reim, where their valuable jets were put into blast pens offering some protection from Allied strikes.

On the next day, 18 April, Galland led a Kette of three Me262s into the air ahead of a second Kette led by 'Macki' Steinhoff. Galland and his wingmen got away clean, but just before he pulled the stick back to rotate one engine on Steinhoff's aircraft blew. With asymmetric thrust the aircraft slewed to one side, its undercarriage toppled as it collided with the embankment, its momentum catapulted the Me262 briefly into the air before it slammed back onto the runway – and 2,730 litres (600gal) of fuel boiled into flames. No one who saw it thought Steinhoff could possibly survive, but out of the top of the blazing fuselage there slowly clambered a terrible, blackened figure. Later that day Galland went to see Steinhoff in hospital; his head was swathed in bandages. Galland told him about the day's events, and said that the end could not be far off. The Americans were approaching Augsburg and advancing on the Brenner Pass. For a while Galland just sat with Steinhoff, deep in thought; then he gently touched him on the arm. 'See you, Macki' he said, and left[5].

Over the next few days JV44 fought back whenever it could, attacking the incessant streams of bombers. Never could the unit raise more than a dozen aircraft, and at times only four or five jets were serviceable. On 24 April the Me262s were in the air attacking B-26s and their escorts from the US 9th Army Air Force when a fierce fight developed, and Guenther Luetzow went down without trace near Donauwoerth. With a score of 108 kills in more than 300 combat missions, he had been a staunch friend in the hardest days of Galland's life. Galland went to tell Steinhoff; the two pilots had been special friends. Steinhoff recalled that Galland was depressed and morose, convinced the end was only days away.

On 25 April 1945 American and Russian troops met on the Elbe. Galland gathered his pilots together and faced them with the reality, offering to remove anyone from the flight list who so wished. Only two chose to do so, citing family reasons.

Adolf Galland's last two victories – his 103rd and 104th – were achieved on 26 April when he led five other pilots against a reported raid of B-26 Marauders from the 17th Bomb Wing and P-47 Thunderbolts from the 27th and 50th Fighter Groups. With seven-tenths cloud obscuring ground references, Galland led the two Ketten over the Danube toward the region of Neuberg. Spotting the Allied aircraft, he found it hard to relate their own speed with that of the slower piston-engined aircraft, and with difficulty made a judgement about their converging rate – a vital factor when making a head-on attack. As they closed on their enemy the jets came under a hail of defensive fire. Galland had forgotten to release the second safety catch for the 24 R4M rockets under his wings. Nevertheless, the four 30mm cannon ripped apart a B-26 which virtually disintegrated before his eyes. Within seconds he had picked off another which went earthward in flames. In a flash the formation was past and the jets were regrouping; but Galland's aircraft had been hit in the fuel intake, and he wanted to make sure his second adversary really was going down.

In that instant of lapsed concentration he was hit by the guns of a P-47 flown by Lt James Finnegan. Bullets shattered his instrument display and flying metal showered the inside of his cockpit. There was a searing pain in his right knee and a dull ache in the lower half of that leg. A second burst of .50 calibre fire hit his starboard engine, and then the port nacelle too. Diving for the cover of cloud he contemplated baling out, convinced that his aircraft was virtually unflyable; but minutes later, after debating with himself the possibility of being shot at on a parachute, he trimmed the aircraft and decided to try to get back onto the ground intact. Power was erratic, the throttle on one engine no longer worked, he had no instruments or radio, and the aircraft was not responding properly to the controls. Nevertheless, below the clouds he could see the autobahn outside Munich, and that gave him his bearings back to Munich-Reim.

Only at the last minute as he banked round on his final approach did he realise that the airfield was at that moment under strafing attack from fast-flying P-47s. Too late to abort, Galland chopped the engines just before touchdown, and rumbled across the cratered runway with a flat nosewheel tyre amid falling bombs, flying bullets and showers of earth and shrapnel. Never has a man with a splintered knee-cap moved so fast as Galland when he leapt for the relative safety of a bomb crater. Minutes later an armoured tractor rumbled toward him at speed, driven by a mechanic who had seen his heroic landing. Relieved to be back on the ground and safe, Galland leaned forward and slapped the man on the back. Soon he was in hospital for X-rays and a plaster cast. For Adolf Galland – the first and the best – the war was finally over.

* * *

In his absence, Obstlt Heinz Bar looked after operational details at JV44. While Galland remained incarcerated in the Luftwaffe hospital at Bad Wiesee the advancing American armies made it impossible for JV44 to remain at Munich-Reim, and on 29 April the jet fighter unit moved to Salzburg-Maxglan with a small number of aircraft being dispersed to Innsbruck. In the last two or three weeks aircraft from other units had been gathering at Munich-Reim. As the advancing Americans forced units to leave their airfields the Me262s were brought to Galland; from all across southern Germany the last jet fighters were rallying to their general. In all, about 60 aircraft flew to Salzburg; but even then there were ominous orders from Berlin requesting that all Me262s gather at Prague to fight the Russians. Mercifully, the orders were shuffled from desk to desk until the German surrender made them irrelevant.

In the meantime, Galland kept in close touch with events from a private villa at Tegernsee. On 30 April, at 15.30, Hitler shot himself. Next day Adolf Galland made the greatest gamble of his life, when he drafted plans to offer the Americans full use of his elite jet fighter unit in their struggle against the Russians, which he was convinced would break out within days. He felt he had a lot to offer: a complete Gruppe-size unit of jet fighters – the only one in the world – with many of Germany's elite fighting aces, ready and trained for air-to-air combat in the world's most advanced aircraft. Rather than see his freshly created unit collapse on the funeral pyre of Nazism he wanted to offer it for a new struggle against an enemy which, he believed, would destroy Europe unless it was itself crushed. He was well aware of the announcements that German surrender must be unconditional; but surely the Americans were not so stupid as to destroy what could be a valuable asset for the coming struggle? Blinded by the moment, Galland had not only failed to understand a political system of which he had no experience; he had also failed to understand – as he should have done, from the example of his own people – that the suffering endured through more than five years of war had left the British and Americans in no mood for more fighting.

Nevertheless, on Tuesday 1 May 1945, Galland arranged for Maj Wilhelm Herget, his aide, and Hptmn Kessler to fly by Fieseler Storch from the villa where Galland was staying to contact the Americans with the offer of delivering JV44 intact. It was a dangerous mission. The country was crawling with fragmented SS units and fanatics on the lookout for 'deserters' to hang from the nearest tree; if discovered, the offer to surrender a complete jet fighter unit to the enemy would have brought instant death for Herget, Kessler and Galland. Written just after midnight, the letter was taken by the two JV44 officers in the Storch on the 45-minute flight to the former Luftwaffe airfield at Schleissheim. Throughout the day Galland waited, not knowing whether the next men to arrive would be his officers returning with a reply or SS men come to kill him. He had time to ponder on the events that had brought him to this moment, time to contemplate all the things left undone.

Long before he had been granted permission to form JV44, during several secret nighttime meetings with Speer, a select group of officers had agreed that when the war was irrevocably lost they would each seize a senior Nazi and hold them prisoner in the hope that they could restore order to Germany. Galland was to have flown to Goering's headquarters to arrest him. In the chaos that now reigned, that was impossible[6].

When Brig Gen Pearson Menoher of the US 15th Army Corps received Maj Herget and Hptmn Kessler at 11.00 on 1 May he drafted a reply to Galland's offer, suggesting that aircraft from Salzburg be flown to Geibelstadt and those at Innsbruck fly to an airfield near Darmstadt. They were to fly with their undercarriages lowered and without ammunition. P-47s of the 64th Fighter Wing were to rendezvous in the air with the Me262s and escort them to their respective fields. When Herget and Kessler returned to Galland they brought a clear message that the local commander had no authority to do anything other than accept total surrender in the manner indicated.

There was nothing left to do. Galland was not going to give the Americans more than 50 perfect examples of the world's most technically advanced fighter without some sort of assurance that they, and their pilots, would be used to help free Germany of the Red Army. It was all over; only two tasks remained. First, he sent a message back to Brig Gen Menoher to say that he was, after all, unable to comply due to poor weather, lack of fuel and technical problems, but that he was at the general's disposal and could be found at Tegernsee hospital. The other thing he did was to order the complete destruction of every Me262 at Salzburg and Innsbruck.

Notes to Chapter 20

1 Obst.Gordon Gollob, a contemporary of Galland, commanded JG3 'Udet' in 1941-2 and JG77 in 1942-4. Credited with 160 kills, he was the third Luftwaffe officer to be awarded the Knight's Cross with Oak Leaves, Swords and Diamonds.

2 Ernst Kaltenbrunner succeeded Heydrich as head of the RSHA, the Reich Main Security Office; in 1944 he also took over the Abwehr or military intelligence agency. He was found guilty of war crimes and hanged after the Nuremberg trials.

3 Lt Heinz Sachsenberg was the cousin of Gotthard Sachsenberg, holder of the Pour le Merite with a reported 31 victories as a naval fighter pilot during World War I. Gotthard died in 1961 aged 69; but his younger cousin, with 104 victories in World War II, only lived until 1951 when, aged 29, he died of wounds received during the war.

4 Hartmann's reward for having stayed on the Eastern Front was ten years in Russian camps; he was finally released in 1955.

5 Steinhoff ended the war with 176 confirmed kills. His badly burned face cost him 70 operations over many years; he was unable to close his eyes for 23 years until an RAF surgeon finally managed to replace his eyelids in 1968. Steinhoff joined the reconstituted Luftwaffe in 1955, rising to chief of staff Allied Air Forces Central Europe and chief of the German air staff. Gen Steinhoff died in February 1994 aged 80.

6 Goering had left Hitler in his Berlin bunker on 20 April and headed for Obersalzburg. When Hitler announced he would remain in Berlin, Koller flew south on the 23rd and urged Goering to seize leadership of the country. Goering sent a telegram to Hitler saying, in effect, that if he did not hear from him to the contrary he would assume the Fuehrer wanted him to take over. Incensed, Hitler responded via a message from Martin Bormann's office saying that unless Goering renounced all titles and offices he would send the SS to assassinate him. Goering, who had nurtured hopes of doing a deal with the Americans, complied; he was arrested by the SS anyway and held at Mautendorf Castle, where he was to be killed if Berlin fell. When Hitler shot himself Kesselring got the SS to leave him to the Americans.

CHAPTER 21

May 1945 –
9 February 1996

When the Americans found Galland on 5 May 1945 he had a plaster cast on his right leg and he wore his full uniform as a Generalleutnant. Everything else he had lived for had been stripped from him.

For almost 15 years he had worked to see his nation restored from the terrible suffering and degradation it had known in his childhood years to its rightful status as a proud and prosperous country; but, like millions more, he had never actively wanted war or rule over foreign lands. Galland had few answers when he reflected on the sacrifices. Of the 97,000 Luftwaffe dead, missing or wounded, 20,300 had been fighter pilots. But they had exacted a grim price from the Allies, accounting for 70,000 of the 120,000 enemy aircraft destroyed by the Luftwaffe. The records of individuals had been extraordinary, and in some cases would probably stand for all time: two pilots, Hartmann and Barkhorn, had each scored more than 300 kills; 13 had scored between 200 and 300; 92 had scored between 100 and 200; in all, 467 Jagdwaffe pilots had achieved more than 40 combat victories.

For three years Galland had led this remarkable band of men, pilots who, for the most part, were ordinary young Germans without political convictions but with a powerful love of their country and a belief in themselves. The fate of the German fighter pilot was to fly and fight until he died; and unlike Allied airmen, their reward for high victory scores was to be allowed to remain at the front in combat.

Now he was a prisoner of the victorious enemy; but grateful, above everything else, for not having been taken by the Russians. Every German knew that there was a wide gulf between the codes of conduct practised by East and West; and very many who had served on the Russian Front knew what reasons there were for Germany to fear a biblical revenge. Many would suffer at the hands of the Red Army; and several hundred thousand would eventually die of disease and hunger in unknown camps deep in the Siberian wastes long after the war – just as millions of Red Army men had died in German captivity, as a deliberate end of Nazi policy.

For several days Galland was held under armed guard at Haus Kathrein, Tegernsee, and a few days later he was driven by ambulance for his first interrogation at Bad Tolz. All across Europe millions of people were on the move; and among them were thousands of Nazis, blending into the grey mass of trudging humanity in a bid to escape their identities and their accusers. Many, like

Galland, had simply done their duty as soldiers should; they had no wish to escape – but even among that group there were widely different attitudes to their individual responsibilities as prisoners of war. Many refused to co-operate; some realised that there was little point in defying their captors; a few, unable to face a bleak future, committed suicide. Galland, having survived such dangers for so many years, decided to fix his eyes on the future; he was only 33 years old,and he knew he still had a lot to give.

Galland underwent his first major interrogation at Heidelberg, conducted by Maj Max von Rossum-Daum of the US Army Air Force, the commanding officer of the Air Prisoner of War Interrogation Unit (APWIU). His was an important job, and Galland was a prize catch. With a reputation in both Britain and America, he was a key figure not only in piecing together the background story of the role played by the Luftwaffe in Hitler's ambitions, but also in helping determine the relative levels of responsibility for many actions which the victorious powers considered as crimes against humanity. Galland got on well with Maj von Rossum-Daum, who quickly established a close rapport with him. When Galland's basic details and personal file had been established he was flown to England for a more extensive interrogation.

Arriving on English soil for the first time in his life on 14 May 1945, with two suitcases and his last few boxes of cigars, he was immediately taken to a special interrogation centre north-west of London. As the prisoners were taken by truck along the winding roads of southern England Galland was surprised to find how much like Germany the countryside looked, but also how relatively little damage had been suffered by the small towns and villages compared with those of continental Europe. He could not help thinking how different had been his expectations of that first trip to England back in 940, when he had seen himself flying in as a proud victor. His destination was the Combined Services Detailed Interrogation Centre, Camp 7, situated on the estate of Lord Chesham at a place called Latimer in Buckinghamshire. There he would be grilled by Maj Ernst Englander, operating under the pseudonym of 'Maj Emery'; in Maj Englander's team was Capt John M. Whitten, referred to as 'Capt Todd' – a 24-year-old interrogator who was to strike up a close friendship with Galland that would last for the remainder of their lives.

Interrogation was a precise and time-consuming business, made the more so by the need to investigate individual cases for possible indictment at the war crimes trials to be held at Nuremberg, the favourite showplace of Nazism. Galland was aware of this, and was fearful that he would be held responsible for the crimes committed against the workers forced to labour in the fighter production programmes. Potentially, every interrogation of a high ranking officer or official of the government was conducted for the initial purpose of finding whether the individual had committed crimes against peace, crimes against the rules of war, crimes against humanity, or conspiracy to commit such crimes. The interrogations at Camp 7 cleared Galland of implication or complicity. Now the real questioning could start.

The Allies wanted to know every minute detail about how the Luftwaffe had been organised, how it had been run, about the technical developments achieved and the operational tactics devised. First and foremost a professional pilot and military officer, Galland had known there would one day be interest in these operations when, in 1943, he had ordered every unit down to Staffel level to write its history and maintain records. No one had foreseen the terrible conditions at the end of the war, and few such records had survived intact. Now, General-leutnant Galland would help the Allies build back that picture.

Naturally, the priority interest focused on the technical details of the Me262, which the Americans and the British wanted to know a lot more about. Captured jet aircraft would be taken back to the United States and flown on test. There was much to learn about them and Galland was pleased to oblige, a level of pride returning to him as he related the general handling and performance characteristics. Leading Allied fighter pilots came to see him at Camp 7 and worked through interpreters to gain answers to their searching questions. Everyone found Galland a total professional, clearly a highly capable pilot and a fine officer. From the outset Galland was willing to co-operate; he was determined to maintain a sense of dignity and purpose, although inside he was bitterly racked by depression and that sense of emptiness that comes with defeat.

What Galland had to say contributed greatly to the Allies' background knowledge of Jagdwaffe operations. But how much of what he said was the truth; how much more might he be concealing, to avoid incriminating himself or others? Galland suddenly found himself with a roommate when Erhard Milch was billeted on him at Camp 7. His room had been secretly wired to record conversations; Galland suspected this, but it seemed that Milch did not. Depressed and maudlin, Milch would wander round the room reminiscing over times past – while Galland patrolled the thin walls, banging gently with the side of his fist to deaden the conversation, which apparently it did quite successfully. Milch was in poor mental condition and feared for his life. Galland was convinced he was going to survive, and had no intention of having his chances destroyed by Milch being overhead saying anything that could be misinterpreted. Milch did little to endear himself to Galland, and kept begging him for some of the last few cigars remaining in his possession. Obligingly, Galland agreed to exchange them for a special hunter's pipe belonging to Milch. When the second most powerful man in the air forces of the Third Reich came to leave, he tried – vainly – to smuggle it away: Galland stood his ground, and kept the pipe.

Some interrogations were held at a special centre at the nearby village of Beaconsfield, where the Americans had a unit dedicated to senior technical officers who had undefined political affiliations. There was still some doubt in the minds of senior controlling investigators about Galland's role in events. Removed from direct contact, they could make objective and dispassionate judgements from the answers and reactions that came under questioning; and for a while Galland's fate hung on the decisions of these faceless men, present in every intelligence community. Milch had been put in with Galland to explore potential conspiracies of silence or confession. His next test would be with a staunch anti-Nazi of high rank, and it was to his amazement that Galland found his new roommate at Beaconsfield to be none other than Gen Franz Halder, formerly of the OKH, who had been arrested on suspicion after the July 1944 bomb plot, and had been found in Dachau concentration camp by US troops. It was Halder who revealed to Galland what he had learned at first hand – what Nazism had truly meant for so many millions, subjected to a debased inhumanity far beyond anything that the Luftwaffe general could have imagined. It was in his room with Halder that Galland learned about the extermination camps for the first time[1]. This time there was no banging on the walls; the obscenities that Halder revealed to him shocked him beyond the power of description, and he would have to have been a moral imbecile not to have brooded over his association with the regime which had committed them. Against the background of such a vast horror, there was even a small, special cruelty which might have been calculated to prevent him, of all people, becoming numbed with the repetition of outrages. He learned about the murder of scores of Allied airmen after the mass escape from Stalag Luft III, and about the atrocities perpetrated by the Gestapo on recaptured airmen who – by Galland's lights – had been doing nothing but their duty.

On 13 June the first report consisting of answers to technical questions had been completed, and a longer series of more protracted interrogations more in the vein of a career debrief began. During the second week in July Galland was taken by an interrogator to RAF Tangmere on the south coast of England for two days of talks. There he met several pilots whom he had flown against. Douglas Bader was there, and provided Galland with some cigars, a small return for the consideration he had received almost four years earlier. The crusty group captain gave Galland the benefit of the doubt, and the two remained friendly until Bader's death in September 1982 at the age of 72. Through meetings such as these Galland, whose reputation was well sung in Britain as a 'fighter pilot's fighter pilot', established friendships that grew from professional respect. His criticism of the Luftwaffe high command for bungling important decisions found sympathy; any professional officer who had fought through a world war could understand his frustration. His apolitical stance, and his acceptance of German atrocities – which, although usually left undiscussed, he never denied or sought to excuse – brought respect for his integrity and professionalism.

On 24 August he was put aboard a B-17 bound for Kaufbeuren in Bavaria. With him were Erhard Milch, the famous Ju88 bomber pilot Werner Baumbach, Edgar Petersen from the Luftwaffe's experimental centre at Rechlin, and several other Luftwaffe officers. As they flew across Germany the view beneath them was strikingly different from the pastoral summer scenery of the England they had just left; there, although the war had left its bitter scars on cities and on lives, total devastation had been avoided. After a refuelling stop at Schweinfurt they flew on to their destination, where the prisoners were put up in their new home, a three-storey villa adjacent to a mental hospital. There, the extraordinarily talented Maj von Rossum-Daum was to begin a long and tedious debrief, in the process of which a vast store of information would be extracted about fighter unit command and operational control tactics. At last they were allowed a modest level of freedom, and in the absence of guards each man swore an oath to his own parole. They were required to report for debrief every day, and every day each one turned up as instructed. There was time for Galland to be taken to Hohenpeissenberg where he hoped to retrieve his hunting guns, special possessions for which he had great fondness, but they had been looted. Gone too from his last temporary home at Tegernsee was his Knight's Cross with Oak Leaves, Swords and Diamonds, many other personal items, and all of the tactical files that had been so carefully preserved. Although the prisoners were denied mail there was discretion through the interrogators for letters which were smuggled out and posted in the local village. A former prisoner of the Americans, but now released and living locally, Obst Walter Dahl served as a safe mailbox for incoming letters. One of Galland's fellow prisoners was Hubertus Hitschold, who impressed the Americans so much with his candour and willingness that they arranged for his wife to spend some time with him nearby. Soon, several families had been located and resettled near Kaufbeuren.

Then there came a change of orders. The Luftwaffe Personnel Holding Unit had moved into Camp 7 in England, and there were other questions for which some of the officers were required to return to England. Less than two months after reaching Kaufbeuren, Galland was taken back to Latimer for further questioning. Evidence was being gathered for the Nuremberg trials, and both Erhard Milch and Albert Speer had been indicted for complicity in Sauckel's slave labour activities. Passages in Goering's interrogation inferred that Galland had pressed for higher production, and that he had put him in contact with Speer, who introduced him to Sauckel. Goering wanted the investigators to believe that it was Galland who had arranged with Sauckel for slave labour to build aircraft, and that he had not been personally involved. There were more questions to which the answers would prove crucial for Galland's immediate future: some Nazis had indicated that Galland knew about oxygen depletion tests conducted on Dachau inmates which provided doctors with information about the reaction of the human body to simulated high altitude flight. Milch claimed that Galland knew nothing about these experiments, a fact which Galland and others confirmed[2].

There were other matters to discuss at Latimer, but there was time for relaxation too; and on 21 October 1945 Galland and Hitschold were told to dress in civilian clothes, and were taken on a sightseeing tour of London by Capt Whitten. Exercising his prerogative, he lunched them at the Cumberland Hotel and took them on a tour of Selfridges. It was a brief respite from the more serious business of interrogation which, as the war crimes trials were getting under way, assumed greater urgency. As part of their preparation for defending the role of the Luftwaffe a high-ranking delegation from the OKL were permitted to assemble signatures on a large sheet of paper absolving them of any responsibility and, collectively, explaining how they had merely followed orders. Galland was incensed by these arrogant and self-righteous statements. What he had so recently learned about Nazi atrocities conducted in the name of ordinary Germans had sickened him. When shown the document and pressed to add his signature, Galland quietly read through the statements in their entirety, and then tore it in two from top to bottom. He personally welcomed the trials, in the hope of learning who had been responsible for the horrors that disgraced the uniform he had been so proud to wear. Forty-five years later he felt an undiminished disgust at their impertinence in expecting him to corroborate their feeble excuses.

Early in December all the outstanding concerns of the Latimer interrogators had been satisfied, and Galland was returned to Kaufbeuren where the real work of writing up the full staff histories of the fighter wings began. For more than a year he was to hand-write notebooks full of detailed accounts and observations concerning his experiences in the Jagdwaffe. These would serve not only as important reference documents for historical purposes but as teaching aids during tutorials at officer training colleges in the eventually reconstituted Luftwaffe. For almost 18 months he would work for the USAAF Historical Division, putting his reports together and attempting to make sense of large quantities of material retrieved from all over Germany. It was not all work, however, and he was able to catch up on overdue visits; one of these, on 21 January 1946, was to the premises of Erich Vollmer, who had been one of the three cigar manufacturers granted licence to market 'General der Jagdflieger' cigars. A few boxes remained, and were borne off in triumph.

Because Galland had made important contacts, he was able to pursue some attempts to find out the whereabouts or fate of old friends. Millions of people throughout Germany were displaced from their own homes and trying to find anyone was an almost impossible task. One person of particular concern to him was the widow of his former aide and friend Oblt Baron Conrad Heinrich von Donner, who had been killed in action in March 1944. Through the kindness of Capt Whitten Galland was able to locate the Baroness Gisela von Donner, and to begin a correspondence which was eventually to lead to a romantic association between the two. His friend Capt Whitten returned to the United States before the end of 1946 but would maintain contact with Galland, supplementing his meagre rations with food parcels.

By early 1947 many of Galland's former associates had dispersed across the country, some being tempted to work for the Russians, others disappearing into the general mass of the population, a very few finding work that would help them re-establish a normal existence. The vast majority of officers and NCOs were left to scratch whatever living they could from manual labour – rebuilding, driving rubble trucks, or pounding spikes into new railway lines. Travel was well nigh impossible and Galland had little opportunity to visit friends or move around the country; he had little money, and no personal transport. Shortly after his first series of interrogations he had been allowed to visit his family at Westerholt, which brought great relief to his mother and father, who for some months at the end of the war had feared he would not survive.

As for the rest, the courts were deciding their fate. From the Luftwaffe, Milch had been indicted for war crimes and would be tried during 1947, eventually serving a prison sentence in Spandau; Goering had been sentenced to death but had cheated the hangman by taking poison; and Sauckel had been hanged for his part in organising slave labour. Speer had made a dignified figure, admitting his complicity in Nazi crimes and declaring his willingness to accept the verdict of the court; he was spared the death penalty, and served 20 years in prison.

During 1946 and early 1947 Gisela von Donner visited Galland many times, travelling by the erratic and unreliable transport system, still in a nightmare state after the years of bombing. Unable to use the roads and forced to ride freight trains, as were the majority of Germans, she found it difficult enough to move anywhere; but her sincerity touched Galland deeply, and a special friendship matured. Finally, on 28 April 1947, Adolf Galland, private citizen, was a free man.

* * *

Released from Heilbronn, Galland's first act was to travel to Schleswig-Holstein and join the Baroness von Donner on the extensive estate in north-west Germany where she lived with her three children. For Adolf Galland it was full circle, for now he was to find employment as a forestry worker. The passage of time and the solace of his beloved woods healed the wounds of so many years of active service, and the sickness of discovering the truth about the Nazi years. Here he reclaimed his hold on life; he could hunt game to supplement the meagre food supplies, and soon he was bringing home enough not only to stock the von Donner table but to trade for essentials in the local villages. He even indulged his inventiveness by growing tobacco and distilling a little schnapps. Life was getting back on an even keel; and soon Galland yearned for more challenges, for some way to exercise his skills again. Flying seemed to be out of the question – until, in the summer of 1948, he received a letter from Kurt Tank, the brilliant designer from Focke-Wulf who had brainstormed the Fw190 and given his design signature to the Ta152 and Ta154.

Tank invited Galland to visit him at an old castle in Minden, where he explained that he had been approached by many people wanting to employ him on various projects since the war ended. The Russians had asked him to go to Moscow and he had narrowly escaped being forcibly seized and flown to the USSR; the British had shown interest in employing him as a consultant. None of these schemes had come to fruition; but then had come an intriguing offer, via a contact in Denmark acting on behalf of the Argentinean government. It seemed that the Argentines wanted to employ Tank to design their first operational jet fighter. The Denmark connection lived in Buenos Aires and had made a living out of getting the right Germans into his country, where their talents could be employed by the Peron government. Tank wanted to know whether Galland would be prepared to join him; the Argentines wanted a team which would include someone to train their pilots to fly the new aircraft, and Tank could only go if the complete organisation was delivered intact. Tank had already secured the services of Otto Behrens, late of the Fw190 project, the leading aerodynamicist Prof Thalau, and many of the original Focke-Wulf design team.

Galland thought long and hard. There would be little opportunity for him in ruined Germany; it would be many years before his own country could develop its own aviation industry, let alone a military air arm. Galland talked it over with Gisela and she agreed that it was too good an opportunity to miss, pledging to join him when he got to Argentina. There was one small problem: none of the people making up the team were supposed to leave Germany, let alone for Argentina, as the Allies were trying very hard to stop the flow of ex-Nazis and military men to South America. Rumours abounded about the whereabouts of several important Nazi fugitives, and the corrupt dictatorships of Latin America were proving to be a haven for many who had good reason to flee for their lives. The Peron government, eager to outdo its chief rival and commercial competitor Brazil, was interested only in securing the services of men who could give it the technology for military might.

So, his passage organised by his contact in Denmark, Kurt Tank slipped out of the country to Copenhagen, from there to London, and finally to Lisbon where an aircraft waited to fly him to Buenos Aires. The main party of technicians and designers were stopped in Denmark and returned to Germany. Galland made it out with the third group and got through, exchanging the shortening days of late autumn for the spring of South America, where the team quickly came together. Given a three-year contract with two optional extensions, Galland quickly settled into life in Argentina. He was introduced to Gen Peron's secretary, to Gen San Martin, head of the national aeronautics and technology institute at Cordoba, and Gen de la Colina, the secretary of state for air. Tank was personally briefed by Gen Peron on the kind of aeroplane he wanted.

Galland was shown the first jet fighter produced in Argentina, with the help of the well known French designer Emilio Dewoitine, and first flown on 9 August 1947. Now, a year on, he was told that this aircraft was not suitable. The *Fuerza Aerea Argentina* wanted a more powerful aircraft to form the backbone of the fighter forces. To get an idea of the air force's requirements Tank and Galland went along to see the secretary of state for air at his headquarters at Juncal 1116, Buenos Aires, where they also met Brig Gen Muratorio, the commander of the air force. It was clear what they wanted.

Kurt Tank had designed a jet fighter for Focke-Wulf incorporating the radical swept wing pioneered in German aeronautical research institutes. Designated Ta183, it was to influence several postwar European jet fighter designs, but in Argentina it formed the basis for Peron's new fighter. Its predecessor, the IAe27 Pulqui I designed by Dewoitine, was a simple straight-wing aircraft powered by a Rolls-Royce Derwent centrifugal gas-flow turbine engine of 1,600kg (3,600lb) thrust; capable of 850kph (528mph), it had a ceiling of 15,200m (50,000ft), and carried four 20mm cannon in the nose. Designated IAe33 Pulqui II, the new fighter would have the same engine – which from 1948 was licence-built in Argentina – but vastly improved aerodynamics, producing an aircraft with a top speed of almost 1,045kph (650mph) with far better handling and performance characteristics.

The aircraft was revolutionary, with a 40-degree sweep on its wings and 45-degree sweep on a vertical tail surmounted by the horizontal control surfaces. It first flew on 27 June 1950, but shortly thereafter it broke up in the air because of faulty welding and killed its Argentinean pilot. Undeterred, Peron had Tank build a second prototype, which flew perfectly; but by this date the aircraft looked a less attractive proposition than existing British aircraft like the Gloster Meteor, and only six Pulqui IIs were built.

For Galland life in Argentina was good. He liked the people, and the relaxed social life was much to his taste. Not long after he arrived in Buenos Aires Gisela von Donner joined him with her three children, and they settled into a house in the fashionable El Palomar district on the outskirts of the city. Galland became something of a figure in the lavish nightlife of this city that never sleeps, and was frequently to be found with the Baroness at parties that rarely finished before dawn. After the rubble and endless shortages in Germany it seemed like life on another planet. Galland quickly got back into the air, and found the hills and mountains suitable for gliding, which appealed greatly to the Argentineans, who were eager to encourage any competitive sport.

Living in a spacious house with lovely gardens, and cared for by servants, the family was assigned an air force interpreter, Capt Luis Grieben, whose fluency in Spanish and German was invaluable when Galland had to deliver lectures to air force officers or translate and explain complex technical concepts written in the native language. Of the family only the children, pupils at a local school, were fluent in Spanish. The Baroness soon became an established part of the social scene; but for Galland and his lady it was the unusual comfort that came from a settled lifestyle that brought true satisfaction. At weekend there were picnics, walks in the country, car rides to the mountains, or clay-pigeon shooting with friends; there was even time for hunting on the pampas. For the first time in his life, Adolf Galland was a family man with responsibilities.

His work focused on the need to build an efficient fighter arm, and the Argentines had not been slow to capitalise on the best equipment around. As early as May 1947 the British agreed to supply 100 Gloster Meteor Mk.4 twin-jet fighters to Argentina, along with 20 redundant Avro Lancaster and Lincoln long-range bombers. The order was challenged by the Americans, who were concerned about the military leadership under Peron, and an additional order agreed in April 1948 for a further 300 Meteors and 30 more bombers was turned down when the US made further protests. The initial order was delivered by September 1948, just as Galland arrived in the country, with 50 Meteors coming from the production line and 50 from redundant RAF stock. When the aircraft began to arrive the Argentines had little idea about what to do with them. It was to be Galland's job to match the pilots to the aircraft through a suitable conversion programme and to develop fighter tactics for the new units. Part of the original agreement with the British allowed for 12 Argentine pilots to receive jet conversion training at the Gloster airfield at Moreton Valance, England.

At first, naturally, Galland had little say in how the Argentines treated their equipment, and he was unaware that the new Meteors were left standing exposed to the weather at Moron airport. Assembled in Argentina under the supervision of a British representative, they waited for their new pilots. By May 1949, with birds' nests sprouting from the slowly corroding airframes, the situation was serious. Only when the British sent test pilot Bill Waterton to sort out the matter did the Argentine agents speed up the final preparations for flight-testing. It was at this point that Galland was able to get the new pilots from England integrated through the Argentine training schools and begin the process of converting pilots to the jets. Galland found the Meteor a fine aircraft with a particularly good engine. Impressed by the technical advances made since he last flew a jet more than four years earlier, he was mindful that this design was in fact a contemporary of the Me262. After flying several Meteors to familiarise himself with its characteristics Galland offered the view that if he could take its engines and fit them to an Me262 he would have the finest jet fighter in the world!

Not all Galland's work took him into the cockpits of single-seat fighters, however, and he managed to become involved with the universal development of the modern *Fuerza Aerea Argentina* in ways that satisfied his lust for flying. With long-range bombers in service the country could afford to take a more strident tone with neighbouring states, and there were many long-range training flights for aircrew unfamiliar with aircraft like the Lancaster and the Lincoln. Once, in 1952, Galland joined the crew of a Lincoln when it flew to Tierra del Fuego and on down into the Antarctic on a flight he would never forget. At other times he would encourage young Argentines to learn gliding, joining them on the hills and teasing them by claiming that it was the first essential step to becoming a general of fighter forces.

Although he enjoyed the work and the rewards it brought, Galland was ever mindful of unfinished business. He had been living with Gisela von Donner for more than four years, and felt that it was time for marriage. The future was as secure as it ever could be amid the changing fortunes of the postwar world, and they talked at length about taking this next step. There was a hurdle that proved insurmountable. Had she married Adolf, restrictions placed upon Gisela's former husband's will would have stripped her of the wealth and freedom she valued as an independent woman. Accordingly, she chose not to marry but to return to her estate in Germany during 1953. Although the two remained on good terms for many years, Galland sorely missed her when she first took the children and left.

As luck would have it Galland was not long in finding another heart to win. The Countess Sylvina von Donhoff, daughter of the former German ambassador to India and an Argentine woman with estates in the country, shared his passion for flying, and it was the gliding clubs which brought them together. Within a few months they had decided to marry. Attractive and charming, the countess became Senora Galland on 12 February 1954; the wedding was a modest affair by Argentine standards. The couple slipped into marital life with ease, and Galland reached a new level of happiness and contentment. There were new adventures to challenge him, too. The Argentine government was looking to increase the size and potential of its armed forces and asked Galland to test-fly several candidate aircraft. In Turin, Italy, he flight-tested a Fiat G80 two-seat trainer, and advised on other aircraft high up the shopping list. In travelling to view and test various aircraft Galland made connections that allowed him to return in a more competitive frame of mind. In June 1954 he teamed up with his old friend Eduard Neumann to fly a Piaggio 149 in an international air rally across Italy. In appalling weather that took the lives of two crew in crashes and seven aircraft, Galland piloted the Piaggio to second place, and received due honours at the President's palace.

Galland's time in Argentina was running out. The Peron government was under increasing threat and his contract had expired. On 7 February 1955, in recognition of his service, Galland received the flamboyantly designed pilot's wings and a citation appointing him 'Honorary Argentine Military Pilot', together with a decree proclaiming the gratitude of the country signed by Brig Gen Juan Francisco Fabri. Fabri had not only done a great deal to encourage Galland in his work for the air force; he had also persuaded him to write his autobiography.

Published in 1953 by Franz Schneekluth under the title *Die Ersten und Die Letzten* ('The First and The Last'), it was a best-seller in 14 languages and sold three million copies. When the British edition appeared in 1955 it was widely acclaimed by RAF and USAF personnel as a frank statement from an honest soldier – the highest compliment possible for a military man. In fact, much was missing from the book that would have enhanced his own profile; he held back from telling the full story, partly for political reasons in those sensitive years after the war.

When Galland returned to a divided Germany with his wife Sylvina he arrived at a propitious time. The Federal Republic of Germany was about to become a full member of NATO and the country was in the throes of reconstituting its own armed services. There was talk of positions to fill within a new air force. Galland was aware of these possible opportunities, but he wanted to set up an aviation consultancy, and settled into a rented house at Neuss where he was to remain for the next two years. Despite his own personal plans, no sooner had he arrived in the country than he received a telephone call from Theodor Blank, a special commissioner for Chancellor Konrad Adenauer. Blank had been charged to gather potential candidates for heading up the new Bundesluftwaffe, and there was widespread support among those he consulted for Adolf Galland to fill that position. Old friends, whom he had served well under more difficult circumstances, had remembered him; but that was not the only reason why men like Steinhoff had recommended him for the job. Under extreme pressure in the past he had shown loyalty to his men and to his conscience, revealing an essential integrity.

Blank told Galland that they were seeking to nominate an 'Inspekteur' as the commander-in-chief of the new Bundesluftwaffe, and that he was the preferred candidate. Galland wanted a more comprehensive briefing on the job and its responsibilities and, above all, time to consider whether he could take on those responsibilities. At face value it could be the highpoint of his career, and no fighter leader would wish to turn down such an opportunity. Nothing seemed to stand in his way; there were no skeletons that could possibly emerge to deny him the post. It would offer him renewed challenge, forging a new air force with new equipment in the strongest military alliance the world had ever seen. For several days he virtually lived at Steinhoff's house, going over every aspect with his old friend and comrade. A day before his week's grace was up he telephoned Blank and accepted the post. Now it was up to the politicians.

He had left it too late: in that short week the political picture changed. France objected to Germany's proposal for a pan-European defence pact, and chose to go its own way with independent armed forces. That changed the way the German government was able to set up its own armed services. The months rolled by, and Galland got on with the business of making a living. In 1956 Franz Josef Strauss became defence minister; and in May of that year he suddenly announced that Gen Josef Kammhuber, who had last held military post as commander of Luftflotte 5, was to head the air force department, eventually to become commander-in-chief of the reconstituted Luftwaffe. What Galland would not immediately know was that he had finally been turned down because of his hurried and technically illegal departure from Germany in 1948, and because of the inevitably slightly gamey flavour of the Argentinean connection.

* * *

From his home at Neuss Galland worked as an aircraft consultant with the firm of Kichfeld, based in Duesseldorf; for more than two years he got to know the people now crucial to the expanding opportunities in Germany's nascent postwar aviation industry. For ten years he had been out of touch with developments in Germany, and the country had changed greatly in his absence. Immediately after the war there had been fears that the victors of 1945 would impose a new Versailles Treaty, and that things would be no better than they had been in 1919. Determination and vision on the part of leaders who, for the most part, had been victims of Nazi excesses themselves helped to transform the country into a model democracy. The general determination to build tall and sound on the ruins, and the American largesse of the Marshall Plan, set Germany firmly on course for economic self-sufficiency. The victors of 1945 had learned from the past, and were concerned to set Germany on the path of self-healing, not to extract a generalised vengeance. Galland wanted to be a part of that process of healing.

He had already gained international respect for the candour and honesty of his lifestory, now widely published around the world; and that helped establish his integrity in the eyes of those for whom he was merely a name on a list of aces. Gradually, his movements around Germany brought him back into contact with ex-Luftwaffe friends and former associates, and he quickly found his way around the newly emerging industries. Many of the wartime manufacturers were getting back into business. After setting up offices in Madrid when Germany was initially forbidden to build aeroplanes, Dornier had returned to Friedrichshafen where it was building light transport and liaison aircraft. Focke-Wulf had re-established itself in Bremen during 1951 with a workforce of just 200 people, and began building gliders. Soon, Messerschmitt would set up offices in Munich, from where it would licence-build French training aircraft. Equally important were the new business opportunities that opened up when Germany became a member of NATO and could legitimately buy aircraft and ancillary equipment from foreign suppliers.

After working for Kichfeld and being part of this expanding wave of opportunity, Galland decided to take the plunge and go into business for himself. In late summer 1957 he moved to Bonn and rented an office on Koblenzerstrasse, from where he could operate his own consultancy. Now he was at the centre of things again, and close to the government offices. Companies from across the United States and Western Europe wanted to gain access to this expanding market. Industry contacts were a treasured asset for linking products with foreign customers. Organisations outside Germany needed introductions and German agents were hired by foreign firms. In the middle were the people who knew both sides of the market, and it was into this niche that Galland fitted well.

It helped for a while that people thought he was heading for the top position in the new air force; when it became clear that Galland was not about to find employment with the Bundesluftwaffe companies still wanted him because he could open doors, explain the lines of communication within the new organisation, and advise on how best to present their products and get business. Early on he became involved with Air Lloyd and was quickly invited onto that company's board of directors, where he helped develop national and international interests.

Although Galland worked hard at building up his business, he ensured he had enough time to play and his weekends were golden opportunities for relaxation and active flying. In September 1955 he participated in the *Flugtag der Nationen*, the Air Show of the Nations, in nearby Duesseldorf, and continued to polish his flying skills on new light and general aircraft that came his way via local flying clubs. During his time in the Argentine Galland maintained contact with many friends and colleagues from the war, and when he returned to Germany he began to gather them around him, socialising and entertaining, hosting hunting trips, or simply reminiscing about close shaves and near misses. In 1956 he was named Honorary Chairman of the *Gemeinschaft der Jagdflieger*, the Association of Fighter Pilots; and it was through this organisation that he came into contact with his contemporaries in Britain and America.

Travel was an increasingly important part of his work, visiting companies on behalf of his clients, representing German companies abroad to foreign investors or potential partners; this gave him the opportunity to visit former enemies and strike up friendships. Business contacts found his offices in Bonn conveniently close to the Federal offices where most of the political decisions were made, and he offered office space for foreign companies or their representatives to work in comfort, affording them business facilities as a complementary service. Key to the smooth running of his new operation was the talented Hannelies Ladwein, his secretary from Duesseldorf. At the end of 1961 he was approached by an insurance group, the Gerling Group of Cologne, who contracted Galland to help them develop the aviation side of their business. Seeking a part of this increasingly lucrative market, with Galland's help Gerling began to open up a network of small airlines feeding the main national and international carriers, and in due course they opened charter operations which were both efficient and successful. All this involvement with aviation served only to heighten the frustration at not having his own aircraft, something he had longed for all his life. With business going well and the bank balance looking healthy, he finally achieved that ambition on his 50th birthday, 19 March 1962, when he purchased a Beechcraft Bonanza registered D-EHEX, which he nicknamed '*Die Dicke*' – 'Fatty'. It was not altogether because the rather bulbous fuselage contrasted sharply with the slim lines of a fighter; he imagined Werner Moelders would have liked that final joke.

Memories of the years in Argentina with Gisela and her children made Galland realise that there was still something missing: children of his own, and a home within which they could grow. He was tired of living in flats and rented housing and wanted a permanent place as an anchor for his own family. Sylvina was unable to bear him children, and increasingly he felt trapped. Hannelies, his secretary, was a younger woman, who found him deeply attractive. According to his many lovers Galland was not the easiest man to live with, and he recognised that in himself. Nevertheless, their relationship blossomed. He was at a critical point in his life and he knew he had to make a decision.

He divorced Sylvina, and on 10 September 1963 he married Hannelies. He found his dream home on the hills of Oberwinter near Bonn, overlooking the Rhine in a house recently completed but with sufficient land for future expansion, an option he was to take up. It was a quiet spot in a secluded part of the town away from the noise and bustle of commercial life, yet a mere 30 minutes away from Bonn where he retained his offices. Hannelies and Adolf moved in during May 1965. He was to remain there for the rest of his life; it was to become a place which took on a part of his character, and reflected it to friends and guests. On 7 November 1966 Galland finally received the son he longed for, when Hannelies delivered him a boy they named Andreas Hubertus. At the age of 54 he had become a father at last, and revelled in the new-found joy that only a child can bring. When it came time for the christening it was the former British air ace Bob Stanford-Tuck whom Galland asked to stand godfather to Andreas.

Stanford-Tuck and Galland had met again, as the latter had predicted, during Galland's first postwar visit to RAF Tangmere. They got on well from the moment they were able to put the war behind them. Both were keen guns; Galland was frequently the guest of Tuck on his mushroom farm in Kent, and when Galland invited him to stay at Oberwinter there were happy days on boar-hunts in the German forests. Their personalities went complementary, and there was a lot of laughter in their company as they endlessly refought World War II. Between 1966 and 1969 they each got the chance to indulge their fantasies when they were appointed advisers to the star-studded feature film *The Battle of Britain*. The actor Manfred Reddemmen played the fictionalised but unmistakable part of the cigar-chewing 'Maj Falcke'; and Heinz Riess played a remarkably convincing Goering. Galland was a trifle ruffled when it was decided that the pilot characters on both sides who were so clearly based on real personalities would bear fictional names.

A lot of the film was made in England but several sequences were shot in Spain, in order to make use of the Spanish air forces' last few Messerschmitts and Heinkels; and Galland had the opportunity to visit old haunts in between keeping an eye on authenticity and helping with technical advice. It was in Sevilla that Galland got to fly a Messerschmitt 109 for the last time – or at least the Spanish licence-built version, with a Rolls-Royce engine, designated HA-1109. In a memorable flight, Galland took Stanford-Tuck into the air in the two-seat trainer version, the HA-1112. With Galland in the front seat and Tuck in the back they cavorted about the sky like two over-exuberant air cadets. When the film premiered in Cologne in September 1969 several former Luftwaffe air aces, including 'Macki' Steinhoff, chief of staff of the new Luftwaffe, were present.

On 29 July 1969 Hannelies gave birth to a second child, a daughter who would be christened Alexandra-Isabelle. Yet all the while there were demands on Adolf's time to pull him from family life. The release and distribution of the film, well received by British and German audiences and, more important, by the fighter pilots themelves, once again made Galland a focus of international attention. He was already sought after as a speaker by organisations and institutions inside and outside aviation. He was particularly amused to be included in that illustrious and hand-picked group of aviation people, the International Order of Characters, among whom were listed astronauts, fighter pilots, test pilots, designers and racers from all over the world. Galland was frequently asked to give after-dinner speeches, and his tale about the four examples of the Knight's Cross with Oak Leaves, Swords and Diamonds which he received from Hitler and Goering always went down well. There were other and rather more serious speeches on his tactical and operational decisions of the war years, which were eagerly requested by air force acadamies and officer training schools.

It was in September 1969 that Galland first met another lady who was to play a significant part in his life: Heidi Horn, who attended a fly-in of women pilots at Ludwigsburg. Galland was with Obst Wolfgang Falck, the head of the Fighter Pilots Association, when he first caught sight of the tall figure that captured his attention. Asking Falck to effect an introduction, he fell at once for this attractive and intelligent woman. For the time being their friendship was nothing more than that, but over the years it would grow to become much more, and would confront Galland with a serious dilemma. Meanwhile he had a family to bring up, and the new decade had further challenges for him. In Spain, the country above all others that held a special place in his heart, he built a holiday home on the Costa Blanca where he could take vacations, entertain friends, enjoy his family and recuperate from the rigours of travel.

Eventually it was time to extend the size of his bungalow home in Oberwinter, and in addition to putting a fighter pilot's bar in the basement he added a wing that bore all the trappings of a hunting lodge. Tastefully integrated with the rest of the house and connected to it in such a manner that it appeared to have been there from the start, it contained hunting trophies, a triple-paned stained glass window, and precious possessions. Comfortably furnished with large rugs and settees, it was the perfect place to sit for endless hours in front of a huge log fire and reminisce. In acknowledging that it bore more than a passing similarity to one of Goering's great hunting lodges he would remark, with more than a glint in his eye, 'The Reichsmarschall built Karinhall East; I have built Karinhall West....' Over time Galland had been able to accumulate several items from his days in the Luftwaffe, including the 1941 portrait by Leo Poeten from which Hitler had had his cigar painted out, and another of his family home in Westerholt where he grew up. He made other homes too, and would frequently visit an apartment he owned at St Gilgen on Lake Wolfgang in Austria.

Far from relaxing, Galland found himself increasingly in demand, and the stresses of life were beginning to tell. In 1965 he had stopped smoking his customary 25 cigars a day and had cut down on the schnapps in efforts to stave off the consequences of a full life. He would not slow down, however, and continued to make the lengthy and frequent journeys demanded by those who sought his time and his energy. In September 1971 he participated in the first Commonwealth Wartime Aircrew Reunion in Winnipeg, Canada, and after delivering a speech which brought sustained applause he was made an honorary citizen of the city.

Back in Germany, his life was drifting further from that of his wife Hannelies; and in 1973 they divorced. Galland lived alone in his spacious house save for the company of a small wire-haired dachsund called Arrax which Heidi gave him. His two children remained close to their father, and both parents worked hard to keep that relationship special. Galland continued to fly for relaxation and in competitive sport, increasingly with Heidi Horn as his navigator. Professional and social life continued unabated. In 1974 he was invited to take part in a wargame – in the professional military sense of the phrase – at the British army's staff college at Camberley; the game was Operation 'Sealion', the planned invasion of Britain in 1940. Later that year he bought an apartment in the Bad Godesberg district of Bonn to which he moved the management of his business interests and where his secretary, Anne-Marie Drinhausen, provided the skills of a dedicated adjutant. In 1975 Galland was a special guest at the unveiling of the German hall in the Battle of Britain Museum, part of the RAF Museum at Hendon, north London, where he was engaged in lengthy conversation by Prince Charles. Throughout these busy years Heidi remained close to Galland, and began to fill a larger place in his daily life. As his health began to wane she looked after him, and served as a shield against unwarranted intrusions.

In 1980 Galland's eyesight became too poor for him to continue flying. In that year, on 16 October, he was finally reunited with his Merkel shotguns, lost since 1945 when an American officer looted them from the cigar-maker Vollmer, in whose safekeeping Galland had left them. Over the years they had passed from owner to owner; on one occasion Galland had located them and tried to buy them back, but was curtly told that they would be worth more after his death. They had been bought from the estate of the last owner by a California industrialist, who believed that Galland deserved to have his rightful property returned. Hunting was still a favourite pastime, and Galland enjoyed showing his son the secrets of the woods, just as his father had shown him so long ago.

Fame and respect brought commercial offers, and Galland's time was increasingly taken up with signing specially commissioned paintings, attending air shows and museums where his autograph was sought by old men and young boys, and being flown to galleries and book shows abroad whenever there was any connection with military aircraft. While visiting the United States in October 1980 he spent some time at the General Dynamics plant at Fort Worth, Texas, and sat in the cockpit of an F-16 fighter before he was made an honorary squadron leader, Evergreen Squadron, of the Confederate Air Force during a three-day show. In Santa Ana, California, he was guest of honour at a special restaurant for flyers; in Canada he was invited on an elk hunt in Yukon Territory; in Dublin he was the guest of the Aviation Division; in Munich he brought together an international group of fighter pilots – and so it went on. Increasingly, Heidi was responsible for organising his daily life in a manner which balanced the pressures of work, the demands of speaking engagements, invitations to social functions, or – with sad frequency now – to the funerals of former friends and fellow pilots.

As the years passed the comrades from his fighting days were being laid to rest. Former adversaries, now lifelong friends, were passing too. On 4 September 1982 Sir Douglas Bader died suddenly after attending a dinner for Sir Arthur 'Bomber' Harris. Galland was invited to attend the memorial service at the RAF church of St Clement Danes in London on 27 October, and drew the attention of crowds who had gathered to pay their last respects to this extraordinary man. Less than three months later he attended the funeral of Gerhard Barkhorn at Tegernsee. In June 1983 Galland fulfilled a promise made many years earlier when he finally managed to track down his crew chief, Gerhard Meyer, and his armourer, Heinrich Olemotz, and met them again in his office outside Bonn. On the 25th of that month he entertained them at his home in Oberwinter, and every year thereafter, for the rest of his life, they returned to talk over old times.

On 10 February 1984 Galland married Heidi Horn and entered the autumn of his life in happiness and contentment. A month later a special reception was held at their home in Oberwinter where pilots gathered for a grand celebration and dignitaries were invited to toast his new wife. There was still little enough respite from the round of talks, dinners, social functions, lectures and tours. Everyone, it seemed, wanted Galland to sit in aircraft or be photographed with them and, as his business career wound down in his seventies, he relaxed increasingly in the light of universal recognition. There were books to promote, and visits to Doug Champlin's fighter museum in Mesa, Arizona, where real Bf109s could be seen and touched. There were symposia to attend, papers to give, or newspaper columnists to talk to whenever there was an anniversary of some great wartime event. On 5 May 1987 his long-standing friend Bob Stanford-Tuck, fighter ace-cum-mushroom farmer, who had been given a welcome drink by Galland 45 yerars before, finally died; and Galland felt his loss greatly.

By the end of the 1980s Galland's health was failing and he had begun to slow down, declining invitations that would at one time have seen him hopping on an aircraft. The world was changing. A divided Germany finally came together and the wall that had separated a people was pushed over in the astonishing anti-climax which ended the Cold War. Galland had always predicted that Communism would collapse from the inside, and he had lived to see it happen. He still made the occasional trip abroad; Heidi and Adolf had friends in many places and were always welcome. His watched his children grow strong and tall. His wife cared for him devotedly through the last peaceful years of his life, and she was with him to the end.

In early 1996, after hospital treatment for a terminal illness, 'Dolfo' was brought home to his house at Oberwinter, where Heidi nursed him through his final days. He had wanted to be at home when he died, to see his faithful dog Chico, to live one last time among his memories. His wife Heidi, his son and daughter-in-law, and his daughter were at the house when he received the last sacraments. He died at 01.15 on the morning of Tuesday 9 February 1996, a little more than a month short of his 84th birthday.

On 21 February, in light snow that fell gently across the hills above Oberwinter, Adolf Galland was buried at the church of St Laurentius with military honours. The Luftwaffe paid its respects to one of its most illustrious commanders by providing six officers as pall-bearers; these were Obersts Wolfgang Fahl (JG71 'Richthofen'), Johannes Hassenewert (JG72), Eicke Krueger (JaboG38), Dieter Reiners (JaboG31 'Boelcke'), Helmut Ruppert (JG74 'Moelders') and Klaus Steiglitz (JG73). Friends and former colleagues from all around the world were there to pay their last respects, including Capt John Whitten who had spent so much time interrogating Generalleutnant Galland in 1945 and 1946. There also to present a valediction was Anton Weiler, the President of the Gemeinschaft der Jagdflieger.

After giving a brief summary of his life, Herr Weiler spoke for those who knew him best and summarised his qualities thus:

'He did not know the word lethargy. He left the slow ones behind. He was realistic but yet idealistic. He enjoyed resistance because it was a challenge. Self-confident, straightforward and at times impatient; always ahead of others and sometimes ahead of himself, he went a long way.'

A memorial service was held in the church of St Laurentius at 11.00 on 31 March 1996, when Adolf Galland, Generalleutnant aD, the last man alive to have worn the Diamonds, was finally put to rest. His life had been a challenge from beginning to end, and fate had taken a hand in giving him an ultimate test. In the face of abominable evil he had maintained his principles, his beliefs and his humanity, and he had never abandoned his dignity, his self-respect or his pride. From the beginning to the end he had never flinched from his lifelong credo, which was never imposed but adopted as his own first principle in life: to be the first and the best. In pursuing that he had succeeded in his quest.

Notes to Chapter 21

1 The author discussed with Galland at some length his awareness of Nazi genocide. The extraordinary efforts to maintain secrecy about this programme from all those not concerned with its prosecution would have been impossible in any political system short of a totalitarian dictatorship. The author believes that it is quite possible for Galland not to have known directly about the gas chambers; but that there was abundant evidence to suspect that mass killings were taking place. Galland remembered flying over Russia in March 1942 in the same aircraft as Himmler and Speer; the Reichsfuehrer-SS looked out the window at thousands of captured Russians, and said that the previous year they had planned to kill them all but that year (1942) they would use them in munitions production. Galland said the comment had puzzled him at the time but he had given it no further thought.

2 In discussion with the author, Galland said that he did know that research was being carried out, but that the method used to get the medical information had been withheld and that he had no means of knowing how it was obtained. The doctor who played the leading part in these experiments – under SS, rather than Luftwaffe sponsorship – was subsequently given immunity from prosecution in order to secure his talents for the USAF aerospace medicine programme at Randolph Air Force Base, San Antonio, Texas.

Index